W9-ABV-914

Gramley Library
Salem College
Winston-Salem, NC 27108

SCIENCE AND LITERATURE

A series edited by George Levine

PR
468
.S34
D35
1989

In Pursuit of
a Scientific Culture

*Science, Art, and Society
in the Victorian Age*

. . . la science est donc une religion.
—Renan

PETER ALLAN DALE

The University of Wisconsin Press

Gramley Library
Salem College
Winston-Salem, NC 27108

The University of Wisconsin Press
114 North Murray Street
Madison, Wisconsin 53715

3 Henrietta Street
London WC2E 8LU, England

Copyright © 1989
The Board of Regents of the University of Wisconsin System
All rights reserved

5 4 3 2 1

Printed in the United States of America

An earlier version of Chapter 10 appeared in *Nature Transfigured,*
edited by S. Shuttleworth and J. Christie (Manchester: Manchester
University Press, 1989).

Cover illustration: "Crabtree Watching the Transit of Venus," by Ford
Madox Brown, one of the twelve murals in the Great Hall of the
Manchester Town Hall in Manchester, England. Kindly reproduced
by permission of Manchester City Council, UK.

Library of Congress Cataloging-in-Publication Data
Dale, Peter Allan, 1943—
    In pursuit of a scientific culture : science, art, and society in the
Victorian age / Peter Allan Dale.
    348 pp.   cm.—(Science and literature)
    (Includes index.)
    1. English literature—19th century—History and criticism.
2. Literature and science—Great Britain—History—19th century.
3. Science—Social aspects—Great Britain—History—19th century.
4. Great Britain—Intellectual life—19th century. 5. Positivism in
literature. 6. Science in literature. I. Title. II. Series.
PR468.S34D35   1989   820.9'008—dc20   89-40251
ISBN 0-299-12260-3
ISBN 0-299-12264-6(pbk.)

For Janet and Allan

Contents

Acknowledgments

THE origins of this book probably go back to conversations in England with another American exile, Professor Walter Simon, who first introduced me to the intriguing story of nineteenth-century positivism. Serious commitment was put aside by doctoral studies at Cambridge, where in the early 1970s it would have been difficult to pursue such a study as this in the English Faculty. But having said this, I cannot fail to note the influence of two Cantabrigeans, Dr. Gillian Beer and her student Dr. Sally Shuttleworth, who not then but later inspired me with their fine work on the relation between Victorian science and literature. Thanks are due as well to two colleagues at the other Cambridge, Professor Jerome Hamilton Buckley and Professor Robert Kiely, who encouraged me when I first began to take on this project in earnest. But, above all, I must acknowledge a profound debt to Professor George Levine, whose comments on the manuscript at several points in its writing were invaluable to me—and no less valuable, his exhortations to get it done.

My research assistants, Stephanie Garber and Linda Voris, stalwartly pursued many no doubt tiresome lines of inquiry for me without complaint. But most long-suffering of all was Diana Dulaney, who "processed" the manuscript with a level of literacy that frequently put its author to shame.

The University of California at Davis was generous in its research and travel grants.

And as usual the greatest help of all was Evelyn Dale, because she would not let me stay discouraged.

Part One

Positivism and the Art of Thinking

1

Modes of Totality: Romantic Metaphysics and Victorian Science

The first step in the analysis of spirit is to take spirit as a realized actual social order. . . . This is social life as an established routine of human adjustments, where the natural characteristics and constitution of its moral individuals are absorbed and built into the single substance of the living social whole. It is spirit as an objectively embodied whole of essentially spiritual individuals, without any consciousness of opposition to one another or to the whole, and with an absolute unbroken sense of their own security and fulfillment within the substance of the social mind.

—Hegel

The supremely important fact [of our era], the gradual reduction of all phenomena within the sphere of established law, which carries as a consequence the rejection of the miraculous, has its determining current in the development of physical science. The great conception of universal regular sequence . . . —the conception which is the most potent force at work in the modification of our faith, and of the practical form given to our sentiments—could only grow out of the patient watching of external fact, and the silencing of preconceived notions, which are urged upon the mind by the problem of physical science.

—J. S. Mill

IN a well-known passage in *Great Expectations*, Joe Gargery speaks to Pip about the inevitable breakdown of their friendship, the one reliable human connection that has stood between Pip and the anarchy of crime, decay, and death in the midst of which he has lived since his first "impression of the identity of things," as he sat a "bundle of shivers" contemplating the world from a graveyard and "growing afraid of it all."

"Pip, dear old chap, life is made of ever so many partings welded together, as I may say, and one man's a blacksmith, and one's a whitesmith, and one's a goldsmith, and one's a coppersmith. Diwisions among such must come, and must be met as they come. . . . You and me is not two figures to be together in London; nor yet anywhere else but what is private. . . ."[1]

What Joe is talking about, of course, is the social "diwision" (the vulgar pronunciation epitomizes the problem) that has sprung up between them as a result of Pip's education as a gentleman. But he is talking as well about the fundamental reality of Dickens' world here as in all the novels: modern society is not a whole, but an aggregate of individuals, divided from one another by all manner of cultural prejudices, engaged in one vast "universal struggle"[2] for survival. Nor in such a society can the individual himself be whole, as we see in Dickens' preoccupation with symbolic doubling (Wemmick, for example, is two different people, one person in London, another in Walworth) and still more in his increasingly realistic portrayals of deep psychological divisions within a single character, Pip being perhaps the most fully explored case in his fiction.

We may generalize further and suggest, following Georg Lukács, that there is no more prevalent theme in classical nineteenth-century fiction than the loss of social "totality," the sense of alienation from what Hegel in the epigraph to this chapter calls a "living social whole."[3]

. . . the mind's attitude within [a properly constructed totality] is a passively visionary acceptance of ready-made, ever-present meaning. The world of meaning can be grasped, it can be taken in at a glance; all that is necessary is to find the *locus* that has been predestined for each individual. . . . For knowledge is only the raising of a veil, creation only the copying of visible and eternal essences, virtue a perfect knowledge of the paths. . . .

. . .

The novel is the epic of an age in which the extensive totality of life is no longer directly given, in which the immanence of meaning in life has become a problem, yet which still thinks in terms of totality.[4]

In Pip's story, as in countless others of the period, there is an effort to reassert the lost totality by returning to its traditional religious ground. Thus, reunited at last with Joe, Pip learns to utter the term that has been missing from his struggle for social meaning: "O God bless this gentle *Christian* man!"[5] But as every careful reader of the novel knows, this resolution of the problem is at best a shaky one. By 1860 the Christian Eden seemed a hopelessly "ruined place" (to borrow *Great Expectations'* closing metaphor), and until a new totality was found society had to remain (to borrow another figure from the same deeply ambivalent closure) under the "shadow of . . . parting," that is, "division."[6]

SCIENTIFIC PHILOSOPHY AND SOCIAL TOTALITY

The essential intellectual history of the nineteenth century may fairly be described as a search for an adequate replacement for the lost Christian totality, an effort to resurrect a saving belief, as Carlyle poignantly put it, on the ashes of the French Revolution. The effort we are most aware of is romanticism, a movement which M. H. Abrams has shown us was bent on remaking Christianity for the modern world, secularizing it as a metaphysical idea of social and individual wholeness, in which all the great enlightenment antinomies, mind and nature, infinite and finite, self and other, might be reconciled anew. "My voice," writes Wordsworth, "proclaims,"

> How exquisitely the individual Mind
> (And the progressive powers perhaps no less
> Of the whole species) to the external World
> Is fitted:—and how exquisitely, too—
> Theme this but little heard of among men—
> The external World is fitted to the Mind;
> And the creation (by no lower name
> Can it be called) which they with blended might
> Accomplish; this is our high argument.
> ("The Recluse," lines 816–24)

This metaphysical gesture at restoring unity cannot, we know, be separated from the mythopoetic powers of its great purveyors. The route to metaphysical transcendence among the romantics is characteristically by way of aesthetic creation. For the "first time in the history of European thought," write Katherine Gilbert and Helmut Kuhn, aesthetics became the "pivot" of philosophy: "An esthetic notion took the lead in metaphysics; and esthetics, in its turn, was remolded from the point of view of idealist metaphysics."[7] This is why Coleridge's definition of imagination (or Schelling's from which it derives) is such a standard reference point for critical and historical discourse on the movement: artistic (secondary) imagination is but the type of divine (primary) imagination, with the signifier "divine" hesitating in true romantic fashion between religious and idealist understandings of the meaning of spirit.

Because of this prominent aesthetic element, the Marxist historian Martin Jay (among others) has called the romantic project for reestablishing social order a "vision of an aesthetic totalization," something available only to the imagination, something "always to be sought, but never fully realized."[8] And, of course, the great romantics themselves were not untroubled by the unreality, the essential fictivity, of

a unity spun from the mind of man rather than God: "Adieu!" Keats
famously complains, "the fancy cannot cheat so well / As she is fam'd
to do, deceiving elf" ("Ode to a Nightingale," lines 73–74). Already
with Keats the romantics' aesthetic totality was fading, and though
poets would luxuriate on the tenderness of night down to the end of
the century, new searches for a unifying belief replaced the romantic
one and with a greater awareness of the need for actual political or
social, as opposed to merely aesthetic, efficacy.

From our twentieth-century vantage point two of these now stand
out as genuinely secular and forward looking, true harbingers of the
future among the many groping efforts (like Dickens') to regain an irrecoverable Christian past. One of little practical relevance in its own
time but extremely potent in ours was that offered by Marx in deliberate opposition to the aesthetic-cum-metaphysical totalities of the romantic period. We may draw again on Lukács, this time the post-
Hegelian Lukács, for an indication of the Marxists' radical emphasis on
the socially real. "The dialectical conception of totality, is the only
method capable of understanding and reproducing reality. Concrete
totality is therefore, the category that governs reality. The rightness of
this view only emerges with complete clarity when we direct our
attention to the real, material substratum of [Marx's] method, viz.
capitalist society with its internal [divisions]. . . ."[9] The empirical social complexity, the genuine historicity of the whole, not an ideological abstraction, is what the Marxist seeks to identify.[10]

The other philosophical project for achieving totality in the postromantic period is one we hear relatively little of as a nineteenth-century phenomenon, though it clearly made far more of an impact on the
contemporary mind than did Marxism. Indeed, I would argue that, because of its widespread currency in the period, the influence of its
promise on virtually every aspect of practical and contemplative life, it
was the true nineteenth-century successor to the romantics' efforts at
totalization. Like Marxism it was militantly realist, but the ground of its
realism lay not in the historical structures of society so much as in the
evolving structures of the natural world, to which it tended to reduce
the historical. And although, like Marxism, it proposed ultimately to
bring about the union of the individual with society and within himself, it began by proposing to fit the structures of mind to those of nature, not in Wordsworth's metaphysical manner of strong romanticism,
but in the materialistic or naturalistic manner that seemed increasingly
to be offered by physical science. The use of "scientific naturalism," as
F. M. Turner has testified, and too few students of the period have taken

sufficiently to heart, was the single most important intellectual phenomenon of the postromantic nineteenth-century: "Not since the genius of the seventeenth-century virtuosi stirred learned imaginations had so many eloquent voices praised the cause of science."[11] The erection of this new scientific spirit into a philosophy of human moral and social life we may call *positivism*, the name given to it by its first and, in many ways, most formidable advocate, Auguste Comte (1789–1857), whose voluminous system stands at the head of later nineteenth-century thought in direct opposition to Hegel's systematization of romantic metaphysics. His was, Louis Althusser has said, "the only mind worthy of interest" produced by French philosophy "in the 130 years following the Revolution of 1789. . . ."[12]

The object of this book is, in general, to explore the development of the positivist project, the attempt to establish something we may fairly call a religion of science, in the Victorian period,[13] as that project works itself out in what I take to be its most sophisticated advocates from John Stuart Mill to Thomas Hardy. And because British positivism, like British romanticism, cannot be separated from its Continental believers, these will also figure prominently in the study with the effect, among other things, of conceptually situating Victorian positivism between two great scientific revolutionaries, Auguste Comte, on the one side, and Sigmund Freud, on the other, with their own great scientific revolutionary, Charles Darwin (not a concentrated object of study here, but a ubiquitous background presence from chapter 5 on), arbitrating, as it were, the movement from one to the other.

This is my general object; my particular approach to it is by way of an unusual, some would even say perverse, route. Positivism, as I have argued, was a reaction against romanticism's pursuit of aesthetic totalization, its supreme privileging of the artist as prophet-deliverer of a moribund social order. But what I have found in examining the history of both British and Continental positivism is that the break between romantic aestheticism and positivist science was far from radical. On the contrary, the position of the aesthetic continued, in the immediate aftermath of the romantic movement, to be a matter of immense concern to scientific thinkers. This is a point I will take up in greater detail in the section "Positivism and the Aesthetic Consciousness," below. For the moment I want simply to observe that the recognition of the nineteenth-century positivists' preoccupation with the meaning of art has placed me, as a humanist, in the awkward position of writing a book that takes seriously, indeed, places at the center of its concerns, positivism's engagement with the problem of art. Awkward because, of course, it has become virtually an axiom of humanistic (not to mention scientific) discourse that the creative procedures of art, its epistemology, if you like, are absolutely different from, alien to, those of science. This axiom, rooted, in fact, in the romantic period, became something like an academic article of faith with the late nineteenth-, early twentieth-century reaction to positivism (about which more in my concluding chapter), which those of us in literature experienced primarily in the form of the New Criticism. Allen Tate's response to the sins of the early I. A. Richards (an apostate as well for his Cambridge contemporary F. R. Leavis), though crude, may still stand as typical of the deeply entrenched "division" this book insufficiently respects. Richards' *Principles of Literary Criticism*, says Tate, is an "instance of the elaborate cheat that the positivistic movement has perpetrated on the human spirit" of attempting to reduce literary phenomena to scientific explanation. That "cheat," moreover, extends beyond the perversion of literary criticism to embrace, it would seem, the Fascistic assault on European civilization (Tate is writing in 1940): "Happily this degraded [positivistic] version of the myth of reason has been discredited by the course of what the liberal mind calls 'world events.'" Happily also Mr. Richards has recanted and now takes the view "that poetry . . . is an independent form of knowledge, a kind of cognition, equal to the knowledge of the sciences at least, perhaps superior."[14] This is the view of the "liberal mind," the mind that, by and large, achieved supremacy in Anglo-American humanistic studies in the postwar era.

Without wishing to defend Richards' *Principles*, which now seem to me to propose an uninteresting conjunction of science and poetry, the product of a latter-day positivism that had all but abandoned the pursuit of larger humanistic and social issues, I take issue with Tate's (and others') belief that science and literature (or art) are utterly independent, mutually antagonistic modes of thought, "two cultures," as the popular phrase (of C. P. Snow) has it. There is an argument to be made against the separation on strictly epistemological grounds, and we will, indeed, shortly see that argument made by virtually all our principal figures—and seconded by some very recent scientific theorists. But of far greater interest to me is the historical argument. It is, in fact, only by a sort of modernist or neo-Kantian hindsight that one thinks of these two modes of thought as having definitively diverged in the romantic era, or, to put the point more polemically, of positivism as having opted for the logic of nature, or, as we might now say, presence, and humanism, for the logic of art, or, as we might now say, rhetoricity. The actual historical process of the disengagement of one discourse from the other was far more complex and its outcome, by the century's close, far more problematical than we are inclined to believe.

So what I am writing is at once revisionary aesthetic (specifically literary) and revisionary intellectual history. A new post-New Critical and, for that matter, post-poststructuralist aesthetic history needs to account more fully, more sympathetically, than the histories we now have for the space between (confining oneself for the moment to the Anglo-American tradition) Coleridge and his New Critical descendants (who have written the standard histories). Such a revision, I suggest, would find in G. H. Lewes (a pivotal figure in the present study), a critical mind of sufficient weight to stand opposite Coleridge as arbiter of the new realist aesthetic, and in George Eliot's novels, an epic embodiment (and modification) of that aesthetic to set against Wordsworth's. Beyond this project and integrally related to it is a need as well for a concomitant revision of intellectual history, one that will account more fully, more sympathetically, for the ethical and social vision that we call positivist and, among other things, show how closely the aesthetic mode of thought bears on and qualifies the scientific enterprise at every step of its nineteenth-century progress.

A HISTORICO-PHILOSOPHICAL DEFINITION OF POSITIVISM

"Positivism" has lately reentered academic debate as a fashionable term for an unfashionable way of thinking. For the deconstructionist it signifies a naive objectivism, the belief that we can somehow "transgress the text towards something other than it," or the related naive belief that we can achieve a "true reading" of a text.[15] For the hermeneuticist, it signifies a naive effort to superimpose the methods of scientific research on the experience of the socio-historical world, the "positivistic view that the only way in which the universal . . . can be known is by means of natural science. . . ."[16] For the "critical theorist" (i.e., new Marxist) it is this as well as a not-so-naive effort to contravene the dialectics of social change by "objectively" legitimating the status quo: "The core of the critique of positivism is that it shuts itself off from both the experience of the blindly dominating [social] totality and the driving desire that it should become something else."[17] The "revolt from positivism," which H. Stuart Hughes long ago located in the late nineteenth, early twentieth centuries, and which, by his account, was pretty well settled in favor of the revolutionaries,[18] evidently continues, and this, of course, suggests that the scientific movement that began in earnest a century and a half ago continues, despite a long list of antagonists, to make its way in the world and to threaten our sense of human dignity. For the generation of the 1950s, for whom Hughes wrote, that dignity seemed to lie in a liberal and humane, vaguely Kantian, devotion to the power of human intelligence to transmute the natural and social world into a suitable home for the soul. In our own generation, the preservation of our sense of human specialness has in many quarters come to reside on a resistance to closure. As Richard Bernstein has written,

There seems to be almost a rush to embrace various forms of relativism. Whether we reflect on the nature of science, or alien societies, or different historical epochs, or sacred and literary texts, we hear voices telling us that there are no hard "facts of the matter" and that almost "anything goes." . . . We have been told that it is an illusion and deep self-deception to think that there is some overarching framework, some neutral descriptive language, some permanent standards of rationality to which we can appeal in order to understand and critically evaluate the competing claims that are made. . . . The dream or hope that many philosophers have had—to grasp the world *sub species aeternitatus*—is, we are told, a deceiving illusion that leads to dogmatism and even terror.[19]

The last freedom, it would seem, is the freedom not to believe in or be determined by our own mental constructions. In such a context positivism, whose very name indicates its commitment to the possibility of discovering a definitive and hence determinative framework for human meaning, becomes a sort of generic enemy.

What this book takes up is the period in which positivism was itself in revolt, in revolt against certain beliefs which it called theistical and metaphysical, but at the same time, and more profoundly, in revolt against the relativist proposition, put forward most notably by Hume, that belief itself is an illusion. "La philosophie positive," wrote one of Comte's greatest disciples even as he was dying, "m'a préserve d'être un simple negateur."[20] The roots of positivism lie in the same empiricism from which Hume's work derived, but, the practical success of natural science in explaining natural phenomena and predicating the laws according to which these phenomena relate to one another took empiricism beyond Hume's radical sense of the word to the point at which it seemed possible to formulate a rational order uniting all natural phenomena. This possibility, in turn, seemed to certain thinkers in the early nineteenth century, notably Comte and Mill, to offer a truly exciting prospect, that of achieving similar certainty in the realm of human behavior. This accomplished, one would have the answer to the characteristic nineteeth-century question, so memorably put by Carlyle, of what to believe in in the post-revolutionary, post-Christian era: " 'The whole world is . . . sold to Unbelief; [the] old Temples . . . crumble down; and men ask now: Where is the Godhead . . . ?' "[21] The answer the positivists offered was decidedly not the one Carlyle was seeking, but it did, nonetheless, promise a new totality, in Comte's well-known phrase, "a religion of Humanity." As one of its most important historians has said, it was "the last, half-heroic, half-desperate, assertion of the esprit de système."[22] Desperate it may have been and far from what most contemporaries were prepared to recognize as a religion, but it became, nonetheless, in its alliance with science, the dominant intellectual force in Europe in the second half of the century.[23] No religious belief, no form of metaphysics, no social philosophy so powerfully affected the thought of educated men and women as this new religion of science.

But what more precisely is positivism? Two extreme definitions, one excessively general, the other excessively narrow, can immediately be discarded. Positivism, as Karl Popper insists, ought not to be confused with a simple admiration for the sciences and belief in their power for promoting human progress.[24] Many admirers of science and, indeed, many scientists are not only not positivists but consciously antipositivist. Nor, on the other hand, should positivism be conceived as a particular doctrine formulated by Comte in the 1850s and promulgated by a handful of devoted followers in the second half of the century. This Positivism, with a capital "P," was of some importance in the period, and its history is told in several excellent books,[25] but the philosophy on which it rested and which it fondly sought to erect into a *"culte"* (Comte's term) had a far wider currency than could be contained under its rubrics or housed in its church. Indeed, with the exception of Comte, the most important positivist thinkers of the nineteenth century were decidedly skeptical of, if not hostile towards, orthodox Positivism.

The positivism that will concern us is not a vague belief in science nor is it a party or a *culte*. Rather, it is a considered philosophical position adopted by a wide variety of intellectuals who have in common simply the conviction that science offers the only viable way of thinking correctly about human affairs. What follows is an attempt to define that position according to its principal categories of analysis,

Gramley Library
Salem College
Winston-Salem, NC 27108

bearing in mind as we go along that the relative importance of the categories shifts as positivism develops through the nineteenth century into the modern period.

As Leszek Kolakowski, the most distinguished of its historians, argues, a full understanding of the meaning of positivism cannot be divorced from this diacritical dimension. For each ensuing generation since the concept first became current with Comte's *Cours de philosophie positive* (1830–1842), the word "positivism" takes on new connotations even as it sheds previous ones, and we may too easily lose sight of the essential kinship between the person who, like Mill, directs us towards the reformation of a political system and the person who, like the early Wittgenstein, directs us towards the reformation of a linguistic system.

THEORY OF KNOWLEDGE

At its most fundamental level philosophical positivism is a theory of knowledge. "Positivism," writes Kolakowski, "is a normative attitude, regulating how we are to use such terms as 'knowledge,' 'science,' 'cognition,' and 'information.'"[26] Its source is in eighteenth-century empiricism, and it maintains with Locke, Hume, Turgot, Condillac, and others, that the experience of the senses must be the basis of all knowledge. Accordingly, positivism rejects as pseudoknowledge the propositions of both theology and metaphysics because these can have no empirical or observational verification. As Comte (upon whom we will initially be relying as our principal authority) writes at the outset of the *Cours*, historically, there have been three theories of knowledge:

the Theological or fictitious; the Metaphysical, or abstract; and the Scientific, or positive. . . . The first is the necessary point of departure of the human understanding, and the third is its fixed and definitive state. The second is merely a state of transition. . . . In the . . . positive state the mind has given over the vain search after Absolute notions, the origin and destination of the universe, and the causes of phenomena, and applies itself to the study of their laws—that is, their invariable relations of succession and resemblance.[27]

If we focus on the *critical* phase of this operation, that is, the attack on pseudoknowledge, we are likely to find, not Comte, but Hume at the fountainhead of positivism, as does Kolakowski. Leslie Stephen would agree. For him Hume marked the "turning-point" of modern thought,[28] the happy catastrophe from which followed the triumphant positivist denouement of the later nineteenth century. If, however, we focus on the *synthetic* side of the positivist theory of knowledge, anchoring the tradition in Hume seems, as I have already indicated, singularly inappropriate. For although nineteenth-century positivism followed Hume in dismissing theological and metaphysical propositions as unreal, it developed, just like Kantianism, as a response to Hume's skepticism. "When I reflect on the natural fallibility of my judgment," writes Hume, "I have less confidence in my opinions than when I only consider the objects concerning which I reason, and when I proceed still farther, to turn the scrutiny against every successive estimation I make of my faculties, all the rules of logic require a continual diminution, and at last a total extinction of belief and evidence."[29] Precisely those "laws" and "invariable relations" that Comte, and after him Mill, confidently expect to establish by the "rules of logic," Hume casts into doubt in favor of a radical empiricism, to which the later positivists were passionately opposed. Positivism is dedicated to nothing if not the belief that a rational and accurate knowledge of the world, as in itself it really is, is possible.

This implies a crucial corollary. Kant sought to go beyond Humean skepticism by positing through philosophical introspection the transcendental forms by which the mind synthesizes or rationalizes the manifold phenomena it receives from experience. Positivists (and others, of course) consider this simply metaphysics by another name. Their response to Hume is quite different. Essentially, positivism is inductivist (though we shall need later to qualify this designation significantly), not apriorist, empiricist, not introspectivist. But having seen the fate of inductivism and empiricism at Hume's hands, it prefers to call itself scientific, thus recognizing what is arguably the most significant intellectual development of the half-century between Hume's death and the formulation of the *Cours*, namely, the apparent contradiction of philosophical skepticism by the immense success of natural science in predicating laws of experience which gave every appearance of being accurate mental constructions of the way nature actually behaves. As Walter Cannon observes, by the early nineteenth century, natural science had succeeded in portraying nature as ruled by empirically grounded laws that "in spite of Hume, do bind the world together."[30] What distinguishes positivism from earlier forms of empiricism, says Maurice Mandelbaum, is the thesis "that the adequacy of our knowledge increases as it approximates the forms of explanation which have been achieved by the most advanced sciences."[31] First Comte and then Mill establish a new, post-Baconian organon of "empiricist" procedures, based on the method of the new physics and, increasingly, the new biology.

The most important consequence of the intimate relation between positivism's theory of knowledge and scientific method is the insistence by its early nineteenth-century promulgators that the final step to be taken in the pursuit of knowledge is the application of the method of the natural sciences to the elucidation of human behavior. By "positive philosophy," writes Comte, "I understand the study of the social as well as all other phenomena [according to] . . . a uniform manner of reasoning that is applicable to all other subject matters that the human spirit can occupy itself with."[32] And Mill fully agrees: "The backward state of the Moral Sciences can only be remedied by applying to them the methods of Physical Science, duly extended and generalized."[33] For positivism the beginning of science may be the explanation of physical phenomena, but its ultimate object is always a human science, whether that science be psychology (as with Mill), sociology (as with Comte, who coined the term), ethics (as with Spencer), or language (as with the Vienna Circle).[34] The difficulties presented by the attempt to apply scientific method to human subjects will not go unnoticed in this study, but what needs to be said clearly at this point is that the attempt itself is nineteenth-century positivism's greatest contribution to philosophy as well as its most revolutionary gesture.

THEORY OF SOCIETY

For Comte, Mill, Lewes, Renan, Spencer, and others, the scientific theory of knowledge was meant, in the end, to lead to the regeneration of social order. This, to be sure, is a *political* objective and, regarded as such, takes us to one of positivism's central problems. To adherents and opponents alike positivism gives the appearance of attempting to transcend politics in the name of an objective science of society, a science in the time-honored tradition of a value- or ideology-free analysis that gives us, at last, "natural laws" as opposed to "interested" prescriptions for the phenomena it explores. What we want to try to do is distinguish between positivism as a program for social analysis and positivism as a political position. Whether it will be possible to maintain such a distinction is another issue.

Positivism's program for *social* analysis we may call, using Comte's neologism, sociology. It rests on the assumption that social relations and processes can be objectively observed, generalized upon, and formulated into lawlike propositions which, as in the case of explanations of natural phenomena, can be used to predict future behavior, "the philosophical principle of the science being," according to

Comte, "that social phenomena are subject to natural laws, admitting of *natural* prevision. . . ." For Comte these laws fall under two headings: "static" and "dynamic." Social statics "consists in the investigation of the laws of action and reaction of the different parts of the social system—apart . . . from the fundamental movement which is always gradually modifying them. . . ." And though this is the "basis of sociology," social dynamics is the more interesting of the two, and "the more marked in its philosophical character, from its being more distinguished from biology [the next science down in Comte's hierarchy] by the master thought of continuous progress, or rather, of the gradual development of humanity. . . ." Social dynamics "studies the laws of [social] succession, while social statics inquires into those of coexistence; so that this use of the first is to furnish the true theory of progress to political practice, while the second performs the same service in regard to order. . . ."[35] In short, in our contemporary terms, the study of social statics is synchronic or structuralist, that of social dynamics is diachronic or historicist. With numerous qualifications, which it is not necessary to explore here, Comte's theory becomes the model for a powerful tradition of social science, probably the most influential to develop over the past century and a half. From Comte one moves to Spencer (who protests too much his independence of the French philosopher), Durkheim, Pareto, Parsons, Lundberg, Popper, and Hans Albert, to name just a few of the more prominent figures.

As a science of human action, this tradition needs to be distinguished from two closely related movements that came out of the same seedbed of eighteenth-century empiricism. One of these, best represented in the later nineteenth century by John Stuart Mill, would maintain that the fundamental science of human action is psychology, which Comte does not recognize as a science. This position will be examined more fully in the next chapter and in chapter 7. For the moment it is enough to observe that the term "positivist" in its nineteenth-century usage and still today connotes the subordination of psychology to sociology. The other great nineteenth-century alternative to positivism's social science is, of course, Marxism. Marxism shares positivism's preference for social over psychological explanation but, drawing on contemporary "political economy," grounds itself in economic exchange as the fundamental social structure. Comte, no less conscious of contemporary political economy than Marx, recognizes the importance of economic causation but rests the possibility of social change ultimately on the praxis of intellectuals. So from the Marxist standpoint, positivism, for all its devotion to material science is, finally, an idealism. Nineteenth-century sociology, as Alan Swingewood has argued, poised itself between these two paradigms with the psychologism and individualism of the utilitarian school being a common point of reaction.[36]

Integral to early positivism's theory of society was a theory of history (as Karl Popper has famously complained[37]), and this can serve us as transition to its political implications. According to Comte's well-known law of the three states, civilization, more specifically man's intellectual and moral presuppositions, develops through three modes, theological, metaphysical, and positive, each of which determines a distinctive social-cum-political organization (or disorganization), roughly speaking the "military" order of the theological stage, the "anarchic" transitional phase of the metaphysical (which culminated in the French Revolution), and the "industrial" organization of the positive stage. This is, for Comte, an ineluctable, natural law of social development. As with his great predecessor in the philosophy of history, Hegel, the present for Comte is the beginning of the end of history, the point of intellectual and moral perfection towards which man has been moving since his first primitive glimmerings of self-consciousness. The difference, of course, is that for Hegel it is the metaphysical state, the enthronement of Absolute Reason, that is the goal of history, whereas for Comte, who is consciously rewriting metaphysical or romantic historicism, there is a further stage, namely, that of the scientific critique of metaphysics, and this, of course, is the positivist stage, the true end of history.

The primary political question raised by Comte's theory of history is whether it is progressivist or reactionary. From the positivist viewpoint it is, needless to say, unambiguously progressivist. Positivism, the goal of history, undermines the theological and metaphysical grounds on which despotism rests. From other viewpoints, most notably in our own time that of the Hegelian Marxists, positivism is reactionary, an apology for the capitalist, technocratic status quo, an apology, indeed, originally designed by Comte as justification for the Second Empire, and used by all Comte's descendants since to suppress the "dialectics" of social change. "The positivist repudiation of metaphysics," maintains Herbert Marcuse, "was . . . coupled with a repudiation of man's claim to alter and reorganize his social institutions in accordance with his rational will. This is the element Comte's positivism shares with the original philosophies of counterrevolution sponsored by Bonald and De Maistre. . . . 'Resignation' is a keynote in Comte's writings, deriving directly from assent to invariable social laws."[38] Jürgen Habermas continues the Marxist critique in still more sophisticated terms. We must "conceptualize society as a totality in the strictly dialectical sense." For the positivist the "relationship of science to [social] praxis rests . . . upon the strict distinction between facts and decisions: history has no more meaning than nature but we can posit a meaning by virtue of arbitrary decision and energetically strive to enforce it gradually in history with the aid of scientific social techniques." By contrast, a dialectical theory of society will "indicate the gaping discrepancy between practical questions and the accomplishments of technical tasks, . . . not to mention the realization of a meaning which, far beyond the domination of nature . . . , would relate to the structure of a social life-context as a whole and would, in fact, demand its emancipation. . . ." The dialectical understanding of history as governed by human interests, as an "interested," rather than an "objective," natural process, is what remains of Hegel after the Marxist demystification. The result is the reassertion of the role of self-reflective, "critical" (versus Hegel's absolute) reason as the cause of historical progress. History is always something "capable of [intentionally] being made," not an automatic process.[39]

His ignorance of the Hegelian dialectic notwithstanding, Comte is as convinced as Marx that the "German ideology" is a mystification of the political interests of a particular class. His appeal to natural law, if not a revolutionary gesture (he is, as Marcuse indicates, adamantly antirevolutionary), is still a progressivist one. Nature's ineluctable processes are evoked to justify the movement of civilization away from the arbitrary enslavement of the many by the few under the "military system" of the theological state. With the hindsight of a century and a half of rising capitalism we may find his faith in the liberalism of the new industrial state rather innocent, but was it consciously reactionary? In fact, the more closely one reads Comte, the more one understands that he shares with Marx an aversion to the excesses of contemporary industrial capitalism and, in particular, the contemporary political economy to which that capitalism looked for theoretical justification. The sixth chapter of book 6 of the *Cours* on "the theory of the Natural Progress of Human Society" is primarily concerned to argue that the "direction of the human evolution" is away from our innate "animality," which Comte sees as essentially the aggressive assertion of self, towards a greater recognition of our innate "social affections":

In man's social infancy, the instincts of subsistence are so preponderant that the sexual instinct itself [the source of our social affections], not withstanding its primitive strength, is at first controlled by them; the domestic affections are then much less pronounced, and the social affections are restricted to an almost imperceptible fraction of humanity. . . . [But] it is unquestionable that civilization leads us on to a further and further development of our noblest dispositions and our most generous [i.e., altruistic] feelings, which are the only possible basis of human association. . . .[40]

Elsewhere and still more definitively he insists that the "final action of the positive philosophy" is "the scientific elevation of the social point of view and of the logical supremacy of collective conceptions." It "will tend more and more to exhibit the happiness of the individual as depending on the complete expansion of benevolent acts and sympathetic emotions towards the whole of our race. . . ."[41]

What Comte is deliberately controverting here is that previous "science" of society set up by the British political economists/utilitarians according to which social order must naturally follow from the free expression of our individuality or, as Comte would say, our "animal appetites." He rejects the political theory of the British school on the grounds that its faulted introspective method has led it to an unscientific—and antisocial—reading of human nature, a reading, we recall, which he classes as a form of metaphysics, for "metaphysics" in the end means for him essentially a "subjective," or in Habermas' term, "interested," interpretation of human nature. Science, says Comte, definitely denies the "ungovernable energy of the 'I,' asserted by the German School."[42] His sociology would challenge "interested" speculation, whether metaphysical or psychological, and show how society can gradually bring out our demonstrable "sympathetic," or cooperative, propensities.

We will be examining a more advanced version of this egoistic-altruistic debate in our discussion of Stephen's argument with the mid-century scion of utilitarian social science Herbert Spencer. For now it is enough to observe that, although it would be inappropriate for a number of reasons to classify Comte as a socialist, he is nonetheless criticizing the same pseudoscientific rationalization of capitalism that Marx later took on, and, by his own scientific lights, seeking to authorize the "supremacy of collectivist conceptions." In his positive polity we have the theoretical roots of a non-Marxist, nondialectical socialism. In England, this socialist tradition begins with John Stuart Mill's Comtean-inspired swerve from classical political economy and carries on through such figures as George Eliot, Frederic Harrison, John Morley, Leslie Stephen, and the Webbs into the early twentieth century.[43]

All this may somewhat vindicate positivist social theory from the charge of being reactionary, according to the crude Marxist equation of scientific method with capitalist technocracy. But the Marxist critique runs deeper. As Marcuse's remarks suggest, the complaint against positivism lies at last not in its supposed tendency to support any particular political structure but in its subordination of the "rational will" to certain inevitable "laws." The good in this, the Marxists would no doubt agree, lies in positivism's demystification of the romantic (Hegelian) notion of the great man as the cause of history. For most positivists individual human action is radically determined by social structure. But for the Marxists positivism goes too far; it overdetermines human potential; it not only eliminates the great man but appears increasingly to dispense altogether with the agency of conscious choice. The "general development of the human race," says Comte, is "completely independent of our control. . . ."[44] But, of course, one need not rely on the Marxists for an attack on positivism's deterministic tendency. We find a parallel objection from quarters with which the Anglo-American reader is more familiar, notably liberalism, on the ground that positivism is anti-individualist, and humanism, on the ground that it is inhumane. What all three of these very different secular traditions—Marxist, liberalist, humanist—have in common against positivism is summed up in the English title to Leszek Kolakowski's book, namely, the "alienation of reason." All in their several ways and for their specific political ends react against what they take to be positivism's elimination of human reason, or, more generally, human will, from the process of social amelioration.

But for all his talk of the "uncontrollable" direction of human evolution, Comte does, in fact, allow for the modifying effect of human intelligence on that evolution in the form of a corporate body of elite instructors who are to educate humanity in the course it is meant to take. This is a theme that is much more pronounced in the second treatise, *Système de politique positive* (1851–1854) with its call for a "philosophic priesthood as the systematic guardian of [the people's] interests against the governing classes," the chosen intellectuals whose "moral force" will eventually bring humankind into an undivided harmonious whole.[45] This priesthood of philosophers, Comte wants us to believe, does not so much change or construct social reality as discover and elucidate by means of its superior insight the natural reality that is already there and guides society accordingly.

THEORY OF MORALITY

The attribution of "moral force" to the new priestly class in the *Système* brings out sharply an issue Comte painstakingly avoids in the *Cours*. Implicit in and, indeed, generating the social theory, providing it with its historical goal or final stasis, is an assumption about morality. In the *Système* Comte's way of acknowledging this is, in effect, to replace sociology with moral science as the "true final science." This is the only science of the individual nature Comte allows, and he places it (in the *Système*) in an intermediary position between biology and sociology, which, we recall, were directly adjacent to one another in the earlier *Cours*.[46] This effort to formulate a scientific morality is perhaps the single most widely characteristic feature of nineteenth-century positivism, as opposed to its early twentieth-century descendant, which effectively eliminates moral propositions from philosophical study as being incapable of verification. But for Mill, Lewes, Spencer, Stephen, and many others, positivism could do nothing if it could not teach the true criteria of moral action.

Comte's concept of morality is thoroughly teleological. He begins scientifically enough by grounding morality in biology and specifically in animal instinct: "Feeling or Instinct stands out as the essential centre of moral existence, in which otherwise there can be no unity." And as we have already seen in our discussion of his social theory, man has two competing instinctual "energies," or "affective forces," "egoistic and altruistic." The "permanent antagonism" between "egoistic and altruistic instincts" is the "natural basis" on which one must construct a "true theory" of morality. The "great problem of human life," the fundamentally ethical problem, "consists in subordinating as far as possible the personal to the social instincts. . . ." We resolve this problem, again, by creating social institutions that educate the affective instincts so that the "greater energy" of egoism is gradually suppressed during the maturation of the individual by the "lesser energy" of altruism. The "germ" of that energy, by the way, lies for Comte in the sexual attraction for an-other-than-self, which must be nurtured and formed until the individual achieves that "ascendancy of the sympathetic instincts" upon which social unity depends. Such ascendancy Comte calls "character," by which he means the artifically conditioned disposition to act rightly.[47] (This process of what amounts to the sublimation of a primitive sexual instinct into an acceptable moral motive so optimistically proposed here by Comte becomes an increasingly problematical transmutation when we come to the later nineteenth-century positivists.)

What is teleological, of course, is Comte's belief that altruism is the necessary goal of human morality, and this, as we will see in the next chapter, requires, in turn, a political decision to structure the state, in particular its educational system, so that it will inculcate and enforce this, in effect, scientifically undemonstrated moral type. The real, if hidden, antagonism in Comte's moral theory is not, after all, between egoism and altruism, but between naturalistic and apriorist justifications of the right. The original biological situation of the self, as far as Comte knows, is ambivalent, at once egoistic and altruistic. The opposing tendencies can be reconciled only by an a priori judgment that the moral is the altruistic, and that judgment is enforced by a system of education (a form of political praxis) which conditions the altruistic and ultimately causes it to appear spontaneous or natural in the educated or cultured individual.

The problem of reconciling the biological and the moral continues to plague subsequent positivists, generating, as we will see, some very ingenious theories. Eventually, however, the problem is resolved by what amounts to a bifurcation of the positivist camp into logical positivists, who, as we have noted, simply exclude moral questions from philosophy proper, and pragmatists, who reinterpret the concept of philosophy itself so that it becomes no longer the pursuit of truth or reality but, in Richard Rorty's phrase, "a tool for coping with reality."[48] Moral propositions become, in this latter context, "true" insofar as they make our corporate existence as human beings possible, not insofar as they correspond to any reality, biological or other.

THEORY OF LANGUAGE

The logical positivists of the early twentieth century are preoccupied, as the name of the school suggests, with the formulation of a scientific theory, not of society or of ethics, but of logic, which amounts, in effect, to a theory of language. The primary reliance on scientific method remains. As Moritz Schlick says, "There is . . . no other testing and corroboration of truths except through observation and empirical science." But every science is now seen as a system of statements. Philosophy accordingly becomes "that activity through which the meaning of statements is revealed or determined. By means of philosophy statements are explained, by means of science they are verified. The latter is concerned with the truth of statements, the former with what they actually mean."[49]

For most logical positivists this means the purification of language through logical analysis so that sentences describe or correspond to relations that actually exist in the world. There are two views of the relation of language to truth, says Schlick; according to one, the "correspondence theory," "the truth of a statement consists in its agreement with the facts"; according to the other, "the coherence theory," "it consists in its agreement with the system of other statements." The only meaningful language is the language of correspondence, the language of "observational statements" whose synthetic or theoretical constructions can be verified by comparison with the facts. "The system of [science's] statements is seen to be . . . a means of finding one's way among the facts; of arriving at the joy of confirmation, the feeling of finality."[50]

There are obviously crucial differences between the logical positivists and their nineteenth-century predecessors.[51] It would be a mistake, however, not to see the roots of the logical positivists' linguistic concerns in the latter. Comte and Mill also had their theories of language, and although they lacked the analytical tool of symbolic logic and hardly placed the linguistic problem at the center of their philosophy, they were at one with the logical positivists in principle. This is more obvious in the case of Mill, who was, after all, trying to devise a "system of logic" and whose effort begins, one recalls, with the "analysis of language."[52] But Comte, who is not generally thought to be interested in such technical problems, also has a theory of language and, indeed, articulates more definitively than Mill the essential positivist position on the subject.

A "*sign*, properly speaking," he writes in the *Système*, describes a "constant relation" between the objective fact of "sensation" (for Comte, what actually happens in the world) and the subjective fact of "movement" within the brain stimulated by that sensation. Thus the "true function of Language" is of a piece with the "cardinal principle of the Positive Philosophy: the universal subordination of the Subjective to the Objective." And further on, "It is only by this union of the world within and that without, that we can give our Spiritual world that cohesion and uniformity, which are the natural attributes of the Material world. . . . It is precisely in giving this fixity that the great force of language consists; which it secures by connecting Man with the World." The linguistic program of positivism, accordingly, becomes that of "giving a systematic form to ordinary language [so that] the word *sign* [expresses] the constant link connecting the objective influence with the subjective impression." In the same context Comte is at pains to insist upon the social dimension of language. Language,

for him, is the "type" of society by which he means that social structure is ultimately reducible to linguistic structure: " . . . the main idea
which I wish to keep in view is the profoundly Collective character of
[linguistic] structure, a point to which Positivism alone has fully done
justice. . . . Thus Language takes on a really sacred character, becoming a part of Religion [meaning what we today would call social total-
ity] itself, by contributing to the Unity of Man." So the critical or
reformist function of positivism becomes, finally, the replacement of
the false or metaphysical structures of "ordinary language" with those
of a properly objective language. This done, humanity will have
realized the "inevitable destiny of . . . Language," which is at the
same time the ultimate unity of "the Order of Man and the Order of
Nature."[53] One of the things we will be discovering in this study is
that the position of language in relation to reality comes increasingly
to absorb Comte's and Mill's Victorian descendants and nowhere more
so than when these descendants are self-conscious artists in words as
in the case of George Eliot and Thomas Hardy.

THEORY OF MIND

One may fairly argue that it was the gradual collapse of nineteenth-
century positivism's efforts to establish a scientific morality that led to
the narrowing of its philosophical horizons, which we find in the
Vienna Circle. But implicit in that collapse, that failure to articulate a
causal relationship between the biological or natural and the moral or
humanly valuable was a larger issue, which the logical positivists
seemed to evade. This we may call a problem in the theory of mind,
more specifically, the origin and ultimate nature of mind.

It is not until the very end of his book that Kolakowski expresses
what he finds most threatening about positivism. "Positivism, when
it is radical, renounces the transcendental meaning of truth and reduces logical values to features of biological behavior. The rejection of
the possibility of synthetic judgments a priori—the fundamental act
constituting positivism as a doctrine—can be identified with the reduction of all knowledge to biological responses. . . ."[54] Comte eliminates psychology from the circle of knowledge, but it does not follow
from this that he was without a theory of mind. The very rejection of
psychology implies such a theory, for it places him in the position of
arguing that the source of mind is biological. In the *Cours* this argument opens, not surprisingly, with the ousting of Descartes from his
foundational position in the modern philosophical tradition and the
replacing of him with a rather unlikely candidate, the phrenologist

Franz Joseph Gall (1758–1828). Descartes is a pioneer of the "old [metaphysical] philosophy," whereas Gall initiates the "happy philosophical revolution" of our own era, namely, the *physiological* study of mind. With him, "the positive theory of the affective and intellectual functions is . . . settled, irreversibly to be this: it consists in the experimental and rational study of the phenomena of interior sensibility proper to the cerebral ganglions, apart from all external apparatus. These phenomena are the most complex and the most special of all belonging to physiology, and therefore they have been the last to attain to a positive analysis. . . ."[55] The implications of Gall's revolution are essentially twofold and were to be developed in great detail over the course of the nineteenth century. These are, first, that mind is ultimately identifiable with brain and consequently thought, no more than a function or epiphenomenon of our organic being, and second, that human intelligence evolves from and is continuous with the "cerebral functions" of lower animals. Both these implications Comte insists upon, and although he himself did no scientific work on the physiology of thought, the biological chapters of the *Cours* provide the early nineteenth century's most important philosophical justification of the new science. Its principal English representative was G. H. Lewes, whose first substantive scientific work, *The Physiology of Common Life*, may be regarded as an elaborate gloss on Comte's observation that, *pace* Descartes, "animals manifest most of our affective and even intellectual faculties." In my discussion of the work of Lewes I will trace in greater detail the rise of what was to become the dominant way of doing psychology from the midcentury down to the revolution initiated by Sigmund Freud, who was himself a product of the physiological school.[56]

For Comte the central philosophical consequence of this "happy revolution" lies in the recognition of the subordinate place of intelligence in our lives. There are for him two fundamental cerebral functions, reason and affection or feeling. Where metaphysics had subordinated the latter to the former and identified man as quintessentially the rational animal, positivism reverses the relationship. There is a "radical fault" in the "ideology" of Descartes and others

—a false estimate of the general relations between the affective and the intellectual faculties. However various may be the theories about the preponderance of the latter, all metaphysicians assert that preponderance by making these faculties their starting point. The intellect is almost exclusively the subject of their speculations, and the affections have been almost entirely neglected and, moreover, always subordinated to the understanding. Now, such a conception represents precisely the reverse of the reality, not only for animals, but also for Man: for daily experience shows that the affections, the propensities, the passions, are the great springs of human life. . . .

Thus subordinated by science to affections, and, indeed, animal instinct, what role is left for intelligence? Comte's answer is, as it were, protopragmatic: ". . . we describe intelligence as the aptitude to modify conduct in conformity to the circumstances [of nature]—which, in fact, is the main practical attribute of reason, in its proper sense. . . ."[57] Intelligence becomes merely a practical, adaptive function that enables man to bring his conduct into alignment with the "logic" of physical nature, the psychological (though Comte would object to the term) manifestations of which are instincts, feelings, and so on.

Comte's theory of society with its vision of science as the basis of a new totality we may call the romantic phase of nineteenth-century positivism. His theory of *mind*, on the other hand, anticipates positivism's next phase, the evolutionist, or Darwinian, phase, which will, in fact, become the principal focus of this study. Comte has absorbed the pre-Darwinian biological concept of mind as the result of a natural development from animal instincts. Lamarck, whose work Comte knew but did not fully assimilate to his theory of mind, adds to this model the concept of organic transformation by adaptation. The *Origin of Species*, of course, refutes Lamarckian evolution in favor of evolution by natural selection, and the early neo-Darwinians further refine the master's work with their research in genetics.

This brief sketch will be fleshed out in subsequent chapters. We now note simply a general tendency: in successive steps the rising concept of evolution impacts upon the positivists' biological theory of mind so that one moves from Comte's fairly simplistic and optimistic notion of mind as somehow developing from animal instinct to a fully moral condition, to George Eliot's, Lewes', and Stephen's biologically more complex, but still melioristic, concept of mind as organically transformed on a Lamarckian model by gradual adaptation to cultural structures; to the fully pessimistic concept implicit in Darwinism, explicit in the later neo-Darwinism, of the mind as an accident of evolution spawned on a universe to whose workings it may well be at once irrelevant and unadaptable. Man wakes at last, writes the mid-twentieth-century evolutionary philosopher, Jacques Monod, "to his total solitude, his fundamental isolation. Now does he at last realize that, like a gypsy, he lives at the boundary of an alien world. A world that is deaf to his music . . ."[58]

If we consider, as we are bound to, that positivism sets out as a philosophy designed to develop knowledge that is positive, not simply in the sense of being real but also in the ordinary sense of being emotionally and morally satisfying, we cannot help but be struck by the fact that the more rigorously evolutionist it becomes the more it tends to undermine any emotionally and morally satisfying knowledge. In its fundamental dedication to the scientific truth as the criterion for all human beliefs, it quite possibly contains the seeds of its own destruction. The aversion to positivism that we have seen for various quarters—Marxist, liberalist, humanist, and so on—tends to focus on its theory of knowledge as the fundamental problem with the philosophy. As Habermas puts it, "Once epistemology has been flattened out to methodology, it loses sight of the constitution of its objects of possible existence . . . [,] the synthetic achievements of the known subject. . . . [Positivists] cannot comprehend as such the foundation of the knowledge. . . ."[59] Both positivists and their opponents, now and in the last century, it seems, prefer to fight their battles on this ground of the origin of knowledge where the issue is not an absolute, but a relative alienation of reason from its object. Neither side, that is, throws into doubt the fundamental proposition that man's reason, however it may come to him, can enable him ultimately to adapt to his world. But one suspects that underlying this epistemological/methodological objection to positivism is a deeper aversion to which Monod draws our attention, the fear that what positivism must inevitably lead to, in spite of itself, is the alienation of reason, not from some particular human activity—politics, morality, education, art, and so on—but from the entire realm of meaningful discourse about the world and man's situation in it. For may not the tendency of modern science be towards the conclusion that reason, being but an accidental and momentary event in a vast evolutionary process, is, after all, a radically ironic tool for coping with our existence?

POSITIVISM AND THE AESTHETIC CONSCIOUSNESS

Let us return for a moment to Dickens. At the beginning of *Hard Times*, an unnamed government official demands of the pupils in Coketown's progressive school, "Would you paper a room with representations of horses?" The correct answer, one remembers, is no, for, as the official explains, horses walking up and down walls are not fact, and the modern scientific world has room for nothing but fact:

"You are to be in all things regulated and governed . . . by fact. . . . You must discard the word Fancy altogether. You have nothing to do with it. . . . You never meet with quadrupeds going up and down walls; you must not have quadrupeds represented on walls. You must use . . . for all these purposes, combinations and modifications . . . of mathematical figures which are susceptible of proof and demonstration. This is the new discovery. This is fact. This is taste."[60]

As I earlier noted, the present study is, broadly speaking, about the development of a scientific faith—such a faith as we see here in Dickens' bureaucrat—among the Victorians. But the study's particular preoccupation, again, is with the relation between the new scientific philosophy and the problem of art, the problem which it seems least equipped to accommodate, and, paradoxically, the problem which can, as we pursue it, lead us to the most intimate understanding of why positivism failed, at last, to realize its grand social designs.

The way we immediately think of the relation of science and art as working is the way Dickens parodies in *Hard Times*: Our understanding of art, like that of all other human constructions, language, ethics, politics, social instruction, and so on, must be reformed by the "new discovery." In a word, our art must become radically realistic; fancy, or imagination, must be suppressed (and with it the romantic aesthetic); taste must be redefined as love of fact. "The actual goal of positivist prohibitions," Theodor Adorno observes, is, at last, fantasy.[61] This relation of positivism to art we will certainly explore, namely, the effect of scientific philosophy on the rise of an antiromantic, realist aesthetic after 1840; and, beyond this, the threat of the new philosophy to the very concept of art and aesthetic, or imaginative, activity.

But what will be of still greater interest to us is another way in which the relation between science and art works, the way, that is, in which what we may call, following Kant, the *aesthetic judgment* persistently refuses to be co-opted by the positivist method. Here we will be exploring in each of our writers a recurring recognition that, far from being able to dispense with the aesthetic in its pursuit of truth, scientific philosophy must in one degree or another fall back upon it, not simply where one would most expect it to be tolerated, in the positivist project for rationalizing the human world, but also at the very basis of the scientific epistemology as it engages the phenomena of the natural world.

Nineteenth-century positivists, largely because of their proximity to the intellectual force of the romantic movement, were not as confident as their twentieth-century descendants were to be of the absolute demarcation between scientific and artistic thinking. Even as they sought to reform the theory and practice of art, to make them more scientific, that is, realistic, they were acutely susceptible to the romantic claim that art was, after all, the arbiter of all human knowledge, its "centre and circumference," in Shelley's memorable phrase. Mill in the very process of constructing the greatest organon of scientific method produced in the nineteenth century could still write of literature that it "is a province of exertion upon which more, of the first value to human nature, depends, than upon any other," a province "which most contribute[s] to form the opinions and shape the characters of subsequent ages. . . ."[62] To the Victorian positivists whose work we will be studying, what came to count most about the romanticism they were reacting against was not its metaphysics, its claims to an intuitive, "poetic" insight into the truth, but its privileging of artistic structures as viable responses to the imponderability of experience.

In other words, although few would have consciously formulated it this way, the romanticism that mattered to them was that which rested finally on Kant's third *Critique* rather than, for example, Schelling's *Philosophy of Nature* or Hegel's *Phenomenology.* In the *Critique of Judgment,* Kant defines atristicu representations as distinct types of "ideas," different from the scientific ideas he had defined in the first *Critique,* the moral ones he had defined in the second. Aesthetic ideas

strive after something which lies beyond the bounds of experience and so seek to approximate to a presentation of concepts of reason (intellectual ideas), thus giving to the latter the appearance of objective reality[;] no concept can be fully adequate to them as internal intuitions. The poet ventures to realize to sense rational ideas of invisible beings . . . —he tries, by means of imagination, . . . to go beyond the limits of experience and to present [ideas] to sense with a completeness of which there is no example in nature.[63]

In short, aesthetic ideas place a tentative shape on the unknowable, whether in physical or human nature, a "purposive" shape, which appears to be necessary if the mind is to avoid the paralysis of skepticism, or, to speak more directly to Mill's point, if the heart is to avoid the despair of alienation from what he and his immediate positivist descendants still assumed must be the saving humane values of "character" and societal "totality."

The crucial and complex functioning in our lives of what Kant was the first to identify clearly and theorize upon as aesthetic judgment has been explored in considerable detail for going on a century now and by no one more fully in our own time that Hans-Georg Gadamer (*Wahrheit und Methode*). For Gadamer, the third *Critique* marks the "turning point" of modern, that is, post-Renaissance, thought.[64] The "transcendental justification of aesthetic judgment [became] initially the basis of the autonomy of aesthetic judgment," and increasingly after Kant, primarily through the modality of Schiller, it became the epistemological basis of the human sciences.

The idea of aesthetic culture [developed by Schiller] . . . consists precisely in no longer permitting any criterion of [realistic] content and dissolving the connection of the work of art with its world. An expression of this is the universal expansion of possessions that the aesthetically-formed consciousness lays claim to. Everything that it acknowledges as having "quality" belongs to it. . . . As aesthetic consciousness it has been derived from defining and definite taste, but has gone beyond it and itself represents [gives shape to] a total lack of definiteness [i.e., the unknown]. . . . [T]he aesthetic consciousness [becomes] the experiencing centre from which everything considered to be art [morality, religion, social codes, etc.] is measured.[65]

From this epistemology follows, for Gadamer, a fundamental concept of social praxis: "It is only the universal form of aesthetic culture that unites everyone."[66] Later in the nineteenth century, aesthetic consciousness, now through the modality of the great German psychologist Hermann von Helmholtz (about whom more in chapter 5), the Kantian aesthetic consciousness, not content with being the arbiter of the human sciences, lays a foundational claim to scientific knowledge (a point that Gadamer insufficiently recognizes). The initial enabling act of scientific hypothesizing, says Helmholtz, who was well read in Kant, is essentially an aesthetic judgment (see below, pages 103ff.).

Gadamer's reluctance to talk about the crossing over of aesthetic judgment into scientific method in a figure such as Helmholtz is characteristic of the late nineteenth-century neo-Kantian tradition from which he descends. Recognition of the all-important role of aesthetic judgment in human sciences and social practice is something that he sees as happening *outside* the scientific or positivist tradition, and something to which that tradition is especially hostile (as we have already noticed, this is *mutatis mutandis*, an outlook Gadamer shares with a number of modern humanists). Hence the opening paragraph of his magnum opus is given over to establishing Mill's *Logic* as the fountainhead of the radically anti-Kantian, anti-aesthetic enemy. With Mill "it is apparent that it is not a question of recognizing that the human sciences have their own logic but, on the contrary, [of showing] that it is the inductive method, basic to all experimental science, which alone is valid in this field too."[67] Insofar as Gadamer is, in fact, paraphrasing here not only what Mill but also what Mill's (and Comte's) positivist descendants among the Victorians say they want to do, his criticism seems unexceptionable. What it ignores, however, is the extent to which Mill and Comte, as well as the most philosophically sophisticated of those who follow them, are forced by their own intellectual honesty and comprehensiveness to take into account the operations of the aesthetic judgment in all areas of human thought. To show how this works, how the aesthetic consciousness irresistibly asserts itself in the very midst of the positivist project, in the very heyday of its power, and, in effect, deconstructs that project, will be a principal objective of this study. The naively inductivist, naively objectivist positivism that philosophers from Nietzsche to Heidegger, Gadamer, Habermas, and Derrida have established as the enemy of the essentially humane, no doubt exists, but we will not encounter much of it here. For the positivist tradition we will explore in the following chapters, the issue is not whether the aesthetic consciousness profoundly conditions our response to reality, but whether there can ever be any reconciliation of intuitive, imaginative ordering of reality with reality itself. What we will find, in effect, is a declining faith in the possibility of such a reconciliation that is perhaps far better understood as a necessary philosophical-cum-historical prelude to the emergence of modern neo-Kantianism and its descendant, postmodern skepticism, than as an inveterate opponent of these more recent movements.

QUALIFICATIONS

Before setting out on the detailed discussion of the interrelation between the scientific and the aesthetic in the Victorian period, a few qualifications are perhaps in order by way of anticipating objections to things either undone or strangely done in this study.

To begin with, the focus on the aesthetic dimension of Victorian positivism must account for some notable omissions. There is very little discussion of the work of those Victorians who have actually come down to us bearing the formal label "Positivist," men such a Richard Congreve, J. H. Bridges, Edward Beesly, John Morley, Edward Lushington, and most prominent of all, Frederic Harrison. Partly this is because their work was been so expertly treated by other scholars. But more important is the fact that none of those epigones of Comte's Religion of Humanity, sympathetic though they were towards aesthetic activity, had anything of serious theoretical interest to say about it, either in itself or in its relation to science. A similar apology needs to be made with regard to Herbert Spencer, whose work I do consider, but not with the extensive attention that might be expected. Again, there are several fine, comprehensive books on Spenser's thought,[68] but more to the point is the fact that Spencer in all his vast synthetic philosophy has virtually nothing of significance to say about art. The reason for this is not far to seek. We find it as early as his 1852 article, "Use and Beauty," where he argues that the "beautiful" is a production of mind which has ceased to matter for the preservation of society. The beautiful is merely the "ornamental." Twenty years later he repeats the point at the very end of *The Principles of Psychology*, almost, one imagines, by way of afterthought. He addresses the "aesthetic sentiments," and "sentiment," it is plain, carries the connotation of excessive emotion. Art is that which "does not subserve . . . the processes conducive to life." In its expression, as in its reception, it operates only in "spheres of superfluous [psychic] activity."[69] Spencer is the one great exception to my earlier generalization about the impact of romanticism on the Victorian positivists. With his radical marginalization of art he would seem almost to anticipate the logical positivists were it not that here, as in so much else in his thought, he simply never got beyond the utilitarians.

The decision to include discussions of two literary artists raises another question of omission. Why these two artists and not a host of others who reflect the impact of scientific philosophy? James Thomson, Samuel Butler, Grant Allen, Robert Louis Stevenson, George Moore, George Gissing, H. G. Wells—and so on. In choosing to write on George Eliot and Hardy, I have concentrated on the Victorian literary artists who were not only the most fully informed on the development of science and scientific philosophy, but also the most concerned to address the relation between that philosophy and what they were doing as artists. What this comes down to, it seems to me, is an exploration of the meaning of symbolic forms, for both writers closely examine the problematical relation of human imagination and natural law. It has also mattered to me that their artistic concerns are intimately related by personal as well as intellectual affiliation to the specifically philosophical discourse of the other writers covered in the book. George Eliot's concept of fiction at once grows from and goes beyond Lewes' scientific work; Hardy is in a similar relation first to Stephen and subsequently to Darwin and Huxley. Finally, what I have not sought to do is trace, in the manner of A. O. Lovejoy, the reflections in literature of ideas formulated by philosophers (or philosophical scientists). That, in any case, has already been well attended to by others, most recently Peter Morton in his comprehensive account of "biology and the literary imagination." There is a telling difference between Morton's approach and mine. He is looking for the "imaginative transformation" of scientific ideas by literary artists, by which he means the writing of a story that illustrates or "exploits" a scientific idea, an idea which in most cases the artist has only partly understood. There tends to be an allegorical and dependent quality in such works which, as Morton is aware, makes them more interesting as examples of the "integration into a culture . . . of a . . . new paradigm" than as original intellectual structures in their own right.[70] I too am concerned with literature's "imaginative transformation" of scientific ideas, but in the quite different sense already alluded to of the subversive transformation of scientific presuppositions by the artist's or scientist's awareness of the operation and effect of the aesthetic consciousness. This particular approach to the relation between literature and "ideas," in which art discovers something rather than "exploits" what others have discovered, necessarily limits the figures available for discussion, but, on the other hand, those who are left give one a good deal more to think about.

2

An Initial Parting of the Ways: Auguste Comte and John Stuart Mill on Logical Fictions

Between poetry and truth there is a natural opposition: false morals, fictitious nature.

—Bentham

Poetry . . . is at once the centre and circumference of knowledge; it is that to which all science must be referred.

—Shelley

THOUGH the philosophical traditions from which Auguste Comte (1789–1857) and John Stuart Mill (1806–1873) came disparaged aesthetic activity as either insignificant or, worse, mischievous insofar as the constructions of imagination distort the reality of nature, both writers took art very seriously even if they did not, like their romantic contemporaries, place it at the center of their thought. "No philosophy should be as favorable to the development of art as positivism,"[1] maintained Comte, and Mill in his more disheartened moments seemed inclined to place the consoling "truths" of poetry on a par with the truth proper of scientific logic. In what these two founders of nineteenth-century positivism have to say about art we find in germ arguments about the relation of art to nature, on the one hand, to moral and social order, on the other, that will in one way and another occupy all the writers subsequently considered.

COMTE'S THEORY OF ART: THE CRITICAL SHIFT FROM THE *COURS* TO THE *SYSTÈME*

In Comte's first system, the *Cours de philosophie positive*, the status of artistic expression, although decidedly on the periphery of his philosophical preoccupations, is, nonetheless, a persistent problem. In re-capitulating the history of civilization he repeatedly returns to the place of art in each successive stage of society's development, and not surprisingly the earliest expression of what we might fairly call a theory of art is the treatment of aesthetic phenomena as effects of particular socio-historical situations—fetishism, polytheism, mono-theism, the metaphysical state, and so on. Art, in this account, as a product of its milieu, evolves according to the same laws of progress at other expressions of civilization. The socio-historical explanation of art will become a central characteristic of later nineteenth-century "scientific" criticism, as we will see, notably, in the cases of two of Comte's most prominent descendants among the critics, Hippolyte Taine (1828–1893) and Leslie Stephen (1832–1904).

The second important point that Comte makes about art in the *Cours* is a more distinctly aesthetic rather than sociological one, though it continues to bear significant social content, albeit now of a more de-terminative rather than determined character. Art, he says, in describ-ing what he (not unlike Hegel) takes to be its finest historical moment in the "polytheistic," or classical, period, mediates between our intel-lectual and moral faculties.

By acting at once on the mind and the heart . . . [art becomes] one of the most important agents of education, intellectual and moral, that we can conceive. [W]ith the great majority of men . . . the intellectual life is benumbed by their affective activity; and the aesthetic development . . . serves as an indispens-able preparation for . . . mental progress. This is the special phase which hu-manity must assume under the direction of polytheism; and thus is attained the first degree of intellectual life, through a gentle and irresistible influence, fraught with delight. . . . [This is how it must be] till the reason gains the ascendency over the imagination.[2]

Although located at a particular historical moment, this mediating function of art constitutes for Comte its universal appeal. What obvi-ously matters to him is the way in which art becomes the means by which the difficult and often uncongenial thought of an intellectual elite is made palatable to the masses in order to achieve social unity. It is for this reason that he ends the *Cours* on the subject of "aesthetic action." Far from being the afterthought it is in Spencer's *Study of Psychology*, aesthetic action is, for Comte, the necessary prelude to the new intellectual order. Art is invoked at this crucial juncture in his sense of his philosophical mission to "fulfil its chief service": "What philosophy elaborates, Art will propagate and adapt for propagation, and will thus fulfill a higher social office than in its most glorious days of old. . . ."[3] The particular philosophy that art is to transmit is, needless to say, the positivist one. Philosophy, in Comte's own person, has brought us to the positivist stage. It is now the turn of art, he says, to make theoretical insight an active force in society at large. Art is the route to political praxis, or "polity," as Comte will call it in his second system.

Not only, then, is art a product of social conditions, it can also be, in a limited sense, a creator of them. But the clear difference from the contemporary romantic aesthetic needs to be borne in mind: imagination is not constructing the intellectual or spiritual basis for the new social order; philosophy, that is, scientific philosophy, is. Imagination, for Comte a faculty for constructing concrete images that appeal to deep emotional proclivities, is philosophy's handmaiden. The broad difference from the specifically Hegelian version of the romantic aesthetic is also worth noticing. The classical standard of aesthetic excellence is not something fixed in the past to which we cannot—and ought not—return, but an ever-present possibility for use in the service of what both Hegel and Comte regard as the ultimate knowledge, that is, philosophy.

This gives art a more substantial role than it had among Comte's empiricist forerunners or will have among his logical positivist descendants, but the difference is only one of degree. In the *Cours* art has a real social and moral function, as it does not with, say, Hume or Condillac, Carnap or Schlick. But it is, nonetheless, extrinsic to the realm of philosophy proper, insofar as that realm is considered to be the *discovery* of truth. With the *Système de politique positive*, published a decade later, this has changed. Comte signals the difference from the outset by the shift he announces from the predominantly "objective" perspective of the *Cours* to a new emphasis on the "subjective," a shift that many have regarded as much more than a matter of emphasis. As his disciple Emile Littré complained in 1863, Comte in the second system lapsed back into metaphysics, an objection Mill would reiterate.[4]

The intellectual core of the first system, what made it for Mill "very nearly the grandest work of the age,"[5] was its advocacy of the objective, or scientific, method and its insistence on applying that method to social phenomena. "The scientific spirit is radically distinguished from the theological and metaphysical," writes Comte, "by the steady subordination of the imagination to observation; and though the positive philosophy offers the vastest and richest field to human imagination, it restricts it to discovering and perfecting the co-ordination of observed facts, and the means of effecting new researches: [It is] above all things necessary to introduce [this spirit] into social researches. . . ."[6] In the preface to the *Système*, Comte shows himself entirely aware of at least appearing to depart along radically new philosophical lines. These two treatises, the *Cours* and *Système*, "will exhibit essential differences" and these differences "correspond to a profound logical diversity. In the first, where the process of scientific preparation is carried to its farthest limit, I have carefully kept the objective method in the ascendant." But having by this "preliminary task [placed myself] at the true universal point of view . . . , [I now proceed on the] subjective method as the only source of the systematization," which comes not as the result of scientific investigation, but of "solitary reflection," the only means of achieving true "conviction." What in particular this conviction is, is not far to seek. The human social order needs to rest on a principle of feeling (the conclusion reached by the objective method of the *Cours*), and "that feeling must be love," that is, altruism: "In the construction of a really complete synthesis, Love is naturally the one universal principle."[7]

Why does Comte make this "profound" change in the direction of his approach to social philosophy? The biographical explanation, that he was experiencing a relapse into his earlier (1826) dementia or that he was infatuated with the memory of Clotilde de Vaux, takes us a very little way. We are on a better track if we begin with Comte's own explanation in the preface, that he was engaged upon two quite different enterprises in the two treatises, requiring two different methods. The first was a "speculative," that is, scientific, analysis of human nature and human society. The second was an attempt to construct a practical political philosophy based on the discoveries reached in the first, a "true Religion," as he calls it.[8] In order to work, such a political philosophy or "religion" needed to speak univocally, conclusively, about the principle upon which social order rests. Scientific method might be the only viable approach to social *research*, but neither a method nor research can be the object of a belief that makes for social unity.

Confronted with what amounts to the gap between theory and practice, Comte makes, in effect, a leap of faith, the faith being that love is the practical unifying principle and that science, in time, will conclusively demonstrate this. The leap may be premature, but for Comte it is necessary. Scientific analysis, as Mill would agree, carries one only so far in the understanding of the reality of human nature; it never at any given moment quite validates the normative judgments that make up the "art of life," the decisions about how to act morally or govern justly.[9] What is intellectually suspect is less the leap itself than the length of the leap. Mill's (and other scientific philosophers') criticism of Comte is ultimately a matter of finding him too impatient with the research of contemporary science, too eager to anticipate the social order he imagined science must eventually affirm, or perhaps more to the point, too fearful of the masses' capacity for tolerating uncertainty in their practical lives.

It will hardly surprise us that in the second system, Comte's theory of art takes on an entirely new dimension. Now art receives its own separate chapter prominently placed in the introductory overview of the positive philosophy. In it Comte starts with the point he had made in the *Cours*: art is fully compatible with the positive philosophy in the sense that that philosophy not only conduces to art's development but also depends upon it for the promulgation of its ideas. Again he takes care to insist that artistic activity must be subordinate to philosophical or scientific activity, only now he qualifies that subordination by saying that it is the way things *should* be in "the normal state of human nature."[10] This qualification effectively points the way to the new turn in his aesthetic theory, for, as Comte makes abundantly clear in this opening section of the *Système*, society is not yet in the normal state, and will not be there until the positive polity, the new religion, is in place. To define that polity in anticipation of its being put into practice is the objective of the *Système*.

What, then, is the nature of art in the non-normal, or incomplete, stage of the positive polity? It is still the means by which we "charm" the masses into believing in that polity, but it is something more besides. Its "sphere" has, in fact, become almost "co-extensive with that of science." In the "true theory of art," art "may be defined as an ideal representation of fact."[11] This definition, unexceptional enough in the context of general aesthetic theory, is, as my discussion in the preceding chapter will have indicated, quite remarkable in the context of a positive philosophy. What it amounts to is a shift of emphasis from the predominantly *affective* treatment of art offered in the *Cours*—art mediates between intellect and action by appealing to the feelings— to a predominantly *expressive* treatment—art is an idealizing projection of the human mind on reality. Initially, art's idealizations are treated, ordinarily enough, as beautifications and/or ennoblements of reality. Science "explains" fact; art "beautifies" it; art's "function is to construct types of the noblest kind."[12] But as the argument progresses, we find Comte integrating art's function more and more completely with the political objective of the *Système* as a whole, so that we have, at last, as the *"principal* function of Art" (my emphasis), its ability "to construct types on the basis furnished by Science," which is "precisely what is required for inaugurating the new social system." There must always be a "void" between social analysis and social synthesis, and into this void "Poetry steps . . . to form prophetic pictures of the regeneration of Man. . . ." Poetry "involves, in fact, the systematic construction of Utopias."[13] Is not Comte, in fact, saying that in the second treatise he, with his subjective method, is performing the role of the poet, the constructor of Utopian types on the basis of scientific analysis?

These remarks on aesthetic idealization were written before 1848. Some four years later Comte developed a fascinating refinement of them in the section of the *Système* devoted to the positivist theory of language, which we have already noticed. There in discussing the logic of signs, which, as we have seen, is for him the logic of properly scientific language, he distinguishes this logic from that of feeling and that of images. The logics of feeling and of signs are parallel, respectively, to the mental faculties of feeling and intellect, which most concern him in the *Cours*. The logic of images belongs to the faculty of imagination, which is, in effect, the central preoccupation of the *Système*. The logic of images, Comte tells us, is essentially the logic of art. The "capacity Language has of assisting the spontaneous combination of mental Images" constitutes "the true domain of Art."[14] This logic/language of images has a special appeal to the emotions and hence inspires us to action, but it also has—and this is the critical point—an epistemological function.

The aid of Art will be specially useful to Scientific Thought in that stage which precedes the work of exposition, and which is less adapted to the use of artificial signs. In this phase our speculative conceptions are more general and less exact, and are thus more easily open to the influence of Poetry, and even that of Images. . . . The Arts supply Language with resources it never can dispense with, even in abstract reasoning. The Positive Theory of human nature, by thus insisting on the regular use of Art as an aid to Reflection, *apart from its reaction upon Feeling*, shows the high importance of calling into play all the resources which can contribute to the difficult task of systematic thought.[15] (my emphasis)

Art, the logic of images, becomes an "aid to reflection," and specifically to scientific reasoning. With these observations Comte brings us back from the moral and political theory that is obviously the main business of the *Système*, to the question that had been fundamental to the *Cours*, the question, that is, of scientific method. What he is talking about, of course, is the role of *hypothesis* ("that stage which precedes the work of [scientific] exposition") in scientific thought, and making an entirely new point (for him), namely, that the logic of the scientist merges with that of the artist at a primary methodological level. "There is, in truth, nothing organically incompatible between scientific and poetic genius . . . ," he observes. "Whether the powers of invention . . . are employed is discovering truth or idealizing it, the cerebral function is always essentially the same."[16] We will return in a moment to Comte's theory of hypothesis, but first, in order to get a fair measure of the revolutionary nature of his thinking, we need to consider Mill's rather more conservative position on the "logic" of art.

J. S. MILL ON ART AS ALTERNATIVE TO ANALYSIS

The beginning of John Stuart Mill's interest in art as an activity worthy of serious philosophical consideration—which it is not among his utilitarian teachers—is, as everyone knows, his mental "crisis," that "dry heavy dejection of the melancholy winter of 1826–1827." He had lost his one object in life, the desire "to be a reformer of the world," because, as he writes in the *Autobiography*, "the habit of [philosophical] analysis" imparted to him by his Benthamite education, had "worn away" his capacity for "Feeling," for experiencing the joy of human life. "My education . . . had failed to create these feelings [of "delight in virtue or the common good"] in sufficient strength to resist the dissolving influences of analysis. . . . I was . . . left stranded at the commencement of my voyage . . . without any real desire for the ends which I had been so carefully fitted out to work for. . . ."[17] What brought him out of his depression was the discovery of the power of art, and, in particular, poetry, to stimulate that capacity for feeling he feared he had lost. Wordsworth, he says, was especially therapeutic: "What made Wordsworth's poems a medicine for my state of mind was that they expressed not mere outward beauty, but states of feeling. . . . They seemed to me the very culture of the feelings, which I was in quest of."[18] Because it occurred to Mill that both his dejection and the experience of poetry's "medicinal" power were not peculiar to himself, he devoted several essays and portions of essays in the 1830s to the discussion of the effects of art. These constitute a rather fragmentary literary theory, which we may, nonetheless, fairly describe as the first philosophically significant attempt in England to move beyond a romantic or metaphysical aesthetic to a scientific or positivist one. We need to be careful, however, of exaggerating the depth of Mill's interest in literary theory. No one was more conscious than himself of his limitations as an interpreter of literature; no one more aware that his true vocation lay in the construction of moral and social theory. Virtually everything he wrote on literature was, in fact, aimed at the development of a moral theory, and it is primarily this connection that we will be pursuing.

The basis of all philosophy, Mill maintains, must be in a "theory of mind," by which he means a theory of psychology. His complaint of Bentham, offered first in anonymous "Remarks" (1833), subsequently (1838) in the famous essay on the philosopher, is, briefly, Bentham's ignorance of the complexity of human feelings, which, in turn, made him a poor moralist. "As an analyst of human nature (the faculty in which above all it is necessary that an ethical philosopher should excel) I cannot rank Mr. Bentham very high." In his consideration of human motives he reduces the causes of human action to a calcula-tion of interest, the fundamental interest of pursuing pleasure and avoiding pain. But "it would be more correct to say that conduct is *sometimes* determined by an interest, that is, by a deliberate and con-scious aim; and sometimes by an *impulse*, that is, by a feeling . . . which has no ulterior end, the act of forebearance becoming an end in itself." It follows from this that Bentham's (and the early utilita-rians') attempt to limit motivation to the predominance of *selfish* in-terest over altruism badly oversimplified the case. "Motives are in-numerable: there is nothing whatever which may not become an object of desire or of dislike by association."[19] Such associations, once securely imbedded in the individual mind, have at least as much to do with human behavior as the abstract principle of natural, inborn egoism, on which Bentham founds his morality. "Knowing so little of human feelings, he knew still less of the influences by which those feelings are formed: all the more subtle workings both of the mind upon itself, and of external things upon the mind, escaped him."[20]

How could Bentham have been so unintelligent? Because—and here Mill indicates the basis of his own divergence from the master—he lacked "imagination," the faculty, understood "by the best writers of the present day, . . . which enables us . . . to conceive the absent as if it were present . . ."; more specifically, "the power by which one human being enters into the mind and circumstances of another. This power constitutes the poet. . . ."[21] Mill is formulating one of the cru-cial connections between art and the objectives of science. What he has done, essentially, is taken the concept of imagination, the basis of romantic philosophy imbibed from Coleridge and Wordsworth, whose work he pored over in the late 1820s, and demystified or psychologized it. It remains, as it was for the romantics, a faculty for perceiving the absent, but the absent is no longer a metaphysical entity. Rather, it is an unnamed or suppressed psychological experience, a feeling within the self which the artist externalizes through his or her art. Implicit then in Mill's concept imagination is what, at the risk of seeming to court paradox, I would call a distinctly realist presupposition, which we will continue to find in the positivist aesthetic as it develops through the century. His "imagination" is essentially the capacity to elucidate and bring before us certain deep "springs of action," or feelings, in the human psyche. Because these are not regarded as metaphysical or theological motivations, but strictly psychological ones, they are real, and the imagination, accordingly, is a faculty of positive research, exposing the levels of motivation that traditional concepts of mind (e.g., Bentham's or James Mill's) overlook.

What psychological realities had Mill found among the poets? Returning to the *Autobiography*, we find that, in his personal experience, poetry, in the first instance, gave expression to, and in doing so validated, his sense of profound depression. The connection between this depression and the absence of love in his life, and, more specifically, the absence of sexual gratification, he only hints at: "If I had loved anyone sufficiently, . . . I should not have been in the condition I was."[22] But it is difficult to believe he entirely missed the point (of sexual malaise) in the two poets, Coleridge and Byron, whom he specifically identifies as having interpreted his feelings at this juncture. More important to him, however, become the positive emotions conveyed by Wordsworth's successful attempts to regain the experience of joy after depression, and Mill admires, in particular, the "Intimations Ode," which, of course, is a response to Coleridge's "dejection." "I found that [Wordsworth] too had had similar experience to mine; . . . that he had sought for compensation, and found it, in the way in which he was teaching me to find it."[23] What Mill probably has in mind here are two things, both of which subsequently lead him to his celebrated revision of the utilitarian ethic.

First Wordsworth teaches the importance of emotional release to mental health, that "cultivation of the feeling," which Mill says had been left out of his own education (and, implicitly, his personal relations). This poetic privileging of feeling, later to be philosophically supported by Mill's reading of Comte's *Cours*, needs to be related to

Mill's developing notion of "spiritual perfection," or character, as moral principle. We must, he insists as early as 1832, build our individual personality on all its sides. "Right self-culture" is "the *spirit of* all morality."[24] In saying this, he is well aware, he departs, in other words, from the utilitarian's traditional measure of the moral as an act's *consequences*. Morality is an inner condition of wholeness, quite apart from the rightness or wrongness of any particular action we may take. "Man is never recognized by [Bentham] as a being capable of pursuing spiritual perfection as an end; of desiring for its own sake, the conformity of his own character to his standard of excellence...."[25] From the standpoint of the strict utilitarian this aretaic morality of inner *disposition* to the good (fully developed in the third chapter of his great ethical treatise *Utilitarianism* [1861], "Of the Ultimate Sanction of the Principle Utility") is a scandal, for it looks very like returning by the back door to the despised intuitionist sanction of an unanalyzable "moral sense." Nowhere does Mill come closer to embracing the precepts of the opponents of utilitarianism, observes J. B. Schneewind, than "in his view of the importance of individual character," his insistence that "the development and perfection of character is the 'highest utility.' "[26] But it is not, at this point, the legitimacy of this departure from utilitarianism that we care about so much as the fact that it comes as a direct result of Mill's willingness to take aesthetic experience seriously. Aesthetic experience and the antiutilitarian morality of "character" (what Mill in the *Logic* calls "ethology") are intimately linked in Mill's thought.

The second Wordsworthian lesson, again reinforced by the later reading of Comte, is more obvious. Not only was Wordsworth's poetry a general culture of the feelings, it also made Mill sympathize with "the general good," "the common destiny of human beings."[27] In other words, it imparted to him the value of sympathy or altruism. As J. M. Robson has argued in what I take to be the finest single essay we have on Mill's poetic theory, poetry (and he is thinking primarily of Wordsworth's poetry) saved Mill by qualifying Bentham's ethical egoism with the expression of "other-regarding affections."[28] Subsequently altruism became for him an essential ingredient of character and hence of moral philosophy: "Though it is only in a very imperfect state of the world's arrangement that anyone can best serve the happiness of others by the absolute sacrifice of his own, yet, so long as the world is in that imperfect state, I fully acknowledge that the readiness to make such a sacrifice is the highest virtue which can be found in man."[29] And he goes on to say that what makes us capable of such altruism is not any Benthamite calculation of pleasure versus pain, but a "disposition" of character that has been developed in us by our education and causes us to act as if spontaneously on behalf of others. Mill tries to argue that this is still utilitarianism, but few have found the argument convincing.[30]

At this point we must pause and consider what amounts to a critical disjunction in Mill's reading of the artistic imagination. In what we may again refer to as its realist mode, it is a faculty of penetrating to and exposing what lies outside conventional morality and social codes, a signal example of which Mill offers us in the Coleridgean experience of dejection: "A grief without a pang, void, dark, and drear" ("Dejection: an Ode," line 21). But artistic imagination evidently functions in another more positive (in the moral sense of that word) way for Mill, the way he finds, above all, in Wordsworth's "cultivation" or structuring of healthful feelings with which to counter disruptive emotional reality (in Mill's and Coleridge's cases the absence of satisfactory love) that makes for dejection.

In this constructivist sense, imagination appears to be doing something that science cannot do—though Mill would be loath to put the point as baldly as that. What he does say in the *Autobiography* is that analysis tends to "undermine" all motivation except "the purely physical and organic." "Higher" motives, notably disinterested love, can be discounted by the scientist as the result of association by "mere feeling" or "sentiment."[31] But for the "great" poet, association by mere feeling is what life is all about; it is what gives life a clear, meaningful, if unverifiable, shape. Such a shape, Mill seems to believe, like Comte in the *Système*, is a necessary basis for personal happiness as well as practical moral action. This, surely, is the "conversion" he writes the *Autobiography* to tell us about. In one who claims to base his moral theory on nothing but experience, this conflation of ethics with aesthetics must necessarily give the appearance of inconsistency. As one commentator has neatly put it, "Mill is essentially a eudaemonist, who claims to know what the desires of men ought to be. . . ."[32] Mill as a theorist of poetry and, by extension, poetic morals is as ready as the later Comte to proceed on the subjective or synthetic method of postulating what ought to be "noble" while looking to science to prove that hypothetical *ought* at some indefinite point in the future. Yet—and this is the critical issue between Mill and Comte—Mill objects strenuously when Comte applies the subjective method to politics, deeming the

Système "the completest system of spiritual and temporal despotism which ever yet emanated from the human brain. . . ."[33]

One's personal morality, evidently, can be the product of an aesthetic projection, but one's governmental polity had better be scientific. The rub here lies in what is probably Mill's most sacred human principle, the principle of individualism: "The free development of individuality is one of the leading essentials of well-being; . . . it is not only a coordinate element with all that is designated by the terms civilization, instruction, education, culture, but is itself a necessary part and condition of all those things."[34] Within the individual self, one is free to "cultivate" whatever feelings one wishes, but one is not free to impose that shape on other selves through an arbitrarily, that is, merely aesthetically, structured polity. Art, feeling—the most important part of morality—and individualism are all closely intertwined in Mill's thought where they define a realm of relative spiritual freedom. Relative, because they seem at last to be circumscribed, indeed undermined, by his most rigorously conceived and, ultimately, most philosophically influential work, the *System of Logic*.

Mill's failure, finally, to integrate his concept of the aesthetic/ethical with his concept of the logical/political is the measure of his positivist conservatism vis-à-vis Comte, his ultimate hesitation before the prospect of an aestheticized scientific epistemology. If we turn now to a comparison of Comte's late work on scientific method with Mill's magnum opus, we will see quite clearly the nature of the difference. It is, if I may anticipate, the difference between, on the one hand, a conventionally positivist need to isolate (even as one emotionally responds to) the constructions of the imagination from the pursuit of truth, and, on the other hand, the recognition that there may well be no such thing as the pursuit of truth without the imagination's constructions.

THE LOGIC OF PROOF VERSUS THE LOGIC OF DISCOVERY

The realm of philosophy from which Mill conscientiously seeks to exclude the aesthetic method is logic. As he observed to that least scientific of his early friends, Thomas Carlyle, "By logic . . . I meant the antithesis of Poetry or Art: in which distinction I am learning to perceive a twofold contrast: the *literal* as opposed to the *symbolical*, and reasoning as opposed to intuition."[35] With the writing of the *Logic*, Mill effectively bifurcates his theory of knowledge, or, more accurately, he separates his theory of knowledge from his psychology. In his psychology he recognizes the determining effect of "casual associations," beliefs that are the result of various social and familial conditions, beliefs that are often mistaken. A recognition of these associations is clearly essential to his concepts of poetry and of morality, as we have seen. The purpose of the *Logic*, on the other hand, is to provide a canon of correct reasoning that will enable us to distinguish "casual" from "causal" associations, and thus gradually obtain an accurate understanding of the world. This logic, in turn, is meant to provide the epistemological basis for a science of society. He wished, at last, to resolve the question

which the decay of old opinions, and the agitation that disturbs European society to its inmost depths, render as important in the present day to the practical interests of human life as . . . to the completeness of our speculative knowledge: *viz.*, . . . how far the methods, by which so many of the laws of the physical world have been numbered among truths irrevocably acquired and universally assented to, can be made instrumental to the formation of a similar body of received doctrine in moral and political science.[36]

Such a doctrine, once established and applied to the "practical interests" of our lives, would presumably replace those erroneous casual associations, and their merely "symbolical" expressions, with true ones, "literally" expressed.

In the *Autobiography* Mill notes that "while as logicians [Comte and himself] were nearly at one, as sociologists we could travel no further,"[37] and he goes on to complain, in a passage we have already quoted, of the despotism implicit in the *Système*. Comte having started out with the appropriate logical basis, evidently failed properly to apply it to the science of society. That basis, of course, is the inductive method, and Comte, in the *Cours*, certainly appears to be at one with Mill in his conviction that induction must be the starting point of all reasoning. However, in the *Système* he writes, perhaps with an eye towards his English colleague's monumental accomplishment in the *Logic*, " . . . it may be said that in proportion as our conceptions recede from the metaphysical stage, induction fills a larger place relatively to deduction, which at first had been supreme. The construction then of Inductive Logic . . . is the principal feature of the modern mind."[38]

But were the two men, after all, "nearly at one" on the subject of logic? Elsewhere Mill does not really seem to believe this. Comte, he writes, is "precise" about the correct, objective method of investigation, but he does not attempt the technical problem of establishing a proof for inductive generalization, nor does he seem even to have "attained a just conception of them."[39] In *Auguste Comte and Positivism* he is still more definitive regarding what he now calls the "hiatus in M. Comte's system": " . . . of induction he has no canons whatever. He does not seem to admit the possibility of any general criterion by which to decide whether a given inductive inference is correct. . . . This indispensable part of Positive Philosophy he not only left to be supplied by others, but did all that depended on him to discourage them from attempting it."[40] What shortly becomes evident is that it is precisely the absence of a commitment to inductive logic, and, consequently, Comte's very substantial difference from Mill as a logician, that accounts for the difference in sociological and, more especially, political theory between the philosophers. The disagreement, as we will see, is not over induction per se but over a correlative function of the inductive process, namely, hypothesis. Comte's failure to develop a canon of induction is but the other side of the privileged place he affords the use of hypothesis and the "logic" of scientific discovery as opposed to proof,[41] and this bears directly on our concern with aesthetic judgment, the formation of scientific hypotheses being, in Comte's understanding, essentially the same "cerebral function" employed by the artist in the construction of his or her fictive worlds.

Induction Mill defines as "the operation of discovering and proving general propositions," of moving from the particulars of experience by a process of inference to general truths or "laws of nature," from which we in turn deduce further truth.[42] What concerns him in the pivotal third book of the *Logic* is establishing the correct method of reaching these general truths and subsequently verifying them. This he realized he must do before he could proceed with any scientific account of social phenomena. He understood as well that it was among the physical scientists, not his philosophical predecessors in the empiricist school, that he had best look for his methodological model. In 1837 his countryman William Whewell supplied him with the one thing needful, a compendium of practical scientific thought (in his *History of the Inductive Sciences*), with which Mill was able to accomplish his task, despite the fact that Whewell was attempting to construct a scientific logic on a radically a priori basis.[43] It is very much what Mill regarded as Whewell's misunderstanding of scientific logic and in particular his idealist concept of hypotheses that he seeks to counter in book 3. Simply put, he finds in Whewell's emphasis upon hypothesis as the *essential* step in scientific method an effort to capture science for the intuitionist or metaphysical school. It "is the peculiarity of [Whewell's] system not to recognize, in cases of Induction, any necessity for proof. If, after assuming an hypothesis and carefully collating it with facts, nothing is brought to light inconsistent with it, that is, if experience does not *dis*prove it, he is content." But to suppose that this exclusively cerebral exercise proves anything about the world "appears to me a radical misconception of the nature of evidence of physical truths"[44]—and, Mill might have added, a radical inability to separate oneself from the notion that "physical truths" must be subordinated to mental conceptions. The object of Mill's argument, on the other hand, is to demonstrate that there really are inferences, that is, mental structures, that are derived from experience, rather than superimposed upon it.

But does Mill, then, reject out of hand the use of hypothesis? Certainly not. Occasions will arise, he says, in describing what he calls the "complete" scientific method, when induction in and of itself is not able to ascertain a cause that explains or a law that rationalizes a particular colligation of facts. In such cases the researcher may formulate a hypothesis to account for the facts, *provided* he formulates it "legitimately." But what constitutes legitimacy?

It is probably Mill's extremely conservative conception of legitimacy that, in the end, most sharply distinguishes his position as a scientific logician. Obviously, he does not want to return to the radical Baconian inductivism characteristic of the previous century, an inductivism that at least theoretically rejects the use of hypothesis.[45] Yet relative to both the idealist Whewell and the positivist Comte, he is much closer to the eighteenth-century position. Hypotheses, he acknowledges, are "indispensable" to scientific investigation, yet it is not true that no scientific generalization whatsoever can go forward without their use, for, again, hypothesis is something to which the scientist must resort when induction has not yielded the requisite law or cause in order, and one must have such a general law or cause "to enable the Deductive Method to be . . . applied to phenomena," in other words, to achieve any practical benefit from scientific generalizations. When hypothesis is required, however, it must be carefully circumscribed. "We may, if we please, imagine, by way of accounting for an effect, some cause of a kind utterly unknown, and acting according to a law altogether fictitious. But as hypotheses of this sort would not have any of the plausibility belonging to those which ally themselves by analogy with known laws of nature . . . there is probably [no such hypothesis] in the history of science. . . ." A "proper" scientific hypothesis is a supposition made "in accordance with facts which are known to be," and the test of its legitimacy—the absolutely critical point for Mill—is its *verifiability*: " . . . it is indispensable that the cause suggested by the hypothesis should be in its own nature susceptible of being proved by other evidence. This seems to be the philosophical import of Newton's maxim. . . . , that the cause assigned for a phenomenon also be a *vera causa*. . . ." And he adds, "The vice of [Descartes'] hypothesis [of the vortices] was that it could not lead to any course of investigation capable of converting it from an hypothesis into a proved fact." The insistence on verifiability is a point deliberately made against "Dr. Whewell, who dissents from the propriety of any such restriction upon the latitude of framing hypotheses. . . ." The flaw in Whewell's logic, as Mill sees it, is that you cannot disprove hypotheses about entities that do not exist.[46]

Mill's conservatism on hypothesis is of a piece with a longstanding empiricist devotion to induction, but the principle of verifiability, interestingly enough, he attributes to Comte, who in book 2 of the *Cours* sets it out as a cardinal rule that scientific hypotheses are those which "are susceptible, by their very nature, of a positive verification, . . . and whose degree of precision accords exactly with what the study of the correspondent phenomena allows of."[47] This is almost certainly what Mill means when he says in a footnote to the *Autobiography* that he learned from Comte "many valuable thoughts, conspicuously in the chapter on 'Hypothesis'" in the *Cours*.[48] As Charles Peirce noted, Comte was probably the first to require that hypotheses be verifiable.[49] Mill also shares with the Comte of the *Cours* a desire to avoid confounding the concept of scientific hypothesis with the patently aesthetic concept of fiction. As Bentham had written, and certainly Mill had read, the word "fiction" is a dangerous one. In "the logical sense" it "has been the coin of necessity"; in the poetic sense, it signifies mere amusement, and in the sense "of the priest and the lawyer, . . . mischievous immorality. . . ."[50] In the *Système*, Comte, Mill evidently believed, came to allow himself the priest's and lawyer's mischievous use of the concept, and the French philosopher's scientific justification for this lay, finally, in the expansion of the concept of fiction "in the logical sense," that is, the confounding of it with hypothesis.

There is, indeed, a liberalization of Comte's concept of hypothesis as one moves from the *Cours* to the *Système*. We see this initially in the statement of "Introductory Principles" where he justifies his shift from the objective to the subjective method as a shift from a "provisional" to a "true" logic, or "Logic in the true religious sense of the word." The use of the objective (inductive) logic advocated in the *Cours* has, says Comte, successfully reformed our understanding of social science. We have learned better than to attribute our subjective mental projections of natural and social order to absolute theological or metaphysical causes. Indeed, the objective method has taught us the futility of trying to say anything about causality at all. What we now understand our subjective projections to be are merely *relative* orders constantly susceptible to change as science discovers more about the world. Subjectivity "in its Positive form" (as opposed to its German idealist or Hegelian form) is purely "social," the product, as I read Comte, of historically determined social beliefs or ideologies. This relativization or historicization of "spirit" has "regenerated" subjective logic allowing the positivist freely to accept structures of belief "based on the direct relation of the sympathies," or the "logic of the Heart," because he now understands these structures as but tentative gestures towards achieving social order. By this regenerated logic, his "political sympathies and . . . scientific tendencies, which hitherto had had no connection with each other, were thenceforth rendered convergent"[51]—a convergence we shall need to come back to.

The new logic, not surprisingly, brings with it a change in outlook towards hypothesis, which we find virtually everywhere in the *Système*. Briefly, this amounts to a movement away from the realist principle of verification we have earlier noticed (in the *Cours*)—hypotheses must be expressed in terms that are verifiable by direct or indirect observation—to what has been called the formalist view of hypothesis. As S. F. Barker describes them, formal hypotheses are not "configurations which . . . [express] statements of a kind that admits of being verified, or . . . inductively confirmed, by observational evidence." Rather, they "are not to be regarded as expressing conjectures that one could literally believe or disbelieve, but that are merely useful strings of marks one may employ." The formalist view "is pragmatic in its intent. It aims to use theoretical hypotheses for deriving predictions about facts, thus getting the 'cash value' out of them, yet without accepting them as literal statements that would need to be confirmed."[52] The first significant mention of hypothesis in the *Système* is in connection with the most basic physical science, astronomy, in which, says Comte, all investigations "relate to phenomena insusceptible of direct examination." This essential "logical characteristic" of astronomy throws light "on the proper mode of constructing scientific hypotheses."[53]

What that mode is, is not very carefully stated at this point, Comte's main concern being to exclude as improper the use of hypothesis to speculate on causes. But later in discussing Dalton's atomic theory, one of the touchstones of the nineteenth-century debate over the use of hypothesis, Comte clarifies his position. Here he speaks of the "relative mode" of regarding hypotheses. Everyone knows that the atomic hypothesis postulates imaginary and hence unobservable entities (atoms), and there is danger that we may endow such "subjective creation with objective existence." On the other hand, "it is perfectly possible," understanding these entities to be merely "logical artifices," to "utilise the great value of the conceptions themselves. . . . It is consistent with sound reasoning to make use of any hypotheses that will assist thought, provided always that they not be inconsistent with what we know of the phenomena."[54] Already we are beyond anything Mill is prepared to allow in the way of scientific hypothesis, and the distance becomes greater still as Comte continues to develop his views on the subject. "As to objective reality, in the mathematical hypothesis [Comte's new term for the relative or formal hypothesis] there is certainly none. But this in no way interferes with its utility, as a mental instrument. . . ."[55] Here we have lost even the qualifying consistency "with what we know of the phenomena," which is no doubt why Mill singled out this particular discussion as an egregious instance of Comte's departure from a scientifically respectable theory of hypothesis.

In his last book, *Synthèse subjective* (1856), which if Mill read he did not choose to discuss, Comte focuses his attention fully on the problem of logic and produces, in effect, an alternative scientific logic to the inductive one Mill had published some dozen years before. The distinctive quality of the new logic, he writes, is that it "replaces the discovery of truths with the inspiration of conceptions." Logic is now defined as the "agreement of feelings, images, and signs in order to inspire in us conceptions which correspond to our moral, intellectual, and physical needs." The processes of induction and deduction must be decisively subordinated to the formation of hypotheses and not necessarily verifiable hypotheses: the new logic, "disengaged from scientific empiricism, no longer restricts itself to the domain of verifiable hypotheses. . . ." The intellectual model for the new logic is a reformed mathematics, an explanation of which is the object of nine-tenths of the *Synthèse subjective*. The informal model, however, is poetry. Having "renounced the poetic domain, logic, in its exclusive

preoccupation with truth, soon finds itself incapable of initiative."
One must "begin by understanding that the beautiful as much as the
true constitutes the normal realm of universal method [logic]." The
point of the reform of mathematics is, indeed, to aestheticize the discipline, to privilege, in Comte's earlier terms, the "logic of images"
over that of "signs."[56] Mill would have bought none of this, but, as
we will see, Mill's student, Lewes came closer and closer to the Comtean position on hypothesis and George Eliot followed at the end of
her career with what I take to be a political application of it.

The political application is, indeed, the crucial one. Disengaging
hypothesis from the canon of inductive logic is the move that enables
Comte to effect his great desideratum, the "convergence" of his "political sympathies with his scientific tendencies." It is his way of justifying in "the fundamental science," the fundamental importance of the
"subjective synthesis," which we may fairly call the *aesthetic* synthesis. Thus adjusted, the logic of science nicely serves the interests
of politics, making something more than merely sentimental sense of
what appears to be an all-too-romantic conviction at the outset of
Synthèse that "to poetry alone belongs . . . [the task] of bringing out
the principal efficacy of [political] institutions. . . ."[57]

For Mill, on the other hand, it is no less politically necessary to re-
strict the conception of hypothesis, precisely because the social sciences
are, for him, all hypothetical sciences. They build on the laws of human
nature established by psychology, which become the premises from
which one hypothetically constructs theories about the behavior of men
in society. Because the construction of hypotheses must provide the
logical ground of a science on which we base decisions for political
change, we need to be especially careful about our rules for constructing them, as we have seen Mill to be in book 3 of the *Logic*. When he
comes to the final and most important part of his great work, the
application of scientific logic to the social sciences, he is no less careful.
He dismisses what he calls the "geometrical, or abstract method," the
erroneous method, which some consider the "type of all deductive science," and which, ignoring the models provided by the physical sciences, fails to take account "of conflicting forces, of causes which coun-
teract or modify one another." By such a method, for example, we have
Bentham's simplistic reduction of social behavior to the pursuit of self-
interest.[58] The objection might well be extended to the geometric concept of hypothesis developed by Comte in the *Synthèse*. The proper
method, says Mill, is the "physical, or concrete deductive method."

The Social Science . . . is a deductive science; not, indeed, after the model of geometry, but after that of the more complex physical sciences. . . . The same objections, which apply to [this method] in this its most difficult employment apply to it, as we formerly showed, in its easiest, and would even there have been insuperable, if there had not existed, as was then fully explained, an appropriate remedy. This remedy consists in the process which, under the name of Verification, we have characterized as the third essential constituent part of the Deductive Method. . . . The ground of confidence in any concrete deductive science is not the *a priori* reasoning itself but the accordance between its results and those of observation *a posteriori*.[59]

The distinction in positivisms we are working towards here is a subtle one, but extremely important. Mill believes it is possible hypothetically to come close enough to the *verae causae* of social life to formulate a plausible course of practical, that is, political, action. If that action proves mistaken, if it proves not to have considered all the relevant causes in the vectoring configurations that make up human motivation, then one adjusts the hypothesis and tries again. It is a recipe that encourages trial and error towards an ever closer approximation of a properly scientific polity, a recipe which we may find rather close to the one offered in our own time by Karl Popper. Comte on the other hand, partly because of his skepticism over ever identifying the *verae causae* of either human or natural phenomena, partly because of his impatience with disorder and individualism, prefers what Mill calls the geometric method, the tendency of which is to allow freer play in our desire for intelligible, emotionally satisfying structures. For Comte the primary function of hypothesis is not, finally, the discovery of true causes but the tentative imposition of order. To Mill's charge that this is metaphysical absolutism or "despotism" as usual, Comte would presumably respond that the radically *relative* nature of his hypothetical structures preserves them from being despotic. What is not claimed as true does not coerce, it simply guides.

POSITIVIST INTENTIONALITY: PURSUING
THE COMTEAN TRADITION

To summarize: We have located in these two founders of nineteenth-century scientific philosophy three distinct attitudes towards art. The first and least complex is the belief that art, like any other human phenomenon, can best be explained by the application of scientific method. This produces a program for criticism: art is reducible either to psychological causes (Mill) or sociological ones (Comte); it has no religious or metaphysical provenance whatsoever. The critical program, in turn, can—and does—modulate into a normative principle for aesthetic production: true art, the art that modern artists ought to produce, is that which conscientiously represents the positive truths of psychology and society as verified by science. This realist criterion, what I will call the new mimesis, is always the primary ingredient in the positivist aesthetic, primary in the sense of being the first and most obvious reform which that aesthetic seeks to initiate. In the next two chapters we will focus on what I take to be its most impressive theoretical and practical expressions among the Victorians in the early work of G. H. Lewes and George Eliot.

Returning to the present theorists, we find that on a deeper level the effort to define the relation between art and science leads Mill and Comte to fundamental questions about how one is to interpret, and live, life itself. For Mill art is, finally, the "antithesis" of science. Its interpretations of human life, emotionally reassuring though they may be, are ultimately subordinate to real, that is, scientific, interpretations. The furthest one can go, philosophically, in accommodating the aesthetic structuring of life is to understand it as a condition of the individual's primitive psychic needs. Mill's distinction between Coleridge and Bentham is very much to the point here: "By Bentham . . . men have been led to ask themselves, in regard to any received opinion, Is it true? and by Coleridge, What is the meaning of it?"[60] (I.e., how does it function to modify practical behavior?) Tolerant as he is of Coleridge's pursuit of "meaning," Mill's loyalty, finally, is to Bentham's "truth."

In the case of the later Comte, this antithetical relationship between scientific and aesthetic "logic" seems to have been significantly revised. The aesthetic faculty, now identified with the process of hypothesizing, becomes the source of the initial, indispensable gesture of theorizing. Without it, Comte eventually comes to say, science, cannot advance. My discussion has emphasized the connection between the French philosopher's gradual "aestheticization" of scientific method and his need to justify certain political predispositions or interests. We may be inclined to dismiss his late theory of method as an elaborate apology for a political program, but we need, at the same time, to recognize that his gradual movement from a realist to a formalist understanding of hypothesis anticipates the principal tendency of modern scientific epistemology. The view that imaginative, nonverifiable projection is a valid instrument of scientific theorizing became commonplace by the close of the century. As Karl Pearson writes in his popular *Grammar of Science* (1892): "There is an element in our being which is not satisfied by the formal processes of reasoning; it is the imaginative or aesthetic side. . . . [D]isciplined imagination has been at the bottom of all great scientific discoveries. . . . [T]he man with no imagination may collect facts, but he cannot make great discoveries."[61] Closer to our own time Popper has reiterated the point. "[T]here is no such thing as a logical method of having new [scientific] ideas, or a logical reconstruction of this process. My view may be expressed by saying that every discovery contains 'an irrational element,' or 'a creative intuition.' . . . 'There is no logical path,' . . . says [Einstein], 'leading to these . . . laws. They can only be reached by intuition, based upon something like an intellectual love. . . .'"[62] And Popper's sometime student Paul Feyerabend goes yet further, arguing the necessity of the "anarchic" exercise of imagination utterly free from any lingering inductivist criteria.

. . . [O]ne of the most striking features of recent discussions in the history and philosophy of science is the realization that events and developments, such as . . . the rise of modern atomism . . . , the gradual emergence of the wave theory of light, occurred only because some thinkers either *decided* not to be bound by certain "obvious" methodological rules, or because the *unwittingly broke* them. . . . [Research] is not guided by a well-defined programme. . . . It is guided rather by a vague urge, by a passion. . . ."[69]

The common denominator between Comte's mid-nineteenth-century subordination of scientific logic to imagination and what we find among our contemporaries is the disengagement of scientific theory from the time-honored realist requirement of correspondence with the world as in itself it really is. As Mary Hesse has observed, "Such studies [as Feyerabend's and Kuhn's] are generally characterized not only by rejection of most of the presuppositions of positivist philosophy of science, but also by explicit rejection of the logical and analytic *style* in a philosophy of science in favour of the persuasive argument from historical examples. . . . Thus discussions of truth criteria are often replaced by descriptions of science wholly within its own context." But, of course, as my argument will have indicated, it is not so easy as Hesse implies to separate new relativist philosophy of science from old "positivist philosophy of science."[64] What I am calling the aesthetic precondition of scientific thought (and Feyerabend and Kuhn would call the ideological or sociological precondition), far from being excluded by the positivist program, lay at its very roots in the last century and has dogged it throughout its history, pressing upon its "truth criteria" in ways that constantly compel reassessment of our assumptions about what these supposedly naive realists were actually about. The detailed working out of this process will be the subject of part 2 of this book.

Before going on, let me expand, in the light of the foregoing discussion, my earlier point about the need for a revisionary history of positivism. According to a widely held view, positivism, having reigned supreme throughout the mid- and later nineteenth century, found itself countered at the end of the century by a new idealism. As one authoritative contemporary account puts it,

> The fundamental intellectual crisis . . . was glaringly epitomized in the direct clash of various systems of thought stemming from the two traditions of idealism and positivism. For the sake of historical exposition, it can be said that idealism tended to dominate German intellectual life in the first half of the century, whereas positivism defined the intellectual development of the latter half [the point may be readily extended to Britain]. . . .
> The idealists asserted that the human mind and its creations represent something wholly originative and unique in the universe. . . . Mind for them constituted the universal condition of reality as apprehended in consciousness. . . . The positivists, on the contrary, were convinced that certain and fruitful knowledge could only come from the extension of the model and methods of the natural sciences across the entire range of human behavior and expression. . . . Positivism treated the mind and human consciousness not as the originary, formative power of the idealists but as a mere adjunct or epiphenomenon of nature.[65]

In this "context of a reigning positivism" various forms of neo-Kantianism and neo-Hegelianism made their appearance from the 1860s on, but none was sufficiently in touch with psychological and social reality to make much headway against the enemy. Then came Wilhelm Dilthey (1833–1911) with a genuine resolution, one that effectively challenged positivism's control of the human sciences.

The remedy Dilthey wished to provide consisted in mediating the barren opposition between a "soulless" naturalism and a "substanceless" spiritualism by means of a proper understanding of a human mind and its creations. He was convinced that the human sciences (*Geisteswissenschaften*) offered a fruitful solution to the sterile dilemma which had impeded the growth of human understanding and threatened to undermine European culture. . . . [These *Geisteswissenschaften*] furnished empirical and "positive" knowledge of man, but not of the same sort as the natural sciences. The human sciences necessitated . . . special . . . methods . . . distinct from those employed by the natural sciences. . . . A new form of reason and self-understanding were to provide the means of overcoming the crisis of the age and the "growing separation between life and scientific knowledge."[66]

Dilthey's new method, the method called *Verstehen* (understanding), rested on the recognition that human action is caused in significant degree by "intentionality," that is, by mental states of desire, expectation, belief, and so on.[67] This is what distinguishes human action from the movement of physical bodies, on the one hand, the behavior of animals, on the other. These intentional states, in one way or another, Dilthey eventually came to recognize as culturally derived. Dilthey's insight is then directly and collaterally elaborated upon in a number of different ways, several of which we have already noticed in our first chapter.

I have no quarrel with the historical account of the idealists' and/or hermeneuticists' reaction against positivism or with the fundamental distinction articulated by that developing movement between causality and intentionality as opposing explanations of human behavior. What I question is the oversimplification of the positivist antagonist. As I have just shown in the cases of Comte and Mill, and will continue to show as we go along, the best of nineteenth-century positivists had a very sophisticated awareness of the problem of intentionality, an awareness which tended to focus itself in their efforts to understand, in scientific terms, the meaning of aesthetic activity.

Part Two

The Prophetic Center

3

The Biological Structure of Thought: G. H. Lewes' Scientific Realism

I believed . . . that I had caught nature in the lawful work of bringing forth living structures as the model for all artifice.

—Goethe

WE remember G. H. Lewes now primarily as the consort of George Eliot. In the last century it was otherwise. Whatever notoriety he may have achieved as a consequence of his irregular relationship with a famous lady novelist was secondary to his reputation as a scientist and a philosopher. For T. H. Green writing in the late 1870s, Lewes was the greatest scientific psychologist of the century, and while Green from his Kantian perspective found less to admire in Lewes as philosopher, others, more sympathetic to his positivist presuppositions, found in him one of the country's most powerful philosophical thinkers since J. S. Mill.[1]

Probably no single Victorian commanded a wider range of knowledge of traditional philosophy (his classic text on the history of philosophy was still standard reading for British undergraduates in the 1930s),[2] the latest developments in science, and, what will be of particular interest to us, the relation of all this to literature and literary theory. Not only was he himself a playwright and a novelist, but he also compiled one of the most extensive and original bodies of criticism that we have among the Victorians (John Halperin considers him the finest theorist of the novel writing in English in the nineteenth century[3]). Indeed, one of the objects of this chapter and chapter 5 will be to show that this much-neglected figure deserves to stand opposite Coleridge (whom he despised) as the great English arbiter of the

59

realist reaction to romanticism, a critic and thinker of intellectual stature surpassing that of the familiar canonical triad of Ruskin, Arnold, and Pater.

FROM SHELLEY TO COMTE

When he visited the grave of the poet Shelley in 1860, Lewes, then 43, could not keep from weeping.[4] The tears were homage to one who was probably his earliest intellectual hero, the writer on whom he wrote his first substantive essay, and the namesake of the hero of his first novel. In Shelley the young Lewes identified with the "high priest-like character" of a man dedicated to the political and spiritual reconstitution of a society still recovering from the trauma of the French Revolution, an event that for Lewes had "proclaimed that the world had outgrown its [traditional religious] clothes," and desperately required the "birth" of a "new credo."[5] The rhetoric, of course, indicates another early influence. Thomas Carlyle, the great historian of the Revolution, was for later Victorians the creator of one of the most persistent patterns of contemporary thought, the notion of an age of unbelief awaiting the prophet, the "great man," who would create the new symbols ("clothes") of belief. Between these two mentors, the young Lewes, like any number of others in his generation, learned to think in essentially romantic terms of the prophetic and revolutionary vocation as the highest to which one could aspire. This was the one romantic paradigm that he was never quite able to cast off (no more could George Eliot).

What distinguishes Lewes from Shelley and Carlyle and from the romantic tradition in general are two crucial turns of mind. First, he early abandoned the idea that it is through art that society will be delivered and focused instead on philosophy as the means of establishing the new credo. This development is implicit in Carlyle, whose best-known hero is not, after all, a Shelleyan poet-prophet but an incomprehensible German philosopher of distinctly Fichtean aspect. But the need for the would-be prophet to shift from art to philosophy is more decisively announced by Hegel, whose work Lewes was one of the first Englishmen to take seriously. The *Vorlesungen über die Ästhetik* (reviewed at length by Lewes in 1842) gives us a magnificently full account of the development of art, but the moral of the history it relates is that art must give way to philosophy, to the mind's pursuit of the Absolute Ideal.[6] Lewes evidently took the point. For all his early efforts at creative writing and literary criticism, his first major work is a history of philosophy (1845–1846), and virtually every succeeding book is an expansion of the philosophical enterprise embarked upon in that history.

The second, far more telling, point at which Lewes diverges from the romantic tradition is in his choice of the *kind* of philosophy he believes will provide the basis for the new social order. Romantic philosophy is unabashedly metaphysical, and in this Hegel is the exemplary romantic thinker. There is a definite tendency in the young Lewes to follow both Coleridge and Carlyle into the arms of German metaphysics (witness the early interest in Hegel), and the tendency, as we shall see, lingers on in later life. But, it is not, in the end, these mentors who determine his course but a quite different influence. As early as age 25 he had met and fallen under the intellectual charm of J. S. Mill. This most determined of Victorian antimetaphysicians steadily drew Lewes away from his youthful flirtation with the Germans[7] and eventually into the circle of a philosopher who would eclipse Mill's own influence, Auguste Comte.

By summer of 1843 Lewes, having read and absorbed the essentials of the *Cours*, was prepared to believe that the "positive method . . . is the only true one." What it offered him, among other things, was what Mill's complexly argued, carefully circumscribed *Logic* did not, a Carlylean vision of the world transformed and saved by a new religion, a religion of science.[8] When he came to the *Biographical History of Philosophy,* Lewes had clearly reached the conclusion that Comte was not only the greatest mind of the century, but one of the greatest of all time. The shape of that *History* everywhere bears the French philosopher's signature as it tells with erudition and clarity the story of the inevitable decline of theology and metaphysics according to the pattern established in Comte's famous theory of intellectual evolution: theological thinking characteristic of the Middle Ages and earlier gives way to metaphysical thinking characteristic of the period from Descartes to Hegel, which in turn gives way to positive thinking and the triumphant rise of scientific knowledge as the only valid form of knowledge.

As Lewes is at pains to point out, the true history of philosophy is not the history of particular philosophical systems: it is the history of *methods* of approaching the problem of knowledge. "The invention of a Method we have always considered as, perhaps, the greatest effort of philosophical genius, and the most deserving of the historian's attention. . . . If a method could be found for Philosophy—if a path of transit from the phenomenal to the noumenal world could be found—

should we not then be quickly in possession of the truth."[9] What his history gives us, finally, is the progress of two "radically" conflicting methods, the metaphysical and the positive, that work out their opposition in one form and another from Thales to Comte. The two are alike in being deductive, but, says Lewes, the metaphysical method is "deductive *a priori*; that is to say, starting from some a priori axiom" (as in the case of mathematics), whereas the positive method is "deductive *a posteriori*": "After much observation, it attains, by the inductive process, to the certainty of a law. . . . From this certain deductions are drawn. . . . [In short, the] one proceeds from an Assumption the other from a Fact."[10] We shall have more to say about the consequences of Lewes' desire to emphasize the deductive procedure rather than the inductive and about this naive devotion to Fact. For now it is enough to note that he follows Comte (and Mill) in the conviction that in the right choice of method, the method which has succeeded in the natural sciences, lies the key to all future intellectual progress. Every division of knowledge is to adopt the positive method until at last one can formulate the laws of human nature itself. At that point, man, led by the scientific elite, will be prepared to construct the ideal (because scientifically based) totality, the "politique positive."

Lewes never properly worked out a positivist social vision of his own, never, that is, achieved his residual romantic ambition. The magnum opus, *Problems of Life and Mind*, only part of which was published in his own lifetime, began in the prophetic key: "The great desire of this age is for a Doctrine which may serve to condense our knowledge, guide our researches and shape our lives. . . . [Religion] must not attempt to imprison the mind in formulas which no longer contain the whole of positive knowledge. . . . It must no longer present a conception of the world and physical laws, or of man and moral laws, which has any other basis than that of scientific induction."[11] But after five thick volumes he still had not formulated the coherent scientific "religion" he longed to offer his contemporaries. He was, as we will see, ultimately too burdened by the criterion of verifiability. It is to George Eliot that we will need to look for the scientific version of the romantic prophetic vocation Lewes never quite realized.

A NEW MIMESIS

We will begin with Lewes' work in literary theory because it is a recurring pattern with him, the reverse of what we find in Mill, for example, that he tends to approach his scientific breakthroughs by way of meditation on art. At the close of his first serious philosophical work, *The Biographical History of Philosophy*, he elevates Comte to precisely the position the latter would have wished: the successor and antithesis to Hegel as consummate arbiter of modern philosophy. When he does this, Lewes inserts a grace note. But "one professor . . . we must name as an associate in the labour of disabusing the public [of its theological and metaphysical prepossessions], and that is O. F. Gruppe, the author of one of the very best books on the Greek Drama."[12] This book, *Ariadne, oder die tragische Kunst der Griechen* . . . (1834) is a thoroughgoing attempt to apply the positivist method to the elucidation of literature at its very roots in Greek tragedy. The title at once signals the antiquity of the subject and the author's confidence that he had found the essential clue to its treatment, the way out of the labyrinth of generations of speculations on the beautiful.

The project obviously attracted Lewes, who had some years before inveighed against the intellectually impoverished condition of contemporary English criticism in a manner that may well recall the complaint of a great twentieth-century critic (to whom we will return) about the egregious absence of a coherent "structure of thought and knowledge" in the "discipline."[13] The "science of criticism," Lewes writes, " . . . is in a truly deplorable condition. No man can read without forming an opinion of some sort . . . ; but this is a distinct thing from formal criticism."[14] Even as he wrote about the "abuses" of criticism, Lewes, as we have seen, was making an extensive study of aesthetics, especially German romantic aesthetics. By 1845 he had already been through not only the obvious British authors, Burke, Wordsworth, Coleridge, Shelley, Carlyle, and Mill, but also a formidable array of Continental critics and theorists: Lessing, Herder, Kant, Goethe, Schiller, the Schlegels, Jean Paul, Schelling, Fichte, Solger, Hegel, Q. de Quincey, Sismondi, Sainte-Beuve, Cousin, Jouffroy, Girardin, Nisard, to name only the more prominent and modern of his sources.[15] Among these, one writer emerges as offering the sort of comprehensive theoretical systemization that he is after: Hegel's "is the most delightful, thought-inciting and instructive work on the subject we have yet met with and . . . four years constant study has only served the more to impress us with its depth and usefulness."[16] But even as he praises Hegel, Lewes, with Mill looking over his shoulder (he gave Mill the essay to read before publication), carefully excuses himself from agreeing with Hegel's "first principles"; Hegel's "science" of art is impressive but it is not scientific enough. What specifically is wrong becomes clear a year later when Lewes, having in the interval read Comte's *Cours*, returns to the subject of the "abuses" of criticism. Now it is no longer the chaos of critical opinion that disturbs him, but a particular method of attempting to order that chaos, the "pseudo-philosophical method" of romantic art theory, associated in this instance with A. W. Schlegel and Schelling, and, in England, Coleridge, who for him is no more than an echo—and "not a very honest one"—of the Germans. A true *"science"* of criticism cannot be a *"metaphysics* of criticism," says Lewes, meaning, we can safely opine, it should be an inductive science.[17]

The task of articulating that science, at least for the English, a task never properly engaged by Mill or by Lewes' own great positivist contemporaries (and close friends), Herbert Spencer (1820–1903) and Alexander Bain (1818–1903), he evidently saw as one of his many intellectual goals. He writes several times in his notebooks of a project, which he calls the Ariadne book, a study in literary theory, modeled no doubt on Gruppe's approach.[18] That book was never developed on anything like Gruppe's scale, not to mention Hegel's. Too many other interests distracted him. Still, we have a large corpus of occasional writing on literature, virtually all of it informed by scientific purpose, as well as a short but penetrating treatise on the "principles of success in literature," probably the bare skeleton of the original Ariadne project. From these materials in conjunction with his extensive writing in other areas we can derive a fair approximation to a theory of literature, and one which, I have suggested, places Lewes as the preeminent representative of the midcentury reaction to romantic theory, the leading voice in Britain and, with Hippolyte Taine (1828–1893),[19] one of the leading in Europe favoring scientific method over metaphysical speculation in aesthetics and, correlatively, realism over romanticism in artistic practice.[20]

In the ongoing debate over the status of art as a form of knowledge we can broadly distinguish two positions. On the one side, as we have seen, is the positivist argument that there is one form of knowledge, science, to which all discourse in whatever field must conform if it is to be called knowledge. Literature, says the positivist philosopher Richard von Mises, precisely because it so thoroughly conditions our perception of the world, must, like all other cultural phenomena which impinge upon our life, be submitted to a "scientific study of the processes of [its] knowledge in their logical and psychological aspects."[21] Opposed to the positivists' position and far more congenial to the contemporary student of literature is a wide range of views from late nineteenth-century aestheticism and symbolism, to twentieth-century New Criticism, phenomenology, and hermeneutics, which have a common ground in the conviction that literary theory, the "science" of literature, if one likes, has a method distinctly its own and radically other than that of the natural sciences, and this because literature is a different kind of knowledge from science. "Up to the time of Kant," writes Ernst Cassirer, "a philosophy of beauty always meant an attempt to reduce our aesthetic experience to an alien principle and to subject art to an alien jurisdiction. Kant in his *Critique of Judgment* was the first to give a clear and convincing proof of the autonomy of art. All former systems had looked for a principle of art within the sphere either of theoretical knowledge or the moral life."[22]

Lewes, as a beginning critic, is at the opposite extreme of this development, at the point where von Mises indicates a critic ought to be. He assumes the "logical and psychological aspects" of literature to be entirely accessible to scientific analysis. What this would mean in an earlier empiricist tradition, one that in England runs from Edmund Burke to Archibald Alison, is that the critical theorist must be preoccupied with the *effect* of art on the senses and the feelings. Mill's other great disciple, Alexander Bain, continues this tradition insofar as he applies scientific method to the problem of art:

Ever since the dawn of philosophical speculation, the nature of the Beautiful has been a matter of discussion. . . . Most of the inquirers laboured under fallacy or misapprehension, rendering the discussion futile as regarded analytic results; they proceeded on the supposition that some single thing could be found entering as a common ingredient into the whole class of things named beautiful. No, *excepting the feeling itself* [experienced in the presence of beauty] . . . , there is no one common thing in all objects of beauty.[23]

And, of course, Mill himself in talking about art as a cultivator of the emotions follows the same line.

Lewes' approach is different. It is self-consciously Aristotelian (Lewes was later to write an entire book on Aristotle), indeed, neoclassical in its focus on mimesis or representation rather than expression and effect. What he wants, above all, to write about is the relation between artistic structure and the *real* structure of the world; what he wants, above all, to recommend is that that relation be literal or transparent, not symbolic. In this we may, in fact, find him even more of a positivist in criticism than Mill, who, after all, allowed poetry its symbolic existence, where one might, for a time, escape from the rigors of scientific analysis. Correlatively, Lewes is still more radically opposed to the romantic aesthetic than is Mill, whose concept of the poetic symbol derives from Coleridge and Carlyle, even as it reduces the symbol's metaphysical referents to psychological ones. Lewes, young and enthusiastic positivist as he is, wants, as it were, a complete sweep of the Romantic aesthetic discourse. To borrow (and pervert) a phrase from Paul de Man, he is engaged as critic primarily in an argument against the "ideology of the symbol," according to de Man the central romantic ideology, the great prophet of which is Hegel. What this ideology insists upon is the existence of a mysterious inwardness that can never be expressed except indirectly or metaphorically by symbols.[24] Art, says Hegel, displays the highest inwardness of spirit sensuously; it "digs an abyss between the appearance and illusion of this bad and perishable world, on the one hand, the true content of events on the other, to reclothe these events and phenomena with a higher reality born of the mind. . . ."[25] Lewes rejects this romantic ideology with its abyss between nature's "appearance" and its "true [rational] content" as a mystification. The romantic symbol signifies a metaphysical entity that is not there. Preoccupation with the "symbolic in Art," Lewes writes, reached its height in the romantic school's desire to create "a new Religion, or at any rate, a new Mythology. . . ." But "the poet who makes symbolism the substance and purpose of his work has mistaken his vocation," symbolism, "being in its very nature *arbitrary*—the indication of a meaning not directly expressed, but arbitrarily thrust under the expression." Incidents "however wonderful, adventures however perilous, are almost as naught when compared with the deep and lasting interest excited by anything like a correct representation of life."[26] Inevitably one compares this with what George Eliot seeks in her early work: "I aspire to give no more than a faithful account of men and things as they have mirrored themselves in my mind."[27] As Comte had said, "The most important and the most difficult object in our intellectual existence consists in transforming the human brain into an exact mirror of the external order."[28]

Modernist descendants of the romantics find the positivist correspondence criterion anathema. "In literature," writes Northrop Frye, "questions of fact or truth are subordinated to the primary literary aim of producing a structure of words for its own sake, and the sign-values of symbols are subordinated to their importance as a structure of interconnected motifs. Whenever we have an autonomous verbal structure of this kind, we have literature."[29] De Man in his objection to the ideology of the symbol would no doubt include such modernists as Frye, as he does the New Critics, among the ideologues, for they in their own essentially neo-Kantian way (Frye is a follower of Cassirer) continue the romantic faith in a metaphysical entity, in this case, something like a universal constructive human reason that transcends the natural world. What de Man advocates, of course, is a radical subversion of this ideology in favor of a Derridean grammatology, according to which language is not a symbol that refers to any entity other than itself, but a *sign* (in de Man's carefully circumscribed sense of the word) that has meaning only as part of a larger system of linguistic differences. "Contrary to the metaphysical, dialectical, 'Hegelian' interpretation of linguistic signs as deferring to an absent presence," writes Derrida, the only possible principle of signification lies in the relation of any given sign to the other terms of its language system: "Essentially and lawfully, every concept is inscribed in a chain of a system within which it refers to the other, to other concepts, by means of the systematic play of differences."[30]

From de Man's standpoint, we do not extricate ourselves from the ideology of the symbol until we have eradicated from our thinking the metaphysics of referentiality. From the standpoint of Lewes' positivism, however, de Man (and Derrida) are, in fact, themselves continuing the ideology of the symbol—the belief that symbols somehow constitute their own reality—to its logical conclusion, a radical relativism that denies any possibility of a relation between the language of art and the laws of nature, physical or human. To be a scientific critic, Lewes maintains, is to insist that art convey accurate information about the world. Or, in the terms (borrowed from Goethe) that come to form the central axis of his early literary criticism, the artist must adhere to a fundamentally *objective* method, avoiding the unreal—and socially unhealthy—subjectivism of the romantic.[31]

The particular reality that Lewes considers it the primary business of literature to represent—and of criticism to urge that literature represent—is psychology: the truth of a work of literature lies not "in the probability and consistency of its incidents, but in the probability and consistency of the motives, passions, and characters" it portrays.[32] Lewes' Aristotelian emphasis on mimesis involves, it appears, a distinctly un-Aristotelian preoccupation with character rather than action as the essential object of literary representation. Why this should be so will be more apparent if we examine for a moment Lewes' developing thought on extra-aesthetic matters.

The Biographical History of Philosophy, as we have seen, is not simply a history. Like most other histories of philosophy it announces its author's fundamental intellectual orientation, his acceptance of Comte and Mill as the arbiters of a new and definitive methodology. If we look carefully at the 1846 volume, however, we see that the end to-

wards which all philosophy moves is not only a method of investigation, but also a particular object of investigation. In his closing pages,
Lewes draws our attention to what he considers the post-Hegelian
muddle in German philosophy, but speaks of one man, F. E. Beneke
(1798–1854), whose *Lehrbuch der Psychologie als Naturwissenschaft* came
out as Lewes was finishing the *History*, as notable for wanting to reduce all philosophy to psychology. Lewes says no more in the 1846
volume about Beneke, but clearly this pioneer in scientific psychology
made a deep impression on him, helping to establish in his mind, as
his reading of Comte would not have done, the idea of psychology as
the new universal human science of the modern era (in the next edition of the *History* [1857], the point is made still more conspicuously).
Positivism, in short, leads him where Edmund Husserl complains it
must inevitably lead, to "psychologism,"[33] to the reduction of mind
to an empirical study of our organs of thought and feeling.

What the early editions of the *History* are, in fact, indicating is
Lewes' movement towards his distinctive intellectual vocation. Since
the history of philosophy has issued in the establishment of psychology as the preeminent human science, should not a young man bent
on revolutionizing contemporary thought focus his attention on that
discipline? Years later, in the preface to the first volume of his great
work, *Problems of Life and Mind*, he speaks of psychology's need for a
new organon, a compilation of "the fundamental data necessary to its
constitution as a science." In this, he says, psychology is in the position of "Chemistry before Lavoisier, or of Biology before Bichat": it
awaits its heroic founder.[34] Clearly he thought of himself as a serious
contender for the role. Although he never really completed his organon—we are left with an extensive collection of related, but incomplete and often disjointed, essays towards a theory of psychology—
Lewes, as T. H. Green indicates, has every right to our consideration
as a great psychological thinker, worthy, indeed, I would argue, to
stand above Alexander Bain, whom most would consider (in the
words of one prominent historian of the subject) "the greatest British
psychologist of this period."[35] Lewes' greatness lies in his un-British
receptivity to Continental, especially German, science. Far more than
Bain or any other British psychologist of the century, including
Spencer, he absorbed into his concept of mind and transmitted to his
countrymen the revolutionary work of Lotze, Fechner, Helmholtz,
and Wundt, men who define, as Bain and the British associationist
tradition do not, the main movement of psychology in the nineteenth
century.

We shall come back to Lewes' particular contributions to psychology. Here we note only that what we see in Lewes' work, both in his historical account of the direction of philosophy and in his deliberate choice of his particular area of scientific research, is a shift in intellectual history as critical in its own period as the "linguistic turn" has been in ours.[36] The consequences of the new perspective were destined to make themselves felt in every imaginable intellectual undertaking, including, as Lewes' example well illustrates, the study of art and literature. The ultimate location of aesthetic value, the center of the "poetic," was no longer, as with the great romantics, some version of "the repetition in the finite mind of the eternal act of creation in the infinite I AM."[37] It had become, rather, a finite psychological condition, observable, radically human, and ultimate. Its truths accordingly replace the romantic vision of "the one Life within us and abroad"[38] as the epiphanic moments of serious art, as we can see in George Eliot.

The waves of her own sorrow, from out of which she was struggling to save another, rushed over Dorothea with a conquering force. She stopped in speechless agitation, not crying, but feeling as if she were being inwardly grappled. . . . Rosamond, taken hold of by an emotion stronger than her own—hurried along in a new movement which gave all things some new, awful, undefined aspect—could find no words, but involuntarily she put her lips to Dorothea's forehead which was very near her, and then for a minute the two women clasped each other as if they had been in a shipwreck.[39]

Such moments as these bear the "religious" value of Lewes' postromantic philosophy and his postromantic aesthetic.

THE UNCONSCIOUS LOGIC OF FEELING

"Not our feelings, but the pattern which we make of our feelings, is the centre of value."[40] These words of T. S. Eliot nicely introduce the problem at the heart of Lewes' search for psychological reality. Psychology must be the essential concern of literature as of philosophy, but what exactly does it mean to present the human mind realistically? It is an issue, we may recall, that Mill confronted in trying to define what he meant by saying poetry must cultivate the feelings. To see how Lewes responds to it, we need first to look at how he studied psychology, not as a literary expression, but in itself.

For Comte the history of philosophy ends not with the triumph of psychology but, on the contrary, with its elimination from the circle of knowledge. Sociology is the highest knowledge, the point to which all science aspires. Psychology becomes a subcategory of biology. To this, J. S. Mill, as we have also seen, takes exception, ending his *Logic* with a call for the establishment of a separate science of psychology: "There is ... [a] grave aberration in M. Comte's view of the method of positive science. . . . He rejects totally, as an invalid process, psychological observation properly so called, or in other words, internal consciousness. . . . The study of mental phenomena . . . has a place in his scheme, under the head of Biology, but only as a branch of physiology. . . . There is little need for an elaborate refutation of a fallacy respecting which the only wonder is it should impose on any one."[41] Lewes obviously was not imposed upon. In his 1853 book on Comte, one of the earliest and most comprehensive English accounts of the philosopher, and throughout his scientific work, he remains fundamentally with Mill in his belief that psychology occupies a separate intellectual province from biology. So in this crucial parting of the ways in the history of the nineteenth-century science of mind, Lewes for all his Continental leanings remains well within the British tradition.

Yet, at the same time, he has learned enough from Comte to take him significantly beyond Mill. The latter, although he recognized in principle that psychology had much to learn from physiology, had no interest in pursuing the connection; he stood, in the last analysis, exclusively on the introspective method. Lewes called in *Comte* for a "new cerebral theory" that would make physiology not simply an adjunct but the very "basis" of psychology. For him, as for Comte, the phrenologist F. J. Gall and the pioneer physiologist P. J. G. Cabanis had made a "philosophical revolution" in the study of mind by urging the necessity of founding that study on biology. The "vision of Psychology as a branch of Biology, subject therefore to all biological laws, and to be pursued on biological methods," he writes, ". . . may be said to have given the science of psychology [a new] basis."[42]

Others in England were moving in the same direction. Alexander Bain had gone to France in 1850 specifically to learn physiology so that he might bring British associationism up to date with the latest Continental developments.[43] For this, one authoritative historian of psychology has given him credit for providing "a completely novel approach in English . . . psychology," moving it from its introspective, associationist base to experimental "psychophysiology."[44] Yet if we compare Lewes' contribution in this direction with Bain's in *Senses and Intellect* (1855), we must recognize that Lewes has at least as much claim to being an innovator and probably a more substantial one. Not only did he precede Bain in announcing in *Comte* that the psychology of the future must be based in physiology, but also his knowledge of the subject was at once deeper and more advanced. As a result, the "transition" in psychology he was promoting was more radical than anything we find in Bain or any other midcentury epigone of the associationist school. Lewes took more time than Bain learning his physiology from the Germans and the French and was several years behind him in publishing his results. But the care was worth the effort, for we find in his work the sort of decisive break with the dominant paradigms of British psychology, paradigms of rationalism, associationism, and individualism that we do not find in Bain, and that does, indeed, make an epoch in the history of the discipline.[45]

Comte may have inspired Lewes to proceed in this direction, but the French philosopher, Lewes observed in 1853, having announced the necessity of reducing psychology to physiology, had failed to keep up with the physiological knowledge necessary to pursue this insight.[46] That knowledge by the mid-1840s was coming not from France so much as from Germany. The first of the great German physiologists Lewes seems to have encountered was Johannes Müller (*Handbuch der Physiologie des Menschen*, 1833–1840), whose dictum, "nemo psychologus nisi physiologus," obviously made a deep impression on him. But still more influential were Müller's followers, and Lewes' own contemporaries, E. W. von Brücke (1819–1892), E. H. Dubois-Reymond (1818–1896), J. Moleschott (1822–1893), and K. Vogt (1817–1895), almost all of whom he had read by at least 1860.[47] These writers (among others) compose what has become known as the German materialist school, and all have in common a "reductionist" approach to the principal psychological problem of the later nineteenth century, the relation between mind and body.[48] All, that is, seek in one way or another to identify the physical causes of mental life. As Dubois-Reymond wrote to C. F. Ludwig, the modern psychological researcher must swear a solemn oath to put in effect "the truth that no other forces are effective [within the human organism] than the purely physical chemical [ones],"[49] It is these writers who define the direction of Lewes' research from 1853 to the early 1860s, at which point other Germans begin to eclipse them, as we will see in chapter 5.

In his reliance on introspection Bain, like Mill, retained an essentially rationalistic, or intellectualist, view of mind, whereas Lewes, under the guidance of Comte and the Germans, pressed forward to a new perspective. Characteristically, we see the beginnings of this in his literary criticism well before he develops it in scientific discourse.

In an early (1844) essay on Honoré de Balzac and George Sand, we find a distinction that runs in one form or another throughout Lewes' thought on psychology. Balzac, he writes, is preoccupied with the question of *motive*, which "is itself a thing of intellect," and in his treatment of motive he considers that the final spring of action is "calculation," the self-conscious, intellectually governed decision to take this or that course: " . . . his persons triumph by ingenuity. They count upon men as they would count upon mathematical data. . . ." George Sand, on the other hand, is concerned, above all, to express profound passions that operate upon her characters spontaneously without their being able intellectually to comprehend them or calculate their consequences. At the same time, the two novelists' methods of presenting the psychology of their characters is "very opposite." Balzac "is a philosopher, and criticizes them"; "he anatomizes and then delivers a learned lecture on them. . . ." George Sand "is a poet and creates characters"; she "places her men and women dramatically before you"; they spontaneously and directly "reveal their characters in their thought and deeds."[50]

This opposition between calculation and spontaneity, intellectualized motive and impulsive feeling, returns repeatedly in his comments on the novel, becoming the pivot on which his critical judgment is most likely to turn. What is psychologically more real, and thus artistically superior, is the representation of the deep emotional or instinctual (later he will call them "unconscious") springs of human action. These the truly modern artist, like George Sand, will present "dramatically," or directly, with a minimum of authorial interpretation. By this criterion, Charlotte Brontë, a touchstone of psychological realism for him, is preferred to her British predecessors, Fielding, Scott, and Austen, as well as her French contemporary Balzac. Her work represents "soul speaking to soul; it is an utterance from the depths of a struggling, suffering, much enduring spirit." In contrast to Mrs. Gaskell, she is far less concerned with convention. Hers is the truly original "utterance" of the feelings; her genius resides in "the depth of her capacity for all passionate emotions." Clearly, she is England's answer to George Sand.[51] Dickens, on the other hand, demonstrates a fundamental shortcoming as novelist precisely because he fails to understand how deeply rooted motivation is in our unconscious nature; how it is not simply a question of holding opinions which can be intellectually changed once we receive the right information. "[We] assert that it is in defiance of all sound psychology to believe in sudden moral conversion following upon an intellectual conversion. . . . Physiology will teach us that this is impossible. Sorrow turning his thoughts inwards, or calamity shattering his pride and confidence, may effect great changes in the outward manifestations, but they will not alter the inward nature. . . ."[52] Again, what is psychologically most real is that which lies below intellect: out of the elemental passions comes the truest poetry.[53]

Turning to Lewes' later scientific writings on psychology, we find this theme developed in extensive, carefully researched detail. It is the main burden of *The Physiology of Common Life* (1859–1860), a two-volume study of the relation between animal and human "mind" and his first original contribution to contemporary psychological research. "It will be understood," he writes," that by the word Mind we do not designate the intellectual operations only. If the term were so restricted, there would be little objection to our calling the Brain the organ of the Mind. But the word Mind has a broader and deeper signification; it includes all Sensation, all Volition, and all Thought; it means the whole psychical Life."[54] Later in his observations on the "unconscious" he speaks of the radical change the new science of psychology has made in our understanding of minds

Descartes—followed by many philosophers—identified Consciousness with Thought. To this day we constantly hear that to have a sensation, and to be conscious of it, is one and the same state; which is only admissible on the understanding that Consciousness means Sentience. . . . The teaching of most modern psychologists is that Consciousness forms but a small item in the total of psychical processes. . . . It is very certain that in every conscious volition . . . the larger part of it is quite unconscious.[55]

The position is somewhat modified in the mature theory of psychology developed in *Problems of Life and Mind*, but the belief that the real basis of human thought and action lies in our subrational, or animal, nature remains intact.

Although it is pretty generally acknowledged that ideas have their origin in sensations, it is rarely acknowledged, and often expressly denied, that all the Feelings, whether those of the Five Senses, specially styled sensation, or those prompted by the Systemic Senses, and more often called impulses, emotions, desires, etc., are the real Motors [of human action]. . . . The intellect, even at its highest, is a guide, not an impulse:—it shows the way, it does not cut it.[56]

Elsewhere the argument is extended to a theory of knowledge , which for Lewes, as for all nineteenth-century positivists, is a subcategory of psychology: "All cognition is primarily emotion. . . . No phenomenon is interesting until it is illuminated by emotion. . . ."[57]

The principal source of Lewes' reversal of the rationalist psychology of his empiricist/associationist predecessors in scientific psychology is, again, Comte. We remember that the French writer, in reducing the psychological to the physiological and dismissing the introspective method, laid the ground for his central point about the relation between the human faculties: ". . . it is impossible to establish permanent harmony between our various impulses, except by giving complete supremacy to the feeling. . . . Without this habitual spring of action [intellect and action] would inevitably waste themselves in barren or incoherent efforts. . . . Unity in our moral nature is, then, impossible, except so far as affection preponderates over intellect and activity."[58] The more physiologists explored the connection between organic processes and consciousness, the more comparative anatomists explored that between animals and humans, the less credible it became, scientifically, to define man as an essentially rational being. From that incredibility follows, for Comte, the necessity of a philosophical revolution, a revolution Herbert Marcuse has aptly described as an attempt to end philosophy's subordination of reality to "transcendental reason." I note in passing that this—and what Lewes and others make of it, is the beginning of the much more familiar psychoanalytic revolution that Sigmund Freud will claim for himself almost a century later, a connection we will explore at length in chapter 11.

We come now to the problem signaled by T. S. Eliot's remark with which we began this section. It is a problem we have already touched upon in our consideration of Mill's concept of poetry as a cultivation of feeling. Far more consciously than Mill, Lewes looked to art as a means of exploring and validating feelings that tend to be suppressed by convention, but which are nonetheless intrinsic to our human nature. The privileging of the psychological over the metaphysical, the emotional over the rational, involves a profound challenge to any morality whose sanction resides in a supernatural being and whose rules closely circumscribe the free expression of certain fundamental emotions. "Realism," Nelson Goodman has said, "is a matter not of any constant or absolute relationship between [art] and its object, but is a relationship between the system of representation employed in the [realist art] and the standard system."[59] Such a definition would have been too indeterminate for Lewes, who, as we have seen, did indeed believe that art could achieve an absolute, nonsymbolic relation with the real, but he would certainly have agreed with Goodman's point that realist art attacks and disrupts the "standard system," whether aesthetic or social. His critical essays of the 1840s and 1850s constantly come back to this opposition between the psychological reality he wishes artists to express and what is conventionally allowed. So far from being "a mirror or expression of *society*" (my emphasis), he writes, the novel with its focus on psychological reality is "under most aspects palpably at variance with society."[60] "Elementary passions" are constant in human nature and are definitely not the same as the "standards of human virtue and vice," which are conventions "modified by advancing civilization."[61] The "illicit passions" that George Sand is accused of portraying are illicit only in a particular, temporary social context.[62] Mrs. Gaskell is admirable in proportion as she shows us how social convention can "blot out the inner life by which we live." Charlotte Brontë's *Villette* is a masterpiece of "contempt of convention in all things" in the interests of portraying a passion that goes so deep that Lewes is made uncomfortable by it.[63]

Yet there are plainly limits to what Lewes will allow in the way of the expression of "elementary passions." There are passions that make him uneasy enough to want to see them excluded from art. His standard in such cases is, predictably, nature. Balzac is something of a touchstone here. Like George Sand, his work seeks to liberate us from certain conventions regarding human sexual expression, but he goes too far when he expresses the "unnatural" sexual desire of an old maid for a young man, or worse still, a young man for his mother. Here the assumption is that there are certain limits—one is hard-pressed not to call them moral—built into nature itself, and these the realist, whose duty is always to the accurate representation of nature, must not violate.[64]

But how are we to know what those limits are? How except by a subjective judgment do we determine that Sand's portrayal of human sexuality is natural and hence healthy realism while Balzac's is unnatural and hence unhealthy or decadent realism? Lewes certainly does not have an answer in the early criticism, though it is apparent he does not consider this a decision that can be left finally to art or the aesthetic judgment. His opinion of Goethe, the most philosophical of artists, is characteristic, and significantly opposed to Carlyle's romantic reading of the poet a decade earlier. Where Carlyle had looked to Goethe as the poet-prophet who could supply the age with a new mythus, for Lewes he is a great genius but not, *as poet*, capable of solving "the great problem[s] of our . . . existence." It is too much to expect of an artist that he present a true solution of the social problem he exposes.[65]

Good positivist that he was by the early 1840s, Lewes considered that it was up to science to establish the natural limits of human passion, which is to say the typical structure of instinct or emotion upon which we must rest both individual morality and social order. This structure, it would then be the "true wisdom" of the artist to "mirror."

Artistic realism, as Lewes is fully aware by the end of the 1840s, could not simply be a matter of empirically representing the unstructured data of human psychology. The realist must register the true *laws* or, to use the term Lewes later employs in his advanced psychological work, the "logic of feeling." "Art," he writes in 1850, "deals with the broad principles of human nature, not with idiosyncracies. . . ."[66] Insofar as the artist follows this rule, he need not surrender his role as a critic of the conventional moral or social order, but he is certainly moving in a direction which, as I have intimated and as we have seen from Comte's remarks on the instinctual basis of altruism, has definite moral implications. This distinction in psychological realisms which I am describing, and which I consider the essential measure of Lewes' development as a critic from the early to late 1840s, closely related to Mill's insistence in the *Logic* that the study of psychology is, finally, the accumulation, not of practical or approximate truths of human nature, but of those truths only as they "can be exhibited as corollaries from the universal laws of human nature on which they rest."[67] Such laws, applied to criticism, would presumably enable Mill to offer a scientific explanation for his spontaneous or "practical" preference for Wordsworth's joy over Coleridge's dejection as the emotional representation proper to the cultivation of the feelings. We shall look in a moment at Lewes' mature concept of "legitimate idealization" in realist art, but before we do, we must follow him through the scientific research that makes it possible for him to affirm theoretically that there is a type or law of human psychological makeup that is actually "there" for the artist to "mirror." This research is markedly different from what Mill proposes in the *Logic* and a continuation of Comtean principles insofar as it begins with the problem of biological structure and not, as Mill would insist, with the laws of association.

LEWES AND GOETHE ON THE NATURAL BASIS
OF ARTISTIC FORM

In 1852 Lewes distinguished between the function of science and that of literature: "Science is the expression of the forms and order of Nature; literature is the expression of the forms and order of human life."[68] We can best describe his mature criticism of the 1850s and 1860s as an effort to overcome theoretically this distinction between natural forms and artistic ones, to make, that is, the scientific search for form and the literary expression of it one and the same enterprise. What propels him in this direction is, beyond question, his concentrated study of Goethe. This began in 1852 when he was finishing up his Comte book. Following Carlyle, he had early recognized Goethe as the foremost literary figure of the age, and the notion of writing a book on the German seems to have been on his mind since at least the mid-1840s. When he came to write that book (1852–1855), he saw Goethe as not only the great representative poet of his age but also its greatest philosopher. What makes this philosophical stature is an extraordinary knowledge of science and a lifelong effort to synthesize the scientific study of nature with the expression of the human spirit in art, subjecting both to the same norms and judgment. "The antithesis to Poetry," writes Lewes, echoing Wordsworth, " . . . is not Prose but Science. Therefore have Poets and Men of Science, in all times, formed two distinct classes, and never, save in one illustrious example, exhibited the twofold manifestation of Poetry and Science working in harmonious unity; that single exception is Goethe."[69] The Goethean ideal is, beyond question, the ideal that Lewes came to set for himself as critic and that in a few years' time he and George Eliot were together to set for her as novelist.

Whatever may be the final decision on Goethe's scientific work, writes Lewes in his *Life of Goethe*, "there must ever remain the great and unique glory of a poet: having created a new branch of science. . . ."[70] Morphology, the study of organic forms, as Lewes correctly observes, first began as a serious science with Goethe. Lewes' lifelong preoccupation with morphology, the "very soul" of natural history, as Darwin was to call it, came not from Comte but emerged with his renewed study of the poet philosopher whom Comte does not even mention in his survey of biology in the *Cours*. We see it again in Lewes' short discussions in 1853–1854 of K. E. von Baer's (1792–1876) embryology, of T. H. Huxley (1825–1895), and of J. M. Schleiden (1804–1888) and T. A. H. Schwann (1810–1882) on cell theory, and, very prominently, in a long essay on Goethe's great French disciple, E. Geoffroy St. Hilaire (1772–1844).[71] The subject fascinated Lewes, and, we may say, provided the gateway into his serious study of science itself as opposed to philosophy and the history of philosophy.

What the science of morphology involved for Lewes, as for Goethe and the others just mentioned, was an effort to discover the fundamental organic form that underlies the multiplicity of the more advanced and complex forms which make up the living world. While conventional biologists were occupied with analyzing and cataloging organic forms, says Lewes, Goethe's philosophical mind

urged him to seek the supreme synthesis, and reduce all diversities to a higher unity. . . . He imagined an ideal typical plant (*Urpflanze*), of which all actual plants were the manifold realisations. . . . [But] he was happier in the conception of all the various organs of the plant as modifications of one fundamental type. . . . [We] must conceive the whole plant as a succession of repetitions of the original type variously modified. . . . It is impossible to be even superficially acquainted with biological speculations, and not to recognize the immense importance of the recognition of a Type. As Helmholtz truly observes, "the labors of botanists and zoologists did little more than collect materials, until they learned to dispose them in such a series that the laws of dependence and a generalized type could be elicited."[72]

Geoffroy takes up the theme and applies it to zoology: "What is the *idée mère* from which all [Geoffroy's] investigations proceed . . . ? It is the *demonstration* . . . that throughout the infinite variety of organic forms there runs one principle of composition. . . . This 'Unity of Composition,' which he [like Goethe] devoted himself to establish is, we believe, the greatest idea contributed by zoology to philosophy."[73]

One can scarcely avoid the obvious connection between Lewes' interest and George Eliot's Lydgate, the student of Xavier Bichat (1771–1802), a pioneer morphologist Comte does mention, and prominently. Lydgate "longed to demonstrate the more intimate relations of living structure and help to define . . . the true order. . . . What was the primitive tissue? In that way Lydgate put the question—not quite in the way required by the awaiting answer."[74] The awaiting answer, which Lewes recognized as early as 1855, was the "cell," "the one primitive universal organ." But more to the point is that what becomes Lewes' central scientific preoccupation, namely the relation between the *Urbild* of biological life and the fundamental structures of mind and hence of culture, becomes the problem on which the meaning of George Eliot's masterpiece turns. She, in fact, gives us two morphologists in *Middlemarch*, a biological one (Lydgate) and a philological (or cultural) one (Casaubon). While the former looks for the primitive tissue, the latter seeks an originary cultural form, the true primitive religion. The question she, no less than Lewes', strives to resolve is whether the two relate to one another and, if so, which is primary.

For her answer (or my version of it) we must wait until chapter 6. Lewes' we can pursue directly.

It is obvious that the biological problem of the *Urbild* had the widest possible implications for Lewes (as it did for Goethe). Science, insofar as it is able to demonstrate the uniformity of organic life, seems to sanction the possibility of a comparable unity in mental life. Lewes is careful not to solve the problem metaphysically as did some of Goethe's followers (notably L. Oken [1789–1851]. Goethe's type, he insists, "was no physical entity." He simply reasons analogically, and tentatively, that the demonstrated existence of fundamental organic types implies the existence of fundamental mental or psychological types. This is the great connection for which he believes he is establishing the basis in *The Physiology of Common Life*. "A basis has been laid . . . for a true zoological classification of mental phenomena. The unity of the nervous system throughout the Animal Kingdom has been generally recognized; but strangely enough, the unity of Consciousness has not been deduced from it. . . . Simple as the forms of Consciousness may be in lower animals, they must be nevertheless essentially akin to the more complex forms in the higher animals."[75] The problem is that there is no logical or empirical ground for making the deduction that Lewes is calling for here, as he himself was well aware. Mill's objection to the use of physiology as the basis of the science of mind was precisely that, given the current state of scientific knowledge, there was no way to make the transition from one to another. Lewes refused to accept this as a permanent situation, but as of 1860, for all his painstaking research, he was still not sure how to solve the problem.

In the meantime, however, the literary criticism of the mid- and late 1850s was written as if the logical transition had been made or rather in the faith that it would inevitably be made. The most striking instance is in the 1858 essay "Realism in Art," the one essay of Lewes' that has survived, just barely, in the modern canon to represent his contribution to criticism. The essay needs to be read in a way it has not yet been, as an outgrowth of his current thought on morphology, for its underlying assumption is that there are primitive mental structures which the literary realist must seek to represent, as opposed to random empirical data. No less interesting is the essay's projection of what those structures are, a projection that is not found in *The Physiology of Common Life* two years later, probably because Lewes felt freer to indicate them in a literary than a scientific context.

Writing on German fiction, Lewes makes his standard objection to
the metaphysical aesthetic. The German bent of mind always wants
to impose an "ideal element" on art. Hence the absence of good
novels in that country. Art is not meant to "beautify" life; it is meant
to give us the "forms of ordinary life."[76] What is distinctive about this
essay, and what readers who take it for one of the manifestoes of midcentury realism do not sufficiently recognize, is that Lewes' principal
objective is not to dismiss the notion of the ideal in art, but to *redefine*
it in terms other than metaphysical. The true antithesis to realism in
art, he writes, is not idealism but "falsism.": We must not, indeed cannot, eliminate the ideal from art, but we can distinguish between true
ideals or forms of life and spurious ones. The only "legitimate style of
idealization . . . consists in presenting the highest form of reality."
That form must be human, not divine or otherworldly, for the
"human soul is the highest thing we know." It must not be idiosyn-
cratic or mean, but present a humanity "such as accords with our
highest conceptions" of the human. Lewes' principal example is
Raphael's "Madonna di San Sisto," a favorite painting of his as well as
George Eliot's. In Raphael's painting, we see "at once the intensest
realization of presentation, with the highest idealism of conception."
The Christ child expresses an "undefinable something" which we feel
is a "perfect truth" of human nature. The virgin mother's expression
is also in the "highest sense ideal" precisely because "it is also in the
highest sense real." This artistic "conception," as Lewes insists, is not
grounded in any theological or metaphysical principle, but is the product of a "sympathetic," a purely psychological, projection of the artist's self into the unapparent emotional center of another human
being. What is "ideal" is the sentiment felt by the artist in the actual
human subjects and then "thrown into" the images on the canvas. We
inevitably note that in this particular image the emotional structure
represented as ideal is a conspicuously altruistic one.[77]

As we will see in *The Principles of Success in Literature* (1865), Lewes
gives fuller theoretical attention to this issue of the ideal-cum-formal
in art. There he objects to what he calls "the [contemporary] rage for
'realism'": realism is "healthy in as far as it insists on truth," but "unhealthy in as far as it confounds truth with . . . predominance of unes-
sential details." A "rational philosophy" of art understands that the
"natural means truth of a kind," or, to use what becomes for him an
absolutely central concept, the truth of "type."[78] This concept of the
"truth of kind," groundable, it is believed, in a scientific morphology
of mind, can be said to be the theoretical mainstay not only of Lewes'

positivist aesthetic but of later Victorian scientific or scientifically inspired criticism in general. We find it implicit in the literary judgments
of Leslie Stephen, John Morley, Grant Allen, and others. As Mill's
late-century follower James Sully, to whom we will return, puts it in
Sensation and Intuition (1874), "The first impulse of an observer is always to measure naturalness [of character] by a subjective standard."
But, repeated psychological observations "lead the mind to supplement its subjective standard by an objective one." This standard in
turn becomes the basis of our aesthetic judgment: " . . . this cultivated
feeling for unity among all types of character . . . affords one of its
principal delights to the aesthetic contemplation. . . ."[79] Sully is drawing heavily on Mill's concept of ethology, or the science of character,
which is not quite what Lewes has in mind when he talks of the logic
of feeling. What both have in common, however, is the understanding
of realism as ultimately a matter, not of "detailism," but of what is
typical in ordinary human nature, and verifiably so. The question of
scientific verifiability aside, one is struck again with the neoclassical
proclivities of this new realist aesthetic.[80]

It should Returning to Lewes' 1858 essay, we cannot help but notice that his
examples of "legitimate idealization" in art are far from morally neutral. On the contrary, the types portrayed by the realistic artist are
"loving," "tender," "sympathetic," "venerable," in no sense a challenge to conventional moral expectations. The exemplary instance,
Raphael's painting, whatever its claims to psychological realism, also
presents, of course, one of the most powerful symbols of Christianity.
Obviously, the more Lewes' notion of a legitimate idealization or truth
of type seems to coincide with values that have their roots in the
Judeo-Christian ethical tradition, the more we feel that, his positivist
protestations notwithstanding, certain metaphysical presuppositions
have, in fact, seeped into his concept of the real.

It should come as no surprise to us that the family piety that Lewes
is responding to in the Sistine Madonna is also a central tenet of
Comte's philosophical vision. The French positivist, as we have seen,
divides his doctrine of social life into two parts, social statics, which
Lewes describes as the "anatomy" of social order, and social dynamics, which is the study of the evolution of humanity. Leaving the question of dynamics for chapter 5, we note that social statics is ultimately
the search for the primitive type that underlies the complex social
structures of contemporary civilization. Thus Comte, following Gall,
wants to establish the originary organic form of human nature. Gall,
he says, has disposed of all metaphysical notions of the "original of

Man's social [i.e., altruistic] tendencies" and "proved" them "to be inherent in his nature."[81] That social instinct or tendency of our nature, he goes on to argue, receives its first structured expression in family life. Lewes, at this point in his career, takes up the point: the family is "not only the effective element of society," he says, it also offers "in every respect the first natural type of its radical constitution."[82] Or as Comte had put it, "There is certainly no natural economy more worthy of admiration than the spontaneous subordination which, first constituting the human family, then becomes the type of all wise social co-ordination."[83] What the *Cours* offers as the original type of social organization becomes in Comte's next system the source of all morality and hence the foundation of the new "religion of humanity" that he is promulgating in that work.[84] We may smile, in our post-Freudian wisdom, at the naiveté of this view of the family, but that does not alter the fact that for Lewes and for Comte it was no less scientific a proposition than the Oedipal *Urbild* of culture was to become for Freud. It is the "cell" to which the social organism can be reduced. For this to change, says Lewes, we must "suppose a transformation of the cerebral organism."[85]

Even the particular choice of the Christ-Madonna relationship as the type of familial or altruistic love was almost certainly suggested to Lewes by Comte, for whom, of course, the future (Positivist) religion of humanity retains some of the most potent symbols of the old religion of Catholicism. The medieval Catholic "acceptance of the worship of Women, . . . is the first step towards the worship of Humanity": "Since the twelfth century, the influence of the Virgin . . . has obtained a growing ascendancy. . . . The special and privileged adoration which this beautiful creation of Poetry is receiving . . . may serve as a connecting link between the religion of our ancestors and that of our descendants, the Virgin becoming gradually regarded as a personification of Humanity."[86] At this point we may make a very interesting "connecting link" of our own between two different "psychologizations" of the principle of Christian *caritas*: Lewes, on the one hand, and that of the woman who by 1858 had become the artist he knew best, on the other.

The image of the Virgin as the essential type of love appears almost contemporaneously in a German philosopher whose reaction against German idealism parallels Comte's own and whose work Lewes would have known very well because of his relationship with its English translator. For Ludwig Feuerbach (1804–1872), as for Comte, human love is the source of all social organization, and its image is

the relation of the Virgin and Child: " . . . the Holy Virgin is a necessary, inherently requisite antithesis to the Father in the bosom of the
Trinity. Moreover we have . . . , implicitly, the feminine principle already in the Son. The Son is the mild, gentle, forgiving, conciliating
being—the womanly sentiment of God. . . . Love is in and by itself
essentially feminine in its nature. The belief in the love of God is the
belief in the feminine principle as divine."[87] Through the intermediary of Feuerbach, as it were, we can see Lewes' (and Comte's)
theory of the biological type of moral and social life merging with
George Eliot's art. From beginning to end of her career she finds in
family life and, more particularly, the maternal instinct, the anchor of
our moral being. "Pity that Offendene was not the home of Miss Harleth's childhood, or endeared to her by family memories! A human life
. . . should be well rooted in some spot of native land, where it may
get the love of tender kinship . . . : a spot where the definiteness of
early memories may be inwrought with affection, and kindly acquaintance with all our neighbours . . . may spread not by sentimental effort and reflection, but as a sweet habit in the blood."[88] Likewise the
image of the Madonna, divested of its symbolic reference to an otherworldly ideal, becomes for George Eliot, no less than for Lewes and
Comte, the "emblem of Humanity." The question of the relationship
between her real heroines and this medieval ideal of loving affection,
as we will see, poses a constant problem for her.

The signal difference between George Eliot's novelistic treatment of
the moral structure of human nature and Lewes' scientific one lies in
a greater willingness on the part of the artist to question whether the
moral type she wants to believe in is, in fact, real. She thought of her
novels, as we frequently hear, as "experiments in life," and indeed
they are, experiments which repeatedly test the positivist proposition,
the fundamentally optimistic proposition, that there is something in
our "cerebral structure" that tends to altruism. Like her own Lydgate, but in greater earnest, she pursues that problematical "poise" in
our psychic structure, which must "determine the growth of happy or
unhappy consciousness."[89] *Adam Bede*, written almost contemporaneously with "Realism in Art," is the closest she comes to an uncritical
acceptance of the Comtean paradigm, with Dinah Morris demonstrating at last that "happy" reconciliation of the germ of sexual desire
(tragic in Hetty's instance) with the altruism that Comte wants so
much to believe in. But when we come to *The Mill on the Floss*, the conflict between desire and disinterested maternal or family love is her
prevalent theme, raising the antipositivistic possibility that "division"

(a key word in that novel), in this case division within the self, may be insurmountable. "[Maggie] hardly ever saw Philip during the remainder of their school life. . . . When they did meet, she remembered her promise to kiss him, but as a young lady who had been at a boarding-school, she knew now that such a greeting was out of the question. . . . The promise was void like so many other sweet, illusory promises made in Eden before the senses were divided . . . —impossible to be fulfilled when the garden gates had been passed."[90] With such an "impossibility" perhaps built into life, the positivist program for a return to reality becomes considerably less appealing. This is a problem to which I have already alluded in the first chapter and to which we will be returning with increasing urgency as we go along. As we will see, it is a problem intimately related to that other question raised in our discussion of Comte's shift to the subjective (i.e., aesthetic) method of whether one must, in the final analysis, project onto reality the ordering *Urbild* that cannot be inductively discovered within it.

4

A World Wrapped in Words: George Eliot and the Irrecoverable Language of Nature

The most primitive germ from which knowledge can be developed is already a perception of fact, which implies the action upon successive sensations of a consciousness which holds them in relation . . .

—T. H. Green

GEORGE ELIOT once wrote that her function as artist was to "rouse the noble emotions which make mankind desire the social right."[1] One cannot read her work with any attention and fail to realize that every novel rests upon one fundamental theme, the necessity of discovering a social order that will embody the "right." What is right, very simply put, is a social order that meets the desires and aspirations of the individual self, an "organic" structure or totality, in which community and individual exist in harmonious interdependence and the individual is at one with himself or herself. As a very accomplished study of George Eliot has lately argued, she ". . . participated in a tradition of social thought that was preoccupied with the rediscovery of community. . . . . Despite many individual differences and internal contradictions, this intellectual tradition includes four principal elements . . . : the perception of a breakdown in traditional values, the belief in a need for social regeneration, the desire . . . to distinguish between fact and value so as to validate both, and the assumption that society could recover a sense of solidarity through a revolution of thought and feeling."[2] The characteristic situation of George Eliot's heroes and heroines is that of living in what Lucien Goldmann has called a "degraded" society, a society in which their deepest values are not realizable.[3] Adam, Maggie, Silas (in Lantern Yard), Romola, Savonarola,

Felix, Dorothea, Lydgate, Daniel—all, in one degree or another, share this condition, the condition of a "blind, unconscious yearning for something that would . . . give [the] soul a sense of a home . . .,"[4] where "home" is understood to be not the otherworldly order that a hero or heroine from Balzac or Dickens or Dostoevsky, caught in the same dilemma, finally turns to, but an earthly order, the order, again, of the *social* right.

A POSITIVIST PERSPECTIVE ON TRAGEDY

George Eliot's way to that order, we begin to understand more and more, was inextricably involved with the rise of scientific theory as the arbiter of all knowledge. "[D]oes not science tell us," writes the narrator of *The Mill on the Floss* (1861), "that its highest striving is after the ascertainment of a unity which shall bind the smallest things with the greatest?"[5] One could do worse than describe George Eliot's career as an extended effort to answer that question in the affirmative. As Sally Shuttleworth has argued,

Science did not, as some of her contemporaries proposed, merely supply her with a source of esoteric imagery. Nor, as more recent critics have argued, was its function merely to lend validation and authority to established views of social order. . . . [N]ineteenth-century scientists and social philosophers shared certain fundamental concerns; mainly a preoccupation with the relationships between part and whole within an historically changing field. George Eliot addresses the social dimensions of this question, employing a biological model of organic interdependence to resolve the ideological conflict between theories of individualism and social integration and, on an historical plane, the demands of continuity and change.[6]

Like Lewes, George Eliot had taken to heart Carlyle's jeremiad on the age "destitute of faith, yet terrified at scepticism," and, like Lewes, she believed that a scientific philosophy could "transform" religion and answer Carlyle's despair, could proclaim (in Lewes' words but with my emphasis), "the supreme importance of *this life*, the supreme value of *human* love, and the grandeur of *human* intellect."[7] Where her work parts most significantly from Lewes', and behind his, Comte's and Mill's, is in its proximity to an almost Carlylean pessimism, its apparently irresistible need to contemplate ironic alternatives to the positivist vision even as she affirms and, after much the same pattern of Lewes, adjusts that vision to accommodate new problems and new discoveries. The underlying motif of her work Lewes, I believe, pays tribute to in a brief, undeveloped aside to some late remarks on the individual's power to reform the "general mind." There is a "striking antithesis," he says, in "the progress of mankind": ". . . the Moral Sense, which in the first instance, was moulded under the influence of [the social factor] comes at last, in the select members of a given generation, to incorporate itself as protest and resistance, as the renunciation of immediate sympathy for the sake of a foreseen general good, as moral defiance of material force, and every form of martyrdom."[8] Martyrdom of the select few in the pursuit of a new "religion" more congruent with that in *Adam Bede* she calls the "language of nature," this is the story George Eliot repeatedly tells. She takes for her theme a consequence of evolution that contemporary scientists were not inclined to emphasize: ". . . that superior power of misery which distinguishes the human being and places him at a proud distance from the most melancholy chimpanzee. . . ."[9]

Another, more familiar, way of putting the point is to say that the dominant form of George Eliot's art is tragedy. She was no less an admirer of Aristotle than was Lewes, and while Lewes in the early 1860s sought to update the Stagirian's scientific thought for the post-Comtean, post-Darwinian era, George Eliot strove to do the same for his principal aesthetic interest, to locate, as she says in *The Mill on the Floss* that $\tau\iota$ $\mu\grave{\epsilon}\gamma\epsilon\theta o\varsigma$ that makes for tragic significance.[10] Essentially, tragedy in the modern world is for George Eliot that experience of martyrdom to inadequate social structures that Lewes alludes to above. To be tragic, she writes in explanation of what she was doing in the *Spanish Gypsy* (1868), is to "represent irreparable collision between the individual and the general . . . ," where the "individual" expresses a "hereditary" or natural condition and the general a social one, "some . . . set of historical and local conditions."[11]

There is another way of reading the "general" in this description of tragic conflict and that is as a transcendent force of nature or the cosmos that she associates here with the ancients, in particular with the Promethean story of an "ineffectual struggle to redeem the small and miserable race of man against the . . . adverse ordinances that govern the frame of things."[12] The understanding of tragedy as a hopeless cosmic battle between man's aspirations and nature's ordinances, George Eliot touches upon throughout her fiction, as when Maggie contemplates the possibility that the human "need for love" is an anomaly in an "insane world," a "world without love," where the "traces" of man are doomed "to be swept in the same oblivion with the generations of ants and beavers."[13] But, ultimately, it is just this irreconcilable conflict between human nature and the "frame of things" that she wishes to leave in the past, among the Greeks, in favor of a more hopeful tragic vision that keeps her, at last, within the pale of the positivist faith that science can discover the unity that binds us together. Her secular martyrs, no less than Christian ones, fail, like Maggie, even die in order to reveal a better world to come. "The art which leaves the soul in despair," she writes at the close of her remarks on tragedy, "is laming to the soul, and is denounced by the healthy sentiment of an active community." The "consolatory element" of the tragedy she seeks to write lies "in the all-sufficiency of the [individual] soul's passions in determining sympathetic action," that is, in moving his or her community back to sanity.[14] For all the suffering of her protagonists, George Eliot's art always strives to affirm (in Lewes' phrase) the "supreme value of human love, and the grandeur of human intellect" as the forces that ultimately govern our destiny.

In my reading, George Eliot's fiction from *Scenes* (1858) through *Silas Marner* (1861) traces a development roughly parallel to what we find in Lewes' scientific and critical theory as he moves from his initial biological and physiological researches of the 1850s to the "Prolegomena" of 1867 (but probably begun in 1862); as he moves, that is, from the belief in a continuum between plant, animal, and human life, from which one may argue, in the manner of the early Comte, for the objective existence of an original, organic moral-cum-social type, to the growing awareness that the search for such a type is quixotic, that moral types are hypothetical or symbolical projections of human consciousness onto nature, not "reals." In Lewes' case, as we will see in the next chapter, this shift in outlook comes of a combination of not being able scientifically to affirm the existence of an original cerebral structure and exposure to the thought of scientific theorist, notably the later Comte, Hermann von Helmholtz (1821–1894), and Wilhelm Wundt (1832–1920), who stressed the subjective or constitutive (intentional) essence of all types of "groupings" of empirical data. In George Eliot's case, a comparable shift in conceptualization comes primarily, one imagines, from her inability to comprehend the empirical realities she committed herself to record or "mirror" within the positivist notion that our highest moral type, namely, the type of altruistic love, has an absolute psychological source in human nature. Some other case needed to be made for validating the "social right" or totality she sought to affirm. Her movement towards a preoccupation with the efficacy of symbolic representation owes something to Lewes' specifically scientific exploration of the same question from the mid-1860s on (the subject of the next chapter). But it owes still more, I think, to a scientific development that Lewes showed little interest in and was, indeed, somewhat hostile towards, a development more closely related to midcentury physics than to the biological revolution that preoccupied him.[15] This too will have to wait for a later chapter. At present we are concerned with her early, self-consciously inductivist efforts to discover and reproduce the true "language of nature," or, as Lewes would call it, the "logic of feeling."

THE LANGUAGE OF NATURE AND THE PROBLEM OF TEXTUALITY

As the dancing begins at Arthur Donnithorne's birthday celebration in *Adam Bede* (1859), Seth Bede, too conscientious a Methodist and too melancholy a lover to join in, watches the scene from a distance and cannot help but see in his imagination that incongruous figure of Dinah Morris superimposed upon the dancers.

> . . . Dinah had never been more constantly present with him than in this scene, where everything was so unlike her. He saw her all the more vividly after looking at the thoughtless faces and gay-colored dresses of the young women—just as one feels the beauty and the greatness of a pictured Madonna the more, when it has been for a moment screened from us by a vulgar head in a bonnet. But this presence of Dinah in his mind only helped him to bear the better with his mother's mood, which had been becoming more and more querulous for the last hour.[16]

The contrast, so puzzling to Seth, between the ideal woman and the vulgar, that is, ordinary, reality of the people around him, including his mother, is a contrast that George Eliot constantly returns to in her fiction. Maggie and her mother, Romola, and Dorothea Brooke are all conspicuously set against the image of the Madonna and, in a late variation on the theme, Mirah Lapidoth, against that of Dante's Beatrice. In all these instances, the problem George Eliot is struggling with is summarized in the last novel. "I wonder," says Daniel Deronda, speaking ostensibly of architectural forms, but also, one suspects, of the woman (Gwendolen Harleth) beside him, "whether one oftener learns to love real objects through their representations, or the representations through the real objects."[17] Or, as I would transpose the problem, are the symbolic representations of things valuable because they transfigure and idealize the real, or because they mirror the ideal *within* the real? The answer George Eliot seems clearly to give in *Daniel Deronda* is the former.

But in *Adam Bede*, close to the outset of her career as artist, it is the second alternative she appears to favor. If we are to believe Seth, the relation between the meaning of the Madonna and an actual women is not in the least problematical. What is, is whether that woman, Dinah Morris, can stand as the type of humankind. The answer, dramatically speaking, is left not to Seth but to his appropriately named brother, Adam. The narrative's conclusion that the madonnaesque Dinah, Adam's choice, represents the morally real, presents us with what amounts to an aesthetic embodiment of the doctrine taught by Lewes' 1858 essay "Realism in Art." *Adam Bede* is George Eliot's analogue to the Sistine Madonna as treated in that essay; the novelist represents in her modern secular language what Raphael needed to represent in the "language" (iconography) of the Church, even as she alludes to the continuity of her language with the earlier Christian one. Both approximate what George Eliot appears to believe in 1859, no less that Lewes contemporaneously, is the true "language of nature": ". . . the mother's yearning, *that completest type* of the life in another life, which is *the essence of real human love,* feels the presence of the cherished child even in the debased, degraded man . . ." (my emphasis).[18] Dinah's cousin and alter ago, Hetty Sorel, on the other hand, is the principal embodiment, not only in this novel but also among all the early novels up to (but not including) *Romola,* of the ironic alternative that love, altruistic maternal love, is not humanity's "truth of kind." For Adam to choose and marry Dinah is a triumphant transcendence of (in George Eliot's key word in the early fiction) "division" in this earthly world, which means not so much that paradise has been regained as that it was never, after all, lost. "I have come to the conclusion that human nature is loveable . . . ." How has she come to this conclusion? Inductively, scientifically, she would have us believe, "by living a great deal among people more or less commonplace or vulgar." This has been the reward of a realism that obliges the artist "to creep servilely after nature and fact . . . ."[19]

If one objects here, as with Lewes' argument in the 1858 essay, that literary realism conforms rather comfortably with convention and has hardly produced any martyrs, one must consider more closely the situation of Hetty. She is the anti-Madonna, guilty of child murder and condemned by her society to die. It is certainly not for this that George Eliot is offering her as a martyr, but there is another sense in which Hetty is more deserving of that role. Idyllic as it is, the community of Hayslope embodies a social structure that at once exploits and condemns another part of Hetty's "hereditary" or biological nature, her sexual instincts—exploits by a system of class division that

at once facilitates her seduction by Arthur Donnithorne and blocks
marriage to him; condemns by a Christian asceticism that finds sexual
expression a necessary evil and tends to locate the source of the problem in woman's Eve-like frailty. George Eliot does not condone Hetty's
extramarital affair (she was far too sensitive on that subject). But it
may be argued that she does allow the proper Madonna to learn from
Hetty.[20]

Every major character in the novel, as throughout George Eliot's fiction, governs his or her life according to some text or image that inter-
poses itself, its symbolic system, between the character and his or her
direct reading of the "language of nature."[21] Donnithorne tends to see
reality through pagan texts; for him Hayslope life is a Greek idyll and
Hetty a Psyche whom he can seduce and desert without consequence. Hetty's text is a kind of spontaneously conceived "romance"
such as one might find in "silly novels by lady novelists,"[22] which she
might have read if she ever read anything. Adam, Seth, Lisbeth, and
Dinah all rely for their reading of life almost exclusively on the words
of the Bible, preferably untainted by interpretation: ". . . let the
words o' the Bible alone!"[23] Adam has occasion to say at the very outset of the story, and thus introduces one of the central questions of
the novel, a question hardly surprising in a work by George Eliot, the
translator of Feuerbach and Strauss: can we let the words of this, the
most pervasive text in Western civilization, go uninterpreted, untrans-
formed by the historical growth of knowledge?

In Dinah's case, the Bible is, of course, interpreted by John Wesley
and his Arminian gospel of divine love as all-encompassing. This Wesleyan reading of scripture, not to mention the purveying of it by a
woman, is itself revolutionary in the Hayslope of the 1790s, as George
Eliot makes clear. Less obvious is the further revolution implicit in
Dinah's own particular moral development in the course of the story.
She begins by insisting upon the all-sufficiency of divine love. "God's
love . . . satisfies the soul, so that no uneasy desire vexes it . . . : the
very temptation to sin is extinguished . . . ."[24] And her reason for not
marrying Seth is that such a marriage would not only interfere with
her prophetic vocation but would also imply a "sinful" desire for
something other than divine love. Seth appropriately attributes her reluctance to the Pauline text against caring too much for husbands. The
final marriage to Adam has been fairly criticized by modern feminism
as a surrender of female independence, a persistent problem, as we
shall see, with George Eliot's treatment of her heroines.[25] But, in this
case, we need also to read that marriage as a conscious liberalization

of the gospel of love to include sexual as well as spiritual love, as a release for Dinah from the biblical and especially Pauline, repression of female sexuality.

The close of the novel focuses on the growing strength of Dinah's "temptation" to sexual love of Adam. When she finally succumbs, it is with a sense of release form inner division: "My soul is so knit with yours that it is but a divided life I live without you. . . . And they kissed each other with a deep joy."[26] George Eliot has learned from Wordsworth, not to mention Feuerbach, the art of transposing the scriptural connotation of "joy" into a fully secular experience, only she goes still further than Wordsworth in explicitly aligning it with the satisfaction of physical rather than metaphysical desire.[27] In the next novel she will combine the cousins, Hetty and Dinah, in the single character of Maggie Tulliver, and there the inability to reconcile sexual desire with the expectations of the social code does, indeed, produce a tragic martyrdom.

What we need to understand is that by her deliberate echoing and transposition of biblical language (I have mentioned the signal instance of "joy"; the closing line from *The Mill on the Floss* is, of course, from Samuel; examples might easily be multiplied) George Eliot is engaged in a reinterpretation or rewriting of scripture. She is refusing to "let the words of the Bible alone." The new scripture she seeks to write—and this is nowhere truer than in *Adam Bede*—is the gospel according to Comte and, still more perhaps, Feuerbach. She has clearly taken up Comte's (and Lewes') point that the "germ" of ideal or altruistic love, what St. Paul calls charity, lies in the human sexual impulse and, in the pilgrim Dinah's progress, has carried us back, in effect, from Pauline or Christian love to its biological origins. Feuerbach is still more insistent, and more revolutionary, on the emotional origins of religious sentiment. "Love is God himself, and apart from it there is no God. Love makes man God and God man. . . . Love is the true unity of God and man, of spirit and nature. . . . What the old mystics said of God, that he is the highest and yet the commonest being, applies in truth to love, a love which has flesh and blood, which vibrates as an almighty force through all living things."[28]

George Eliot's conclusion that human beings are typically loving and loveable is not, then, as socially comfortable as it may at first appear to be. If we fail to take the point in *Adam Bede*, we can hardly miss it in *The Mill on the Floss*, where Maggie's desire for sexual love, the post-adolescent expression of her irrepressible animal impulses, puts her at tragic odds with the general mind of St. Ogg's, and does, indeed, make her just such a martyr on behalf of moral progress as Lewes describes, a Feuerbachian prophetess whose time has not yet come, but whose biblical epitaph—"In their death they were not divided"—seems to look forward to some future world of "saner" human relationships.

When we perceive the connections between the new gospel of love that George Eliot is trying to write in *Adam Bede* and the similar visions of Feuerbach, Comte, and Lewes, we may reasonably ask ourselves how accurate her claim is that she has come to the conclusion that human nature is typically loving and loveable (in the sense of those words we have been pursuing) a posteriori, inductively, by way of direct observation. May one not as well argue that the type of human nature, the fundamental moral reality embodied in the novel, owes at least as much to George Eliot's reading in philosophy as to her empirical experience, that it is no less textual, after all, than her characters' interpretations of life, that it is very much an a priori *projection* onto reality of other people's writing?

Very much, but not entirely, which brings us back to Hetty. Hetty is more than is dreamed of, or at least written of, in the philosophy of Comte, Lewes, or even Feuerbach. The experience she represents I take to be George Eliot's most adventuresome, least textually mediated exploration of psychological reality. She does not fit into the positivist closure we have been considering, and it is this lack of fit, more than anything else, that probably pushes George Eliot to reassess and redefine what she has been given by the philosophers. In Hetty's story, if you like, lies the germ of deconstruction that will constantly shadow George Eliot's search for a scientific totality, down to the murderous hysteria of Gwendolen Harleth.

Hetty alone of all the characters in the novel experiences utter isolation from her fellow man and, as a result, stares directly on the possibility of the meaninglessness of human life. Here is the "hidden dread" that tastes "the bitterest of life's bitterness. . . . Such things are sometimes hidden among the sunny fields and behind the blossoming orchards; and the sound of the gurgling brook, if you come close to one spot behind a small bush, would be mingled for your ear with a despairing human sob."[29] In the economy of this narrative it must be Dinah, the priestess of love, who ministers to Hetty's suicidal alienation, as she does in the climactic prison interview after Hetty has been condemned for child murder. Dinah seeks a confession of guilt and remorse that will show her (and the reader) that deeper than this archetypal crime against love is a still more archetypal moral nature that can recognize it as crime. She gets the confession, but not the remorse. Instead Hetty presents her with an overwhelming question: "Dinah, do you think God will take away that crying [of the abandoned child] . . . in the wood . . .?"[30] And Dinah, for all her faith in love, cannot respond yes. In that silence resides the possibility not simply of the absence of redeeming *divine* order (something George Eliot was prepared to do without), but of any redeeming moral order whatsoever.

The silence, we can say, is ultimately drowned out by the joyous sound of marriage bells in the last chapter. But is it really? There remains the epilogue, the outside-the-text, graphically reminding us of what is left out of the positivist text that I am arguing provides George Eliot with the essential moral structure of this novel. The epilogue returns us to the problem of the long-suffering and now dead Hetty and at last expresses explicitly what was implicit in Dinah's silence: " 'There's a sort of wrong that can never be made up for' "— a wrong or a flaw felt empirically within the self, a "something behind" the reality of human lovableness, that needs to be accounted for.[31]

At this point we come back to the problem that confronted both Mill and Lewes in their advocacy of a scientific aesthetic. The artistic imagination in its realist, as opposed to constructivist, mode discovers the psychological "springs of action" that lie outside conventional morality and the social code. These it brings out, in good "scientific" fashion, without regard to the disorientation or, to recur to Coleridge's signal experience referred to by Mill, the dejection they may cause. The question then becomes for George Eliot, as for Mill and Lewes, How is the intelligence to accommodate these disruptive discoveries about the mind? Through the scientific reconstitution of our moral and social expectations, is the pat positivist response. But it is the process of reconstitution itself that is the problem and resolving that problem requires that we look more closely at the function of imagination in its constructivist or intentionalist sense. As soon as we do, this realism, whether as artistic or scientific doctrine, begins to lose its earlier unproblematical—vulgar positivist, if you like—authority.

THE PROBLEM OF "DIVISION" ONCE MORE

In *The Mill on the Floss* there is no expression of despair quite so deep as Hetty's, but what lies behind that despair, the recognition of the deeply problematical status of human nature, is thematized to a degree not found in the earlier novel. If *Adam Bede* strives to regain

Paradise by locating in human nature itself an objective, unifying structure of love, The *Mill on the Floss* sets us disconcertingly back in the "wilderness," reducing the notion of an originary principle of love to the dream of childhood with which the narrative opens. The reality is soon expressed by the character in this novel who perhaps comes closest to Hetty's dread at the confrontation with absolute meaninglessness, Edward Tulliver. The world, says Tulliver, has not "been left as God made it . . .; but things have got so twisted round and wrapped up i' unreasonable words, as arn't a bit like 'em, as I'm clean at fault, often an often. Everything winds about so—the more straightforward you are, the more you're puzzled."[32] We have here at the very outset George Eliot's most persistent metaphor for life in the mature work: it is a labyrinth, a puzzle for which we perpetually seek the clue. Like Adam and Dinah before him, Tulliver believes in the existence of some fundamental "language of nature" that has been obscured by countless interpretations or rewritings until nothing is intelligible, "straightforward"; Causabon will work on the same presupposition. Unlike Adam and Dinah, however, Tulliver never finds his way back to that original language, but dies virtually without language, far more deeply and tragically puzzled than when we first encounter his troubles in the above passage: "This world's . . . too many . . . honest man . . . puzzling . . . ."[33]

Tulliver longs for a "reasonable" world, a positivist world, in which words reflect how things actually are, but what George Eliot now appears to concede is that there is no such language of nature, that everything is experienced through one symbolic system or another. It is a position not unrelated to Lewes' discussion of method in the contemporaneous *Aristotle* (the first draft of which was completed in early 1862). The psychologist's analysis, he writes (and we will explore the point more fully in the next chapter), "discloses that facts are indissolubly ideal—the appearances of things to us, not the things *per se*, and that so far from any fact being the unadulterated image of its object, the conditions of our consciousness are necessarily mingled with it."[34] Lewes here is making a point about perception, George Eliot is extending the point to language (there is no transparent language of nature), and Aristotle plays a not inconsequential role of her own textualist, as opposed to his perceptivist, position. "Aristotle! if you had had the advantage of being 'the freshest modern' instead of the greatest ancient, would you not have mingled your praise of metaphorical speech as a sign of high intelligence, with a lamentation that intelligence so rarely shows itself in speech without metaphor—that

we can so seldom declare what a thing is, except by saying it is something else?"[35] It is still a matter of lamentation that this should be so,
for the narrator as the Edward Tulliver, but the form, unlike the latter,
recognizes it as unavoidable. Metaphor, as George Eliot would have
learned from the great contemporary philologist Max Müller, is the
source of myth[36] (Lewes, also influenced by Müller, will make it the
source of scientific hypothesis). Through myth, language interprets
the world but never gives it to us directly, only as a "something else."
Whereas texts and the myths they inscribe are presented in *Adam Bede*
as illusions that obscure reality and must be broken through, in *The
Mill on the Floss* there is no getting behind them to some original structure, either in nature or in the human mind.

What I think most concerns George Eliot in *The Mill on the Floss*,
given the lamentable unlikelihood of getting beneath the "wrapping"
of language, is the process by which language and its symbolic struc-
turings of reality change through time. *The Mill on the Floss* is the first
of her novels to focus fully on the movement of history rather than
the simple resurrection of the past. In this novel she is herself a kind
of Bossuet recording the major phases, or "variations," through
which religious belief has passed to arrive at the debased condition in
which we find it in St. Ogg's in the 1830's, a society "irradiated by no
sublime principles, no romantic visions, no active, self-renouncing
[i.e., altruistic] faith. . . . "[37]

The two central characters suffer tragically from want of such a
sustaining faith, a faith that will make the world a "home" for them.
In the legend of St. Ogg (related in the first Book, chapter 12), with
its emblematic figure of the Madonna rescuing man from the deluge
and "shedding a light around us of the moon in its brightness, so
that the rowers in the gathering darkness took heart . . . ,"[38] we have
an image of the Christian faith in all its Catholic medieval strength.
Maggie's adolescent resort to the fifteenth-century à Kempis as
spiritual guide, like Dr. Kenn's adult Tractarianism, represents a desire
to return to that early Christian communion and community when
"the Church in its original constitution . . . [watched] over its children
to the last—never abandoning them . . . ," when that Church represented "the feeling of the community, so that every parish should
be a family knit together by Christian brotherhood under a spiritual
father."[39] With significant allusion to the Protestant revolt against
Catholicism—its great texts, *Paradise Lost* and *Pilgrim's Progress*, weave
their way throughout the narrative—George Eliot, in effect, traces the
progress of the Christian mythus to its early nineteenth-century con-

dition. This latest "variation of Protestantism"—the key Darwinian word is consciously deployed—is the religion of capitalism, the fetishistic worship of money and goods and respectability. All the Dodson sisters and their spouses (except Edward Tulliver) practice it, and most notably Deane; the lawyer Wakem is its Levite and Tom Tulliver its upcoming acolyte. "The World goes at a smarter pace now," says Uncle Deane to Tom. Fifty years ago, "everything was on a lower scale, sir—in point of expenditure, I mean. It's this steam, you see, that has made the difference—it drives on every wheel double pace and the wheel of Fortune along with 'em . . . . I don't find fault with the change, as some people do. Trade, sir, opens a man's eyes . . . . [It's] a fine thing . . . to further the exchange of commodities . . . ."[40]

To such "wide commercial views" George Eliot has a deep aversion, an aversion not unlike what she would have found in Carlyle, Balzac, George Sand, Dickens, and many other Christian and quasi-Christian opponents of the new faith.[41] Fundamentally, she regrets the utilitarian doctrine of egoism or self-advancement that philosophically underpinned the capitalistic "faith" with the consequent fragmentation of community into an aggregate of individuals pursuing their own interests at the expense of the whole. The new faith has little patience with Maggie's vague "need of love, [her] hunger of the heart."[42] It has even less time for those who wander from the prudent path of respectability. There are no strong Adams here to rescue Maggie when she goes astray, only a deformed artist, an anachronistic priest, a self-preoccupied brother, and a dilettante lover.

Self-rescue is an alternative. The protagonist can attempt to find for herself a better belief than the contemporary world offers, and the intellectual center of the story is perhaps the recognition—and failure—of this alternative. "She wanted some explanation of this hard, real-life: . . . the . . . oppressive emptiness of weary joyless leisure; the need of some tender, demonstrative love . . .: she wanted some key that would enable her to understand and, in understanding, endure the heavy weight that had fallen on her young heart. If she had been taught 'real learning and wisdom, such as great men knew,' she thought she should have held the secret of life; if she had only books that she might learn for herself what wise men knew!"[43] But self-rescue also comes through the readings of others' symbolic constructions of the world. The texts she finds, a dictionary, a grammar, a geometry, a logic, an epic (I have rearranged them in ascending order of moral relevance), all offer possible beginning, but what immediately works is à Kempis' *Imitation of Christ*, a book which, as we will see, Lewes later uses as an exemplary instance of the creation of a new "moral ideal."[44]

But this symbolic system, while it has supplied her need for the presence of divine love in the world, cannot accommodate the sexual feelings stimulated by Stephen Guest. One needs to make again the point that George Eliot is pursuing a *transfigured* gospel of love, and the books Maggie really needs, *Das Wesen der Christendom* (1841) and *Système de politique positive* (1854), were yet to be written. Having failed to find the rescuing text, the new mythus, Maggie sinks beneath the flood, her boat shattered by floating fragments of the new industrial society. This, of course, is how George Eliot had planned it from the outset. A viable system of belief embodied in its symbolic text, a system such as contemporary St. Ogg's lacks, would float us above the flood of meaningless, unstructured natural energy, much as the Madonna in the St. Ogg legend floats upon the waters, spreading light and order. Implicit in this image is the fact that the relationship between unstructured and unfathomable nature and the interpreting belief is radically discontinuous or metaphorical. The belief is a "something else" that, at least temporarily, preserves us from sinking. We are not meant to despair that Maggie fails to find her saving belief/ text. Her story, as I have suggested, is a tragedy of the "healthy" sort (as opposed to Hetty's story); it looks forward to the construction of some future symbolic social system along the lines indicated by the martyred protagonist's unfulfilled needs. We are not entirely in the position of the reader of the early Carlyle or, for that matter, the late Lewes, looking confidently forward to some "mighty new birth."[45] Maggie's prophetic status is more problematical even than Teufelsdröckh's. But we are in a comparable state of reasonable expectation, rather than hopeless inarticulate puzzlement, which is the end of Edward Tulliver's story.

What we need to ask before going forward is why Maggie's effort at self-rescue fails, for the answer to this question points us toward the principal concern of George Eliot's later fiction, which, simply put, is to design or postulate a self-rescue that will work. The obvious explanation, the historicist one, is that Maggie was simply born at the wrong time. In another period, another place, another class, she might well have found what she was looking for. But this does not take into account the many indications George Eliot gives us that Maggie's problem is not only in the uncongenial historical/social moment, but also in herself. That problem comes down to a lack of sufficient force of personality. Her search for the clue to the labyrinth is, after all, a conspicuously passive one. She hopes to discover in the texts of others the explanation of life she seeks; she neither desires an explanation nor has the ability to create one for herself. Rebellious as she is, her "power of defiance," as George Eliot signals early on in the story, is "feeble,"[46] too feeble, it turns out, to enable her to extricate herself from the containing web of contemporary "religion," let along construct a new one.

Too feeble as well in another, more significant, sense. She assumes that the texts in which she would find deliverance must be written by males, the product of "masculine wisdom." She is all too willing to be rescued by a father, either biological or spiritual, and to lean on the arm of a brother or a lover. As with Stephen at the outset of their "elopement," so with all men, "Maggie felt that she was being led . . . by [a] stronger presence that seemed to bear her along without any act of her own will, like the added self which comes with the sudden exalting influence of a strong tonic—and she felt nothing else."[47] This is not to say that all women or even Maggie herself are utterly without the power to initiate a "variation" in the ongoing development of the symbolic code, for a "girl . . . may still hold forces within her as the living plant-seed does, which will make a way for themselves. . . ."[48] Not only for themselves, but also for others; the metaphor of seed takes us forward, as George Eliot intends it should, to the "spiritual seed" of religion that in her discussion of a "variation of Protestantism unknown to Bossuet" requires "favorable circumstances" in which to grow.[49] It takes us still further forward to the "seed of fire" that impels Deronda's search for the New Jerusalem in the final novel.[50] Maggie's problem is passivity, which George Eliot deliberately portrays as part of her sex. But although it may ultimately make Maggie's personal tragedy, it is not, as George Eliot comes more and more to insist, irremediable, not, that is, built into the "hereditary" nature of sex but the effect of "local conditions"—to return to that all-important distinction in her definition of tragedy.

Before closing this chapter we need to consider one further, and as it turns out, crucial implication of the seed metaphor. George Eliot's remarks on Aristotle and metaphor occur in the context of a discussion of Mr. Stelling's concept of the human mind (it is a field to be plowed by the classics in preparation for any future intellectual seed). But, says George Eliot, "what a different result one gets by changing the metaphor!"[51] The concept of consciousness as originating in a seed or germ which contains its *Urbild* had been, as we have seen, the staple of Lewes' early scientific psychology. The tenor of the metaphor, however, is slightly but significantly different in *The Mill on the*

Floss. There the seed matters less as a structure than as the source of an amorphous force, comparable to Maggie's "blind, unconscious yearning." That is, as George Eliot moves away from the notion of getting back to an original moral structure in human nature and towards the recognition that moral order is imposed, subjectively, or textually, if you like, from without, what becomes of prime importance to her is the problem of generating a force sufficient to make one's subjective constructions prevail. This is a problem she is just beginning to explore in *The Mill on the Floss,* and it will take her eventually to that revision of the metaphor for mind just noticed in *Daniel Deronda.* The seed, again, becomes a "seed of *fire.*" To understand mind as a force rather than a structure, thus to revise one's metaphors, I will want to argue, implies a different kind of scientific preoccupation from what we find in Lewes, or for that matter, in Comte or Mill.

The gradual movement of George Eliot's art away from what one may call a program of scientific sociological realism (as expressed, for example, in the early essay on Riehl and the well-known seventeenth chapter of *Adam Bede*) towards the "poetic," that is, the symbolic, is a theme that has been explored by several critics. Felicia Bonaparte, for a notable example, has shown us the change that takes place in George Eliot's art as she moves from *The Mill on the Floss* towards *Romola*: ". . . to understand *Romola* completely and to understand its pivotal place in the evolution of Eliot's fiction, we must [recognize that it] . . . is not merely a poetic novel but, in its entirety a poem. It is a work, that is, in which the prose narrative is at the same time a symbolic narrative in which every character, every event, every detail—every word, in fact—is an image in an intricate symbolic pattern."[52] What preoccupies George Eliot in *Romola* is "that force of outward symbols by which our active life is knit together. . . ."[53] Bonaparte convincingly argues that *Silas Marner* is a "preliminary exercise" for this sustained and extremely sophisticated experiment in symbolic expression.[54] The same thing needs to be said of "Brother Jacob" and with emphasis, for even more than *Silas Marner* it is, like *Romola,* an attempt to place symbolic or "poetic" form on history.[55]

In *Romola* (as in *Silas Marner*), the doubtful, analytical voice, so prominent in *The Mill on the Floss,* gives way to the prophetic. Unlike Maggie, Romola, who is a study in self-sacrificing love, does not drown in the ongoing flood of nature, but lives on to reaffirm the symbolic power of the Madonna legend, the legend of "a woman [who] had done beautiful loving deeds there, rescuing those who were ready to perish."[56] The possibility of that rescue depends on Romola's instinctual goodness, but it depends no less on her creator's new faith in symbolic expression, a faith announced at the outset of the novel in the image of Giotto's tower: "a prophetic symbol, telling that human life must somehow and sometime shape itself into accord with that pure aspiring beauty."[57] The same notion of human aspiration occurs in *The Mill on the Floss* only in terms distinctly Darwinian: ". . . is not the striving after something better and better in our surroundings, the grand characteristic that distinguishes man from the brute . . .?"[58] The difference is that by the time she comes to *Romola*, George Eliot has begun to understand what Darwin himself never fully accepted, that the most distinctive means of survival available to the human, as opposed to the animal, mind is the power of symbolic expression.

What we now turn to is Lewes' movement, virtually contemporaneous with George Eliot's, towards a revised and painstakingly scientific understanding of the place of symbolization in our lives, an understanding no doubt supported by George Eliot's literary experiments, but inspired as well by some prominent German revisions of Comte's revolution in the theory of mind and society.

5

A New Theory of the Symbol: The Impact of Helmholtz and Darwin on Lewes' Mature Theory of Mind

Our nimble souls . . .
Can spin an unsubstantial universe
Suiting our mood, and call it possible
Sooner than see one grain with eye exact,
And give strict record of it.
—George Eliot

IN the early 1860s Lewes' thought negotiates a distinct turn from a predominantly objectivist to a guardedly subjectivist position, paralleling, but certainly not reproducing, the comparable shift in Comte's thought from the *Cours* to the *Système*. Where he differs from Comte is, first, in the development of what we may very broadly call a neo-Kantian epistemology, second, in his engagement with the implications of Darwinism, a revolution Comte had nothing to say about. The result, largely recorded in the five-volume *Problems of Life and Mind* (1874–1879) is what I take to be perhaps the single most important scientific speculation on the nature of mind in the later (i.e., post-Darwinian) Victorian era. What it does, among other things, is to bring together in a precarious synthesis the two great philosophical developments of the second half of the century, the rise of neo-Kantianism and Darwinism, before the two go on their separate and radically antithetic ways.

LEWES AND HELMHOLTZ:
RECONCILING COMTE AND KANT

For Lewes as scientist not the problemizing of the wholeness of things but its demonstration is the objective, and this means going beyond the Comtean *faith* in the existence of a real moral type to a *proof* of it. Towards this end he turned in the early 1860s to a new and very powerful influence, the German physiologist Hermann von Helmholtz (1821–1894), and with that influence came a new preoccupation with structure as a condition of knowing rather than being. We now recognize Helmholtz as the foremost psychologist of the nineteenth century, and, thanks largely to the work of Ernst Cassirer and Maurice Mandelbaum, we may extend that recognition a step further and see in his work the expression of a decisive turn in nineteenth-century philosophy.[1] Closely related to the German materialist school that in the 1840s and 1850s worked to reduce mind to entirely physiological or chemical causes, Helmholtz concerns himself with the purely physiological mechanism of perception, in particular, vision. As John Merz was to put it, "Through Helmholtz's analysis of the formation of our space perceptions by the eye in connection with tactile and muscular senses, psychology and metaphysics were brought into immediate contact with physics and physiology."[2] But from a more carefully considered point of view, Helmholtz, far from being the principal supporter of the materialist school, turns out to be one of its most formidable critics, the scientist who, more than any other, delivered the final blow to the crude identity of mind and matter that enabled Karl Vogt to make his notorious comparison of thought to gall.[3]

To the German *Materialismusstreit* of the early 1850s, Helmholtz contributed a classic treatise on optics ("Über des Sehen des Menchen"). Here we find a scientifically based theory of knowledge that at once invalidates the position of the materialists and announces a new direction in the study of mind or rather a new version of an old direction. Helmholtz, ultimately, is a disciple of Kant.[4] Ernst Cassirer has seen him as leading the post-Hegelian generation back to Kant. Helmholtz's Kant, however, is a radically naturalistic or psychologistic Kant in the sense that Kant's "forms" of perception (the "transcendental aesthetic") have become for Helmholtz purely physical or organic forms.

Perceptions of external objects being . . . of the nature of ideas, and ideas themselves being invariably activities of our psychic energy, perceptions also can only be the result of psychic energy. Accordingly, strictly speaking the theory of perceptions belongs properly in the domain of psychology. This is particularly true with respect to the mode of the mental activities in the case of the perceptions. . . . Yet even here there is a wide field of investigation in both physics and physiology, inasmuch as we have to determine, scientifically as far as possible what special properties of the physical stimulus and of the physiological stimulation are responsible for the formation of this or that particular idea as to its direction and as to its distance. . . . Thus our main purpose will be simply to investigate the material of sensation whereby we are enabled to form ideas, in those relations that are important for the perceptions obtained from them. This problem can be solved entirely by scientific methods.

This, Helmholtz later says, is the "naturalistic view" of "Kant's assertion . . . that the general apperception of space is an original form of our imagination."[5] As Mandelbaum has put it, "The universal and necessary forms of experience were interpreted by Helmholtz as consequences of the nature of our sensing organs."[6]

Helmholtz effectively reconciled the formalism of Kant with the physicalism of both the British associationist school and the emerging school of positivist, physiological psychology discussed in chapter 3. The result was a new model of mind, according to which cognition, although grounded in sensation, is not a mere aggregate of sensation, but the superimposition of a form or structure on experience, a structure which is innate, in a *biological* sense, in each individual member of the species. The critical philosophy, in short, became Gestalt psychology. As Cassirer observes, Goethe and Geoffroy de St. Hilaire initiate a way of thinking ("structuralist") that transforms the empirical study of mind. "It remained an empirical science, using empirical methods. But in this field, too, we now meet with a new concept and a new description of empirical science. When studying the phenomena of sense-perception, the Gestalt-psychologist had become aware of the fact that sense-perception has a definite structure. It is not a piecemeal of 'simple ideas.'"[7] What Goethe and Geoffroy initiate Helmholtz brings to fruition.

There is no doubt that Lewes was profoundly influenced by Helmholtz's work. He had, as we have seen, read Helmholtz on Goethe by 1854; indeed, it is likely that Helmholtz provided him with the basis of his discussion of Goethe's "philosophic" method of doing science. He probably would have read Helmholtz's major work, *Handbuch der physiologischen Optik*, when it began coming out in 1856; in any case, we know from his journals that he was reading the complete version by the mid-1860s. In 1868 he made a special point of visiting Helmholtz in Heidelburg,[8] and by the time he published his first sustained study of psychological principles (1874), he was ready to place Helmholtz with Shakespeare, Bacon, Newton, and Comte on his short list of the great minds of the modern world,[9] the implication being that he regarded Helmholtz as the successor of Comte in the ongoing development of scientific philosophy.

In the preface to the first volume of *Problems of Life and Mind* (1874), Lewes speaks of a significant change in his approach to psychology that occurred sometime between 1860 and 1862. Up until 1860 he had proceeded on the "plausible supposition that the complex phenomena in Man might be better interpreted by approaching them through this simpler phenomena in Animals" (the assumption underlying *The Physiology of Common Life*). But, Lewes continues, "rightly to understand the mental condition of Animals we must first gain a clear vision of the fundamental process in Man. . . ."[10] This is not particularly expansive, but it probably marks the point at which Helmholtz's Kantian concept of organic perceptional forms emerges as the governing principle of Lewes' psychological theory. Certainly what we see in his publications immediately following *The Physiology of Common Life* is a movement away from the investigation of lower forms of life towards the study of human mental processes, in particular the process of perception. When we come to the lengthy Prolegomena to the 1867 edition of the *History of Philosophy*, which Lewes seems to have begun working on as early as 1862, the influence of Helmholtz is unmistakable. Turning to the "great question" of necessary truths, he immediately makes the concession, anathema to the empiricist tradition, that "the mind is in possession of many ideas which would never have been directly given in Experience. . . ." He then proceeds to tread a careful path between the "sensational school" (utilitarians) and the "apriorists." We are born, he says, with certain "Laws of Consciousness," which have been "evolved through successive modification." His elaboration of the point is worth regarding at length, for it contains the Helmholtzian heart of his mature theory of mind.

The sensational School has greatly obscured [the question of whether the Laws of Consciousness are evolved] by the unscientific conception of the mind as a *tabula rasa* upon which Things inscribe their characters—a mirror passively reflecting the images of objects. This presupposes that Consciousness is absolved from the universal law of action and reaction, presupposes that the Organism has no movements of its own; and thus Psychology is separated from its only true biological ground. The *a priori* School commits the opposite mistake of conceiving Consciousness as a pure spontaneity, undetermined by the conditions of the Organism and its environment; a spontaneity which brings Laws, not evolved from relations, and organised as results but derived from a supra-mundane, supra-vital source.

We cannot take a step unless we admit that Consciousness is an active reagent, even in its first stage of evolution. Sensibility is not passive, cannot be conceived otherwise than as an excitation. Nor is this all. Biology teaches that the Sensitive Organism inherits certain aptitudes, as it inherits the structure, from its progenitors, so that the individual may be said to resume the Experience of the race. Faculties grow up in the development of the race. Forms of Thought, which are essential parts of the mechanism of Experience, are evolved, just like the Forms of other vital processes.[11]

This is Lewes' new post-Comtean, post-Darwinian morphology of the mind. The "forms of consciousness" are not metaphysical entities, but biological ones, the structures of the physical organism, from which, indeed, they evolve. The mind does preconstruct reality, as Kant says, according to intelligible forms, but these forms are not "anterior to the existence of the animal"; they emerge "in the successive phases of the animal's development . . . . With Mind as with Body, there is not preformation or preexistence, but evolution and epigenesis."[12]

Through this "biological doctrine of Innate Ideas," as he will later call it, Lewes believes he has made a decisive step in crossing the formidable gap between the order of mind and the order of things. "Psychogeny [the science of the growth of individual psychology]," he writes in the first volume of *Problems of Life and Mind*, "tracing the evolution of [human] Sensibility in the organic world, must conclude that it is the External Order which *determines* the Internal Order, by determining the organic structure of which sensibility is the property. . . ." Therefore,

I regard the Subject in no . . . alienation from the object; and regard perception as the assimilation of the Object by the Subject, in the same way that Nutrition is the assimilation of the Medium by the Organism. Out of the general web of Existence certain threads may be detached and rewoven into a special group—the Subject—and this sentient group will insofar be different from the larger group—the Object, but whatever different arrangement the threads may take on, they are always threads of the original web. . . .[13]

This Lewes calls "reasoned realism": "realism" because it affirms the reality of what is given in feeling; "reasoned" because it rests on verified scientific research. And he insists on the crucial difference between his realism and a comparable one offered by Spencer (in *The Study of Psychology*) and another by Helmholtz, which he calls "transfigured realism." Helmholtz "declares Perception to be symbolical," whereas Lewes maintains that the object perceived "exists precisely *as* it is felt." Perception does not "symbolically" alter the order of reality, it mirrors it.[14]

So far so good, but we observe that the "forms of thought" which Lewes argues are also forms of reality are, after all, very primitive forms of thought, that is, perceptions. We are a long way from a demonstration that the more advanced *conceptual* forms, the moral and social forms that Lewes would like to ground in reality, are, in fact, thus groundable. Still, an essential step has been taken. If the forms of perception (he calls them the "logic of feeling") are demonstrably continuous with the forms of things, the mind has at its disposal the fundamental means of testing the reality of its more complex conceptions. The "biological doctrine of Innate Ideas" seems to establish the possibility of analytically verifying any proposition whether about the physical or the moral world. Lewes' version of that process, which he, like Comte and Mill, identifies with the logic of science, we must now examine more closely.

LEWES' DEPARTURE FROM MILL ON METHOD

The 1867 Prolegomena is, in fact, a treatise on scientific method, the first original and systematic one attempted by Lewes. Its second chapter opens with a statement that leaves us in no doubt about its subject or the importance of that subject to its author: ". . . the question of Method rules, and in one sense comprehends, all philosophical questions, being indeed Philosophy in action."[15] These are words that would have warmed the heart of the author of *A System of Logic*. Lewes had forecast the particular character of his approach first in *Aristotle* (1864), which was primarily on the Greek philosopher's "revolutionary" method, and then in two substantial articles of 1866 on Mill's dispute with Comte over the question of subjective versus objective method. In the earlier work, criticizing Aristotle, on the one hand, Whewell, on the other, for an excessive and uncritical reliance of hypothesis, he emphasized (with Mill and the early Comte) the paramount importance of *verifying* hypothetical speculation. But, he complained, this "supreme law [of verification] . . . has been taken for granted, rather than articulately expressed. . . ."[16] In the articles on Comte and Mill he repeated the point from a different direction. The subjective method, as developed in Comte's later works, was essentially the use of hypothetical concepts without regard to verification, and he, Lewes, was no less "antagonistic" to such a procedure than Mill. At the same time, he felt that the subjective method might be "regenerated" if it could be accompanied by a proper logic of verification. In the Prolegomena Lewes defines scientific logic as requiring two "successive stages of inquiry": "from Observation to Conjecture, and from Conjecture to Verification"[17] Comte had focused on the first (the "logic of discovery"), Mill, on the second (the "logic of proof"), but the latter not, evidently, to Lewes' satisfaction, for what he is about to offer is a new theory of verification. While his obvious target, like Mill's, is still the "incompetent" metaphysical method, the more significant antagonist is probably Mill himself.

The problem with verification is the supposed unreliability of the human faculties. "Facts are inextricably mingled with Inferences, and . . . both Perception and Reasoning are processes of *mental vision*. . . ." It will doubtless then occur to the reader "that since Consciousness is the ultimate ground of appeal, and since Consciousness can never transcend its own sphere, we cannot possibly have a test of Objective Truth."[18] This is the problem, under the name of the "relativity of knowledge," which Mill had been wrestling with in his recent book on William Hamilton (1865). Lewes' first response to it is not unlike Mill's. Science is contended with "relative certainty," that which enables us to predict the course of natural (or social) phenomena with a degree of accuracy sufficient to our practical needs. But to this "test of truth" Lewes now adds a second, "biological," argument, which Mill, ignorant as he is of physiological psychology, does not consider. Under the classical metaphysical category of "Necessary Truths," which, as a positivist, he should be rejecting outright, Lewes argues in deliberate opposition to Mill that there may, in fact, be such truths: "Mr. Mill insists, that a necessity of Thought cannot be a necessity of Things. Perhaps not; perhaps it can."[19] That, indeed, it can be, in the biological sense which Lewes subsequently develops in the Prolegomena, is the new and still more positive principle of verification which he has to add to Mill's logic. Verification is, finally, a process of reducing the ideal or hypothetical constructions of science to the "logic of feeling." When this is done, we know these constructions are real because, as Lewes believes he has demonstrated, the logic of feeling is an "untransfigured," utterly reliable reflection of the logic of nature.

At the beginning of *Problems of Life and Mind*, Lewes returns to the problem of scientific method, reasserting with greater sophistication and more elaborate terminology, the biological argument for verification. But this does not fully characterize all that he is doing. The "indispensable principal" of verification remains the anchor of his theory of method, but his rhetorical bias has shifted significantly, as we see from his opening announcement of what he now considers his special contribution to the wider positivist search for a "Religion founded on Science." Having gone in his principle of verification beyond Mill, he will now go beyond Comte and extend the scientific method to metaphysics: "I propose to show that . . . when scientifically treated, [metaphysical problems] are capable of solutions not less satisfactory and certain than those of physics." This, Lewes insists, will involve no retreat from his commitment to scientific method, only an "extension" of it: "Scientific Method, *rightly interpreted*, will find its employment . . . [in metaphysics]."[20]

His first problem is to make his position respectable in the eyes of his fellow positivists. This requires a crucial demarcation between metaphysics and what he now calls "metempirics." Metaphysics "embraces the ultimate generalizations of Research" and, therefore, is "a term for the science of the most general conceptions." These conceptions ultimately grow out of experience, though they may not be deducible from it, and though they may not themselves refer to real entities, they contribute to the scientific resolution of real problems. Lewes focuses in particular on the concepts of force, matter, and cause, all of which positivists characteristically reject as being "metaphysical" because unsusceptible of physical verification, and hence pseudoentities. "Metempirics" he reserves as a term to cover what he used to mean by "metaphysics"; it "designates whatever lies beyond the limits of possible Experience, it characterises inquiries which are vain and futile." With the introduction of this term he hopes he can detach "from Metaphysics a vast range of insoluble problems." This means that the key problem of logic or method now becomes that of articulating, not a principle of verification (which he has already done), but a principle of scientifically legitimate generalization or speculation. "It is a serious error to imagine that the true scientific spirit is opposed to the speculative, because it is opposed to the metempirical. The error arises partly because the Logic of Speculation has not yet been organised with sufficient precision,—its tests and canons are left undisciplined. . . ."[21] Clearly, Lewes sees himself as correcting this deficiency, as writing a "Logic of Speculation."

The logic of speculation, or conception (he uses the words interchangeably), Lewes also calls the "logic of signs" and specifically opposes to the "logic of feeling," which is employed in verification. All logic is about "laws of grouping." The logic of feeling describes how we group sensation, perception, emotion, and instinct; the logic of signs, how we organize the "laws of conception" and, significantly, the "formation of symbols." To speculate or conceive is to construct a symbolic interpretation of reality, as opposed to perceiving, which directly reflects reality. For Lewes the epitome of conceptualization in science is the formation of the symbolic structures called hypotheses: "Without Hypothesis no step [in Science] could be taken." And he later expands his point to a generalization on the history of science: "The grandest discoveries, and the grandest applications to practice, have not only outstripped the slow march of Observation, but have revealed by the telescope of Imagination what the microscope of Observation could never have seen. . . ."[22] Lewes' new logic of speculation, at this point, is aimed primarily at providing rules for the formation of hypotheses for use in scientific research. We are still well within the bounds of traditional understandings of scientific method though we have shifted to the more creative or innovative pole of that method relative to Lewes' earlier concern with proofs.

What we may say about Lewes' 1874 position on hypothesis, in the general context of nineteenth-century discourse on the subject, is that it is extremely liberal.[23] "Ultimate verification" by the logic of feeling remains the "one indispensable condition," but this caveat made, Lewes seems at times almost to believe with Feyerabend that "anything goes." The formation of hypothesis is, he says, an "analogical" or "metaphorical" operation. The mind does not proceed inductively, slowly relating contiguous phenomena to one another but makes an imaginative leap over the unknown to draw a plausible order or explanation from an entirely separate but related experience. This seems, in still later writing, to be the only sense in which hypothesis is anchored in experience. "Our mental vision is a reproduction of the past and application to the present. . . . We are not at liberty to *invent* Experience, not to infer anything *contrary* to it, only to extend it analogically." This condition being met, the scientist is at liberty to "mount on the wings of Imagination into regions of the Invisible and Impalpable, peopling these regions with Fictions more remote from fact than the phantasies of Arabian Nights are from the occurrences of Oxford Street."[24]

Most distinctive about what Lewes is prepared to allow as legitimate in hypothesis, as against what Mill and, he seems to believe, Comte would allow, is the use of absolutely unverifiable agents or entities if such entities will serve to forward the progress of scientific generalization. The scientist may employ a "conscious fiction by which Imagination pictures what would be the effect of a given Agent or Agency, *if present*. It is purely a tentative process, like that of assigning an arbitrary value to an unknown quantity."[25] In this view of hypothesis there is no requirement, as with Mill, that the hypothesis be reduced to an inductive law (see above, pages 46–48). All that Lewes requires is that the hypothesis be an "auxiliary" to the establishment of such a law somewhere down the line and that in the process the researcher never lose sight of its fictionality. In thus allowing conscious fictions, Lewes places himself as a revolutionary in methodology: "I am not aware of any philosopher having boldly . . . proclaimed the introduction of Fiction to be a necessary procedure of Research,"[26] and if the emphasis is placed on "necessary," as Lewes probably intends it to be, he is correct. But we need to bear in mind that Comte came to much the same conclusions about conscious and unverifiable fictions as Lewes (see above, pages 50–52). Knowing that Lewes read the last of Comte's works (*Synthèse subjective*), we may object that he is being less than forthright about the influence of his predecessor.

But one has still less sympathy with a more fashionable philosopher of scientific method who would claim revolutionary status almost 40 years after the publication of *Problems of Life and Mind* for something very close to what Lewes is saying. Hans Vaihinger, perhaps even now in the process of canonization,[27] looked back in 1912 to Kant's *Critique of Judgment* and announced that for over a century Kant's "As-if approach," his reliance upon "heuristic fictions," had gone "unnoticed."[28] One cannot authoritatively speak for Comte's acquaintance with the third critique, but Lewes in addition to what he was learning from Comte's late works was carefully rereading Kant in the 1860s.[29] An epigraph from Kant stands just under one from Mill at the outset of *Problems of Life and Mind* in what we can certainly take to be a symbolic gesture at synthesis. Neither Kant nor the scientific implications of aesthetic judgment had gone unnoticed.

Intimately related to the subjective movement in Lewes' concept of scientific method—and we come round now to the critical point—is a new theory of *types*. Under the heading of "ideal Constructions in Science," Lewes returns to the question of biological morphology and to the efforts of Goethe and Geoffroy de St. Hilaire—to which he now adds those of Lamarck and Darwin—to identify the "typical forms" of plant and animal life and establish the "series" by which these primitive forms evolve into complex organisms. It is a "profound mistake," he now says, "in regard to nature" no less than "in regard to method" to "wrest" these types from their status as "ideals" and offer them as "real." A truly "positive doctrine of Morphology" rejects the notion of types as existent structures whether in the Divine Mind or in Nature. "The Scientific value of Types is that of being ideal *guides*, not real facts." Like any hypotheses their value lies not in their truth but in their "effect," their "vast power" as auxiliaries to research.[30]

Having thus asserted the radical fictivity of biological types, he moves rather abruptly to the question of moral types, abruptly because he has, up to this point in *Problems*, been talking almost exclusively about natural, not social, science. The "Creation of Moral Types," he says, is a form of hypothesizing.[31] They are not meant to be laws of nature by which we must live, but, again, tentative guides "by which we measure all deviation from a perfect life."

We all place before ourselves the ideal of a noble life, the type of a grander character than our infirmities enable us to realise [his example, interestingly, is Maggie Tulliver's adolescent inspiration, Thomas à Kempis]; and we do not look on that ideal as a fiction, on that type of character as a falsehood, because we fail to realise it. Like the typical laws of physical processes, these conceptions are solid truths although they exist only as ideals. . . .[32]

What a more conservative scientific methodology had not been able to accomplish, the objectivication of human moral and social structure, a "regenerated" subjective methodology, seems to remedy. The category of moral ideal, like that of hypothesis, in the new "logic of speculation" does not correspond to any objective reality; it only suggests a coherent structure of action, the truth or falseness of which is bracketed.

But the transition from scientific hypothesis to moral ideal is not altogether satisfactory in Lewes' account. One accepts "conscious fiction" in scientific reasoning on the understanding—and Lewes is very clear about this—that it will lead to results, propositions that can be verified against the primitive logic of feeling. Scientific ideas, he constantly reminds us, must ultimately be reduced to reals. The hypothetical structures of science are, from this standpoint, genuinely tentative; they tend towards verifiable statements about the world. But can this be so of moral ideas? By what principle of verification are they to be tested? They are, he says, "solid truths"[33] even though merely ideal. But in what sense "solid"?

The clue to an answer, I believe, lies in the phrase quoted above. We "do not look on [the moral] ideal as a fiction. . . ." Lewes had insisted in his discussion of the use of fiction in scientific hypothesis that the researcher take special pains never to forget the fictivity of his hypothetical projections. Apparently this is not to be true of moral hypotheses. So on this critical question of the subject's *attitude* towards the ideal structure he or she is using as a "guide," there is a significant discontinuity as Lewes moves from scientific to moral ideals. A Kempis certainly did not look on the moral ideal he "created" as a fiction, nor did Maggie Tulliver seek to follow it as a fiction. They had to believe it as an absolute imperative, a present, "solid truth," not a tentative gesture. What Lewes here calls solid truth, I suspect, is better named symbolic truth. To make sense of this apparent paradox, I need to return for a moment to his aesthetic or literary theory, recalling, as I do, that aesthetic meditation with Lewes characteristically precedes and leads the way to scientific and social concepts.

THE PRINCIPLES OF SUCCESS IN LITERATURE: REHABILITATING THE SYMBOL

Lewes' *Principles of Success in Literature*, which first appeared as a series of essays in the *Fortnightly* of 1865 (when Lewes was the journal's editor), is the nearest he came to producing a systematic theory of literature. It begins with the problem of "legitimate idealization," which had become his central preoccupation as critic by the late 1850s. His way of dealing with the problem now, however, is altogether different from what it had been seven years earlier, a difference which reflects, as we might expect, the larger changes introduced into his concepts of psychology and of methodology in the interval.

The first principle of success is the "principle of vision," which, initially, appears to be the principle of "truth of kind" he had developed in the earlier "Realism in Art." The artist represents not empirical reality but its inner, typical form; for this he needs a kind of intuitive "vision." But "vision" now has a subjective connotation; it is very much Helmholtz's constitutive vision. Typical form is not something we passively receive from without; it is built into the very act of perceiving; it is, in E. H. Gombrich's terms, the artist's *schema*. From the most fundamental level of perception to the highest expression of reason and imagination the mind projects an order onto nature, and this is true whether that mind belongs to artist or scientist: "Both poet and [scientific] philosopher draw their power from the energy of their mental vision—an energy which disengages the mind from the somnolence of habit and from the pressure of obtrusive sensation."[34]

The idealization or typicality that derives from artistic "vision" is clearly moral as well as perceptual, and the issue arises here, as we have seen it does in the later *Problems of Life and Mind*, of how we know these aesthetic projections of moral order are "real," how we verify them. Lewes' answer in this aesthetic context is to introduce the second principle of literary success, "sincerity." If the artist is writing as he sincerely feels, he is, Lewes maintains, writing "truly." We object when it is said that an artist is trying to achieve an "effect," but, in fact, "to produce an effect is the aim" of art. What we need to be sure of is the "legitimacy" of the effect, and this is a factor of the artist's sincerity: ". . .the real method of security the legitimate effect is not to aim at it, but to aim at the truth, relying on that for securing effect. The condemnation of whatever is 'done for effect' obviously springs from indignation at the disclosed insincerity in the artist, who is self-convicted of having neglected truth for the sake of our applause. . . ."[35] This begins to look like Carlyle's anti-self-conscious theory of belief or simply a retreat to intuitionism: what we spontaneously feel to be moral is moral. What we need to notice is the way the principle of verification has shifted from the ordinary positivist standard of correspondence to the order of nature, to an entirely new standard of "effect." What is true in art appears now to depend not on what art says about the structure of the world but on how it affects us. Art "depends on sympathy"; "belief creates belief."[36] Lewes' discussion of art for the first time in his career is out from under the controlling concept of scientific truth and working on a distinctively *aesthetic* concept of truth.

With Lewes' third and final principle of success, the "principle of beauty," the distance between artistic and scientific truth widens. The artist's vision and sincerity, he says, are useless unless he can express himself in "fit" symbols.

It is not enough that a man has clearness of Vision, and reliance on Sincerity, he must also have the art of Expression. . . . Any instructed person can write . . . , but . . . to express ideas with felicity and force, is not an accomplishment but a talent. The power of seizing unapparent relations of things is not always conjoined with the power of selecting the fittest verbal symbols by which they can be made apparent to others: the one is the power of the thinker, the other the power of the writer. . . . [The latter requires] the delicate selective instinct to guide us in the choice and arrangement of . . . symbols, so that the rhythm and cadence may agreeably attune the mind, rendering it receptive to the impressions meant to be communicated.[37]

Sincere belief, it appears, does not in itself spontaneously create belief, but requires the medium of carefully chosen or constructed symbols which "attune" the mind of one's audience and render it "receptive."[38] Thus after many years of alienation in the interests of scientific realism Lewes returns to the value of the symbol. This is not, to be sure, the romantic or metaphysical concept of symbolization he earlier rejected. Rather, Lewes' symbols here refer to nothing outside themselves but an inarticulate feeling. Their function is, indeed, not to refer at all but to move and organize responses in their recipients. They are, in short, essentially rhetorical.

In *Problems of Life and Mind* Lewes insists on a distinction between the scientist's disciplined flights of imagination and the artist's unlicensed ones. Yet it seems clear that the concept of a decentered, that is, nonreferential, but effective or rhetorical symbol, developed in his 1865 theory of literature, has by the 1870s overflowed into his scientific discourse. The theory of the consciously fictitious, unverifiable hypothesis, we have seen, owes much to the late Comte, but it owes much as well to Lewes' sensitivity as critic and artist to the way symbols condition belief, a sensitivity certainly heightened by George Eliot's growing preoccupation with the function of symbols after the failure of *The Mill on the Floss* to arrive at an "undivided" vision of the human condition. But in *Problems of Life and Mind*, as we have seen, scientific symbols, though unverifiable in themselves, must tend towards the formulation of propositions that are verifiable, that do tell us about the objective order of things. Knowledge is what constitutes their "success."

The question raised as Lewes tries to move in that text from scientific to moral ideals is the very different one of how symbols function to guide behavior rather than produce knowledge. By speaking, as he does, of their immediate "potency" to "move" us and of our spontaneous, unreasoned reception of them as "solid truths," he seems beyond question to be thinking of them as functioning in the manner of artistic symbols. At the close of the first volume of *Problems of Life and Mind*, he returns with greater clarity to this most problematical area of his search for a scientific religion. Confronting the still unresolved "place of [moral] sentiment in philosophy," he now makes a crucial distinction between cases where Verification and those where Conviction is "the immediate object of research." In the latter category we must include "Moral Instincts and Aesthetic Instincts which determine conduct and magnify existence; but of these . . . we can give no better account than that we find them as facts of human nature; and no better justification . . . than that they [they] are beneficial." These "Sentiments" seem to be like "facts of the human organism," beyond the capacity of reason or science to verify. Is it, then, legitimate to allow them to determine belief and regulate conduct? This, says Lewes, is a "delicate question."[39] Indeed, it is the most delicate question in his philosophy. If we think of moral (or aesthetic) "sentiments" as instincts, part of the "logic of feeling" and hence part of the web of nature, clearly, we are justified in following them. But Lewes knows better, knows that moral beliefs, however much they may become matters of habit and thus seem to be instinctual, are originally symbols "created" by historical individuals, like Thomas à Kempis, subjectively, without recourse to objective verification, like the symbols of art.

Lewes' ambivalence about the status of moral ideals or symbols continues right down to the close of this first volume, but at last his positivism prevails and he falls back on the criterion of verification. Moral ideals are "admirable as an inspiration, when duly controlled by verification," "disasterous" when, as in art, feeling "takes the place of verification and substitutes personal for impersonal relations."[40]

In the final volume of *Problems of Life and Mind* published posthumously and edited by George Eliot,[41] we find Lewes returning, inevitably, to the question of nonreferring symbols. He repeats and clarifies much that he has already said on the subject. There are in the human consciousness three logics, the logic of feeling, the logic of images, and the logic of signs, or symbols. The first, insofar as it is a matter of perception, gives us an objective presentation of external experience. The second is a re-presentation or reinstatement of sensation, "excited by subjective sensation." The third is a "substitution" for the second and still more subjective; it is ideal and abstract, where the second is pictorial and representative. Above all, it is "conventional," the product of the "social factor," and, more specifically, linguistic. Symbols, the expression of ideation or conceptualization, are now for Lewes essentially words. "Ideation" is "the formation of conceptions, and the combination of a series of feelings by means of verbal symbols."[42] Lewes in the mid-1870s has begun, it appears, to make the "linguistic turn."

The object of science is, as always, to reduce symbolic substitutions to the logic of images and thence to the logic of feeling. This process, which Lewes describes as assigning symbols their values (as in algebra), is "verification," the "translation" of symbols to reals: ". . . words are vacant sounds, ideas are blank forms unless they symbolise images and sensations, which are their values." But again (as Lewes earlier argued in his theory of scientific hypothesis) we can "carry on very extensive operations with blank forms, never pausing to supply the symbols with values . . . until the calculation is completed. . . .

[A]lthough it is impossible to feel non-existence, it is possible to think it."[43] What distinguishes this final discussion of symbols from what has gone before, however, is a far greater willingness, not simply to tolerate those symbolic operations that never achieve verification as a fact of human life, but also to recognize that they are quite possibly the *only* means man has of achieving moral and social order (and here, of course, we recall the late Comte). It is the "power of thinking by means of symbols," Lewes says in "The Potency of Symbols" the very last chapter of *Problems of Life and Mind*, "which demarcates man from the animals, and gives one nation the superiority over others." Language overcomes the contingency and indeterminacy of existence by bringing it into a "living synthesis." Its power "over feelings and actions is incalculable." Most important, in view of Lewes' previous efforts to ground morality in an objective order of nature, it is now verbal symbols alone, without regard to verification, which make man the "only moral animal" and unify society: "Language is to the Social Organism very much what the Nervous System is to the Body—a connecting medium. . . . It links together man with man." Finally, in language alone lies the possibility of human progress: it "generalises experience and opens a vista of experiences about to be"; "the invention of a new symbol is a step in the advancement of civilization."[44]

Lewes in this last "problem" has reached the outer edge of positivism. We are reminded of the pattern to be traced by Ludwig Wittgenstein (1889–1951) some half a century later as he moves away from the logical positivism of the *Tractatus* to a new understanding of the "ordinary" function of words, or the "potency of symbols," if you like, as conditioners of behavior: "What do the words of . . . language *signify*, if not the kind of use they have?" And again, ". . . without language we cannot influence other people in such-and-such ways; cannot build roads and machines, etc."[45] Wittgenstein's preeminent modern disciple among sociologists, Peter Winch, draws from his later language theory conclusions that apply no less relevantly to the outcome of Lewes' voluminous effort to found totality on scientific method. We cannot, says Winch, treat the conventional ideas that govern human social behavior as if they were precisely what the scientific observer must put out of the way in order to get at the reality of social life itself. Man's social relations are "permeated" by his ideas about reality; they are, indeed, nothing if not "expressions of ideas about reality." These ideas in turn are reducible to language and must be approached by methods specifically suited to the understanding of language. The issue of the social sciences is *"not a question of what empiri-*

cal research may show to be the case, but of what philosophical analysis reveals about what it makes sense to say. I want to show that the notion of a human society involves a scheme of concepts which is logically incompatible with the kinds of explanation offered in the rational sciences" (my emphasis).[46] Whether Lewes fully understood the direction his thought would take when he began *Problems of Life and Mind* by saying that it was his special task to bring metaphysics within the range of scientific method is uncertain. His neo-Kantian contemporary T. H. Green believed (as Lewes feared many would) that Lewes had ended at last by coming over to the right side. His "untenable compromise," says Green, collapsed into the tacit admission that mind is the ultimate reality that gives us the world. Perhaps, but is it not more accurate to say that what the subsumption of metaphysics under scientific method produced in Lewes' case was a precocious reduction of the problem of "spirit" to a problem of symbolization or language, of the search for noumena to the search for meaning?

ACCOMMODATING THE DARWINIAN REVOLUTION: LEWES AND WILHELM WUNDT

Having pulled Lewes thus far forward into our own time, I must end by pushing him back again to Victoria's. Wittgenstein may have "deeply respected" the search for moral and religious order, but he did not, as philosopher, see it as his business to join in it. This, on the other hand, was precisely Lewes' business. His growing understanding of language came into it, but from first to last his ultimate reference was to psychology and, inevitably after 1860, psychology in the context of the Darwinian revolution. Lewes uses this revolution, or his own version of it, to establish what he was unable to establish by his morphological approach of the 1850s, a ground for the naturalness of altruism and a cooperative social order.

Lewes was among Darwin's earliest and most enthusiastic readers. But it is not for nothing that Darwin is left off the earlier-mentioned short list of the modern world's greatest thinkers in favor of Helmholtz. Lewes admired Darwin in many ways, but like most mid-Victorian evolutionists, he was fundamentally a Lamarckian. Darwinism did not allow, except in a very limited sense, the possibility of consciously *directed* evolution, and hence effectively precluded the melioristic faith that Lewes as well as George Eliot needed to believe in. Whatever might have preceded man in the dark abyss of time, Lewes considered that, with the emergence of mind, evolution ceased to be

random and purposeless and took on the structure and the direction
that intelligent beings chose to place upon it. The particular moral ideals created by man spread abroad to become part of the "web" of civilization and, in the slow progress of generations, instantiate themselves in mind; they are, that is, "acquired" and passed on by heredity. Thus, if they are not original biological structures or, to return to
Lewes' key word, *types* of human behavior, they virtually become so.

Lewes applauds Darwin's theory for its rejection of teleology or the
long-standing metaphysical notion of the unfolding throughout organic life of a preformed plan impelled by some mysterious "vital
force." He agrees with Darwin in the reduction of the evolutionary
process to entirely natural causes and accepts the doctrine of natural
selection as the mechanism by which variation in individuals produces new species. Where he differs most significantly is in his understanding of the cause of variation and of the struggle for survival.

The *Origin* gives little play to external conditions as the cause of
species formation. The variations that initiate species changes are
placed decisively within the organism itself as accidental and inexplic-
able mutations. "The crucial difference between Darwin's view of variation and his opponents'," writes Ernst Mayr, is that, with the
former, "variation was not given any special direction by the environment. . . . Implicit [in Darwin's writing] . . . is the conviction that the
genetic material is usually not affected by the environment."[47] Lewes
is adamant in this insistence on environment or "conditions" as the
principal cause of variation.

Natural Selection is only the expression of the results of obscure physiological
processes. . . . [T]o understand Natural Selection . . . we must analyse the
"conditions of existence." As a preliminary analysis we find *external conditions*, among which are included not only the dependence of the organism on
the inorganic medium, but also the dependence of one organism on
another—the competition and antagonism of the whole organic world. . . .

Far "too much stress," he continues, "is laid on . . . blood, and not
enough on . . . conditions."[48] The influence of Lamarck and the neo-
Lamarckians of Lewes' own period is apparent: the principal occasion, if not strictly speaking the cause, of diversity among organisms
is to be found in changes of environment to which they adapt.

But Lewes also recognizes an internal cause of variation. Indeed,
much of his argument against Darwin is aimed at elucidating those
"obscure physiological processes" behind variation, which Darwin
leaves unexamined. The struggle for existence, Lewes argues, cannot
be restricted to that of organism against organism. It takes place

within the organism itself between competing "organic affinities." There is, at any given moment in the evolution of an organism, a "primary and more important struggle" between inner affinities or "organites" that determines which develops and which degenerates.[49] We will see in a moment how this theory serves Lewes' moral and social philosophy. For now we note only that this version of the internal cause of variation leaves more room than Darwin's theory for an element of *choice* between competing organic possibilities and hence of intelligent guidance, provided, of course, one can work into the notion of the conditioning environment some mechanism of conscious (as opposed to natural) selection. This, not surprisingly, is precisely what Lewes attempts to do.

His mature observations on Darwin's theory first come out in the 1868 *Fortnightly* and, much expanded, later introduced the third volume of *Problems of Life and Mind* (*The Physical Basis of Mind*, 1877). The centerpiece of that volume is the "problem" entitled "Animal Automatism," in which Lewes is concerned to controvert Thomas Huxley's (and other contemporary materialists') reduction of mind to physical causes. It is the centerpiece, because it seems to me that the final objective of *The Physical Basis of Mind* is the vindication of conscious psychic causality as a force of evolutionary change and hence a refutation of the thesis, strikingly put forward by Huxley and closely related to his role as Darwin's "bulldog," that consciousness being the effect of physical or bodily causes can itself do nothing to modify those causes or the behavior they determine.

It may be assumed [writes Huxley] that molecular changes in the brain are the causes of all the states of consciousness of brutes. Is there any evidence that these states of consciousness may conversely cause these molecular changes . . . ? I see no such evidence. . . . The consciousness of brutes would appear to be related to the mechanism of their body simply as a collateral product without any power of modifying that working as the steam-whistle which accompanies a locomotive engine is without influence upon its machinery.[50]

Lewes is quick to indicate that he is not arguing against Huxley from an idealist point of view. He recognizes and accepts, with Huxley, the dependency of mind upon matter, the evolution of mental from physical structures. What he denies is that consciousness, once evolved, lacks an independent causality of its own, that it is unable to turn back upon and modify the physical structures (Huxley's "locomotive") from which it has evolved.[51]

The way in which consciousness acts to modify organic structure—

and this, we should be clear, is the real issue between Lewes and Huxley (and behind Huxley, Darwin)—is, Lewes argues, historical and social. A machine

has no *historical* factor manifest in its functions. It has no experience. It reacts at last as at first. How different the organism . . . ! Every organism has its *primary* constitution in the adjustment of parts peculiar to the species; it also has its *secondary* or modified constitution. . . .

. . . I need not dwell on the profound modifications which the human inherited mechanism undergoes in the course of experience—how social influence and moral and religious teaching redirect, or even suppress, many primary tendencies; so that "moral habits" become organised, and replace the original tendencies of the organism. These, when organised, become the inevitable modes of reaction, and are sometimes called secondarily-automatic.[52]

This social conditioning of the human constitution, much more fully developed in the ensuing volume of *Problems of Life and Mind* (*The Study of Psychology*, 1879), is the key to Lewes' revision of Darwin.

When Lewes turns from *The Physical Basis of Mind* to *The Study of Psychology*, his principal anatgonist is no longer Huxley but Charles Darwin himself. In *The Descent of Man* (1871) Darwin had insisted— and Lewes quotes him—that "there is no fundamental difference between man and the higher animals in their mental faculties." His own purpose, says Lewes, is "to bring out the distinctive position of Human Psychology" and demonstrate, against Darwin, that man's higher mental faculties do decisively "demarcate" him from the lower animals. What makes the distinction is the "social factor," or "general mind," the accumulated tradition of human beliefs into which each individual is born. Returning to his insistence on the importance of external conditions in the process of evolution, we now see that this general mind is part of what he means by environment in the case of human evolution:

. . .Centuries of culture have modified [man's] organism. . . . [M]y object [is] to make prominent the effect of social factor, and to take man in his developed state as the peculiar exemplar of its power. The distinguishing character of Human Psychology is, that to the three factors of Organism, External Medium, and Heredity, which it has in common with Animal Psychology, it adds a fourth, namely, relation to a Social Medium, with its product the General Mind. . . . [H]ow supremely important is this social medium.

The recognition of the "supreme importance" of the social medium, Lewes now maintains, represents his distinctive contribution to psychology. Whereas metaphysicians attribute our higher mental faculties, notably, moral beliefs, to innate ideas, and materialists attribute them to "germs" of the animal constitution which have spontaneously evolved, he, Lewes, insists on the specifically human "mental forms" as the product of the social factor. Thus, he says, he reconciles the a priori intuitional with the experiential theory.[53]

Lewes was almost certainly helped to this solution to the Darwinian problem by yet another German psychologist. At one point in his argument against animal automatism, Lewes notes that he had long been unable to overcome the materialistic/Darwinian subordination of mind to physical causality and that the way out of this determinism had only recently come to him in the form of the theory of *parallel psychic and physical causation*.[54] What he does not mention—and perhaps should have—is that he was almost certainly led to this theory and its consequences by Wilhelm Wundt (1832–1920), the "senior psychologist in the history of psychology," according to Edwin Boring, because Wundt is the first one "who without reservation is properly called a psychologist."[55] Lewes began reading Wundt extensively in the late 1860s,[56] and it is certainly not without significance that the epigraph to *The Study of Psychology* is from the German's first major work, *Vorlesungen über die Menschen und Thierseele* (1863). There Lewes would have found an argument for the parallelism of physical and psychic causality very close to that which he uses in *The Physical Basis of Mind*. The connection of mind and matter, writes Wundt, "can only be regarded as a *parallelism* of two causal series existing side by side, but never directly interfering with each other in virtue of the incomparability of their terms. . . . Over against [the bodily processes] stands the circle of the psychical phenomena . . . , an equally independent sphere of investigation, not admitting of causal explanation in terms of . . . motions of matter."[57]

No less important, Lewes would also have found in Wundt the notion of the social factor as the historical embodiment of psychic causality: ". . . *psychical* causes . . . form part of a . . . general conscious nexus, of which the individual mind constitutes only one link. The general direction of the individual will is . . . determined by the *collective will of the community* in which its possessor lives. . . ."[58] With Wundt's insistence on the psychic causality of the general will, the nineteenth-century positivist interpretation of mind, whether in its Millian associationist or Comtean physiological phase, turns a significant corner. It is Ernst Mach (1836–1916) and Richard Avenarius (1843–1896) who continue the positivist reduction of mind to physical causality. Wundt attacks both these writers in a series of articles during 1896–1898 and through his influence on Wilhelm Dilthey stands as a historical bridge between the positivist tradition and the burgeoning neo-Kantian and hermeneutical movements. With Wundt, Dilthey observed in 1894, the scientific psychology at last confronts the inability of reductionism to explain the more complex synthetic functions of mind.[59] Lewes performs something of the same role for British thought.

Clearly the problem Lewes is most concerned to solve via the "social factor" is that which we have already found at the heart of both Comte's and Mill's moral philosophy: how to justify man's evolution from an egoistic to an altruistic being. There are two "conflicting motions" in man, an "animal" and a "social" one. The former is an "egoist impulse," the latter an altruistic "restraint" on that impulse. What the social factor produces "are certain organised predispositions that spontaneously . . . issue in the beneficent forms of action which the experience of society has classed as right. . . . It is a great progress . . . when love of approbation attains to the ideal force which renders social rule . . . an habitually felt restraint and guidance." As with Comte, the sexual impulse appears to contain within it the "germ" of the social or altruistic principle: animals "have scarcely any sympathetic or altruistic impulses beyond the sexual and parental." But much more than with Comte that germ needs the social factor to assure its proper development into the highest moral value. Although animals and man share the sexual instinct, animals "know nothing of Love."[60] Returning to Lewes' internalization of Darwin's struggle for existence, we see that the social factor, or general mind, works as an external causal force upon the human mind, promoting one competing organic affinity or another until the successful tendency becomes, as it were, the natural, the spontaneous, motive of behavior. Insofar as this social factor is the product of conscious intention, deliberately constructed beliefs or institutions, the evolution of human morality or character is liberated from the randomness of evolution prior to man. Consciousness creates its own moral teleology, transforming human nature by the instrumentality of the social medium.

In trying to carve out for himself an original position on this question of the social transmutation of our biological nature, Lewes says that, although others have shown themselves fully aware of the impact of the social factor on individual behavior, none has so far shown its *"mode of operation,"*[61] including presumably Wundt himself. What he means depends on where one reads him. In fact, he has two explanations of this mode of operation, the difference between the two being of considerable consequence.

In the first volume of *Problems of Life and Mind* and as late as the early part of *The Study of Psychology* (volume 4), Lewes seems to believe that the social factor causes variation in humans by gradually but directly modifying the cerebral functions, which, in turn, are passed on to subsequent generations by heredity. In this belief in "acquired characteristics," or "soft inheritance," he follows the neo-Lamarckian majority of contemporary evolutionists, represented perhaps most notably in his own generation by Samuel Butler (1835–1902), who squabbled with Darwin over the latter's "hard" reading of inheritance.[62] Instinct, argues Lewes, including in the concept spontaneous moral proclivities and aversions, is "lapsed or undiscursive Intelligence," an original Consciousness that has "sunk" into "Sub-Consciousness." It is "the fixed action of an acquired organization, transmitted from ancestors who acquired it through Adaptation [to the social factor], whereby what was facultative became fixed, what was voluntary became involuntary." And again, "the Organism is an evolution, bringing with it, in its structure, evolved modes of action inherited from ancestors. . . . [The Kantian forms of thought, are] an inheritance of acquired modification. . . . In this sense we have Moral and Intellectual Instincts. . . ." This is from the first volume of *Problems, The Foundation of a Creed*.[63] The point is reiterated in the discussion of evolution in the third volume, *The Physical Basis of Mind*.

The argument for acquired and inherited mental forms appears to continue in the early chapters of the fourth volume of *Problems, The Study of Psychology*: "Culture transforms . . . the selfish savage into the sympathetic citizen. The organism adjusts itself to the external medium; it creates and is in turn modified by, the social medium."[64] But some three-quarters of the way through the book comes a disarming observation. "Moral intuitions" are the product of "experienced" social belief, but, "some writers who are disposed to exaggerate the action of Heredity believe that certain specific experiences of social utility in the race become organized in descendants, and are thus transmitted as instincts. With the demonstrated wonders of heredity before us, it is rash to fix limits to the specific determinations it may include. . . ."[65] It is possible that Lewes is simply responding to an excessive specificity in certain neo-Lamarckian claims for acquired moral intuition (again one thinks of Butler). But Lewes' observation is continuous with his tendency throughout the book to emphasize the "evolution" of the general consciousness, rather than the race, and to speak of the determining effect of that general consciousness on the individual's development in the course of his own individual lifetime. There is never a clear statement, such as we find in the earlier volumes of *Problems of Life and Mind*, that moral habits acquired in one generation are transmittable by heredity to a subsequent generation. This is partly a mark of Wundt's emphasis on the independent historical development of the general will. But I suspect it is also a reflection of the beginnings of the movement away from neo-Lamarckianism in the late 1870s. Lewes would not have been able to benefit from August Weismann's (1834–1914) decisive refutation of the principle of soft inheritance (to which we will return in chapter 10) but quite possibly would have known of Francis Galton's (1822–1911) and, among the German physiologists, Wilhelm His's (1831–1904) movements in that neo-Darwinian direction.[66]

In any case, the difference between the "soft" and "hard" positions on the role of the social factor as a principle of variation implies a great difference in one's concept of human progress. According to Lewes' earlier position, the moral ideals that make for altruism can biologically transform the human race from its animal or egoistic nature into a new species, as it were. That is, although it had not been possible for Lewes to argue morphologically for a primitive type of altruism which evolves into a universal moral structure that is "natural" to human beings, he had, by way of his neo-Lamarckian adjustment of Darwin, reached a position in which the wished-for moral type might be developed from various "organic affinities" and over the course of generations be "acquired" in the race as a natural form. One might hope, that is, for the ultimate repression of all those animal affinities that "divide" us from the truly moral ideal and a consequent end of the conflict of man within himself and with his fellow men. Human nature might thus evolve into complete and spontaneous congruity with social law. In proportion, however, as one moves from this evolutionary model to a more strictly social model according to which the social factor does not modify the race (because this is genetically impossible), but simply constrains animal instincts from one generation to the next, starting anew with each individual, one is bound to be considerably less sanguine about the future. There is no vision of an ultimate reconciliation of the biological and the social, but rather the prospect of endless conflict between the two. Lewes is only beginning to move in the direction of the latter position and shows no real awareness of or concern for the difference it might make in his confident meliorism. In *The Study of Psychology* he still trusts, no less than

Comte or Mill, that the necessary movement of human history is progressive, and that increased scientific knowledge will do nothing but assure this.

SYMBOLISM AND THE VARIATION OF THE SPECIES

Whether Lewes believes in soft inheritance or hard, one thing is clear, his faith in mankind ultimately rests on the development of the "ideal force" of the general mind, the "shifting panorama of History [that] presents a continuous evolution, a fuller and more luminous tradition, an intenser consciousness of a wider life." This is, he says, reminiscent of Hegel's World Spirit, but, at the same time, radically different, being no metaphysical abstraction separated from actual historical beliefs and social structures. Like Wundt's "general will" his general mind assumes no spiritual substance independent of the various historical manifestations of mental life. This mental substance is "for ever germinating, for ever evolving," and forever "fashioning the Experience of the individual."[67] But what, one wants to know, propels it, if not some metaphysical force? It may cause variations in human nature, but what causes variation in it? This is a question which, as we shall see, comes to concern George Eliot a good deal more than Lewes. By gathering together observations from several places in *Problems of Life and Mind*, we may confidently suggest that Lewes at the close of his career was still romantic or Shelleyan enough to believe that the force for change resides, finally, in something like individual genius. "Society can, and does, compel the individual," he writes, but "this does not prevent the individual from initiating a change, which may be passed on from one to another like yeast cells growing in a fermenting mass. . . ."[68]

One great difference between men and animals, Lewes maintains at one point, is that the latter have "imperfect individuality" (or "personality").[69] The individual, he says in the chapter of *The Study of Psychology* devoted to a justification of free will, is "as subject to causal determination" as the movements of the planets, but he is a "system of forces" that "has within itself the conditions of its special actions; just as our world . . . [is] in some sense independent of the solar system." In the case of the human personality the "special action" of force that constitutes its freedom, is the act of *choosing* between conflicting motives and endowing one of these with a "superior energy" for action. "In this way . . . our Personality intervenes to shape our conduct." Closely related to this power of choice is another power which

Lewes elsewhere associates with the scientist's formulation of hypotheses and, more generally, with imagination. "Our consciousness tells us we are free in the sense that we have a range of motives surveyed by a Personality which is the incorporation of our past experiences *and carries the prevision of alternative future*" (my emphasis). Prevision and resultant choice of alternative futures constitute what Lewes means by "Will," or the "generalised expression of all the personality's volitional impulses" brought to bear on individual belief and action, which, in turn, can "ferment" among others, causing a new initiative in the development of the general mind.[70] It is a position not too far from what Lewes would have found in Wundt's concept of the relation between general and individual will: "The [community] relations in which the individual is . . . placed are the principal determinants of his voluntary actions. But the general will . . . is usually in its turn determined by the wills of the more energetic individuals, . . . which are acquiesced in by the individual wills of the majority."[71]

The fundamental exertion of individual will in prevision, Lewes tends to call by its romantic name, "imagination," while making clear, as usual, that he is not talking about a metaphysical force, but an "energetic [neural] impulse" which is no more than the "reinstatement" of sensation, "another form of Perception." "In men of artistic and scientific genius it is the intentional or plastic Imagination which prevails. "Whether in fiction or in hypothesis a " 'cerebral rehearsal' of future experiences" makes progress possible. "Were it not for this facultative property of images which allows of their being recombined differently from the order of sensations, there would be no enlargement of Experience. . . ."[72] But more important for Lewes than this "logic of images" is the further abstraction of images into signs or symbols. Language, as we have seen, is Lewes' essential ideal force. The general consciousness "rests on the evolution of Language. . . ."[73] The epitome of individual will or personality is the embodiment of a new "intentionality" in language. Again, the "invention of a new symbol is a step in the advancement of civilization."[74]

The symbol introduced by any particular individual and made to prevail in the general consciousness, it appears, determines the evolution of the race. Insofar as the symbol is a scientific hypothesis, it is subject eventually to verification, and hence objectification. But insofar as it is a moral hypothesis, such as the Comtean "we should live for others," Lewes seems at last to concede no verification is possible. "Objectification" in this case becomes a matter of embedding that moral belief in the evolving mental type of the race (if one accepts soft inheritance) or in the "unconscious" of each member of each succes-sive generation (if one does not). This may seem a liberal enough pro-ceeding, but is it really any less "despotic" than the subjective method of social organization Mill complained of in Comte's second system and Lewes was no less critical of in his 1866 essay on Comte and Mill? The source of social morality is, as we see, an individual subjective will, and Lewes has none but either a priori or aesthetic reasons for preferring the effects of an altruistic to an egoistic will. The only thing that makes his proposal for the controlled evolution of the human species less autocratic than the more obviously objectionable attempts at genetic engineering we associate with the Social Darwinians, and worse, is the liberal stipulation that individuals must be *educated*, not coerced into the "previsioned" mode of moral behavior. This is no doubt preferable to Karl Pearson's late-Victorian program for legislat-ing human reproductivity,[75] but, one way or the other, the state, as with Comte, is still being invoked to implement an ideal that for all its scientific surroundings rests on the "intention" of the hero, to revert to Carlyle's notorious cutting of the knot, as man of letters.

6

From New Physics to New Jerusalem: George Eliot's Scientific Pragmatism

Fragile reed as he may be, man, as Pascal says, is a thinking reed: there lies within him a fund of energy, operating intelligently and so far akin to that which pervades the universe, that it is competent to influence and modify the cosmic process.

—T. H. Huxley

IN a striking correlation of the "internal" and "external" history of science, Stuart Peterfreund has lately argued that the early nineteenth-century revival of the concept of energy, whatever its scientific antecedence, was facilitated by a theological problem. The "interpretative strategy" of Protestant hermeneutics in its "first [Lutheran] phase," he argues, aimed at delivering the "immediate truth of God" as expressed in scripture. This was a project, "driven by a terrible nostalgia for the plenitude of the prelapsarian state, in which unmediated knowledge, conveyed by a language that bears witness to a perfect fit between word and object, banishes all uncertainty. . . ." The scientific counterpart of this nostalgia was to be found, Peterfreund continues, in the Baconian search for the unmediated laws of nature. In a world "underwritten by Protestant hermeneutics," which in turn underwrote empirical science, "there was simply no place for *energeia* in language," only *enargeia*, or exactness of expression, the pursuit of a precise linguistic image of the real. The breakdown of the hermeneuts' search for an "Adamic" correspondence of word and thing, the recognition that all language, even scriptural language, is radically interpretative, not representative, of things (an intellectual development Peterfreund places in the last quarter of the eighteenth century) leads

129

to a correspondent rise in respect for *energeia*, not only in language, but also in nature. One ceases to think of the divine as a primordial order to which man must strive to return, and begins, instead, to think of it as an ongoing creative force, the highest expression of which is an evolving language. In terms of biblical hermeneutics, this means that one begins to worry less about discovering the original meaning of scripture, from which centuries of interpretation have separated us, and to think, rather, of interpretation as a value in itself, a foundational act of mind, and language, in the process of growth.[1]

Obviously the appeal of this argument to me lies in the light it sheds on the transition in George Eliot's fiction from *Adam Bede* to *The Mill on the Floss*. Failure to realize the archetypal positivist objective of exact correspondence between the structures of mind and the structure of nature, recognition of the inescapability of metaphor/interpretation, pushes her towards an understanding of mind as an independent expression of energy, constituting an order of its own, rather than seeking to conform to some putative primordial order outside itself. What I want now to consider, with Peterfreund's point very much in mind, is the manner in which the developing preoccupation with energy physics in the later nineteenth century comes to the aid of a project that one might otherwise consider purely literary and enables George Eliot to continue to claim a scientific basis for her concepts of mind and of art.

THE OTHER REVOLUTION: THE RETURN OF ENERGY/ENERGIA

Writing to Sara Hennell in December of 1865, George Eliot recommended to her friend a "splendid piece" in the first edition of the *Fortnightly Review*. The article, "The Constitution of the Nature," by John Tyndall (1820–1893) was, she said, about the "higher physics."[2] More particularly, Tyndall was drawing attention to the overwhelming importance of the first law of thermodynamics (the conservation of energy), which, he argued, was bound to bring about "momentous changes in human thought."[3] As he was to maintain, quite correctly, in a later, more famous, essay (the "Belfast Address" of 1874), this was one of the two great scientific doctrines of "our day," of "still wider grasp and more radical significance" than the other, Darwin's theory of evolution.[4] What we will be exploring in this section is the impact of this genuinely revolutionary development in physics, the equivalent in its day to the doctrine of relativity in ours, on George Eliot, and how it seems to have drawn her away from Lewes' positivism in the late 1860s and early 1870s and given her the basis for a neo-romantic theory of art and society.

In the 1850s after well over a century of existing in an aura of scientific disrepute, the concept of energy again became not only a current but also an indispensable concept of physics. The proximate scientific reason for this was the discovery and mathematical formulation of the law of conservation of force or energy (we will come back to the distinction between the terms). There is no need to rehearse here the history of this development,[5] except to note that it was Lewes' hero Hermann von Helmholtz, working from a basis in physiology, and in particular the phenomenon of animal heat, who first gave full expression to the law in 1847 ("Über die Erhaltung der Kraft"). By the 1850s the concept of energy, virtually ruled out of court by Newton as an unreal entity, one of Aristotle's mysterious "qualities," had, as a result of further applications of Helmholtz's law, provided the science of physics with a unifying principal beyond anything it had known in its earlier, "mechanical phase," "subsuming," as one historian of the subject has said, "the phenomena of heat, light, electricity, and magnetism within the framework of mechanical principles."[6] What the law affirms is, essentially, that the energy in the universe can neither be added to nor annihilated but is constant and indestructible. From this follows the crucial implication that energy forms are interconvertible. A form of energy which may seem to disappear has merely been converted to another form. From Helmholtz's physiological point of view this meant that life was, not an energy or *vis viva* supplied *ab extra* by some divine fiat, but evolved from forces found in inorganic nature, light, heat, electricity.

In Tyndall's writing (and others in the 1860s and 1870s) the principle expands to cosmic proportions, as we see in this dramatic expression, which would certainly have caught George Eliot's attention. Are we to suppose, asks Tyndall, that the universe was created at once by the fiat of divine omnipotence? "In presence of the revelations of science this view is fading more and more. Behind the orbs, we now discern the nebulae from which they have been condensed. And without going so far back as the nebulae, the man of science can prove that out of common non-luminous matter this whole pomp of stars have been evolved."[7] In the hands of not only Tyndall but also (confining oneself to Great Britain) W. J. M. Rankine (1820–1872), William Thomson (Lord Kelvin [1824–1907]), Peter G. Tait (1831–1901), and Clerk Maxwell (1831–1879), the concept of energy became in the second half of the century the basis at once for the unification of science and nature. Darwinian evolution, in terms of the new energetics, became but one (biological and terrestrial) expression of an entity that develops throughout time and the universe.

The word "entity" shows us the way to the problem this "higher physics" presents for an earlier positivism. The concept of force or energy is intimately involved with that of causality, and causality is precisely what both Comte and Mill urge a properly scientific method to avoid discussing: ". . . the first characteristic of the Positive Philosophy," insists Comte, "is that it regards all phenomena as subjected to invariable natural *Laws*. Our business is—seeing how vain is any research into what are called *Causes*, whether first or final—to pursue an accurate discovery of these Laws. . . ."[8] Mill is somewhat more compromising, but only by virtue of carefully restricting what he is prepared to admit under the name of "cause": "I make no research into the ultimate or ontological cause of anything. . . . The Law of Causation . . . is but the familiar truth that invariability of succession is found by observation to obtain between every fact in nature and some other fact which has preceded it. . . ."[9] Both founders of the nineteenth-century scientific philosophy, in short, share Hume's skepticism about the ontological reality of cause, as well as his fear that any discussion of causality must lead sooner or later to metaphysics, to the explanation of phenomena in terms of some unobservable, all-comprising, all-moving entity.

Because of the implication of force/energy in the concept of causality, there is an extreme reluctance to talk about it, except as a heuristic aid implying no existent entity, but serviceable in explaining certain phenomena. "Force," says Mill, is a "logical fiction" resorted to in order to avoid "giving the name cause to anything which had existed for an indeterminate length of time before the effect."[10] "Force," in this understanding, becomes a word by which we sanitize the concept of cause, allow ourselves, that is, to talk about "cause" without hypostasizing it. This critical linguistic trick of eighteenth- and early nineteenth-century physics, as we will see, lies behind the later nineteenth-century debate over the difference between force and energy.

The question of causality in Mill's *Logic* relates to methodology in another way developed by Alvar Ellegård many years ago. Mill on causality, as in so much else, consciously aims to refute the doctrines of William Whewell. We must apply the term "cause," writes Whewell in *The Philosophy of Inductive Science*, "to a certain conception of *force* abstracted from all . . . special events, and considered as a quality . . . by which one body affects the motion of the other. And in like manner . . . cause is to be conceived as some abstract quality, power, or efficacy, by which change is produced; a quality not identical with the events, but disclosed by means of them."[11] This understanding of force as an actual, effective cause, Ellegård argues, bears significantly on Whewell's concept of scientific hypothesis. The mental ideal which the scientist superimposes on facts was, for Whewell, in some cases more than simply an imaginative construction. It was the expression of a spiritual force that really exists in the world, much in the same manner as Coleridgean imagination is a repetition in the finite mind of the infinite I AM. "Indeed," writes Ellegård, "it appears that theoretical [hypothetical] concepts were acceptable to Whewell to the extent that they could be assimilated with such entites as he already believed in, mainly on religious grounds."[12] To hypothesize correctly was to participate in the divine mind and, in effect, to reproduce its ordering force for the scientific elucidation of one's fellow man. Mill, as we have seen in chapter 2, accepted Whewell's point about the necessity of hypothesis, but only on the understanding that such hypotheses were fictions to be verified, hardly in the faith that they partook of some arcane metaphysical force.

The formulation of the law of the conservation of energy and the subsequent rise of the new physics undermined Mill's (and Comte's) careful strictures. Force (now increasingly called energy, by way of demarcating it from Mill's "logical fiction") and, with it, causality again became respectable topics of scientific discourse, observable realms in which experiments could be performed and results measured. As Thomson and Tait insisted, ". . .according to modern experimental results . . . Energy is as real and indestructible as Matter."[13] Whether this also meant the reintroduction of Whewell's theistic program, depended on the researcher. In the case of Stewart, Tait, Thomson, and Maxwell, it certainly seems to have done. As the first two conclude in what was to become Victorian England's most prominent popular statement of the new energetics, *The Unseen Universe* (1877), "When we regard the universe from [the] point of view [of the law of the conservation of energy], we are led to a scientific conception of it which is strikingly analogous to the system which is presented to us in the Christian religion."[14] But not so with Tyndall or Huxley,[15] for whom the word "energy" had no theological content whatsoever, only a material one. The force of mind was a random evolution from more fundamental physical forces, not the working out of some divine plan.

Where was Lewes in this ongoing discussion of energy and causality? His primary scientific interest, as we have seen, lay not in physics but in the life sciences, biology and psychology. Still, he had certainly read Helmholtz on the conservation principle and by the writing of *Aristotle* (published 1864) recognized the importance of what he called the Indestructibility of Force in modern science. "It is now so obvious that no physicist disputes it, whatever may be his views on the *nature* of Force—whether he believes it to be an Entity, or a Relation." On the crucial question raised here of the nature of force, Lewes at this point is essentially with Mill. We cannot, he argues, altogether "banish" the words "force" and "causality" from our scientific vocabulary, as some (e.g., Comte) would wish, but when we do use them, we must take care not to take them as entities. The danger of the terms "lies in our tendency to forget that they are introduced into our calculations solely as unknown agents acting through known laws." We must not assume anything of force "which has not already been verified."[16] Over the next decade the concepts of force and cause obviously become increasingly important to Lewes, for when he sets it out as his purpose in the first volume of *Problems of Life and Mind* (1874) to apply the positive method to metaphysics, the specific metaphysical problems he has in mind to treat "positively" are force, matter, and cause. The result, we recall, was not an ontological resolution of these problems but a theory of scientific method in which to treat such concepts scientifically was, in effect, to formulate the logical rules that would permit them to be used as aids to induction of "relations," not as "entities." A positive "metaphysics," as we have noted, turns out with Lewes to be a theory of scientifically useful fictions. It is perhaps worth noting that he took pains to get Peter Tait to read the proofs of this first volume, the object presumably being to get one of the premier energy physicists of the day to check his views on the properly scientific treatment of the subject, views which, not surprisingly, Tait did not find congenial.[17]

A year later in the second volume of *Problems of Life and Mind* (*The Foundations of a Creed*, ii, 1875), Lewes takes on directly the problem of "Force and Cause." That in doing so he consciously situates himself in opposition to the new physics is suggested by his letter to George Eliot expressing impatience with their friend Tyndall's "baseless" theory "founded on the [supposed] *reality* of atoms,"[18] belief in the reality of atoms having become a mainstay of contemporary energetics. This theory he promises to demolish in the second volume of *Problems*. Opposition to the new physics is suggested as well by his deliberate decision to speak of the "grand law" of the "conservation of *Force*," rather than "energy," although he knows well that "many English authorities" (read, Tyndall, Rankine, Thomson, Tait, Maxwell) condemn the phrase,[19] the use of "energy" rather than "force" having become by the 1870s a shibboleth separating the believers in energy as an entity from those who continued, after Comte and Mill, to consider it a logical fiction. It does appear that Lewes has gone a considerable way with the new physicists; he freely uses the word "energy," defining it as an "indwelling capacity of doing work"; he regrets the "wearisomely iterated statement [made, in fact, by himself in *Aristotle*] that man can know nothing of Force, because he can never know causes, only effects"; and he criticizes Mill (in Mill's *Sir William Hamilton*) for being "unable to rid himself of the traditional [empiricist] idea that a cause is simply an antecedent. . . ." But close reading of the argument reveals nothing so much as an effort to accommodate the increasingly unavoidable arguments of the new physicists without at last slipping into the "metempiric" fallacy of reifying or personifying a heuristic abstraction. Mill's "confusion," it turns out, lies in the continued assumption that cause and effect are separable from one another. In fact, claims Lewes, they are aspects of an integrated process: "Once recognise the identity of cause and effect under obverse aspects, and these aspects may be interpreted . . . without necessitating any mysterious intermediation" (the argument is very close to the Wundtian one we have seen him develop on the parallelism of physical and mental activity; the one does not *cause* the other; they are, again, "aspects," objective and subjective, of a single process).[20]

The separation of cause from effect, then, becomes a verbal or symbolic problem. Once we clear it up, we are freed from the necessity of thinking in terms of "mysterious intermediation." Lewes' object here, the criticism of the master notwithstanding, is to update and make more defensible Mill's (and Comte's) fundamental objection to the concept of force as a temptation to metaphysics. "Force and cause" remain for Lewes symbolic abstractions, not realities. With a view towards the discussion of George Eliot to follow, it is worth noting that for Lewes, at this juncture, one of the most egregious of "mysterious intermediaries" is that which we refer to as "Will." "Even to this day, in all the glare of Science, the clouds which gather round the conception of Cause are wafted from the mysterious region of Will, and many thinkers hold that no explanation of causation is possible except that which is furnished by volition. . . . [T]he identification of Causation with Volition is not acceptable."[21] The fact that the hero of

George Eliot's *Middlemarch* (1872), written almost contemporaneously with Lewes' preparation of the first two volumes of *Problems of Life and Mind*, is named Will may suggest to us, at least tentatively, a parting of the ways between the two companions on an issue, which, if we are to believe Tyndall, was of still greater scientific moment than the Darwinian revolution.

In the later volumes of *Problems of Life and Mind*, those published after *Daniel Deronda* (1876), Lewes, as our consideration of his concept of personality in the last chapter suggests, became significantly more accommodating of energy physics—or at least in George Eliot's editing of that late work he certainly appears to have become so.[22] Still, there is never anything approaching the commitment to *energeia* that we will find in George Eliot's last works. Lewes retains, to the end, a certain Comtean/Millian reservation about unreal entities that makes it more appropriate to relate his late "metaphysics" of the symbol, as I have done, to the later Wittgenstein's treatment of fictive propositions. George Eliot's late work, on the other hand, looks more towards the preoccupation with actual spiritual energy we find in William James and Henri Bergson. The difference is a subtle one (though perhaps not so subtle when one juxtaposes Wittgenstein and Bergson), but it seems real enough, involving, as it does, two quite distinct levels of belief in the binding authority of mental force/energy (the ambivalent notation seems, finally, unavoidable).

DOROTHEA'S CHOICE: A CONFLICT OF PARADIGMS

Dorothea Brooke's story is a continuation of Maggie Tulliver's. She begins at almost the same age at which Maggie ends, is allowed, as Maggie is not, to marry, not just once but twice, and discovers, as Maggie does not, at least the beginnings of a solution to the labyrinthine problem of how to achieve the "social right." But only the beginnings, for Dorothea, though she does not die in the end, is nonetheless a martyr. Both Maggie and Dorothea are Christianas in George Eliot's reworking of Bunyan's fable, but neither can actually arrive at the New Jerusalem. They are, in Dorothea's words, "always . . . finding out [their] religion . . . ,"[23] never quite finding it.

Like Maggie, Dorothea is an idealist from the beginning ("all Dorothea's passion was transfused through a mind struggling towards an ideal life. . .") to the end ("She yearned towards the perfect Right, that it might make a throne within her . . .") of her story. And like Maggie's, her vague longing for the right lacks a "theoretic" structure, an "effective shape," which is a crucial deficiency, for, as George Eliot has come increasingly to understand, a clear conceptual framework is the necessary preliminary to praxis. If Dorothea is to act in the world, to reform it, which is what she wants above all to do, she must have some coherent philosophy of life, a "binding theory," a "more complete teaching" that will dissipate the oppressive "indefiniteness which hung in her mind, like a think summer haze, over all her desire to make her life greatly effective." Put another way, she suffers from the same untoward historical situation in which we found Maggie, as George Eliot is at pains to emphasize even before the story begins. Her heroine will be a modern St. Theresa, whose soul "soared after some illimitable satisfaction, some object . . . which would reconcile self-despair with the rapturous consciousness of life beyond self." But unlike Theresa, she will be "helped by no coherent social faith and order which could perform the function of knowledge for the ardently willing soul."[24]

Rather, Dorothea lives, like Maggie, in a world of degraded Protestantism (unknown to Bossuet), that is, a world governed by advanced capitalism, represented in this novel by the "web" of Middlemarch with its interconnected families of Bulstrode, Vincy, and Featherstone, for whom (by and large) "religious activity could not be incompatible with . . . business." Finally, Dorothea is like Maggie in believing that the solution to her theoretic needs must come from a strong male intellect: ". . . masculine knowledge seemed to her a standing-ground from which all truth could be seen more truly."[25] (Maggie, we recall, desires to "learn for herself what wise men knew.") Ideally, such knowledge would come from a marriageable "wise man," the full "soul-hunger" with Dorothea, as with Maggie, being at once for knowledge and for love.

While Maggie's story was virtually without a wise man to rescue the heroine, Dorothea has no fewer than three, Edward Casaubon, Tertius Lydgate, and Will Ladislaw, two of whom she marries and the third of whom she might have married were he not, after all, so firmly fixed not only to another woman but also, as we will see, to another story. The inadequacy of Casaubon's masculine knowledge (I am not concerned at this point with his failure of personality) is too well known to need another exposition here.[26] One point only I need to make: his work is, in principle, at one with the hermeneutic pursuit of an original, uninterpreted religious or moral order that seemed to motivate George Eliot herself in *Adam Bede*. Casaubon attempts to penetrate all religious texts to discover the primordial Ur-myth, the germ or type from which all subsequent beliefs have, in his view, devolved, "to show . . . that all the mythical systems or erratic mythical fragments in the world were corruptions of a tradition originally revealed."[27] What Dorothea eventually realizes is what I take George Eliot to have begun to realize between the writing of *Adam Bede* and *The Mill on the Floss*, namely, that this particular form of masculine knowledge is flawed in its very conception. It offers no "binding theory" of life, only "mixed heaps of material": "Mr. Casaubon's theory of the elements which made the seed of all tradition . . . floated among flexible conjectures no more solid than those etymologies which seemed strong because of likeness in sound . . . ; it was a method of interpretation which was not tested by the necessity [of any correspondence with reality]: it was as free from interruption as a plan for threading the stars together."[28] In other words, Casaubon's theory is in the category of an unverifiable hypothesis not unlike Comte's theory in the *Cours* of an original structure of human nature.

With the realization of the pointlessness of her husband's research, Dorothea receives a glimmering, a (David) Straussean glimmering, if you like, of an alternative theory. Myths do not descend from an original structure or "seed"; they are "mosaics" put together from the ruins of previous myths; as far back as one goes, one finds only mosaics,[29] that is, hermeneutical reconstructions of earlier constructions which have ceased to work as "coherent social faiths." Will Ladislaw, the wise man Dorothea does at last choose, is as synthetic a thinker as Casaubon is an analytic one, as much a constructor of mosaics as Casaubon is a sorter of fragments. What exactly he offers Dorothea—as well as denies her—we will consider at the close of this section. Now however we need to consider closely the wise man not chosen, paradoxically not chosen, for his wisdom is as near as anything we find in George Eliot's fiction to that of the man she herself chose.[30]

Lydgate is not available as a husband for Dorothea. Even were both of them free, she is not, he says, his "style of woman"; in short, she thinks too much.[31] Nor does Dorothea ever contemplate Lydgate as a lover, much as he may share her interest in social reform. Yet at the moment of her first great spiritual crisis when she must confront not only the emptiness of her husband's "wisdom" but the prospect of his imminent death—and her own frightening independence—she turns immediately, desperately, to Lydgate for guidance.

"Oh, you are a wise man, are you not? You know all about life and death. Advise me. Think what I can do. He [Casaubon] has been laboring all his life and looking forward. He minds about nothing else. And I mind about nothing else."

For years after Lydgate remembered the impression produced in him by this involuntary appeal—this cry from soul to soul, without other consciousness than their moving in the same embroiled medium, the same troublous fitfully-illuminated life.

Confronted with death and meaninglessness (nothing to look forward to) the heroine, quite reasonably, appeals to the most advanced thinker in her acquaintance for a "plan" of life. His response? A silence that takes us right back to Dinah Morris: "But what could he say now except that he should see Mr. Casaubon again to-morrow?"[32] What we need to ask is why Lydgate here, as throughout the novel, is unable to supply Dorothea or anyone else with the one thing needful, the elusive "binding theory of life," despite the fact that he is deliberately portrayed by his creator as marching in the absolute vanguard of the contemporary European mind.

Like Flaubert's Bovary, Lydgate is a provincial physician, but he is, of course, far more. A theoretical scientist with an ambition to reform not only the medical profession but also society at large, "he meant to be a unit who would make a certain amount of difference towards the spreading change which would one day tell appreciably on the averages. . . ." He had early experienced his "moment of vocation"[33] and gone on to study medical science in Paris, the scene of the most advanced work in life sciences in the early nineteenth century. Like his near contemporary Comte, he was inspired by the work of Xavier Bichat (for Comte a father of modern biological science who carried that science to the "threshold of the ultimate domain of Positive thought,"[34] sociology): Lydgate "felt the need for that fundamental knowledge of [organic] structure which just at the beginning of the century had been illuminated by the brief and glorious career of Bichat." The Frenchman's research had been, "as the turning of gas-light . . . on a dim, oil-lit street, showing new connections and hitherto hidden facts of structure. . . ." Lydgate's own research program is essentially a continuation of Bichat's: ". . . he longed to demonstrate the more intimate relations of living structure and help to define men's thought more accurately after the true order. . . . What was the primitive tissue?"[35]

What Lydgate is after, as I earlier indicated, is what his German contemporary Theodor Schwann would introduce a decade later in his "Mikroskopische Untersuchungen . . . " (1839), and what Huxley and Lewes would only begin informing the general British public of in the late 1840s, early 1850s, namely, cell theory.[36] Beyond this, Lydgate in 1829 has distinct intimations of the new physiological psychology. He hopes "to pierce the obscurity of those minute processes which prepare human misery and joy, those invisible thoroughfares which are the first lurking places of anguish, mania, and crime. . . ."[37] Indeed, he is looking to bring positive science over the threshold into the study of mind, connecting "the operations of intelligence and volition with the origins of all vital movements."[38] as Lewes had put it in describing the revolutionary work of the physician P. J. G. Cabanis (*Rapports du physique et du moral de l'homme*, published as a separate book in 1802, and no doubt read by Lydgate in his student days in Paris). In Lydgate, then, we are talking about a thinker who is as up-to-date, as revolutionary, as any young man could have been in the Britain of 1829, a proto-positivist, who, had he realized his promise (and been real), would have anticipated much of what Lewes was to try to do by way of bringing about that "mighty new birth," that new scientific totality, which George Eliot hints in *The Mill on the Floss* might have answered Maggie's needs.

In his scientific wisdom Lydgate does not hesitate to condescend to Casaubon's antiquated philological research. But beyond Lydgate is a narrator who herself, I will argue, ultimately presents his knowledge no less ironically than Casaubon's. For Lydgate, although he has radically redefined the concept of the ultimate structure, that is, seen it as biological not theological, evolving, not devolving, has, at the same time, retained the same Platonic paradigm that underpins Casaubon's research. He seeks the primordial structure, the true originary order. In short, his science has found a new *object* of inquiry but hardly a new principle of order. The underlying metaphor for truth remains the same, an archetypal, objectively existent *form*, which we must go beneath present appearances of phenomena to discover, the "going beneath" being, essentially, an attempt to reverse the flow of time. We all, says George Eliot, act fatally on the basis of metaphors. Lydgate, whose metaphor for truth is, after all, the same as Casaubon's, is doomed no less definitively to fail. And, of course, we need to add at this point that Lydgate's metaphor is also Comte's and the early Lewes'.

It may well be objected that Lydgate's real fatality, the tragedy of his wasted life, is the result, after all, not of any flaws in his theoretical position, but the conspicuous flaws of his character, his well-known "spots of commonness."[39] I would not so much want to deny this as to argue that the characterological problem, the stuff of George Eliot's psychological realism, is quite carefully linked, thematically, with the theoretical problem. More specifically, Lydgate's essential spot of commonness dramatically illustrates the inadequacy of his theory, even as it points the way towards not only the construction of a better theory but also the reason George Eliot chose, finally, to unite his story (originally, of course, conceived as a novel in itself) with that of "Miss Brooke."[40]

Lydgate's theoretical precocity goes beyond what we have so far explored to touch upon what we recall was Lewes' fundamental concern, the problem of method. In a second, extended, description of Lydgate's scientific program, George Eliot says that he is committed to "that delightful labour of imagination which is not mere arbitrariness [as the artistic imagination tends to be], but the exercise of disciplined power—combining and constructing with the clearest eye for probabilities and the fullest obedience to knowledge; and then, in yet more energetic alliance with impartial Nature, standing aloof to invent tests by which to try its own work." Such an imagination "reveals subtle actions inaccessible by any sort of lens, but tracked in that outer darkness through long pathways of necessary sequence, by the inward light which is the last refinement of Energy, capable of bathing even the ethereal atoms in its deeply illuminated space. . . .[He] was enamoured of that arduous invention which is the very eye of research, provisionally framing its object and correcting it to more and more exactness of relation. . . ."[41] At a time when the dominant concept of scientific method was, as we have seen, overwhelmingly inductivist, a time when the first great British defender of the indespensability of hypothesis in scientific method was still a decade away from *The Philosophy of the Inductive Sciences* and the first great British formulator of the criteria of legitimate hypothesizing, the necessity of their initial "probability" and their ultimate "verification" was even further from book 3 of *A System of Logic*, Lydgate is doing very well indeed. Not surprisingly, we note, he even anticipates the later Lewes, who was refining his own concept of scientific hypothesis even as George Eliot was writing her novel. The very description of Lydgate's method here reads, as George Eliot surely means it to, like a synopsis of the opening move in *Problems of Life and Mind*.[42]

The obvious way to relate this account of Lydgate's method to his character is to note the ironic contrast George Eliot carefully constructs between the use of the imagination Lydgate, as scientist, insists upon and his decidedly artistic, that is, arbitrary, use of it in his ordinary life, most notably, in his relation with Rosamond, where he weaves a "web" of love for himself "made of spontaneous belief and indefinable joys," a web spun "from his inward self with wonderful rapidity, in spite of experience" and "in spite too of medicine and biology. . . ."[43] We may read this as lamentable inconsistency on the part of a fallible individual, or we may read it, as the later George Eliot everywhere encourages us to read her "realism," in parabolic terms ("there never was a true story which could not be told in parables"[44]). In the latter case, Lydgate's story becomes a parable of the radical disjunction between the use of the imagination in science and its use in practical life, a disjunction which, we recall, vexed Lewes as he tried contemporaneously to relate scientific hypotheses to moral ones. This is a point to which we will return.

The less obvious but more significant way of relating the statement of method to Lydgate's life is to focus on that twice-repeated reference to *energy*: the imagination is the "last refinement of Energy," working in "energetic alliance" with nature. Now the ironic distance between theory and practice becomes, if anything, more complex. "Energy," as we have seen, is not a word that Lewes is entirely comfortable with, and it is not a word which he applies to the use of imaginative projection in science.[45] The notion of imagination as the last refinement of an actual physical energy originating in "impartial Nature" is far more likely to come to George Eliot from John Tyndall. For him the "ultimate problem of physical science" is to trace the flow of "structural energy" running throughout the universe: "Everywhere . . . throughout inorganic nature, we have this formative power, as Fichte would call it—this structural energy ready to come into play, and build the ultimate particles of matter into definite shapes." From inorganic nature we follow the path of energy into plants and on to animals: "Animal heat . . . is the same in kind as the heat of a fire, being produced by the same chemical process. . . . As regards matter, the animal body creates nothing; as regards force, it creates nothing."[46] From the energy of animal heat evolves the energy of mind: ". . . not along the exquisite and wonderful mechanism of the human body, but . . . the human mind itself—emotion, intellect, will, and all their phenomena—were once latent in a fiery cloud. . . ." And from this it follows that "all our philosophy, all our poetry, all our science, and all our art . . . are potential in the fires of the sun." Scientific hypothesis becomes the ultimate expression of these "successive exhibitions of creative energy," and Tyndall's discussions of method inevitably come down to a defense of imaginative energy as nature's means of revealing itself, a "creative power" that leads us "into a world not less real than that of the senses, and of which the world of sense is the suggestion and, to a great extent, the outcome."[47]

This faith in imaginative energy as the expression of the ultimate structural energies of the universe does not lead Tyndall to ignore the necessity of verifying imaginative constructs or hypotheses, but it does make him considerably more tolerant of unverified hypotheses than, say, Lewes is, and more inclined to believe in the reality of the entities they postulate: ". . . many chemists of the present day refuse to speak of atoms and molecules as real things. . . . I respect [their] caution, though I think it misplaced. . . . The scientific imagination, which is here authoritative, demands, as the origin and cause of a series of ether-waves [which are definitely real] a particle of matter quite . . . definite. . . . Such a particle we name an atom. . . ."[48] In George Eliot's passage, we recall, it is precisely these "ethereal atoms," rejected by Lewes as unreal, that the energy of imagination reveals.

Yet—and this is the crucial point—whatever powers of imaginative speculation Lydgate may have, energy of a less refined sort, energy necessary for practical action in the world, is conspicuously what he most lacks. This deficiency George Eliot repeatedly and with increasing emphasis draws to our attention as he declines towards ignominy and despair. His fatal tendency, we learn in the election of Tyke to the hospital chaplaincy, is to rely on "the energy which is begotten by circumstances,"[49] rather than that which is generated from within the self. At the last, unable to shape anything in his own life, let along Middlemarch, he turns to gambling, which, says the narrator, is nothing but the "suspension of the whole nervous energy [of the self] on . . . chance," the complete abandonment of belief in the power of the will to change one's life or the lives around one. From this point his failure is inevitable: "If his energy could have borne down the check, he might still have wrought on Rosamond's vision and will. We cannot be sure that any natures, however inflexible . . . , will resist this effect from a more massive being than their own. . . . But poor Lydgate had a throbbing pain within him, and his energy had fallen short of its task." Without the "massive being" (a central concept in the late novels) that generates an energy that works on the will of others, Lydgate is entirely at the mercy of the "embroiled medium." Ever more restrained by the "threadlike pressures" of the corporate will of the "Social Medium," as Lewes will call it in The Study of Psychology, Lydgate slides "into that pleasureless yielding to the small solicitations of circumstance, which is a commoner history of perdition than any single momentous bargain."[50] This, as the allusion to the Faust legend implies, is the new tragic condition of man.

If we return, then, to the relation between Lydgate's scientific vision and his failure, we see that that vision, advanced as it is, aims at an undiscoverable reality (the primordial order) while ignoring the available reality of an ongoing formative energy of mind, the energy that makes theory itself possible. What Lydgate's scientific project fails to grasp adequately, his personal life demonstrates to be the one thing necessary for anyone who would shape the world rather than "be shapen" by it.[51]

What Lydgate lacks Will Ladislaw, identified from the outset as a kind of solar deity,[52] has in abundance. When at last he transfers his creative power from art to politics, and his immense stores of energy are focused on social reform, he works, as the newspaper says, with "the violence of an energumen."[53] Eventually elected to Parliament, he places himself in the position of actually being able to accomplish what Lydgate can only "plan," social reform. To Lydgate's facetious objections to the makeshift, the "hocus-pocus" of politics, Ladislaw responds in a way that is emblematic of the difference between them: ". . . your cure must begin somewhere. . . . Wait for wisdom . . . in public agents—fiddlestick! The only conscience we can trust is the massive sense of wrong in a class, and the best wisdom that will work is the wisdom of balancing claims. That's my text. . . . [Are we] to try for nothing till we find immaculate men to work with? Should you go on that plan?"[54] That search for "immaculate men" suggests Lydgate's (as well as Casaubon's) Platonist "plan" to get back to primordial origins. But Lydgate himself, with his "spots of commonness," his "old Adam," is the most maculate of men, and, given a society of such men, it is the "massive sense" of the right and the energetic will to realize it, however imperfectly conceived, that constitute "wisdom." This is the male wisdom that George Eliot's heroine at last chooses.[55]

ENERGY AND GENDER

So far I have described a dramatic structure in which the principal problem of *Middlemarch* is Dorothea Brooke's search for a binding theory of life as embodied in an appropriate "wise man," and I have treated the final choice of Ladislaw, parabolically, as an expression of preference for one contemporary scientific paradigm over another. The choice having been made, Dorothea, unlike Maggie, has her clue to the labyrinth and can live happily ever after "at home" in a potentially intelligible world, the governing principle of which is an ongoing human energy of structuration, rather than an irrecoverable dream of lost wholeness or totality. But, of course, this is not quite the way things work out, for it is not at all clear that Dorothea does live happily ever after. On the contrary, as George Eliot indicates in the prelude, the story of her "later-born" Theresa must end in failure, in the establishment of "nothing," a prophecy that is confirmed in the closing pages. Dorothea, "whose story we [now] know" may have achieved the "home epic," the "complete union" with the right man, but she has done so at the expense of a "sad sacrifice."[56] What has been sacrificed is a hidden fourth choice. She might, after all, have chosen herself, have worked out her own "theoretic" deliverance without relying upon male wisdom.

From this perspective, we ask why, indeed, Dorothea needs Will Ladislaw's energy, since, surely, there is no greater focus of personal energy in the novel than she herself. From the outset she is described as having a "hereditary strain of Puritan energy," which, as the story proceeds, George Eliot develops more ecumenically into a "full current of sympathetic motive," a "reaching forward of the whole consciousness towards the fullest truth, the least partial good. . . ."[57] This, George Eliot insists, is a spontaneous energy for the good of others, an altruistic energy, that directly affects and moves those around her. The loveless relation with Casaubon comes close to shutting this energy off altogether: ". . . her ardour, continually repulsed, served . . . to heighten her dread, as thwarted energy subsides into a shudder. . . ." But with the death of her husband and the recognition of Ladislaw as a possible object of love comes a "metamorphosis," and the hereditary energy bursts out with unprecedented strength: "Dorothea's native strength of will was no longer all converted into resolute submission. . . ." As with Maggie, her "native" energy is, on one side, distinctly sexual; she seeks a man who does not suffer from Casaubon's conspicuous lack of "masculine passion." But on the other side, George Eliot would have us believe the more powerful side, that energy has great, if unrealized, political potential; hers is "an ardent faith in efforts of justice and mercy, which would conquer by their emotional force,"[58] a faith that forms a common bond between her and the mature Ladislaw.

Denied the opportunity of political expression, Dorothea's emotional energy probably achieves its highest altruistic (as opposed to sexual) objective in the rescue of Lydgate from despondency over the failure of his "great work." In a scene that deliberately echoes the earlier one in which Dorothea turns to this wise man for deliverance, Lydgate at the close of her story turns to her. But where he had been unable to do anything for her, she does rescue him, restoring, at least temporarily, his faith in himself and in life, and this rescue is the occasion for one of George Eliot's most characteristic expressions of her humanistic faith: "The presence of a noble nature, generous in its wishes, ardent in its charity, changes the lights for us: we begin to see things again in their larger quieter masses. . . . That influence was beginning to act on Lydgate. . . . He sat down and felt that he was recovering his old self in the consciousness that he was with one who believed in it."[59] This is the point at which the meanings of Lydgate's story and Dorothea's come closest to one another. A few pages before, in a passage already cited, George Eliot showed us the failed scientist, his energy "checked," unable to exert the force of a "massive being." Now comes the heroine, herself so long in need of rescue, but mature, independent, and, above all, exhibiting precisely that "massive being" that Lydgate cannot muster, the being whose energy "changes the lights for us." If she does not resolve his tragedy, she at least gives us something beyond that tragedy to believe in.

Thus juxtaposed, the two stories present complementary images, first, of male theoretic brilliance failing for lack of a "conquering" emotional and moral energy; second, of female emotional and moral energy supplying that absence. Or, we may extend the point to my larger argument about conflicting paradigms. In Dorothea's "energetic" rescue we may perhaps read a dramatic embodiment of George Eliot's effort to distinguish her own application of science to life from Lewes', to find in the new physics and its hypostatization of energy a possibility of justifying her residual romantic faith in the power of the individual will to redeem man's tragic situation. It is not for nothing that the chapter in which Dorothea rescues the despairing Lydgate has for epigraph a quotation from Blake.

But Dorothea does not, at last, find her way to the New Jerusalem. Her story, less obviously than Maggie's but, I would argue, no less definitively, comes round to the tragic key. Effective as her moral energy may be in transforming the lives of *individuals* around her, Lydgate, Ladislaw, Rosamond, and so on, it has no force in the world at large. Her Theresean ambition to become the heroine of a "national epic" and help make society new is doomed to frustration. The best she can manage, again, is to become the heroine of the "home epic," the unifier of the hearth, not the state. This matters immensely to George Eliot, for *Middlemarch*, like virtually every other work of fiction she produced, is finally about the historical (rather than domestic) process,[60] about the problem, that is, of society's need to change as a whole, to find a new totality.

On Dorothea's Roman honeymoon the spectacle of the ruins of empire merges with her recognition of ruined love to produce a profound depression. Rome becomes "the city of visible history, where the past of a whole hemisphere seems moving in funereal procession. . . ."[61] The possibility of a parallel between ancient imperial decline and contemporary Britain, a commonplace of Victorian historicism, is clearly suggested in the novel with Mr. Vincy predicting apocalypse as a result of the impending Reform Bill and the appropriately named newspaper, The Trumpet, "blasting . . . against Rome."[62] George Eliot, like Lewes, is inclined to a more progressivist reading of history. Dorothea's marriage to Will Ladislaw is a marriage to one who can at once make sense of the "stupendous fragmentariness" of history by symbolically or aesthetically reconstructing it[63] and, no less important, act in a spirit of confident hope in the future. The narrator's several gestures of identification with Herodotus, the first of ancient historians to interpret the process of historical change progressively, bears out this desire on George Eliot's part to write as if history in general and the Reform Act in particular were movements forward towards the "social right."[64]

Yet the invocation of Herodotus is also the occasion of a more problematical reading of history. The Greek historian, she tells us, like herself, takes "a woman's lot for his starting-point."[65] The reference, beyond the obvious one to Io, is to Herodotus' persistent association of national decline with the subjugation of women. Even more, George Eliot may have in mind Herodotus' related account and apparent approval of the matriarch of the Lycians, who "have . . . one singular custom in which they differ from every other nation in the world: naming themselves by their mothers, not their fathers."[66] Such foregrounding of the status of women in history, I suspect, influenced George Eliot's desire to write in Middlemarch about whether it is possible to have in the modern era a woman capable of performing world-historical acts of reformation rather than the merely "unhistoric acts" to which at last Dorothea is relegated. It is, of course, Will who becomes the "ardent public man," and marriage to him, is, for Dorothea, politically an "absorption."[67] Her story, like Lydgate's, is that of wasted or misdirected energy: "Her full nature, like the river which Cyrus broke the strength, spent itself in channels which had no great name on earth."[68] The reference here is again to Herodotus, to his contrast of the conspicuously imperial male's power with specifically female weakness,[69] and it implies volumes of frustration on the part of the "belated historian"[70] of *Middlemarch*, who finds the political potential of female energy in much the same situation her ancient forebear had found it. Dorothea is not a new Theresa, but, as her creator makes clear at the close, she is a new Antigone buried alive by a "social medium" of (men's) rules she cannot transcend. Finally, we need to note that in this tragic reading of woman's situation we may find a profound protest against that aspect of the positivist faith, so prominent in Comte and, as we have seen, accepted by the early George Eliot, which mythologized a putative principal of passive, altruistic love (as opposed to active, constructive intellectual energy) as feminine. Maggie may leave behind her the light of a modern Madonna, but that sort of energy is hardly enough for Dorothea.

It was John Morley, Lewes' successor as editor of the *Fortnightly* and a man well versed in Comte's positivism, who argued that as late as *Middlemarch* George Eliot had still not extricated herself from what he took to be the principal political consequence of Comte's version of a scientific social theory: "The scientific quality of [her] work may be considered to have stood in the way of her own aim. . . . The sense of the iron limitations that are set to improvement by inexorable forces . . . is stronger in her than any intrepid resolution to press on to whatever improvement may chance to be within reach. . . . In energy . . . in the kindling of living faith in social effort, George Sand . . . takes a higher place."[71] Surely, there is a side of *Middlemarch* that supports Morley's judgment, a side on which even the powerful Shelleyan (Tyndallian) energy of Will Ladislaw, in which we are clearly meant to place our faith in the political future, seems to become, in the finale's long retrospect of years, perhaps as futile as that of everyone else in the novel. He performed his historic acts of reform in "those times," the narrator wistfully observes, "when reforms were begun with a young hopefulness of immediate good which has been much checked in our days."[72] We seem here to be moving back to that deeper, pagan tragic vision which, as I have indicated, always shadows George Eliot's meliorism, the vision of a "blight of irony over all our higher effort."[73] Put another way, the "lot of woman," with which this particular historian begins as well as ends, seems to take on a distressingly transsexual implication: we are, all of us, no matter how energetic, essentially in the condition of female impotency, doomed to be subjugated and martyred to the "embroiled medium."

But the failures that dominate *Middlemarch* are not George Eliot's last work on the subject. She was no more prepared than Morley to abandon a "living faith" in human will. Rather it was a question with her of finding an argument that, while not metaphysical, would nonetheless demonstrate what romantic writers like George Sand assumed, the efficacy of individual will in the historical process. The emphasis on the energy of ongoing structuration, rather than the search for the true primordial Edenic structure, was a critical step in that direction. That is, George Eliot seems clearly to be saying in this novel that if there is not an Ur-structure, there is certainly an Ur-energy, apart from any particular structures, that one can identify as a universal good in itself. In *Middlemarch*, Dorothea's energy, her ardent longing for the "least partial good," is treated not only as an ontological reality but also as a moral absolute. We are not left in any real doubt on either of these scores, and for this reason it is difficult to accept J. Hillis Miller's celebrated reading of the novel: "*Middlemarch* itself is an example of form arising from unlikeness and difference, a form governed by no absolute center, origin, or end."[74] Dorothea's spontaneous altruistic desire or impulse is the novel's center, it is the psychological reality underlying all particular forms and, specifically, all particular linguistic forms. In an early conversation with Will on the nature of her "religion," Dorothea tells him it consists simply in "desiring what is perfectly good, even when we do not know quite what is . . ." When Will responds by calling this a "beautiful mysticism," Dorothea reacts sharply, refusing not just that name but any name for it: "Please not to call it by any name. . . . You shall say it is Persian, or something else geographical. It is my life."[75]

George Eliot in *Middlemarch*, as Miller points out, does recognize "the deconstructive powers of . . . language, its undoing of any attempt to make a complete, and completely coherent, picture of human life,"[76] but in a far more conservative sense than he has in mind (and for which "deconstructive" is really not the appropriate term). What Dorothea is saying is that, because the structure of language (or any symbolic form) inevitably departs from the reality of inarticulate desire, we must finally place our faith in the latter, in the vague experience of the energy itself. Her faith, and George Eliot's, in this novel requires that all particular, historical structures must, to return to that crucial positivist expectation, be *verifiable* against this more primitive, authoritative, and universal "logic of feeling." The "idea [must be] wrought back to the directness of sense like the solidity of objects," for "our good depends on the quality and breadth of our emotion."[77]

Where Miller best reads the novel is in his recognition that George Eliot is hesitating profoundly over whether her model of true "religion" can, indeed, provide the source of the social totality she everywhere seeks in her work. For Miller this hesitation is the consequence of recognizing the merely formal or metaphorical nature of all totalities, recognizing "one can get a different kind of totality depending on what metaphorical model is used. . . ."[78] George Eliot, as we saw in our examination of *The Mill on the Floss*, has long understood the metaphorical or textual nature of beliefs and consequently the futility of the search for the true text/tissue of the sort Casaubon, Lydgate, the early Lewes, and her own early self engage in. What she has held in reserve, and what comes out most clearly in *Middlemarch*, is the belief that the formative, but itself formless, energy of the human will is our proper moral center.

As she moves into the last novel, however, George Eliot's perspective shifts towards the position imputed to her by Miller to the extent that she understands that this energy in order to have a widespread *social* or *historical* effect must have a specific symbolic/metaphoric form. Dorothea's one great spot of commonness is in the "hereditary" Puritanism of her energy, which amounts to a failure to understand how the symbolic forms of art can have anything to do with the social reform she seeks to effect. Ladislaw does not suffer from this deficiency, and though we see relatively little of what he actually believes in in *Middlemarch*, his story will, in effect, continue in the next novel.

SYMBOLIC REPRESENTATION AND THE MEANS
OF REVOLUTION

"Heat," writes George Eliot in the first book of *Daniel Deronda*, "is a great agent," but before it can become a "means of explaining the universe it requires an extensive knowledge of differences."[79] In this way does she signal what I take to be her principal object in the novel: to define that specific difference in heat which we know as the energy of mind, and, still more subtly, to define those differences within the category of mental energy which make, to borrow a phrase from the previous novel, the "growth of happy or unhappy consciousness." *Daniel Deronda* is her version of the Prometheus story, of man's transmutation of the cosmic fire into his cultural world. We begin with Prometheus bound, with "those moments of intense suffering— which . . . like the cry of Prometheus . . . [seem] a greater energy than the sea and sky he invokes and the deity he defies,"[80] and end with him unbound. It is, one recalls, Shelley's play which is under discussion when Mordecai takes the neophyte Daniel to the debate on historical change at The Hand and Banner, an event that perhaps marks Daniel's first decisive step towards the prophetic vocation. Of course, the concern with the prophetic vocation, so overwhelmingly present in this last novel,[81] reminds us that it is also George Eliot's "Book of Daniel," her story of the vision of a New Jerusalem beyond the "embroiled medium" of her particular historical moment. Whether viewed from the perspective of classical or biblical precursor the result is the same: this is the work in which she comes closest to transcending the tragic and attaining the epic voice, though, as we will see, the irremediably tragic lingers on in the figures of Gwendolen and the Alcharisi.

Daniel Deronda is a continuation of Ladislaw or, as George Levine has nicely put it, "Will Ladislaw [is] a more trivial, or less solemn, anticipation of Deronda."[82] What makes for the solemnity, we shall shortly consider, but first we need to explore a less obvious connection between *Daniel Deronda* and the previous novel, for, the sexual difference notwithstanding, a case can be made that, before he continues the character of Will, Daniel, in a certain sense, continues that of Dorothea. Indeed, it is not altogether certain that we need to put sexual difference aside. As Henry James was probably the first to notice, at least in print, George Eliot takes care to bring out the androgyny of the early Daniel. "He is the most irresistible man in the literature of fiction," Theodora observes in James's "conversation" on the novel. To which Pulcheria perspicaciously responds, "He is not a man at all!"[83]

"What," asks George Eliot, "in the midst of [the] mighty drama [of world history] are girls and their blind visions?" And she disarmingly answers—disarmingly in that she has just been developing a portrait of one of the most self-preoccupied and "demonic" women in her fiction: "They are the Yea or Nay of that good for which men are enduring and fighting. In these delicate vessels is borne onward through the ages the treasure of human affections."[84] As she had learned from Comte, women are the distinctively "affectionate" sex, the sex in which we are most likely to find the emotion of love in its highest forms of asexual tenderness and disinterested sympathy or altruism. This had been Dorothea's great strength; she is one of George Eliot's many priestesses of the "religion of sympathy," a sister of Dinah Morris, Maggie Tulliver, and Romola de Bardi. Now it is the (nominal) male Daniel who is the single most important "vessel of affection" or

sympathy. He has the "ardently affectionate nature," the "inborn lov-
ingness," the "precocious" interest in "how human miseries are
wrought." He is "moved by an affectionateness such as we are apt to
call feminine, disposing him to yield . . ."; "all the woman lacking in
[his mother] was present in him. . . ." It is this "too diffusive sympathy" (George Eliot picks up the central metaphor of Dorothea's martyrdom), this "wandering energy," that makes Daniel, like Dorothea,
unable to do great works in the world, that lets him simply "drift"
amidst the "hopelessly entangled scheme" of things rather than work
actively to change them.[85]

At the same time, this very force of affection this extraordinarily
sympathetic nature also makes of him, as it does of Dorothea, one of
those "massive beings" who can transform the lives of the individuals
around them, and George Eliot explores through his character again
and in still greater depth the power of "personality" that can "change
the [moral] lights" of another. The test case here is the misery of
Gwendolen Harleth, and, far more than in Dorothea's relation with
Lydgate, in Daniel's with Gwendolen we see a complexly developed
exchange of strength from one character to another, an exchange of
emotional energy that George Eliot actually seems to regard as something like a chemical reaction. From the moment of their first encounter, before a word is even exchanged between them, the image of
Deronda becomes for Gwendolen a kind of icon. His person and,
eventually, his personality "by some hidden affinity" "bite" themselves "into the most permanent layers of [her] feeling." He takes
hold of her mind, "as one who had an unknown standard by which
he judged her. . . . It is one of the secrets in that change of mental
poise which has been fitly named conversion, that to many among us
neither heaven nor earth has any revelation till some personality
touches theirs with a peculiar influence, subduing them to receptive-
ness. . . . [Deronda's] influence had entered into the current of that
self-suspicion and self-blame which awakens a new consciousness."
And, ultimately, almost certainly holding her back from madness and
even suicide, his "words were like the touch of a miraculous hand to
Gwendolen. . . . So pregnant is the divine hope of moral recovery
with the energy that fulfills it. So potent in us is the infused action of
another soul. . . ."[86]

What we see in the extended depiction of the relation between
Daniel and Gwendolen, and, indeed, between Daniel and virtually
everyone else of significance in the novel, is George Eliot elaborating
more fully than ever before the psychological doctrine that has to this

point been at the center of her writing. It is a doctrine, as we have seen, which Lewes touches upon in *The Study of Psychology,* written almost contemporaneously with the writing of *Daniel Deronda.* Each organism, he argues, is a *"system* of forces," and in man we call this system "personality": ". . . over and above the particular motives . . . we are conscious of a Will, a Personality, which determines these to be what they are."[87] With Lewes, however, the principal interest of personality as a psychological category is in its capacity for spontaneous moral decision. He has virtually nothing to say about what has become most important to George Eliot, personality as a force for the transformation of another self.[88]

As always with George Eliot, it is not just private lives that need rescuing, but society in general. The theory of a personal moral force must become a theory of history. Deronda, as Promethean hero, is not "unbound" until he chooses to make his force of personality part of a larger historical process, to adopt, that is, the prophetic vocation that Mordecai thrusts upon him: "[T]he fuller nature desires to be an agent, to create, and not merely to look on. . . . And while there is warmth in the sun to feed an energetic life, there will still be men to feel, 'I am lord of this moment's change, and will change it with my soul.' "[89] But how does one convert the energy of sympathetic love into an energy that changes society?

One must begin by abandoning "a many-sided sympathy," the "imaginative" "habit of seeing things as they probably appeared to others," abandoning, in short, that fundamental positivist value of objectivity or "impartiality" in favor of "that *selectness* of fellowship which [is] the [condition] of moral force" (my emphasis).[90] Or as George Eliot puts it when Daniel has selected his particular religious fellowship and set himself the task of establishing a Jewish homeland, "There was a release of all the energy which had long been spent in self-checking and suppression. . . . It was as if he had found an added soul in finding his ancestry—his judgment no longer wandering in the mazes of impartial sympathy, but choosing, *with the noble partiality which is man's best strength*, the closer fellowship that makes sympathy practical" (my emphasis).[91] In terms of the dramatic structure of the novel, Daniel must make a painful choice between ministering to the "wounded" individual, Gwendolen, or submitting to the "grasp of Mordecai's dying hand,"[92] which carries with it the mission of imposing a definite, partial, and quite possibly mistaken shape on mankind's moral and social life. Daniel, of course, chooses Mordecai and becomes the only hero/heroine in George Eliot's fiction to make so decisive a move from the religion of sympathy to what we may regard as an early form of pragmatism, a religion, as it were, of the efficacious form.[93]

The necessity of the selective, or "partial," representation of reality is announced at the very outset of the novel ("Men can do nothing without the make-believe of a beginning"[94]) and is reiterated throughout. Nowhere is this more evident than in the carefully orchestrated motif of the "image." Every character comes to the consciousness of every other as well as to the reader, conspicuously mediated by an image. Thus we readers begin, not with Gwendolen herself, but with Gwendolen through Deronda's perception of her as we enact with Deronda the primary psychic process of trying to interpret the "problematic sylph" (the pun is surely intended). Daniel applies to the problem one image after another from his (our) aesthetic experience. Is she a "sylph," a "goddess of luck," a "Nereid," a "Lamia"? Or, again Daniel, himself is, for the Meyrick sisters, an image from the Arabian Nights, for Mirah, an image from the Old Testament, for himself, an image from various historical narratives (Pericles, Robert Bruce, Washington), for the narrator, an image from Titian, and so on.[95] Nowhere else in George Eliot's fiction has imaging, which is to say the aesthetic transfiguring of reality, been so consistently and self-consciously portrayed as the inevitable way the mind reads reality. But still more important, nowhere else has the positivist requirement of relating these images back to reality, rendering them "impartial," seemed so irrelevant. Truth, Mirah tells us at one point, lies in the image not the thing behind the image.[96]

Given the spontaneous tendency of the mind to prefigure reality in terms of coherent images, images that flatter us with the belief that we live in an intelligible moral order, the key to effecting a change in the historical situation, George Eliot comes to argue, lies in the power of constructing new images of reality. Thus Mordecai's visionary power is essentially a matter of image-making. He has that "second sight" in which "yearnings, conceptions . . . continually take the form of images which have a fore-shadowing power: the deed they would do starts up before them in complete shape, making a coercive type. . . ."[97] Daniel has a similar talent for imagistic projection, which is what makes him such a suitable continuator of Mordecai's prophetic mission. As a child he seeks to understand his origin by transferring images drawn from his copious reading to his own life: "The ardour which he had given to the imaginary world in his books suddenly rushed towards his own history and spent its pictorial

energy there, . . . representing the unknown. . . . The impetuous advent of new images took possession of him with the force of fact. . . ."
What keeps Daniel from fully releasing or expressing this "pictorial
energy"[98] is a positivistic hesitancy over the reality of the projective
images formed by desire or yearning. This hesitancy continues to rest-
rain his Promethean/prophetic impulse right up to the climactic encounter with Mordecai, in which the latter identifies him as the second self who must carry on his (Mordecai's) vocation. What if Mordecai's visionary images of a New Jerusalem, that is, a Jewish homeland, are the products of monomania? "What such a temper of mind
likely to accompany that wise estimate of consequences which is the
only safeguard from fatal error . . .?" The narrator responds, in effect,
that our scientific preoccupation with verification or correspondence
may not be an appropriate criterion in the case of the visionary's second sight. "Faith in preconception" is necessary "even [to] strictly
measuring science," and,

in relation to human motives and actions, passionate belief has a fuller efficacy. Here enthusiasm may have the validity of proof, and, happening in one
soul, give the type of what will one day be general. . . . [P]erhaps an emotional intellect may have absorbed into its passionate vision of possibilities
some truth of what will be—the more comprehensive massive life feeding
theory with new material, as the sensibility of the artist seizes combinations
which science explains and justifies. . . . We must be patient with the inevitable makeshift of our human thinking. . . .[99]

Deronda does, of course, eventually give himself over to the unverified and unverifiable force of Mordecai's visionary image-making: "'It is you [Mordecai] who have given shape to what, I believe,
was an inherited yearning. . . . Since I began to read and know, I
have always longed for some ideal task, in which I might feel myself
the heart and brain of a multitude—some social captainship. . . . You
have raised the image of such a task for me—to bind our race together. . . .'"[100] The particular image which Deronda takes from Mordecai—and vows to enlarge—the image which focuses and gives efficacy to his amorphous yearning for the social good is far more universal than it may at first appear. The ideal of Israel, for Mordecai, as for
George Eliot, is the quintessential ideal of social and moral unity, or
totality: "'. . . the *Shemah*, wherein we briefly confess the divine Unity,
is the chief devotional exercise of the Hebrew; and this made our religion the fundamental religion for the whole world; for the divine Unity
embraced as its consequence the ultimate unity of mankind. . . . Now,
in complete unity a part possesses the whole as the whole possesses

every part: and in this way human life is tending toward the *image* of the Supreme Unity. . . .' "[101] The paradox George Eliot has most at heart in this novel here comes squarely before us: in the separateness, the partiality, of specific form, lies the principle of unity. Only through the arbitrary imposition of form, only through the act of placing an ideal shape on vague, "hereditary" yearnings, does the energy of mind become an effective political, that is, polity-making, and binding power.[102]

This is the answer to the problem so troublesome to Dorothea of how aesthetic activity can possibly have anything to do with the social right: "Gods and men wrought deeds that poets wrought in song."[103] Art provides us with the image of unity which appeals to an apparently innate "tendency" in the human mind and commands assent. Recalling our discussion of the late Comte, we see that it is a position that, among other things, owes much to the French philosopher's regeneration of the "subjective principle." Maintaining that the objective method had accomplished its mission of demonstrating that man's history is subject to the same invariable laws as nature, Comte announced in the *Système* that the time was right to reassert the supreme importance of subjective synthesis in establishing social/political unity. "Thus the . . . [symbolic] logic under which Man's primitive belief arose adapts itself, when regenerated by Positivism, to his final constructions."[104] From Comte as well, George Eliot would have learned of the pivotal importance of art, and more particularly images or poetic language that approaches the condition of images, in instilling the principle of social unity in the population at large.

The principal function of Art [in the modern world] is to construct types on the basis furnished by Science. Now this is precisely what is required for inaugurating the new social system. . . . [I]n Sociology . . . the conclusion of Science [will] fall always far short of that degree of fulness, precision, and clearness, without which no principle can be thoroughly popularised. . . . Poetry steps in and stimulates practical action. . . . In his effort to accomplish this object the Positivist poet will naturally be led to form prophetic pictures of the regeneration of Man, viewed in every aspect that admits of being ideally represented.[105]

Science, inadequate in its tentativeness and its abstractness, needs "prophetic pictures of the regeneration of Man" to make its new synthesis a political reality. This is very close, indeed, to what George Eliot is saying in *Daniel Deronda*.

But it is not the same thing. What Comte insists upon is that the subjective synthesis regenerated by positivism has been validated by the objective or scientific analysis of the "external" order of nature.

The social instincts [altruism] would never gain mastery [in human feelings] were they not sustained . . . by the economy of the external world. . . . The phenomena of human life, though more modifiable than many others, are yet equally subject to invariable laws. . . . Now the benevolent affections, which themselves act in harmony with the laws of social developments, incline us to submit to all other laws as soon as the intellect has discovered their existence. The possibility of moral unity depends, therefore, even in the case of the individual, but still more in that of society, upon the necessity of recognising our subjection to an external power. By this means our self-regarding instincts are rendered susceptible of discipline. In themselves they are strong enough to neutralise all sympathetic tendencies, *were it not for the support that the latter find in this External Order*.[106] (my emphasis)

In *Daniel Deronda* George Eliot has no such confidence that the subjective synthesis she is seeking is grounded in any external order or natural law. On the contrary, what she has come increasingly to believe is that it is the expression of an energy which, whatever its origins in nature, now operates independently of nature in the interest of specifically human desires. The images of unity constructed by this mental energy are spontaneous, aesthetic "previsions" of order which may or may not have a correspondent reality. Their "reality" lies, rather, in their causal effect on individual and social behavior.

What this modification of Comte's still essentially positivist argument allows George Eliot to do is vindicate the efficacy of individual free will, more particularly, the aesthetic will to form, as a causal force in human, historical development. It is her way out of the determinism alluded to by Morley and endemic to positivism, a determinism she would have found in one form and another in her contemporaries Spencer, Harrison, John Fiske, and W. K. Clifford (to name only those whose influence she felt most strongly), all of whom, in the interests of a scientific social theory, reduce the process of history to an impersonal law of nature with little or no room for individual "resistance." On the other hand, Tyndall's tendency to associate his own materialist concept of human mental energy with the idealism of Fichte and Fichte's greatest English disciple Carlyle, may serve to bring home the point that George Eliot (herself an admirer of Carlyle) very much in the spirit of Tyndall and the "higher physics," reasserts, at last, the possibility of heroism in history. Something of this impulse we have found in Lewes, most conspicuously in the works written after *Daniel Deronda*, but even still his own allowance for the causality of will and, correlatively, the effect of symbols falls considerably short of the absolutely central, virtually Carlylean role[107] George Eliot gives them as the arbiter of human destiny.

To find an analogue among contemporary, or nearly contemporary, philosophers for what George Eliot is doing in *Daniel Deronda* one needs to look not to Comte or for that matter to any of the properly positivist thinkers to whom she owes so much, but to William James (1842–1910). James, himself initially a physiological psychologist and as such the student of Lewes, Helmholtz, and Wundt, as well as a great admirer of Darwin, sought, like George Eliot, to vindicate, above all, the force of individual personality in the process of history. His "defense of the primary importance of individual experience and personal freedom," writes Philip Wiener, is the "Ariadne thread" that pulls together his entire philosophy.[108] And, as with the George Eliot of *Daniel Deronda*, the "will to believe" displaces in his Pragmatism the positivists' persistent attempt to establish a correspondence theory of truth and, what is intimately related, a natural-law theory of moral and social right.

The vulgar notion of correspondence . . . is that thoughts must *copy* the reality . . . ; and philosophy, without having ever fairly sat down to the question, seems to have instinctively accepted this idea. . . . The notion of a world complete in itself, to which thought comes as a passive mirror, adding nothing to fact, Lotze says, is irrational. Rather is thought itself a most momentous part of fact, and the whole mission of the pre-existing and insufficient world of matter may simply be to provoke thought to produce its far more precious supplement. . . . It seems obvious that the pragmatic [rather than correspondence] account of [knowing] is accurate. Truth here is a relation, not of our ideas to non-human realities, but of conceptual parts of our experience to sensational parts. Those thoughts are true which guide us to *beneficial interaction* with sensible particulars as they occur, whether they copy these in advance or not.[109]

As the reference to Hermann Lotze (1817–1881), one of the earliest researchers into the physiological energy of mind, serves to suggest, James participated in much the same movement of psychological theory as that which we have seen influencing George Eliot.[110] As he writes in *The Meaning of Truth* (1914), "Energetics . . . is the last word" of the new pragmatism; it "makes our whole notion of scientific truth more flexible and general than it used to be."[111] The understanding of truth as that which guides men to a "beneficial interaction" with each other and their environment, or, as James puts it in a more popular lecture, of faith as "faith in some one else's faith," belief as "a passionate affirmation of desire," fairly describes the nature of "working truth,"[112] as George Eliot comes finally to understand it in her Daniel story.

Richard Rorty distinguishes between the preeminent concern of traditional philosophy, to know the truth, and the concerns of pragmatism. In his account, the transcendentalists and the empiricists or Platonists and positivists, though their opposition had "crystalized" by the nineteenth century, were, in the end, after the same impossible object, the correspondence of their propositions to reality, or truth. Pragmatism, on the other hand, "cuts across this transcendental/ empirical distinction between the true and the not true, *episteme* and *doxa*."

For the pragmatist true sentences are not true because they correspond to reality, and so there is no need to worry what sort of reality, if any, a given sentence corresponds to—no need to worry about what "makes" it true. . . . One difficulty [he] . . . has . . . is that he must struggle with the positivist for the position of radical anti-Platonist. He wants to attack Plato with different weapons from those of the positivist, but at first glance he looks like just another variety of positivist. He shares with the positivist the Baconian and Hobbesian notion that knowledge is power, a tool for coping with reality. But he carries this Baconian point through to its extreme, as the positivist does not. He drops the notion of truth as correspondence with reality altogether, and says that modern science does not enable us to cope because it corresponds, it just plain enables us to cope.[113]

What we find in George Eliot's last novel is just such a crucial parting of the ways with positivism as Rorty is describing here. She, at the close of her career in the mid-1870s, was turning the same epistemological-cum-political corner James, at the beginning of his career, was turning at virtually the same moment across the Atlantic, that is, through physics to what their more orthodox scientific brethren might well—and in James's case did—regard as a new metaphysics. James lived on to parlay the turn into a school. George Eliot in her fiction, we may say, gives us an image or prevision of philosophical things to come; both make their move, ultimately, in defense of a residual humanism, a humanism that the ongoing logic of contemporary scientific philosophy, as we will see in later chapters, increasingly threatened.

THE PROBLEM OF RELATIVISM

Leszek Kolakowski correctly sees pragmatism as an outgrowth of positivism and hence as another step in the "alienation of reason."[114] What he tends to overlook is what I have argued is its humanistic provenance. James's (and George Eliot's) end in view was to reaffirm the autonomy of human structures and the efficacy of the individual will in the face of a positivism that was progressively reducing mind to an utterly "impartial," that is, undifferentiated, alliance with nature.

Kolakowski's principal criticism of pragmatism, that it leads "naturally" to a "radical relativism," needs further consideration, not with regard to James, who is not our principal concern, but George Eliot insofar as her own position in *Daniel Deronda*, whether we want to call it pragmatist or not, is certainly susceptible to the charge of relativism. She herself is well aware of this and the difficulties it presents for her, as we see perhaps nowhere more powerfully than in the novel's epigraph (which was almost certainly composed by her).

> Let thy chief terror be of thine own soul:
> There, 'mid the throng of hurrying desires
> That trample o'er the dead to seize their spoil,
> Lurks vengeance, footless, irresistible
> As exhalations laden with slow death,
> And o'er the fairest troop of captured joys
> Breathes pallid pestilence.

Do we need stronger evidence of the author's anxiety over the dangers of partiality, the dangers of a coercive image of life formed, not in accord with objective nature, but with what may be simply wrong-headed, not to say insane, desires? Clearly, George Eliot, unlike Nietzsche (with whom we might, like J. H. Miller, be inclined to compare her "aestheticization" of belief[115]), is not beyond good or evil. It matters immensely to her that the energy of "soul," which shapes any given image of totality, be, in its essence, morally good, and she does attempt to establish a criterion for determining whether this is the case. The image or figure or trace is not, for her, the ultimate reality it is for Nietzsche and his followers; the ultimate reality, again, is the psychic energy that generates the image. In *Deronda*, precisely because that energy is disengaged from any originary structure or germ, she engages more fully than ever before the issue of what it is that distinguishes a good or wholesome energy or will from a bad or demonic one, a Deronda, or a Mirah, if you like, from a Gwendolen or a Leonora Halm-Eberstein. The answer she comes up with, as we will see, is intimately related to that unresolved problem of gender that we found underlying Dorothea's tragedy.

Daniel wonders on first seeing Gwendolen whether the "genius" in her, metaphorically associated with energy, is good or evil. The answer, announced by the title of the first book, is that she is, if not quite evil, "spoiled." What has spoiled her is, in a word, the absence of adequate love, and in particular maternal love, in her early childhood. As we have seen, she had not an infancy "well-rooted in some spot of a native land, where it may get the love of tender kinship for the face of the earth . . ." a spot where the definiteness of early memories may be inwrought with affection, and . . . may spread . . . as a sort of habit of the blood."[116] What we see George Eliot exploring here as elsewhere is the question of how "habits" or emotional dispositions are "inwrought" in the child. In Gwendolen's case, parental absence or insouciance has been the dominant childhood experience and hence the "spoiling"[117] that in the adult shows itself as a compensatory "energy of egoistic desire."[118] But it shows itself more profoundly, I believe, in a susceptibility to existential "dread"[119] and a related capacity for intense hatred, the "lurking" vengeance George Eliot speaks of in the epigraph. Gwendolen's native energy is rendered at last demonic, and the image that most coerces her is the image of herself as murderess.

Mirah's situation is diametrically opposite. Awful as her adolescence may have been, she has, George Eliot takes pains to emphasize, imbibed in her earliest childhood the love of an extraordinarily tender mother. For Mirah the dominant image of her life is a vision of the Madonna singing a Hebrew lullaby over her "before self-consciousness was born." This is the source of her almost infallible capacity to realize an otherwise very ugly life. As she tells Daniel, " 'When the best thing comes into [my] thoughts, it is like what my mother has been to me.' "[120]

Daniel is in a more problematical position. Never having known a mother's love, he has filled that absence with an image of the mother he believes he had, the mother in need of rescue from the world's miseries, an image which Mirah comes to embody for him. When at last he discovers the lost mother, the reality of her desertion of him blends with the image of Gwendolen to create his moment of profoundest disillusionment, "a mood in which Gwendolen and her equivocal fate moved as busy images of what was amiss in this world along with the concealments which he had felt as hardships in his own life, and were acting on him now under the form of an affecting doubtfulness about the mother who had announced herself coldly and still kept away."[121] Fortunately, Mirah supplies him with a reassuring image of the proper mother even as her male counterpart, Mordecai, releases in him the energy of prophetic vocation. This novel closes with a double marriage, as it were, to sister and brother, "the very best of human possibilities," as George Eliot says, "the blending of a complete personal love in one current with a larger duty."[122]

What obviously continues to disturb George Eliot and to disrupt this closure is the alternative possibility, always in the background of George Eliot's work, that fundamental divisions between people and within the self are not, after all, transcendable. We find this, most apparently, in Daniel's need to escape (as several critics have complained) the real social complexities of England—and psychical complexities of Gwendolen—for the merely promised totality of Israel. But we find it more subtly, and at the same time more poignantly, in the situation of the successful female artist Leonora Halm-Eberstein. "You can never imagine," she tells her son, "what it is to have a man's force of genius in you, and yet suffer the slavery of being a girl."[123] To release that force of male genius, to become a successful artist requires abandoning the role of the loving mother, which George Eliot (like Comte and Lewes) still needs to think of as the source or center of morality and, by extension, the criterion by which we distinguish the benevolent image of unity from the demonic.

Leonora shows us still more graphically than Dorothea what this novelist comes to understand as the fundamental disabling division, the block that perversely stands in the route to the New Jerusalem. For a woman to become the heroine in the national epic, a vocation now plainly identified with the formative power of the artist, is to betray her essential moral function as the "vessel . . . of human affections." To overcome this inner division, George Eliot at last understands intellectually, if she does not quite accept emotionally, requires eradicating in herself and in society an extremely coercive image of what a woman ought to be and remaking that image. When Mirah objects to her otherwise enlightened brother's image of woman as "especially framed for the love which feels possession in renouncing," his response implies what remains for George Eliot to do: " 'My sister, thou hast read too many plays, where the writers delight in showing the human passions as indwelling demons. . . . Thou judgest by the plays, and not by thy own heart, which is like our mother's.' Mirah made no answer."[124] Like Will in the last novel, Mirah in this one is conceivably the hero/heroine of the next novel, the woman who will write the play that will change the (corporate) heart.

This has a hopeful ring about it, which fits well with the faith I imagine George Eliot, no less than Lewes or William James, wills to believe, the faith in the power of individual genius or energy to transform the human condition. But how, finally, are we to understand that energy? As an articulate yearning for love or the "last refinement" of image or symbol-making? Does the heart generate (and validate) the sign, or the sign define and form the heart? If the former, then one can still evade the charge of radical relativism; if the latter, then that charge, surely, is inescapable. George Eliot's reluctance to liberate her heroines, understandably regretted by recent feminists, needs perhaps to be understood as symptomatic of a larger philosophical reluctance. To abandon belief in the reality of the maternal heart, to see that belief as yet another image superimposed on the vacancy of the soul, is to risk conceding that the transformative power of the imagination is, after all, disengaged from any moral sanction, without a center (as Miller would argue), and this she is too much of a realist and too much of a moralist to allow. The belief that "Mighty Love"[125] has somehow laid his hand on the human race is a "habit of the blood" she cannot shake off.

There is no question but that George Eliot's intellectual poise is, at last, a precarious one. The shift in scientific paradigm from the pursuit of original organic structures to the tracing of energy's conversion processes (its "differences") and the parallel shift, to return to Peterfreund's point, in linguistic paradigms from *enargeia* to *energeia*, work only if one can continue to believe, as she wants so much to do, in some ultimate principle of good underlying the supposed continuum from energy to *energeia*, nature to culture. The future history of positivism will find that belief already threatened from within by George Eliot's own deconstructive perceptions (concentrated, I have suggested, in Gwendolen) and from without by further developments in the two scientific revolutions that have, in fact, underlain our concerns in the last two chapters, Darwinism and the new physics. First, however, there is another and still hopeful phase of positivism to negotiate, one which, in effect, preserves Lewes' and George Eliot's faith in an essential natural good—albeit at the expense of their scientific humanism.

Part Three

The Social Determination
of the Self

7

Beyond Humanism:
Leslie Stephen's Scientific Ethics

Everytime a social phenomenon is directly explained by a psychological
phenomenon we may be sure that explanation is false.
                                                —Durkheim

WITH Stephen we come to a scientific philosopher (and, of course,
literary critic) who is at once more conservative and more advanced
than George Eliot—and for that matter Lewes. More conservative in
that he has little use for the aestheticist aspect of scientific thought,
with its relativistic implications, that we find in the older writers'
later work; more advanced in that he is prepared, as the other two are
not, to abandon the sacred humanistic principle of individual free
will. On both counts this means Stephen goes a step farther down the
road towards the complete naturalization of man's view of himself,
but then he takes that step with a rather uncritical faith in the essential
humanness of the natural. His ultimate focus is not on psychology or
epistemology, art or politics, but on ethics. His great work, *The Science
of Ethics* (1882), though now virtually ignored, is surely the finest
treatise on positivist morality to come out of the Victorian era and a
work that struggles with questions of human motivation that remain
pertinent in our own day.

AGAINST THE "RELIGION OF FINE ART"

The problem of relativism confronts Leslie Stephen at the outset of his
career, but not in the work of George Eliot, whom he, like too many
of his contemporaries, regarded as preeminently the artist of a lost
idyllic age.[1] Rather it is a distinctly antiscientific relativism, with its

attendant pessimism, that brings him out in a new positivist defense of the language of nature, which, in his account, is a demonstrably moral, demonstrably healthy language. His principal antagonist was a formidable figure, a figure whom no account of culture in the Victorian period can ignore.

Stephen's first philosophically significant book, *Freethinking and Plainspeaking*, came out in 1873 when he was 41. It is a collection of essays published separately over the previous three years. He himself seems to have thought of it as something of an ad hoc production, the binding together of some of the better "rubbish" he was doggedly producing for the periodical press.[2] He was more than a little apologetic to his American friend Charles Norton for having dedicated it to him. But while it is certainly not "the great book"[3] that he had been promising Norton and others for the past two or three years, it is still an important book, not only for his own development but also as an expression of the times. Far more coherent than he himself probably realized at the time, it is thoroughly positivistic, announcing the inadequacy of Christianity or theism of any sort as a viable mode of belief for the modern age, and calling, just as Lewes would do in the opening volume of *Problems of Life and Mind* the following year, for the construction of a new social belief based on science. What we must ask ourselves as the nineteenth century draws into its last quarter, he writes, is "are we Christians?" The answer, as he sees it, can no longer be the easy affirmative of even a generation earlier. The "opiate" of religion has lost its hold on the "intellectual classes" and it can be only a matter of time before it loses its "sway over the 'proletariate.' " It is to reason and Mr. Darwin "as the best modern expounder of the universe" that we must now turn for our guide and "go boldly forwards to whatever may be in store for us."[4]

A major inspiration for the book, or rather for making a book out of his published essays, is, as Stephen suggests in the title essay, John Stuart Mill, whose death early in that year he must have wanted in some way to memorialize, for beyond Darwin, Mill was unquestionably the English contemporary who most significantly influenced Stephen's thought. It is not simply that Stephen believed in Mill's doctrine of scientific knowledge as the only valid knowledge; it is that Mill had conspicuously stood for the untrammeled expression of unorthodox opinion, for "plainspeaking." The conjunction in Stephen's title is very much the point: not only freethinking but also plainspeaking. The greatest danger of our day, he writes, is not the absence or inaccessibility of truth, but the "general atmosphere of insincerity," which is fast producing a skepticism "as to the very existence of intellectual good faith."[5]

The object of Stephen's criticism, then, is not really Christianity, which he assumes is a dying belief,[6] nor is it a repressive political regime that imposes this outmoded belief on its citizens. What he is after is a certain kind of liberalism which sees clearly the movement of modern thought away from theism yet from fear of moral and social consequences argues for the retention of the traditional forms of belief, for the Bible and the Church establishment. He is after the Broad Churchmen, and for reasons not unlike J. H. Newman's, though from a radically different philosophical basis. Just as Newman had regarded the liberal Anglicans as obscuring the necessity of an unqualified commitment to Church dogma, so Stephen found their penchant for accomodating modern scientific truth to the language and forms of Christianity not only insincere but also perversely obstructive of science's efforts to establish a "living creed" that would provide for the "social solidity" (totality) that contemporary Europe had not known since the French Revolution. In the category of Broad Churchmen he included the usual figures, notably Coleridge and Maurice. But he was, finally, more concerned with an eloquent, egregiously unclerical descendant of the tradition. The great negative inspiration of *Freethinking and Plainspeaking* is almost certainly Matthew Arnold, who emerged in the late 1860s as the Victorian era's latest prophet, the promulgator of what Stephen calls "religion as a fine art."[7] It was an enterprise that Stephen, for all that he stood in awe of the older man, regarded as an extraordinary piece of "cheek"[8] in its efforts to undermine the true prophecy of Mill.

Arnold's first extended attempt at articulating his new "gospel" (the word, of course, is his own) occurs in *St. Paul and Protestantism*, published in the *Cornhill Magazine* (1869–1870) just before Stephen took over as editor. What may have immediately prodded Stephen to respond was Arnold's cutting reference in the final number of his series to Stephen's favorite tutor at Cambridge, the political economist Henry Fawcett,[9] who by Arnold's account is an epigone of Mill, full of "mere blatancy" and "truculent hardness."[10] In "Mr. Matthew Arnold and the Church of England," published in *Fraser's* in 1870 (but not included in *Freethinking and Plainspeaking*), Stephen begins by mocking the eloquence with which Arnold attacks his victims and carries on with a critique that, in fact, keeps returning to what for Stephen is Arnold's central problem, his excessive fondness for rhetoric, and its corollary, an inadequate commitment to truth.[11]

At first glance Arnold seems to have much in common with Stephen in his view of religion. What he is doing, he insists, is reinterpreting the language of St. Paul in a way that will yield its essentially humanistic or psychological meaning and dispose of the theological and miraculous excrescence that it has hitherto carried. This, he says (taking his cue from Ernest Renan), is what one must do to accommodate scripture to the scientific age:

Paul does not begin outside the sphere of science; he begins with an appeal to reality and experience. . . . [F]or he appeals to a rational conception which is a part, and perhaps the chief part of our experience; the conception of the law of *righteousness*, the very law and ground of human nature so far as this nature is moral. Things as they truly are, facts, are the object-matter of science; and the moral law in human nature, however this law may have originated, is in our actual experience among the greatest of facts.[12]

This "scientific appreciation" of Paul will, says Arnold in a characteristically impertinent figure of speech, resurrect his doctrine "from the tomb where . . . it has lain buried" so that it may "edify," literally build, the "church of the future."[13] So often does he invoke the authority of science, so strongly does he insist that it is morality and not miracle that must be the basis of the new faith, so earnestly does he seek by this new faith to unify the spiritual anarchy of his generation, that one is hard pressed to see why Stephen, the attack on his tutor Fawcett notwithstanding, should not have embraced the resurrector of Paul's true meaning as an ally.

What Stephen perceives, however, is that Arnold's argument, for all its gestures towards science, comes down finally, in good Broad Church fashion, to a defense of the Church of England against its opponents, in this case Dissenters, to whom he attributes an "unscientific" conception of God and hence one that cannot hope to stand as the basis of social order in modern England. Stephen sees here an intellectual dishonesty of two sorts. First, Arnold, holding, as Stephen believes, the atheistical beliefs of a Hume (he might more appropriately have named Spinoza), insists, as Hume did not, on maintaining the traditional social and political structures associated with theism. Second, and more hypocritically, while ostensibly playing the part of a scientific reformer, Arnold, in fact, ends by associating the new scientific philosophers with the old religious dissenters as enemies of the establishment. Hence the neat alliterative collocation of Mialism and Millism at the close of the series, and the memorable image, certainly offensive to Stephen, of Mill and his "youthful henchmen and apparitors" burning all the prayer books on the altar of science.[14] Stephen, in short, had not failed to understand that Arnold in his mastery of rhetoric had invoked the concept of "science" expressly to undermine it.

In the sequel to *St. Paul and Protestantism*, Arnold shifts to more honest ground. Under pressure from those who, like Stephen, objected to what they took to be at once an absurd distortion of St. Paul's words and a misuse of the authority of science, Arnold makes what may seem to us a distinctly modern hermeneutic move. *Literature and Dogma* (1873) is essentially a book about language. Its object is to distinguish between two different uses of language, scientific and poetic. Having acted in *St. Paul and Protestantism* as if he were at one with the scientists in seeking the reality behind the forms of language, he now leans very heavily on what he regards as the method peculiar to the literary critic. The critic is not, after all, so concerned with the positive reality signified by words as with their symbolic meaning. Culture, as usual for Arnold, is the necessary basis of criticism, but now he appears to mean by culture an intense sensitivity to semiotics, to the way words sign: ". . . thus we come back to our old remedy of *culture*,—knowing the best that has been thought and known in the world; which turns out to be, in another shape, . . . *getting the power through reading to estimate the proportion and relation in what we read. . . .* Now this is really the very foundation of any sane criticism." Endowed with the hermeneutic powers that come with the understanding of culture, the critic (as opposed to the theist, on one hand, the scientist, on the other) understands that "the language of the Bible is fluid, passing, and literary, not rigid, fixed, and scientific."[15] It is a great mistake, says Arnold, to treat the word "God" as if "it stood for a perfectly definite and ascertained idea" from which we can "extract propositions and draw inferences. . . . [T]he word 'God' is used in most cases as by no means a term of science or exact knowledge, but a term of poetry and eloquence, a term thrown out, so to speak, at a not fully grasped object of the speaker's consciousness, a literary term, in short; and mankind mean different things by it as their consciousness differs."[16] We do not need to dwell here on Arnold's own notorious definition of God as a "power not ourselves that makes for righteousness"[17] and on how the need to fix the meaning of God with such a cumbersome definition limits the fluidity he claims for literary or biblical language. It is enough to note that in his distinction between poetic and scientific language he is not, as he believes, "making his peace"[18] with the scientific philosophers, but assaulting the foundation of their position. As we have seen, that position had insisted—George Eliot's late divagation notwithstanding—that truth is univocal, that the form of human thought, the "logic of symbols," as Lewes calls it, can and must at some point be brought into conformity with an independent objective reality. In Arnold's concept of poetic language we find the quite contradictory notion that the logic of symbols is "fluid" in the sense that it need not definitely refer to any objective entity or condition outside itself.

Arnold lacks the courage of his convictions. He will not, ultimately, let his poetic language float with complete indeterminacy. But this matters less than that he has distinctly raised the possibility that it can. In later essays he will go further. Having set up a duality of language—and implicitly of truth—he writes as if that duality, after all, gives too much to science. In "Wordsworth" (1879), an essay which, as we will see, has Leslie Stephen and the scientific community very much in view, he dismisses the notion that Wordsworth's poetry is valuable because it expresses a "scientific system" and announces, in words that were to become dear to future practitioners of the critical art, that the poetry is the reality, the philosophy (i.e., the scientific system) the illusion. Later, in "The Study of Poetry" (1880), Arnold makes that critical dictum into something like a philosophical principle. "More and more mankind will discover that we have to turn to poetry to interpret life for us, to console us. . . . Without poetry, our science will appear incomplete; and most of what now passes with us for religion and philosophy will be replaced by poetry."[19] Part of this doctrine—the incompleteness of science without poetry—we have already seen Lewes developing more systematically in the 1860s and 1870s. The rest of it—the replacement of religion and philosophy with poetry—we have seen, had a great appeal to George Eliot.

But as with George Eliot, there is always a practical moral bent to Arnold's thought, which keeps the skeptical tendency to reduce the real to the aesthetic under control. The essence of poetic language turns out to be not its tentativeness or indeterminacy but its emotional effect. More particularly, it is the kind of language which provides us with the necessary emotional impetus towards good conduct or "righteousness" (the object of all Arnold's biblical criticism is to establish a practical morality for the modern age). Reason can tell us rules of conduct but we need an "irresistible force of motive power" to adhere to these rules. In "the words Israel has uttered for us, carers for conduct will find a glow and a force they could find nowhere else."[20] For all their differences in emphasis, then, *St. Paul and Protestantism* and *Literature and Dogma* are coming back to the same point.

Traditional religion is essential to maintaining the moral order of the individual as well as the political order of the state. The function of criticism, in Arnold's hands, is to reclaim the damage done by science to religion at the very source by releasing the language of religion from science's requirement of objectivity and thus freeing it to exert its customary effect on human action.

Stephen's response to *Literature and Dogma* came in the following year in "Religion as a Fine Art," which he tactfully published in *Fraser's* rather than in his own *Cornhill Magazine*, where Arnold's articles had been appearing.[21] We cannot, he writes, construct a barrier across the brain and exist in a cataleptic state, one side of our thought dealing with "Darwinism, and blue books, and political economy," the other wandering through a "beautiful shadowy region, where romance takes the place of history, and poetry of reasoning." Everywhere around us we see the decay of the "old symbols." The conflict between science and theology becomes "daily more implacable." A reconciliation is required, but all the establishmentarian liberal produces is the doctrine of the two truths:

We are to believe dogmas, not because their truth can be established by the ordinary process of observation and induction, but partly also because they give a certain satisfaction to our emotions. . . . The division between faith and reason is a half-measure, till it is frankly admitted that faith has to do with fiction, and reason with fact. Then the two spheres of thought may be divided by so profound a gulf that each of the rivals may be allowed its full scope without interfering with the other.

Attractive as this solution may be, says Stephen, it is unworkable. One cannot, finally, "evade the conflict between science and theology." The "ridicule of artistic minds" notwithstanding, ordinary people will "persist in thinking that the words 'I believe' are to be interpreted in the same sense in a creed or a scientific statement."[22]

This is the intellectual core of *Freethinking and Plainspeaking*. With Stephen as with Arnold it comes down to a linguistic issue: what are the propositions of belief to signify? Stephen's positivist position is that they must strive to signify the world as it actually is; Arnold's aestheticist response is that the entire question of signification or reference is irrelevant. What matters is what the language of belief makes us feel and do. Beyond the linguistic issue, again, is the political one. Arnold's aestheticism, while radically different from the metaphysical intuitionism against which Mill had persistently argued, has, as Stephen sees it, essentially the same political consequences. "The cultivated classes are invited to acquiesce in a creed which they do not believe, or, in plainer language, to sanction systematic lying on consideration that the priests will keep the dangerous classes quiet. The dangerous classes are to give up their objectionable schemes and receive in exchange a good comfortable religious narcotic."[23]

The phrase "religious narcotic" will serve to remind us of the precise nature of the dialectic that Stephen is engaged in. The enemy for him in the 1870s is not, as it was for an earlier generation of positivist thinkers, theism or metaphysics, but a sophisticated, again, aesthetic substitute for both, which he sees as a form of narcosis, an "acquiescence" in the arbitrary structures of fiction simply for the sake of maintaining order. The threat to the positivist program, as Stephen perceives it, is not absolutism but skepticism, by which he means doubt, not about any particular belief, but about the competency of human reason in general to define the real as in itself it is. We are back again—though perhaps now with lines more sharply drawn—at that recurring conflict we have witnessed among all our would-be realists—Mill versus the later Comte, Lewes versus the later George Eliot—over what ultimately authorizes the structures of human meaning once we have dispensed with the metaphysical.

Freethinking and Plainspeaking is a critical undertaking rather than an attempt at a constructive philosophy. Yet Stephen, no less than Matthew Arnold, had heard the seminal voice of Carlyle announcing the era's need for a new belief, and no less than Arnold he felt a responsibility to make a contribution towards that new belief, to the task of providing a "modern social revolution."[24] Emerging at every point in his ciriticism we see glimpses of the "living creed" that he has it in mind to substitute for religion. "We can best fortify ourselves . . . by anchoring our minds on the firmest holding ground. Science will tell us that by working with the great forces that move the world, we may contribute some fragment to an edifice that will not be broken down. . . . The goal is clearly in sight. . . ."[25] The contemporary writers pointing him towards this goal, Mill, primarily, but also Comte and Darwin, make notable appearances throughout the essays that constitute *Freethinking and Plainspeaking*. Stephen knows already his particular contribution to the new edifice will, like Arnold's retrograde one, be a type of moral philosophy,[26] but what its precise shape will be he is yet unprepared to say.

SCIENTIFIC ETHICS AFTER UTILITARIANISM

When J. S. Mill called in 1843 for a science of morality, he already considered that the foundations of the science had been laid by Jeremy

Bentham. "What Bacon did for physical knowledge, Mr. Bentham did for Philosophical legislation [and ethics]. . . . [H]e was the first who attempted regularly to deduce all the secondary and intermediate principles of law, by direct and systematic inference from the one great axiom or principle of general utility."[27] Mill himself continued in the footsteps of Bentham and became what most would agree is the most important philosophical advocate of utilitarian ethics in the nineteenth century and probably for all time.

What makes utilitarianism scientific, according to its followers, are essentially two things which are interdependent, its *consequentialism* and its *psychologism*. The emphasis placed on one or another of these qualities varies as we move from the early to later utilitarians. For Bentham it is, above all, consequentialism, by which he means that the criterion of morality ceases to reside in an intuitive or metaphysical principle and comes to reside in the observable consequences of one's actions, consequences which are supposed to be objectively measurable. Mill, while agreeing on the necessity of shifting the grounds of morality from intuitionism to consequentialism, found that Bentham had gone too far in the latter direction. He "confounded the principle of Utility with the principle of specific consequences" and, as a result, paid too little attention to the question of the "*character*" or "*state of mind*" that motivates moral actions.[28] We will return to the already noticed and frequently mooted question of how far Mill's concern with moral character violates the fundamental principle of the philosophy he claims to represent, but for now we need only note that when he talks of the "state of mind" or "disposition" that causes an action, he is talking in strictly psychological terms of instincts and conditioned mental associations.

Whether the emphasis is on the effects of actions called moral or their psychological causes, ethics for the utilitarian becomes a "naturalistic" study, in G. E. Moore's celebrated understanding of the word. Goodness is reduced to some property of a natural phenomenon, and hence becomes the subject matter of the natural sciences rather than something *sui generis*. Thus Moore:

I have . . . appropriated the name Naturalism to a particular method of approaching Ethics—a method which, strictly speaking, is inconsistent with the possibility of any Ethics whatsoever. This method consists in substituting for "good" some one property of a natural object or a collection of natural objects; and in thus replacing Ethics by some one of the natural sciences. . . . In general, Psychology has been the science substituted, as by J. S. Mill. . . . But any other science might equally well be substituted.[29]

For Bentham the naturalistic argument is conducted against the "moral-sense" descendants of the Cartesian tradition. For Mill the argument is still against the Cartesian tradition but a tradition now formidably buttressed by Kant and the categorical imperative. Against Kant's principal British representative in the first half of the century, William Whewell, Mill, as we have seen, waged persistent battle: ". . . the tone of religious metaphysics, and of ethical speculation connected with religion, is now altogether Germanized; and Dr. Whewell, by his writings, has done no little work to impress upon the metaphysics of orthodoxy this change of character."[30] But Kant and Whewell and the ancient religious prejudices that Mill sees informing their work notwithstanding, the naturalistic approach of utilitarianism, supported on the one hand by the advance of science, on the other, by the success of political economy, was clearly the avant-garde philosophy when Mill published its great manifesto in 1861 and Leslie Stephen, newly appointed examiner for moral sciences at Cambridge, threw his weight behind the "Millite" Henry Fawcett for university professor of political economy. As one historian has put it, the utilitarians were "once in England what the Marxists were for a few decades in Germany, the social and political thinkers whose ideas had the widest currency though they were also the most vigorously attacked."[31]

Stephen's commitment to utilitarianism's naturalistic ethic is apparent in his admiration for Hume but no less telling is his response to his friend Henry Sidgwick's (1839–1900) monumental *Methods of Ethics* (1874), easily the generation's most influential treatise on the subject and, many would argue, the Victorian period's finest contribution to moral philosophy.[32] Sidgwick, widely regarded as a continuator of the utilitarian tradition, in fact, diverges from it at its most fundamental level and becomes one of the primary sources of the modern case against naturalism.[33] Like Moore, who was his student,[34] he is concerned to argue that the nature of moral judgment is something distinct in itself, something which cannot be reduced to psychology or any other extrinsic science.

Most men wish not only to understand human action, but also to regulate it; they apply the ideas "good" or "bad," "right" or "wrong," to the conduct or institutions which they describe; and thus pass, as I should say, from the point of view of Psychology or Sociology to the point of view of Ethics. . . . [An] attempt to ascertain the general laws of uniformities by which the varieties of human conduct, and of man's sentiments and judgments respecting conduct, may be *explained*, is essentially different from an attempt to determine which among these varieties of conduct is *right* and which of the divergent judgments *valid*.[35]

This leads to the assertion, ordinarily associated with the intuitionists, that the moral judgment is ultimately a question, not of feeling or impulse or association, but of rational decision to do the right: ". . . an ethical judgment cannot be explained as affirming merely the existence of . . . a [moral sentiment]: indeed it is an essential characteristic of a moral feeling that it is bound up with an apparent cognition of something more than mere feeling. . . ."[36] In short, Sidgwick is firmly drawing moral philosophy away from the psychological-cum-physiological base that Stephen considers essential to its scientific credibility, drawing it back in the direction of, if not quite to, Kant's categorical imperative.

As Stephen sees it, such attempts to establish the rationality of our moral decisions must end in skepticism, in the inability of reason to provide a reliable ground for moral action. Here he may, in fact, be reflecting Sidgwick's own sense at the close of *Methods* that he has arrived at an irresolvable antinomy in his efforts to produce a rational morality without resort to some overriding metaphysical principle that will reconcile the opposing dictates of reason. "For, if we find [as we have found] an ultimate and fundamental contradiction in our apparent intuitions of what is Reasonable in conduct, we seem forced to the conclusion that they are not really intuitions at all, and that the apparently intuitive operation of the Practical Reason is illusory."[37] On this method, this assumption that there is something "right or reasonable" to do under all circumstances, and that we can by a "web of logic" discover what it is, moral philosophers, says Stephen, will go on "puzzling themselves for ever, with no more danger of any final yes or no terminating their doubts than if they were trying to invent perpetual motion."[38] All moral judgment, he insists, contains an element of instinct, which is the result at once of our inherent psychological makeup and the conditioning factors of changing social environments. Therefore, as the utilitarian school has maintained, "scientific morality" must "be based upon the psychological and social data"[39] that underlie our moral decisions and may or may not have anything to do with reason. As he will later argue, every attempt to twist morality out of pure reason is foredoomed to failure.[40] We now need to consider the ways in which Stephen sought to distinguish himself from the utilitarians without, as he believes Sidgwick to be doing, slipping over into the Kantian or metaphysical camp (the two being not synonymous for him so much as continuous).

By 1880 after completing the *History of English Thought in the Eighteenth Century* (1876) and almost all the essays that would later go into *An Agnostic's Apology* (1893), Stephen had reached a mature understanding of the historical situation of utilitarianism and his own relation to it, which he expresses in "An Attempted Philosophy of History." His immediate subject is the voluminous work on the history of Europe since the Renaissance by Adam Smith's and J. S. Mill's devoted follower Thomas Buckle (1821–1862). Stephen argues that this is one of the great books of the nineteenth century, comparable in its impact to Darwin's *Origin of Species*, but with the critical difference that, where the *Origin* opens an entirely new intellectual era, Buckle's contemporaneous *History of Civilization* (1857–1860) marks the close of an old one. Buckle's "philosophy of history" is, finally, mistaken because he continues to operate on the assumption of preevolutionary science. For Stephen a truly modern scientific concept of society and history must begin with the impact of Darwin's theory, to which the utilitarians as late as the 1880s remained virtually impervious. In the process of arguing this point he expresses a further regret that the utilitarian mentality pays too little attention to a still earlier scientific writer, Auguste Comte. Buckle, who, of course, could not have been expected to incorporate Darwin's theory into his history, would, nonetheless, have benefited, Stephen believes, from a reading of Comte's "far clearer view of history as a process of organic development."[41] Taking our cue from this essay written just a few years before *The Science of Ethics*, we may see in that later book Stephen's most significant contribution to Victorian philosophy: an attempt to synthesize Comte and Darwin in a system designed to supplant utilitarianism as the true scientific morality for the modern age.

EVOLUTIONARY ALTRUISM

If he had gone to Oxford rather than to Cambridge, Stephen once remarked, he might well have become a Comtist,[42] might well, that is, have followed his friends Frederic Harrison and John Morley in their devotion to the teachings of the Oxford Positivist Richard Congreve. Even so, Comtist doctrines seem to have found him at Cambridge and somehow escaped the vigilance of Fawcett, to whom, as to all good utilitarians, they represented a serious challenge. What first attracted Stephen's attention to the system we do not know. But after Lewes' and Congreve's enthusiastic summaries of it at midcentury and Mill's essays of 1865, no one seriously interested in scientific philosophy could afford not to know about it. Stephen's notebooks show him reading the *Cours de philosophie positive* by at least May of 1859 (at age 26).[43] By the late 1860s when the influence of Comte was at its height among young English intellectuals, we find Stephen duly writing as essay on that "remarkable phenomenon," the development of the "Comtist school." Although he is not uncritical of Comtism, he is clearly drawn to it. In particular, he notes Comte's "radical" opposition to the doctrine of Mill's *On Liberty*. "Without pretending to decide between opinions so radically antagonistic, it is easy to understand the influence which Comte exercises over certain minds, and especially in England at the present moment. It is the great difficulty of the present stage of civilization that we are suffering from intellectual and social anarchy. . . ." On "scientific questions," however, we have "reached a certain harmony," and Comte proposes to make this growing scientific synthesis the basis of a new social order.[44]

As we have seen, the French philosopher's social and historical thought rests on a single ethical presupposition, a presupposition held in conscious opposition to utilitarianism, that there is in human nature an altruistic principle that is no less real and operative than the egoistic one from which the utilitarian begins. The basis of all social organization lies in our "inherent tendency to universal love. No calculation of self-interest can rival this social instinct, whether in promptitude and breadth of intuition, or in boldness and tenacity of purpose."[45] Comte, again, believed that science had demonstrated the existence of an instinctive tendency towards universal love or altruism in the human brain. From Comte, Stephen, like Lewes and George Eliot, takes this fundamental principle but moves it several steps closer to the socialistic resolution towards which, as I suggested in my opening chapter, it is headed by the century's close.[46]

Definite signs of dissatisfaction with the utilitarian ethic begin to surface in Stephen's moral and political writing in the early 1870s. An essay on Bernard de Mandeville (1873), for example, finds in this disciple of Thomas Hobbes an expression of ethical naturalism that obviously repulses Stephen. Mandeville considers all rules enjoining social responsibilities and altruism illusory. The reality underlying human behavior is the pursuit of self-interest. According to this "bestial theory of human nature," selfishness is to human beings what gravitation is to the planets. One may find in Mandeville's psychological assumptions, moreover, the anticipation of the "spirit" of "natural selection" as well as "glorification of the passions for accumulating wealth" characteristic of the modern "industrial view of morality." Stephen is careful to note that Mandeville's position is only a "preposterous caricature of modern utilitarianism,"[47] yet it is apparent in Stephen's later writing on utilitarianism that he considers the morality of even its most sophisticated adherents tainted with an excess of what Sidgwick had called "egoistic hedonism."[48]

From the Mandeville essay we may move, I hope without too great a leap, to a brief outline of the metahistorical structure underlying Stephen's thought. The *History of English Thought in the Eighteenth Century*, in effect, tells the story of the progress of English philosophy from metaphysical to scientific presuppositions, a story Stephen would, of course, have found prominently developed in both Comte and Lewes. Stephen's insistence on pushing the origin of English scientific moral philosophy back to David Hume, rather than to Hobbes, in the *History* presupposes the goal he wants civilization to reach, the goal to which he himself sought to contribute. For Hume, in addition to calling for a truly scientific rather than metaphysical morality, deliberately rejected Hobbes's (and Mandeville's) gestures in that direction in favor of an ethic that would allow for the possibility of altruism as a native principle of human nature:[49] ". . . there is some benevolence, however small, infused into our bosom; . . . some particle of the dove kneaded into our frame, along with the elements of the wolf and serpent."[50] For Stephen, the scientific revolution in general displaces theology and metaphysics, but the true line of succession, in so far as it relates to what most matters to him, moral theory, is from Hume to Comte, not Hobbes to Mandeville to Mill.

And from Comte to Darwin, for important as Comte was to Stephen, the guiding spirit of *The Science of Ethics*, as of his thought in general, is, finally, the author of *The Descent of Man*. "His reverence for Darwin was unbounded," writes his friend and biographer, F. W. Maitland, ". . . it went near to hero worship."[51] Had Buckle "lived into a later period and absorbed the teaching of evolution," notes Stephen in the 1880 essay, "he would have found the clue of which he was in want."[52]

We have seen how Darwinism began to influence the later work of Lewes and, to a lesser degree, the novels of George Eliot. With Stephen we come to the generation for which that influence had become all-pervasive, for which virtually every intellectual issue had to be placed before the bar of "the evolutionary criterion." As J. H. Bridges observed in 1877 (the year after George Eliot's last novel was completed): "A new intellectual era is supposed to have begun.

Natural selection, or the survival of the fittest, is applied as a master-key to unravel all manner of problems, not biological merely, but social and moral questions of every kind."[53] Bridges was a leading British Comtist, and, as his ironical tone suggests, there was little love lost between Comtists and Darwinians. Of the several reasons for this, the most important, surely, was the Comtist belief that Darwinism with its talk of survival of the fittest was contradicting the Comtean reading of human nature as essentially altruistic.[54] The principal determinant of this reading of Darwin's moral meaning was, clearly, Herbert Spencer, who had effectively turned the theory of evolution into a scientific justification of a radical utilitarianism with its focus on egoism firmly back in place after J. S. Mill's Comte-inspired digressions in the direction of socialism noticed in chapter 2. Our twentieth-century sense of what was involved in nineteenth-century evolutionary ethics in still largely determined by the spectre of Herbert Spencer and the Social Darwinism that issued from his philosophy. What we believe is that evolution's primary effect on morality—when it did not subvert it altogether—was to authorize what Thomas Huxley (with Spencer specifically in mind) called "fanatical individualism,"[55] and we trace a direct line running from Malthus on population through Darwin and Spencer to J. D. Rockefeller: "The growth of a large business is merely a survival of the fittest. . . . This is not an evil tendency in business. It is merely the working out of a law of nature and a law of God."[56]

The utilitarian philosophers, having provided Darwin with the essential clue for his doctrine of the survival of the fittest, noted the American J. G. Schurman long before our contemporary Marxist critiques of Darwin's theory, realized a substantial return on their investment in the form of a biological theory that seemed to make aggressive individualism a law of nature: ". . . the essence of utilitarianism and the essence of Darwinism . . . have such strong elective affinities that to effect their continuation nothing was required but to bring them together."[57] But there is another tradition of evolutionary ethics besides Spencer's, one which Comtists would, and late-century socialists did, find more congenial.[58] In this tradition Stephen plays a major role, and his *Science of Ethics* stands in need of resurrection if for no other reason than to show us that already as early as 1882 Spencer had a formidable competitor among the scientific moralists.

Darwin, as Steven Gould has pointed out, was an extremely cautious materialist,[59] scarcely less fearful than his religious antagonists of the moral and social implications of his doctrine. When he at last applied that doctrine to the human species in *The Descent of Man* (1871), he applied it in such a way as to allow those who placed their faith in man's capacity for altruism ample room to continue in that belief. Natural selection might well confirm the wisdom of Hobbes, but it might also support Hume. "The following proposition seems to me in a high degree probable—namely, that any animal whatever, endowed with well-marked social instincts, the parental and filial affections being here included, would inevitably acquire a moral sense or conscience, as soon as its intellectual powers had become as well, or nearly as well developed, as in man." The "social instinct" leads an animal to take pleasure in society. Of this instinct "sympathy," or fellow-feeling, is an "essential part," and sympathy may be nurtured by society into a fully developed "moral sense." This "moral sense," derived from the social instinct, Darwin opposed to the "instinct for self-preservation." There is, indeed, cause to expect, although—and this is a significant hedge to which we must return—no cause to be certain, that the moral sense will continue to advance in the human species. "Looking to future generations . . . we may expect that virtuous habits will grow stronger, becoming perhaps fixed by inheritance."[60]

What is it, in a context in which only the fittest survive, that will allow an essentially non-self-regarding virtue to triumph? Darwin's answer, apparently, is that the survival of the species depends upon the development of the social instinct. The desire to preserve the species or group takes precedence over the desire to preserve the individual. The argument becomes much neater a few years later in W. K. Clifford's (1847–1879) "On the Scientific Basis of Morals" (1875), a brilliant pioneering essay on evolutionary ethics derived from the *Descent*. One of the primary units on which natural selection works among *homo sapiens*, he argues, is the "tribe."

The tribe, *qua* tribe, has to exist, and it can only exist by aid of such an organic artifice as the conception of the tribal self in the minds of its members. Hence the natural selection of those races in which this conception is the most powerful and most habitually predominant as a motive over immediate desires. To such an extent has this proceeded that we may fairly doubt whether the selfhood of the tribe is not earlier in point of development than that of the individual. In the process of time it becomes a matter of hereditary transmission and thus is fixed as a specific character in the constitution of social man. . . . Self-regarding excellences are brought out by the natural selection of individuals; the tribal self is developed by the natural selection of groups.[61]

We have here the beginning of the debate on the individual versus group selection, which continues to exercise modern adherents of evolutionary ethics. The answer to those who, like Richard Dawkins or E. O. Wilson, base human moral behavior on egoism is offered by those who, like Marshal Sahlins or Maynard Smith, find a ground for morality in the altruistic principle of group selection.[62]

Stephen, the editor of Clifford's essays, knew the 1875 article as well as Darwin's *Descent*, and a version of their defense of altruism appears early on in *The Science of Ethics*. Distinguishing between instincts/ habits which are essential or nonessential to the organism, Stephen finds that the test is whether that instinct or habit contributes to the survival of the species or race, not the individual: "An instinct grows and decays not on account of its effects on the individual, but on account of its effects upon the race. The animal which on the whole is better for continuing its species will have an advantage in the struggle even though it may not be so well adapted for pursuing its own happiness."[63] Later the principle of group selection is used to account for the evolution of moral character within the race. Altruistic dispositions are implanted or "constituted" in the individual by rules which have been selected for group rather than individual survival: ". . . the development of the society implies the development of certain moral instincts in the individual, or that the individual must be so constituted as to be capable of identifying himself with the society, and of finding his pleasure and pain in conduct which is socially beneficial or pernicious. The necessary condition for morality is altruism."[64]

Neither Stephen nor Darwin postulates a primary instinct inherent and fixed in human nature from which altruism necessarily develops. What both are saying, rather, is that *homo sapiens*, at whatever moment he crossed over from the apes, had in his constitution a collection of instincts, "germs"[65] of behavior, capable of further development. Among them was a social instinct as well as the instinct for self-preservation. It was altogether possible, then, to read Darwin in a way that allowed precisely what Comte had argued to be true of man's underlying biological nature, an innate altruism, on which one might build an entirely different moral vision from what the utilitarians were currently offering. The question which remained was, given that the archetypal germ of altruism is in Darwin's account in competition with that of egoism, what determines the survival of one or the other? To answer this, Stephen needed to shift to Comte's other way of explaining human behavior, that is, by the premier science of sociology, to which, in an ingenious effort at synthesis, he applied the Darwinian principle of natural selection.

THE SOCIAL CONSTRUCTION OF MORALITY

In another early essay, "Social Macadamisation" (1872), the focus of which is more political than ethical, Stephen broaches a second problem he has with contemporary utilitarianism. Noting that Mill's *On Liberty* is regarded by many as the "gospel of the nineteenth century" with its "apotheosis of individualism," he wonders whether this is, in fact, the one thing needful for contemporary society. Mill's gospel seems, rather, to promote social disintegration rather than unity. Individualism is "a desirable thing within certain limits," but at the moment we are more in need of "centralization" and "cooperation."[66] If we may judge from *Freethinking and Plainspeaking*, Stephen found Arnold's gospel of culture ultimately more threatening than Mill's scientific one of individualism in the early 1870s. Still, "Social Macadamisation" reveals misgivings about Mill's political outlook that would have registered well with Arnold.

In the late *English Utilitarians* (1905) Stephen discusses more comprehensively than anywhere else the ramifications of Mill's individualism as well as its unfortunate roots in the "old utilitarianism" of the previous century. We learn that the scope Mill insists on giving to the individual leads him to an "unscientific" conception both of society and the individual character. The tendency of the utilitarian is to regard society as an "aggregate" instead of an "organism," to see it "as a number of independent beings, simply bound together by the legal or quasi-legal sanctions. Morality itself [is] treated as a case of external 'law.' The individual . . . [is] a bundle of ideas, bound together by 'associations which could be indefinitely-modified.' . . . [And] therefore the whole structure of individual character [becomes] in some sense 'artificial.'" Political and economic individualism, Stephen believes, involves the utilitarian in a methodological error which vitiates his efforts to produce a scientific ethic. He is virtually blind to a whole class of causes that condition individual behavior, namely, social phenomena. Since for Mill, for example, "the laws of . . . society are . . . nothing but the actions and passions of human beings, the laws of individual human behavior," it follows that the primary method of explaining social phenomena is to generalize upon the laws of individual human nature. Stephen, on the other hand, insists that one must proceed on the very different methodological assumption, characteristic of Comte, that social phenomena are not the effect but the cause of individual human behavior. To grasp the "sociological" side of morality requires "a real historical sense," which, he maintains, is precisely what utilitarians lack. They fail to understand that social institutions are not products of "conscious manufacture" by various extraordinary individuals but the result of slow, "organic" growth, in which we understand each individual as a product rather than a producer of social structure.[67]

In his review of Stephen's *Science of Ethics*, which, unfortunately, is the most comprehensive and attentive review it received, Henry Sidgwick found some things to admire, but much more to blame. The criticism that probably came closest to home and certainly seems most to have affected Stephen is that the book lacks an intelligible theoretical structure. It begins, says Sigdwick, as a psychological treatise, becomes a sociological-cum-evolutionary one, and only towards the very end becomes properly ethical discourse when it attempts to determine an ideal code of morality. Stephen wrote to Sidgwick about the review and granted that he had certainly "failed in a literary sense," since he had not succeeded in making so qualified a reader as Sidgwick understand the "logical framework" of his argument. Yet, he continued, he could not accept Sidgwick's charge that the disorder in his presentation "implies real confusion of thought."[68] Modern readers of *The Science of Ethics* will, if anything, experience a still greater sense of disorder than Sidgwick's remarks suggest, because we are so far removed from the contemporary context of ethical debate from which the book grows. On the other hand, one might make the case that Sidgwick is perhaps too imbedded in that context, and in particular in the dialectic of intuitionism versus utilitarianism, to perceive what it is Stephen is attempting to do. The distinctiveness of Stephen's approach lies precisely in his effort to distance himself from the utilitarians by establishing a new methodological approach to explaining the *cause* of moral action. For him the entire issue of intuitionism versus utilitarianism had been effectively settled by Comte, Mill, and the general advance of scientific thought. What had now become the real crux of debate was the issue of whether the primary cause of moral action was individual will or community pressure, or, in Spencer's celebrated phrase, the issue of "man versus the state."[69]

The opening chapters, which Sidgwick more or less automatically read as "subjective psychology" on the "mainly introspective" method,[70] or utilitarianism as usual, are, in fact, an argument against subjective psychology and introspection. What Stephen is saying is that the attempt to determine the nature of morality by the examination of individual psychology is doomed to failure, for we are in a profound state of ignorance regarding "the elementary [psychological] faculties; what their relative strength; what relations hold amongst them in virtue of the unity of the subject . . . ," and so on.[71] What, then, can a scientific theory of ethics use as its ground?

The answer, as our foregoing discussion will have anticipated, is sociology. "If our psychological armoury is so scantily provided," can we not "find effective weapons in the nascent science of sociology?"

The members of a given society are forced to accommodate themselves to certain fixed conditions as much as the iron which is poured into a given mould. . . . [They] are . . . being constantly educated in a thousand ways by the persistent conditions of the social organism; and thus there are secondary or derivative laws of conduct dependent upon these conditions and producing uniformities not affected by the variation of individual idiosyncrasy.[72]

If we thus shift the focus of our inquiry from the individual psychology to the social medium, or "social tissue,"[73] as Stephen comes to call it, we find a phenomenon that is available to definitive scientific analysis, a phenomenon that "forms a whole" and "the laws of whose growth can be studied apart from those of the individual atom."[74] This is, indeed, a new departure in British ethical theory. Stephen is, effectively, relegating individualism to the realm of metaphysics. He is sociologizing what even the most scientifically sophisticated thinkers among his contemporaries—Mill, Lewes, Spencer, George Eliot—still were inclined to consider the last bastion of the sacred, the *individual moral will*. Three "inspiring trumpet calls" have traditionally moved men, George Eliot is supposed to have said, "*God, Immortality, and Duty*"; "how inconceivable . . . the *first*, how unbelievable . . . the *second*, and yet how peremptory and absolute the *third*."[75] One might go so far as to concede the impossibility of the individual changing the course of history—as Spencer, of course, did—but to suggest that his or her moral consciousness was the product of impersonal social conditions was scarcely less demoralizing than to suggest, with the radical materialists, that it was the product of a chemical reaction.

This methodological basis having been laid, Stephen devotes his attentions to elaborating not so much the specific content of the social tissue as its general process of development and the means by which it determines individual behavior, both of which he interprets, as we will see, in Darwinian or at least evolutionist terms.

Beyond question, the source of Stephen's social definition of morality is Comte, for whom, as we recall from our first chapter, it is the collective life of society that explains human behavior once biology has given us its instinctual basis. "The chief problem of human life" as revealed by biology, writes Comte, is shown to be the subordination of egoism to altruism. "The whole of social science consists . . .

in working out the problem, the essential principle being the reaction of collective over individual life."[76] Lewes would also have influenced Stephen here, his claim to originality in *The Study of Psychology* being, again, that he had recognized more fully than any predecessor the mechanism by which the social medium becomes part of individual behavior. Beyond this, Lewes may even have provided Stephen with the one specific example of the "social issue" that he develops in any detail in *The Science of Ethics*, for like Lewes, Stephen seems ultimately to reduce the social to the linguistic. Our morality, he maintains, is always determined by the "code" of our era and our nation,[77] and the "most striking illustration" of how this social code impacts upon our lives is the instance of language. Language is "clearly a product of the social organism . . . gradually elaborated . . . by the race under pressure of social needs." Each child "accepts it as a ready-made instrument," and implicit in its symbols is the entire philosophical outlook of the society which uses it.[78] As Lewes had said, " . . . without Language, no Society."

The difference between Stephen's use of this concept and Lewes', however, takes us to the heart of the younger man's new bearings. Lewes reduced the social to the linguistic with the residually romantic end in view of justifying the power of individual will to change society. Language, for Lewes, is not an autonomous, impersonal system, but the product of individual, creative, that is, aesthetic, construction. Again, "the invention of a new symbol is the first step in the advance of civilization." With Stephen the focus on language takes us in a contrary direction. Language is the primary source of social conditioning, the earliest structure in which the individual is enmeshed. Far from being indefinitely modifiable by individual genius, it is, like all other social codes, a structure on which the individual can "impress" at "rare intervals" only some "relatively trifling improvement."[79] Language, we may say, had become in the 1870s a kind of touchstone on this question of individualism. Lewes and George Eliot still found in it much the same thing their romantic predecessors found there: "Who shall tell what may be the effect of writing?"[80] Stephen, on the other hand, has crossed the Rubicon and found in the linguistic *system* something like that ultimate determiner of human thought another, more distant, descendant of Comte has spoken so persuasively of in our own era. "Linguistics," writes Claude Lévi-Strauss, presents us with a "totalizing entity, . . . but one outside (or beneath) consciousness and will. Language, an unreflecting totalization, is human reason which has its reasons and of which man knows nothing."[81]

But there is a still more plausible French analogue for Stephen and that is the man who is probably, after all, Comte's greatest disciple,[82] Emile Durkheim (1858-1917). Stephen occupies a position in the history of British thought comparable to Durkheim's in his reaction against the "metaphysics" of individual personality and individual will. For him no less than for Durkheim the "social fact" has become the ultimate reality underlying human mental life in general and moral life in particular. As the French sociologist was to write in his first major book (*The Division of Labor* [1893]), more than a decade after Stephen's *Science of Ethics*, "Of what value are our individual pleasures, which are so empty and short? This is the greatest objection to utilitarianism and individualist ethics. . . . Could not one say, on the contrary: morality is first and foremost a social function, and it is only by a fortunate circumstance, because societies are infinitely more long-lived than individuals, that they permit us to taste satisfactions which are not merely ephemeral?"[83] In Talcott Parsons' classic study, *The Structure of Social Action*, Durkheim quite correctly takes his place as the revolutionary theorist who reversed the course of nineteenth-century scientific social theory, largely British and individualist in its presuppositions, and established it on its modern collectivist, or holistic, model.[84] My reading of Stephen's *Ethics* may be taken as a modest qualification of Parsons' historical schema. Stephen, although hardly the monumental thinker Durkheim was, nonetheless anticipated his position and from within the British camp. Indeed, in his reduction of social fact to language he even glances, as I have intimated, beyond Durkheim to the latter's student Lévi-Strauss.

Stephen's anticipation of Durkheim may be appropriately extended in one further direction, and hardly a surprising one. Durkheim's bête noire in *The Division of Labor*, as elsewhere, is Herbert Spencer, for him the very embodiment of the evils of individualist sociology and individualist ethics. In the *Ethics* Stephen's intuitionist target is Sidgwick. He means to write a scientific ethic that will counter Sidgwick's objections, but to do this he must dissociate himself from that ethic as Sidgwick had understood it, and this in the early 1880s meant he must dissociate himself from the work of Hebert Spencer. *The Science of Ethics*, then, no less than *The Division of Labor* (and, again, 10 years earlier) sets itself the task of offering an alternative to the moral vision of a man widely regarded by contemporaries as the century's most formidable scientific philosopher. But quite apart from its interest as an anticipation of Durkheim, Stephen's engagement with Spencer helps point the way to a consideration of an issue still not addressed, and that is the issue of where Darwinism comes into the concept of a sociological morality.

SOCIETIES FIT TO SURVIVE

Stephen makes, in effect, two applications of evolutionary theory to ethics, one to explain why individuals adapt themselves to society's moral rules—in order to survive—and the other, far more interesting, to explain why a particularly "type" of moral order evolves in the social organism. This latter application we need to consider more closely. Society, Stephen says, "has in some sense a life of its own. And this . . . implies no mystical or non-natural sense." It is not a "single consciousness" developing along a predetermined path (à la Hegel, and, for that matter, Spencer), but a complex competition of interests struggling for survival. Just as the formation of our organic structure is determined by natural selection, so also is the formation of the "social factor." The criterion that determines which of the many moral types generated by the social tissue is "selected" is, as with organic nature, the "vitality" of the organism, that is, the capacity of the social tissue to conduce to the continued life and health of the society as a whole:

. . . every society, beginning from the simplest germ of social union, where the state is not yet differentiated from the family [the family being for Stephen as for Comte and foundation of social organization], requires the action of all the social instincts. The more elaborate fhe structure the greater the number and force of the instincts which must be called into play. All that is implied in loyalty, patriotism, respect for order, mutual confidence . . . , is essential to the vitality of a complex social organization.

What we call moral are all beliefs which make for social unity.[85]

The truly "vital" social tissue is one which has slowly evolved by a long historical process of trial and error. It cannot be created by genius or imposed by the state. It is, in a word central to Stephen's argument, a web of *custom*: " . . . the power of making a constitution presupposes a readiness to act together and accept certain rules as binding, and this again implies a whole set of established customs, such as are necessary to the constitution and authority of a representative body."[86] As we have seen, Stephen, following Comte and bolstered by Darwin's *Descent*, accepts as a biological reality the presence, *inter alia*, of an other-regarding social instinct in human beings. It requires, however, the slow elaboration of the social tissue to develop that instinct to the point that it becomes in the individual a habitual disposition for moral and political action. The emphasis on custom (as against law) as the real source of social integrity may well remind us of the Coleridgean concept of culture (as opposed to civilization), with the difference that Stephen believes he has found in evolutionary theory what Coleridge lacked, namely, a nonmetaphysical way of affirming the "naturalness" of our motive for adhering to the traditional binding values of community and cooperation. He has also, one notes, found a justification for gradual rather than revolutionary social change. It is the instinctual structure of people that must be modified if we are to have a truly vital or living community. Morality, in particular, "is the variation of the most intimate structure and the deepest instincts, not of the superficial sentiments or of the special modifications of society," which means, again, that moral change is radically unavailable to, independent of, the individual will: the moral law "must be natural, not artificial; it must grow, and not be made . . . ; [it is] incapable of being abruptly altered by the action of any particular person or in obedience to any subordinate series of events. . . ."[87]

In this way Stephen explains the origin or cause of morality, identified by him, as we see clearly enough as this juncture, with the subordination of the egoistic to the altruistic instinct. A given social entity in order to survive requires self-repression on the part of its members and, more than that, a positive devotion to the "good of society" itself. Through its various institutions and customs it inculcates and elaborates these other-regarding, holistic values until they become second nature. The consequence of failing to do so is societal extinction in the face of competition from other more cohesive societies. From this standpoint, egoistic self-interest, when it becomes a dominant motive among the members of any given society, while it may be a sign of the individual will to survive, is, more significantly, the sign of the society's decay or devolution. Its social tissue has weakened to the point that it cannot command self-restraint in the interest of the whole. Durkheim will later find such a disintegration of society's sense of its integrity, and, correlatively, of the individual's sense of belonging to a meaningful community, the occasion for despair and suicide. Whenever society loses what it normally possesses—whenever the individual dissociates himself from collective goals in order to seek only his own interest, suicide increases. Man is the more vulnerable to self destruction the more he lives as an "egoist."[88] What is "natural" or "evolutionary," then, about Stephen's explanation of morality is not the deduction of morality from any biological data so much as the location of the source of moral, that is, altruistic, self-sacrificing behavior in the practical tendency of any particular society to want to perpetuate its wholesomeness, its condition of being a discrete whole or a totality.

When we read Durkheim on suicide or, for that matter, George Eliot on Gwendolen Harleth's susceptibility to existentialist terror, we have little difficulty approving this "evolutionist criterion" (Stephen prefers the expression to "social criterion")[89] of morality. From another standpoint, however, and one perhaps closer to Stephen's own concern, the invocation of the social factor, and with it the evolutionist threat of societal extinction, has about it an uncomfortable air of constraint. This is particularly pronounced when Stephen, in the closing chapters of *The Science of Ethics*, turns from the cause to the *sanction* of morality. What is it, he asks, that makes an individual follow the moral law, makes him habitually repress his self-interest in favor of the interest of society? His answer, for all its convolutions, comes down to fear of social disapproval: " . . . the virtuous man means simply the man who corresponds to the best social type, and will therefore act on all occasions in conformity with the character so defined."[90] Reading these last chapters on the social sanction of morality, we note that the immoral or egoistic behavior that seems to disturb Stephen still more than the antisocial economic self-interest that Spencer advocates in the unrestrained expression of "sensual" desire, and we recall the editor of *Cornhill* who worried Thomas Hardy over his sexual explicitness with an "excessive prudery of which I am ashamed."[91] We will need to return to this point in our discussion of another of Stephen's literary heirs, George Meredith.

There is, then, in Stephen a cultural and ethical conservativism, which, as I earlier intimated, may remind us of Arnold against anarchy, and which, as in the case of Arnold, no doubt owes a debt to Coleridge's seminal nineteenth-century defense of the necessity of ecclesiastical polity, the Church in this case being the autonomously evolving "social tissue." Where Stephen and Arnold part ways, and this marks as well the difference between Stephen and his fellow believers in scientific philosophy, Lewes and George Eliot, is in the category of the aesthetic or symbolic. To measure the difference, we need to return to his quarrel with Arnold, but in this instance, the issue will be, not religion or ethics, but the aesthetic judgment.

8

Science and the Comedic Vision: Stephen's Criticism and George Meredith's Art

The comical is always the mark of maturity; but it is important that the new shoot should be ready to appear under this maturity, and that the *vis comica* should not stifle the pathetic, but rather serve as an indication that a new pathos is beginning.

—Kierkegaard

STEPHEN is the other great scientific critic of the Victorian period after Lewes. He is, as critic, less interesting, but he has benefited from a better press. The Leavises and the "Cambridge Tradition" of English studies no doubt bear a large responsibility for this. In a *Scrutiny* piece of 1939, Queenie Leavis places Stephen among the saints of humanism: ". . . after Johnson, Coleridge, and Arnold who was there who was any help? (Certainly not Pater or Symons or Saintsbury or . . .). . . . He seemed to be in the best line of the best tradition of our literary criticism . . ." Leavis' target in this article is another sort of tradition, closely associated with late nineteenth-century Oxford (Pater, Symons, and Saintsbury) and rooted in the less "responsible" side of Matthew Arnold's critical mission, a tradition we may broadly call art-for-art, or "aestheticist." A descendant of that mistaken tradition, Desmond MacCarthy, had recently given her the occasion for her essay:

Delivered at Cambridge in 1937, his [MacCarthy's lecture on Stephen] can only be described as an insolent performance. For if the humanistic side of Cambridge studies has any justification for existing[,] it is in standing in the eyes of the world—as it does—for a critical position descended from Leslie Stephen's and antagonistic to Mr. MacCarthy. . . . Those of us who do not choose to linger in the aesthetic vacuum of the 'nineties can afford the courage of asserting that we agree with Leslie Stephen and not Mr. MacCarthy. . . .[1]

What MacCarthy had regretted in Stephen, as Leavis' strictures suggest, was an absence of concern for, or worse, an inability to perceive, the specifically aesthetic or formal qualities of a literary work. Stephen, he complained, judged literature in moral and philosophical terms; he "is the least aesthetic of noteworthy critics."[2] MacCarthy was drawing on Matthew Arnold's 1879 essay on Wordsworth, one of the monuments of Victorian criticism, in which Stephen had been made to stand for the wrong-headed sort of taste which admired the poet for his ideas, not his art: "The Wordsworthians are apt to praise him for the wrong things, and to lay too much stress on his philosophy. His poetry is the reality, his philosophy . . . is the illusion."[3] "It is impossible," MacCarthy provocatively remarked, "to imagine a Matthew Arnold who had never been at Oxford and a Leslie Stephen who had never been at Cambridge,"[4] throwing out a challenge the Leavises could hardly ignore.

Queenie's answer is that Stephen's Cambridge position, is, after all, the only one that matters to serious critics, the one, that is, that finds in moral and philosophical seriousness "something more profound than an 'aesthetic' theory can explain."[5] She then completely disarms MacCarthy by, in effect, making Arnold an honorary Cantabrigean. "We recollect that Arnold . . . also practised this method when [he was] most effectual."[6] Her "effectual" Arnold, no less available than MacCarthy's aesthetic one, is the critic for whom, we recall from elsewhere in the Wordsworth essay, "a poetry of revolt against moral ideas is a poetry of revolt against *life*."[7] Another Cambridge admirer of Stephen has put Leavis' point more straightforwardly. Stephen, writes Noel Annan, is "Arnold's disciple," who "did for English fiction what Arnold did for poetry."[8]

But all this strained effort to defend Stephen from the aesthetes by associating him with the good, the morally, philosophically serious Arnold, and the "best tradition" of "humanistic" criticism, is, in the end, rather parochial. Stephen, as we have had occasion to see, is at a very substantial intellectual distance from Arnold, and that difference continues unabated in their criticism. Stephen is as far as possible from pursuing the same critical method as Arnold, whichever Arnold we are talking about, aestheticist or humanist. The most important point Leavis has to make about Stephen, in the end, is that he left Cambridge (as he would have left Oxford) for reasons of conscience. These were reservations about the validity of established religion. But they were also reservations about the ancient universities' unestablished religion of humane letters, reservations that should, really, bring the Leavises and MacCarthy together in allied indignation at Stephen's apostasy.

SOCIALIZING THE AESTHETIC

There is no mention of Arnold in Stephen's 1876 essay "Wordsworth's Ethics," but here, not less than in the earlier essays that constitute *Freethinking and Plainspeaking*, the need to respond to him is a condition of Stephen's writing. For some 20 years, in poetry and in prose, Arnold had been treating Wordsworth as the greatest of modern British poets, the continuator of Milton, the rival of Goethe. Yet even as he admired Wordsworth, Arnold had persistently condescended to his philosophical intelligence, associating his ideas not with the "modern spirit"—the mainstay of Arnold's critical and cultural project—but with an era of spiritual innocence before the "disease of modern life": "The greatest of the [English romantics] Wordsworth, retired . . . into a monastery. I mean, he plunged himself in the inward life, he voluntarily cut himself off from the modern spirit. . . . [His] works have this defect,—they do not belong to that which is the main current of the literature of modern epochs, they do not apply modern ideas to life; they constitute, therefore, *minor currents*. . . ."[9] Arnold's most recent mention of Wordsworth had been in the preface to *God and the Bible*, where he presents lines from the "Intimations Ode" by way of demonstrating the nineteenth-century mind's reluctance to awaken from its religious illusions.[10]

What Stephen, no less an admirer of Wordsworth than Arnold, wants clearly to do in his essay is vindicate the poet's claim to philosophical seriousness. Wordsworth, as a *moralist*, he writes, shows an "intuitive" grasp of the direction in which modern philosophy is moving. The Platonic philosophy of the "Intimations Ode," which Arnold had found utterly passé, becomes for Stephen a "symbol" of the most advanced scientific thought. The prenatal experience that Wordsworth celebrates in the poem is now made intelligible by the evolutionist as the prompting of instincts "embodying the past [social] experience of the race." It would be "too daring" to attribute to Wordsworth the "most remarkable" discovery of modern "scientific doctrine," that is, evolution, but it is entirely appropriate to see in this poem, as throughout his poetry, a precious awareness of how the moral character of the race and the individual develops from certain primitive emotions.[11] The essay, as we see, is a prelude to *The Science of Ethics*, and if we look at it in terms of Stephen's larger historical perspective, we see that Wordsworth becomes for him a key transitional figure between eighteenth-century deism and contemporary science. Far from being Arnold's backward-looking metaphysician, Wordsworth is a very pioneer of the modern spirit in Stephen's positivist reading of that spirit.

Arnold in composing his response in his own essay on Wordsworth (written two months later) chose to attack Stephen, not at the center of his argument, but on its periphery. Stephen, he says, is too preoccupied with Wordsworth's ideas and insufficiently attuned to his "poetic truth and poetic beauty." Conceding that he himself has long advocated the crucial importance of a poet's ideas in our estimate of his work, Arnold, nonetheless, finds that Stephen has dwelt too exclusively and literally with those ideas in attempting to extract from the poet " 'a scientific system of thought.' "[12] What Arnold rather disingenuously ignores is, first, Stephen's very plausible argument for Wordsworth's modernity and, second, his careful effort to excuse himself from discussion of poetic form in this particular essay. Stephen might well feel hard done by. Having attempted fairly to answer Arnold's own intellectualist attack on Wordsworth's "inadequate" ideas, he finds his opponent complaining of his failure to understand that Wordsworth's ideas are not, after all, what really matters about his poetry.

What is almost certainly bothering Arnold is less the intellectualist approach as such than the particular type of intellectualist approach. Wordsworth's ideas were not to be redeemed as "scientific"; he was not to be "placed" as an intuitive forerunner of Darwin. Similarly, the insistence that a true estimate of Wordsworth must rest on the "laws of poetic truth and poetic beauty" should probably not be taken as the statement of fundamental *critical* method it is usually taken to be. Rather, it is more likely the statement of an alternative *philosophical* position to the positivist one Stephen represents, a position we examined at the outset of the previous chapter.

There we saw Arnold at first writing (in *St. Paul and Protestantism*) as if he were in wholehearted sympathy with the modern scientific spirit and then (in *Literature and Dogma*) trying to distinguish his own concept of "poetic truth" from the scientist's positive truth. This new awareness of science (rather than religion) as the real threat to the humanistic philosophy he himself is attempting to purvey is characteristic of his writing from the mid-1870s onward. When Arnold speaks of "poetic truth" in the Wordsworth essay, he refers, not to some undefined formalist criterion for poetry, but to the same poetic (as opposed to scientific) truth he was speaking of in *Literature and Dogma*, and he is, in fact, rather precise in explaining what he means. What we admire in Wordsworth is not his philosophical system (which Arnold continues to treat as outmoded metaphysics) but a kind of concrete emotive language that evokes "primary affection," primitive feelings of "commonalty" with nature.[13]

This attempt to find, in a particular kind of language or style, the essence of religious feeling, lies behind the provocative claim we have already noticed that poetry is the reality, philosophy and science the illusion. "More and more mankind will discover that we have to turn to poetry to interpret life for us, to console us, to sustain us. Without poetry, our science will appear incomplete; and much of what now passes with us for religion and philosophy will be replaced by poetry. . . ."[14] I said earlier that Arnold ignores Stephen's careful distinction between Wordsworth as philospher and Wordsworth as artist. It would be more accurate to say that Arnold is making a philosophy of what Stephen has bracketed as aesthetic and therefore not philosophical. For Stephen poetry works according to a "logic" of "symbolic representation," an "imaginative power which harmonizes the strongest and subtlest emotions. . . ."[15] What he does in defense of Wordsworth as philosopher is *translate* the symbolic logic into a scientific belief, putting the symbols aside, as it were, in favor of the psychological concept they seem to him to stand for or, better, intuitively point towards. Arnold, in effect, refuses to translate the symbolic logic; it is an end in itself, conveying its own form of emotional truth.

Stephen's essay on Wordsworth has been taken by both admirers and detractors as representative of his critical position, which is unfortunate, for, as I have suggested, his object in that essay was self-consciously philosophical. Its title is "Wordsworth's *Ethics*," and it is probably more important as a prelude to his *Science of Ethics* than as a contribution to literary theory. For what is most distinctive about his literary theory we must look elsewhere. It is neither the moral seriousness that his early twentieth-century defender, Queenie Leavis, has admired nor the intellectualism that Arnold regretted which should "place" Stephen in the history of criticism; rather, it is his self-consciously scientific approach to the study of literature.

This does not take the form, as with Lewes, of trying to construct the theoretical basis for a new realism. Realism is certainly important for Stephen, but what preoccupies him as a theorist of literature is a problem continuous with his approach to ethics. He is first and foremost a sociologist of literature and the first significant one to write in English. For him a scientific criticism means understanding artistic phenomena as products of particular historical situations, situations characterized by particular social-cum-institutional arrangements and, though he does not use the word, particular ideologies. This approach, as he was able to recognize clearly only towards the end of his life, represented a revolutionary change in criticism in the later nineteenth century. The critic comes to realize that, in addition to being an individual, every artist is also "an organ of the society in which he has been brought up. The material upon which he works is the whole complex of conceptions, religious, imaginative and ethical, which forms his mental atmosphere. . . . He is also dependent upon what in modern phrase we call his 'environment'—the social structure of which he forms a part . . . ." To appreciate any great artist fully, it is necessary to grasp "the characteristics due to his special modification by the existing stage of social and intellectual development."[16] This new historical, or, as I prefer to call it, sociological, attitude towards literary production has certain obvious critical consequences, which Stephen duly notes. The critic becomes less "dogmatic," more ecumenical, in his tastes, and what is related, he becomes less concerned with formal issues, inasmuch as these are seen to be the result of individual genius or idiosyncrasy.[17] But the sociological approach to criticism has another culturally more encompassing consequence, and it is this that I shall be focusing upon and, in the process, marking what I take to be a significant new departure in the Victorians' pursuit of a scientific culture.

The principal inspiration for Stephen's sociological method is, certainly, Hippolyte Taine (1828–1893), the "founder," as René Wellek writes, "of a sociological science of criticism,"[18] and for Stephen the "beginning of modern scientific criticism." Stephen read the French critic's *Histoire de la littérature anglaise* (1863) by the early 1870s, and reviewed it for the *Fortnightly* in 1873. The "new theory" that we must study the literary work "in connection with its medium"[19] begins almost immediately to affect his criticism. We see it, for example, in his treatment of Pope's poetry as reflecting the "position of the best thinkers of his day";[20] of Crabbe's poetry as the product of working-class realism;[21] or of Johnson's "limitations" as determined by his "social medium," in particular the quality of his readers.[22] But, of course, the new method is most fully embodied in the extensive discussion of literature, society, and thought in volume 2 of *English Thought in the Eighteenth Century*, to which we will return in a moment.

But we need to consider the important adjustment Stephen makes to Taine's new theory. Wellek, while acknowledging Taine as the founder of sociological criticism, immediately qualifies the point by observing that he is, nonetheless, a very poor practitioner of the sociological method: "On every point he fails to show the complete concrete determination of literature by race-milieu-moment."[23] Stephen's essay, admiring as it is, conveys a very similar complaint, which he expresses, characteristically, as a failure on Taine's part to be adequately scientific in his analysis. By this Stephen clearly means what Wellek means: Taine fails to give us a concrete account of social and ideological structures and how specifically they determine literary phenomena. But Stephen means something more fundamental as well, though he is not ready to articulate it in 1873.

In his introduction to the *Histoire de la littérature anglaise*, which is actually a theory of history rather than of literature, Taine distinguishes three phases of modern historiography, of which the last, the only one we need concern ourselves with, is the most scientific. This is the point at which the historian, having determined the psychological "type" of a given age, then proceeds to analyze its "causes," which, of course, turn out to be the "primordial forces" of "race" (the "internal mainspring"), "milieu" (the "external pressure"), and epoch (the "acquired momentum"). Taine thinks of a period's type as organic, analogous to the "physical structure of a family of plants or order of animals" (we are reminded of Goethe and Lewes). Similarly, the causes that determine it are seen in organic terms as analogous to forces and nutrients. History is like a "chemical problem."[24] But these scientific analogies are, at last, merely rhetorical. They do not lead to precise historical or sociological explanations. What they do lead to here, as throughout Taine, is an understanding of literature, not as determined by social or ideological factors, but as expressing a type or symbol of the age. What "wealth . . . may be drawn from a literary work: when the work is rich . . . we find there the psychology of . . . an age . . . . In this light the great poem, a fine novel . . . are more instructive than a heap of historians with their histories. . . . It is . . . chiefly by the study of literatures that one may construct a moral history. . . . I intend to write the history of a literature, and to seek in it for the psychology of a people. . . ."[25] For all its scientific paraphernalia, this is idealist or romantic history as usual, and its underlying inspiration, as others have observed,[26] owes far more to Hegel than to any positivist sources. (Taine, of course, is often seen as a student of Comte.) Here, as throughout his work, Taine's "sociological" approach is really what we may more appropriately call a *historicist* one. His interest is not really in analyzing the social and ideological causes of artistic phenomena, but in reading art as an index of history. Again, the introduction to the *Histoire* is not a theory of literature, but of history, an essentially Hegelian theory in which history expresses itself symbolically in the work of great men. (Not surprisingly the introduction singles out Stendhal as the artist who best illustrates Taine's theory.)

We have already seen how in his ethical theory Stephen rejects not only Carlyle's doctrine of the hero but also Mill's methodological individualism, both of which would reduce the causes of history to the individual will. Clearly, the same thing is happening in his literary theory, and it is this which makes the difference between his approach to the sociology of literature and that of the French critic. What this comes down to is a new reading of the social status of the literary symbol, and Stephen's views on this topic mark, in my reading, one of the most decisive breaks with romantic theory in the Victorian period. We may see this not only in his relation to Taine but also, as I earlier intimated, in his relation to those far more informed scientific interpreters of literature, Lewes and George Eliot.

We can fairly easily locate the moment of transition in Stephen's attitude towards the literary symbol and its relation to society. In one of his earliest theoretical essays, "Art and Morality" (1875), we find him expressing a characteristic view: art and morality are inseparable. He then goes on to develop the point along distinctly romantic lines (he might almost have been reading *Daniel Deronda*). The moral value of art lies in its "powerful effect upon human beings": "Art is the means by which the men who feel most strongly and think most powerfully appeal to the passions of their weaker brethren. . . . [A]ll literature may be . . . regarded as forming the electric chain by which the great centres of spiritual force exercise an influence over the wide circle of their fellow-creatures."[27] What in particular gives these centers of spiritual force their power? The romantic symbol. The power of art's influence lies in its direct appeal to the emotion, and this appeal is, in turn, expressed in the symbol. These are "moral ideas in solution, . . . doctrines which are embodied in . . . imaginative symbols." The analytical critic may analyze these symbols and translate them into doctrine (as we have seen Stephen do in the case of Wordsworth), but in doing so he obliterates the unmediated "logic of sentiment" (as opposed to the "logic of proposition") by which they achieve their powerful effect, by which they "insinuate" themselves "into the mind in disguise, instead of openly taking it by storm. . . ."[28]

Within two years, Stephen has adjusted his position significantly. In "Genius and Vanity" he is again taking a theoretical position on art's relation to society. His point is that genius, or rather the worship of genius, is vanity. He begins, interestingly enough, with a reference to George Eliot's story (in *Middlemarch*) of genius forestalled or "martyred" by entanglement in the social "labyrinth."[29] But rather than going on to celebrate genius triumphant, as George Eliot will do (with the qualifications we have noted) in her ensuing novel, he argues, in effect, that our regret over the "martyrdom" of genius is the result of romantic illusion, a "lack of philosophic insight." In reference to the same Shakespeare whose symbolic power over society's morality he had celebrated in the earlier essay he asks,

What, after all, is the worth of any creation of human genius? . . . What—for this seems to be the real question—is the value to the world of its greatest men? . . . The more we know, the more clearly we realise the vastness of the debt which even the greatest owe to their obscure contemporaries. . . . History sees everywhere, not the work of a solitary legislator, but processes implying the slow growth of many generations. . . . In art the importance of the social medium, relative to the single performer, assumes ever greater proportions. But what is this but to diminish the extravagant value attributed to single performances? Their intrinsic excellence may not be lessened but we must lower our estimate of their importance as self-originated and creative forces.

We must also, evidently, lower our estimate of their influence on the course of events. Artists count "almost for zero in the great forces which really move mankind." A sentiment, Stephen's says, "not to be indulged even in private,"[30] recalling, no doubt, that the vast majority of his literary readers were still romantic enough to believe, with Matthew Arnold, that the "future of poetry is immense," and with it the individual poetic genius, not to mention the prophet-as-critic who prepares his way.

But then what becomes of the morality of literature and the logic of the symbol in Stephen's theory? Between "Art and Morality" and "Genius and Vanity" Stephen made his fullest practical application of the sociological theory of literature in the section entitled "Characteristics" of his *English Thought in the Eighteenth Century*. No doubt the requirement, implicit in the book's conception, to interrelate all the principal strands of the period's intellectual activity, went a long way towards convincing him of the philosophical innocence of privileging literature or literary symbolism as the governing force in society. "The character of imaginative literature," he says at the outset of "Characteristics," is "a function of many forces," the current philosophy, peculiarities of the race, social and political relations, as well as individual idiosyncracies.[31] There is much to be said of the way in which Stephen distinguishes and interweaves the various causes underlying eighteenth-century literature; in general, the account is far more sophisticated historically and sociologically than anything we find in Taine's *Histoire.* But one particular line of argument needs to be developed: the connection Stephen now articulates between literature and symbolic expression. This in turn will relate to what remains, after all, his overriding concern as a literary critic no less than as a philosopher: morality.

Individual literary artists are no longer seen as generating symbolic representations of belief, but as receiving them from a culture characterized by a "common faith" that "generates a symbolism universally understood and appealing to genuine beliefs. . . ." What was distinctive about eighteenth-century England was the deterioration of the "common faith" and, consequently, the growing deadness of its symbols. Deism is, by definition, a rationalization and abstraction of faith in a personal god. The living symbols of Christianity, its mythic force, were no longer available to Pope as they had been to Milton: "The mere dead forms of extinct thought are useless in a form of literature which men judge by their spontaneous feelings. . . ." Into the intellectual and aesthetic vacuum created by the decline of religious belief come, not the creative geniuses of romantic mythology, but the more modest phenomena of the essayist and the novelist, who are characterized by a "common sense" realism, which is expressed in a rejection at once of skepticism and philosophical speculation in favor of certain traditional social and moral laws: "When a creed is dying, the importance of preserving the moral law naturally becomes a pressing consideration. . . ." The rise of these new literary artists, particularly the novelists and their "new form of art," is not attributed to individual genius but, again, to a kind of commonsense desperation and, more interestingly, to the rise of a "new social form," the bourgeoisie, for whom common sense, moral law, and realism are saving values.[32]

Society, however, still needs its universalizing creed and this begins to "evolve" at the century's close. Its source, again, is not the poetic myth-maker of romantic imagination, but a general sense of spiritual want that generates certain "blind impulses." "The greatest thinkers of the century are not the first to show the working of the new leaven." This is found, rather, in various "subterranean channels of society," marginal classes and beliefs that begin in the midst of "intellectual chaos" to push forward. Which of these survives to define the new creed and how it survives, Stephen here, as in the later *Science of Ethics*, leaves to a kind of natural selection. Late-century "Sentimentalism" and "Gothicism" do not survive, being of little use for social cohesion. The desire for a "return to nature" does survive—expressed (not created) in literature by Burns and Cowper, in philosophy by Bentham—and involves, above all, an effort to "bring fact and philosophy together, so that the highest truths might be embodied in laws of experience, and not dismissed to a distinct world of transcendental entities."[33]

The coming new creed, as the above remarks suggest, is not, for Stephen, romanticism; the romantic movement is not discussed in *English Thought in the Eighteenth Century*. But in the late *English Literature and Society*, Stephen returns to the topic with greater confidence to declare "what is called the Romantic movement" not at all the "revelation of a new . . . creed" it is ordinarily taken to be, but a conglomeration of "divergent and inconsistent schools" that have in common, essentially, the negative quality of dissatisfaction with eighteenth-century institutions, religious, political, literary, and so on.[34] Clearly, he believes the new creed to be the positive or scientific philosophy adumbrated by Betham and developed by Mill, Comte, and Spencer. What then happens to the concept of symbolic or imaginative logic if science is to be the basis of the new "common faith"? Will scientific philosophy "generate," like the Christian totality that preceded it, a living symbolism of which poets may avail themselves? Comte certainly thought something like this would happen, and Stephen in his discussion of the one romantic he considers was actually on the right track sounds at times as if he believes Wordsworth's pantheism had led the poet to a new symbolic language. But, as we have seen, he chooses not to talk about this language. The fact is that Stephen, while recognizing the crucial importance of symbolic or figurative expression for poetic effect, has by 1876 become too scientific a thinker to believe in the possibility of reviving such a language in the modern world.

We find a similar skepticism in his contemporaries, the great Oxford philologist Max Müller and the father of British anthropology (and disciple of Spencer), Edward Tylor. The research of these and others[35] seemed to confirm that a vital symbolic language and the mythology associated with it were the product not only of certain cultural conditions but also of conditions either fixed in the past or, if found in the present, found only among primitive peoples. According to Tylor, these conditions were essentially two: "The teachings of a childlike primeval philosophy ascribing personal life to nature at large [i.e., animism], and the early tyranny of speech over the human mind, have been the two great . . . agents in mythologic development." His elaboration of the latter condition is particularly worth nothing.

Language not only acts in thorough unison with imagination whose product it expresses, but it goes on producing of itself, and thus . . . we have [symbolic conceptions] in which language has led and imagination has followed. . . . [This is the usual state] among ancient and savage peoples, intermediate between the conditions of a healthy prosaic modern citizen and of a raving fanatic. . . . A poet of our own day [Wordsworth] has still much in common with the minds of uncultured tribes in the mythologic stage of thought. . . . Both share in that sense of the reality of ideas [as signified by analogical language], which fortunately or unfortunately modern education has proved so powerful to destroy.[36]

Whether Stephen actually read Tylor on the evolution of language is not the point. What matters is that Tylor is articulating a theory of language and, implicitly, of poetry that was becoming current among positivist thinkers in the last decades of the century (we have seen the early Lewes anticipating and then withdrawing from it). The power of symbolic language, which has been at the heart of romantic theory not only of poetry but also of history and politics, was at last reduced to a product of certain social conditions which the "healthy prosaic modern citizen" had gone beyond once and for all. Accordingly, we find Stephen, having celebrated the poet's symbolic logic in "Art and Morality," expressing doubts about its reality in *English Thought in the Eighteenth Century* ("The poet . . . sometimes . . . fuses into a whole very inconsistent materials"[37]), and finally seeming to reject it altogether as, for example, in his essay on Sterne's "astonishing" and utterly irresponsible skill with words, an essay which turns into something very like a case against literature itself: "There is a good deal to be said for the thesis that all fiction is really a kind of lying, and that art in general is a luxurious indulgence, to which we have no right. . . ."[38]

This is Stephen in a particularly exasperated mood writing against an artist he detested. He does not, in fact, abandon either literature or literary criticism as irrelevant, primitive pursuits in the face of modern science. What he does is definitively reject the romantic preoccupation with genius and the power of poetic language, to which Lewes and Eliot, as we have seen, still cling, and, of course, Matthew Arnold as well. Stephen's last published word on that persistent rival is worth noting as a nice measure of the distance between them. Their "intellectual types," writes Stephen in 1893, were, after all, utterly different. Arnold was an "eddy in an intellectual revolution" (romanticism) that had had its day, a "musical moaner" over spilt milk. He had "too much hearty loyalty to the Zeitgeist and scientific thought" to believe in the truths of religion, but too little to be able to dispense with the "symbols" of religious emotion. His was an intelligible position only for one who despaired of science's ability to minister to our human needs. For the "prosaic" person, like himself, Stephen concludes, the advance of science was not something to fear but to celebrate.[39] It was not poetry (or criticism) but science that would save us, not symbols but truth.

EVOLUTIONARY OPTIMISM

Stephen regrets Arnold's pessimism over the effects of the "advance of science" on man's self-esteem. As Arnold argues in "Literature and Science" (1882), the study of humane letters becomes more crucial precisely in proportion as science seems to undermine our faith in the value of humanity: ". . . under the shock of hearing from modern science that 'the world is not subordinated to man's use, and that man is not the cynosure of things territorial' [Arnold is quoting Huxley], I could, for my own part, desire no better comfort than Homer's line . . . , 'for an enduring heart have the destinies appointed to the children of men!' "[40] Pessimism, whether in Arnold or Samuel Johnson, George Eliot or the late Huxley, is a sentiment Stephen vehemently resists. The greatest men, he writes, will always be "the most profoundly sensitive to the sadness of the world," but our "real interest" must finally be in that which ennobles us.[41]

Henry Sidgwick complains of both Spencer's and Stephen's ethical systems that they use the doctrine of evolution illegitimately as a "short-cut" to optimism. "The principle of evolution," he insists, ". . . decides nothing as to the issue between Optimism and Pessimism; Von Hartmann and Mr. Herbert Spencer may equally hold it. . . ."[42] What Sidgwick's criticism reflects is the growing prevalence of philosophical pessimism in the last two decades of the century (about which more in chapter 9) and the sense one has that Spencer and, still more, Stephen are straining after an optimistic conclusion to the Darwinian story.[43] Lewes, Spencer, Stephen, Clifford, Tyndall, Darwin himself, and many others attempted to turn evolutionism to good account. But for this, two formidable problems needed to be overcome: first, the moral iniquity of natural selection; second, the randomness of variation. As Sidgwick argued in 1876, before either Spencer's or Stephen's ethical treatises came out, it is simply not possible to get from the principle of natural selection to moral consciousness.[44]

Spencer's answer to the problem is to submerge the pain of natural selection in the luminous glow of a perfect organic efficiency, the end to which it is the necessary means. The specifically moral problem he resolves teleologically by defining the highest goal of evolution as the ideal reconciliation of egoistic and altruistic ends. Stephen's solution is more sophisticated. Evolution by natural selection in the organic world is bracketed and reapplied with laudable ingenuity to the development of the social tissue, fitness being defined as the organic wholeness or cohesiveness of any given group. Natural selection thus becomes a bloodless competition (or so Stephen wants to believe) among social structures based on their relative capacities to promote altruism and control egoism. The successful structure gradually imbeds itself in and modifies our instinctual nature or character in a Lamarckian process similar to what we have found in Lewes. This concept of moral evolution seems to be shared, as we have seen, by Darwin himself: it "appears probable . . . that [virtuous tendencies] become first impressed on the mental organization through habit, instruction and example, continued during several generations in the same family, and in a quite subordinate degree, or not at all, by the individuals possessing such virtues having succeeded best in the struggle for life." In all cases, "mental organization" is in some important sense the direct result of cultural factors that transcend and operate independently of the biological struggle for existence. Insofar as this seems scientifically plausible—as Darwin so cautiously puts it, not without "inherent improbability"—one may think, optimistically or at least melioristically, of the gradual eradication of "immoral" impulses by "instruction" rather than an unending war of each with all.[45] But one thinks this way, as Sidgwick is, in effect, objecting, at the expense of a unified theory of evolution.

The problem of the randomness of variation is one that British scientists in the nineteenth century preferred not to address directly, no doubt because it was so unthinkably demoralizing. The American Jacob Schurman, writing five years after Stephen's *Science of Ethics*, points out that the "fundamental assumption" of a consistent evolutionism must be that the origin of ethical belief is "mechanical," that is, without conscious or meaningful direction. But, "the accredited expounders of the subject have in their exoteric writings enveloped this point in such a wrapping of extraneous discussions that even a master in ethics like Professor Sidgwick has hazarded the declaration that evolution . . . can make no difference at all in our ethical theories." On the contrary, continues Schurman, it makes all the difference in the world, for once you accept the principle of natural selection as the cause of moral consciousness, the

question of an ethical end . . . becomes unmeaning, since there cannot, in a literal sense, be any ends or aims for a being conceived as a mere mechanism, even though its random acts have through natural selection been solidified into habits, and habits on the supervention of consciousness, been reflected as rules. . . . An individual who really [accepts Darwinism] must regard moral responsibility as illusory, as nothing but an echo of the modes of conduct which enabled the human species to overcome what . . . threatened its extinction.[46]

This conclusion was not publicly accepted by Spencer or Stephen or any British evolutionist of stature. It is not even proposed as a position to be refuted. Yet it is not difficult to see that the neo-Lamarckian argument for the culturally directed evolution of human nature is, implicitly, a recognition of the specter of ethical pyrrhonism raised by Darwin, a pyrrhonism worse than any Hume envisaged.

Its origin aside, the optimist argues, once mind evolves, it becomes the order-giving principle. One may think of the process in quasi-metaphysical terms as a development of unconscious spirit or force towards consciousness. Such a fusion of romantic idealism with evolution we find in many of Stephen's contemporaries, Balfour Stewart, Peter Tait, J. A. Symonds, F. W. Hutton, *inter alia*. It is what is finally behind Spencer's "synthetic philosophy" with his notion of "God" as the "unknowable" energy propelling man towards the telos of the industrial state. Or one may, more consistently with the Darwinian revolution, take the "accident" of mind independently of any metaphysical grounding and concern oneself simply with how it orders and transmutes nature. This is what Lewes, Tyndall, George Eliot, Stephen, and ultimately Huxley, attempt to do. Here, as John Dewey says, "interest shifts from the wholesale essence back of special changes to the question of how special changes serve and defeat concrete purposes; shifts from an intelligence that shaped things once for all to the particular intelligences which things are even now shaping. . . ."[47] Here the evolutionist struggles to achieve a residual humanism, to establish the concept of culture as a self-creating and self-validating order that has become man's principal adaptive instrument,[48] and in this way he seeks to avoid what Darwin saw as an unacceptable confrontation with "blind chance,"[49] or what we might now prefer (as literary critics) to call absence. The confrontation was nonetheless bound to come, forced, as we will see, by further developments in science, and with it devastating effects on the positivist effort to ground culture in nature.

Stephen was increasingly troubled in the last two decades of the century by what he took to be the tendency of contemporary European civilization towards decadence. *Fin-de-siècle* aestheticism, the renewed interest in Schopenhauer's philosophical pessimism, and, above all, literary "naturalism," the excess of realism that insists upon the bestiality and/or pointlessness of human life were, for him, all disconcerting signs of the times, signs that science had not yet accomplished its mission of establishing the new unifying creed. His way of retaining his faith in that mission was to treat the apparent decadence as a "morbid" direction in the social tissue that was bound, in the nature of things, to be corrected by the "cosmic" reality of our healthy instincts. The "energy of the race," he writes at the close of one of his own most pessimistic essays ("The Decay of Literature," 1882), "continues unabated" and "will . . . throw out again . . . a group of dazzling luminaries."[50] There is no backsliding here to the "great man" theory. The process is still thoroughly deterministic, only what Stephen is reassuring his reader of, no less than himself, is that the determining element, the social tissue, remains healthy.

The difference from George Eliot's way of evading contemporary science's pessimistic implications needs emphasizing. The focus on personality and, beyond that, individual imagination, that "seed of fire," as the last refinement of cosmic energy, enables her to assert a scientific philosophy according to which the energy of the "massive being," like Daniel or Dorothea, constantly generates new and better social orders. Stephen believes in no such transformative power of individual genius and is too much of a realist to give symbolic expression more than its minimal due. Yet at the same time he is as uncritically optimistic as the early Comte in his dependence on that "germ" of altruism at the root of human nature, which, in fact, functions for him as the agent of "natural" selection. It is the instinct that makes it possible for the race to choose the "healthy" social structure. In this we may say that Stephen shares that Wordsworthian innocence the pessimistic Arnold complains of. For Stephen, as we have seen, the romantic poet intuitively anticipated Darwin. It might be more accurate to say that, for him, Wordsworth interprets Darwin. The emerging "shoot" of pathos that Kierkegaard speaks of in our epigraph is visible in Stephen, but it is, at last, stifled by the *vis comica*.

Stephen had two great literary descendants (other than Virginia); one carried on his optimistic, if not his scientific, spirit; the other reversed the priorities. The first of these, George Meredith, we will consider briefly, briefly because he is only tangentially part of the tradition I am exploring. The second, Thomas Hardy, will require more attention, occupying, as he does, a place at least equal to George Eilot's as an artist philosophically committed to measuring the impact of scientific thought on human culture.

GEORGE MEREDITH'S NEW LANGUAGE OF NATURE: SCIENCE AND HUMAN SEXUALITY

Meredith's admiration for Stephen was immense. He began to know him well in the early 1870s and came to consider him one of the foremost philosophers of the age as well as a model of personal integrity.[51] As most readers know, Stephen appears in *The Egoist* (1879) as Vernon Whitford,[52] the self-effacing scholar who turns out to be a modern Perseus. But it is not simply the character of Stephen that Meredith, always inclined to draw his heroes and heroines from people he actually knew, wishes to memorialize, but his ideas, or better, the *spirit* of his ideas.[53] Vernon represents, as Lionel Stevenson has observed, the "spirit of comedy," which is tantamount to saying that he represents the intellectual center of all Meredith's work, for Meredith, no less than Dante, seeks to reveal the essentially wholesome shape of things.[54]

The dominant metaphor for this wholesomeness, not only in *The Egoist* but throughout his late fiction, is an Alpine setting, almost certainly another tribute to Stephen, a famous climber of the Alps. "I had often fancied," writes Stephen in an article Meredith read just before beginning *The Egoist*, that in the "dreamland" of the Alps

access might be attained to those lofty reveries in which the true mystic imagines time to be annihilated, and rises into beatific visions untroubled by the accidental and the temporary. Pure undefined emotion, indifferent to any logical embodiment, undisturbed by external perception, seems to be the sphere of the transcendental. Few people have the power to rise often to such regions or remain in them long. . . . We—the positive and matter-of-fact part of the world—need be no more afraid of dreaming too much than the London rough need be warned against an excessive devotion to the Fine Arts. Our danger is the reverse.[55]

For Clara and Vernon, for Clotilde and Alvan (*The Tragic Comedians*, 1881), for Diana and Percy (*Diana of the Crossways*, 1885), and for Norman Radnor (*One of Our Conquerors*, 1889), the Alps are the symbolic setting in which one may realize the full potential of human love, untrammeled by social convention ("this land of social policy"). This is the "transcendental," the region of the truly comedic: ". . . the two lovers [Clara and Vernon] met [at last] between the Swiss and Tyrol Alps over the Lake of Constance. Sitting beside them [was] the Comic Muse. . . ."[56]

What Meredith shares with Stephen, what must have inspired him in Stephen's work, is, first, the agnostic's "plainspoken" refusal to compromise with a theism he could not intellectually accept and, second, his search for an alternative ground for belief in "nature." Like Stephen, Meredith considers that the central issue of such an ethic must turn on whether we are, in nature, more inclined to egoism or to altruism, and, like Stephen, he works in the faith that it is the latter principle which ultimately governs us and that any social structure which fails to recognize this is unnatural and hence unhealthy. Finally, he agrees with Stephen in believing that contemporary social structures show a distinct tendency towards decadence. Stephen, on the other hand, is not as inclined as Meredith to dwell on the departure of English society from the norm of nature, nor does he believe, as Meredith clearly wants to believe, that the solution to this problem lies in the hands of the great man, whether politician or artist. Like George Eliot, Meredith owes a substantial debt to Carlyle, only, in the end, it is not the Carlylean spirit of heroic prophecy so much as the Carlylean spirit of comedy that moves him. "Comedy is a game played to throw reflections upon social life. . . ." Its mission, ultimately, is to reassure us that, the distortions of "social life," once removed, we are at heart good and loving people.[57]

The Egoist is self-consciously a story of evolution, one might say, a parable of evolution.[58] It rests on the issue of sexual selection developed by Darwin in his long-awaited application of evolutionary theory to humanity: "A deeper student of Science than his rivals, [Willoughby] appreciated Nature's compliment in the fair one's choice of you. We now scientifically know that in this department of the universal struggle, success is awarded to the bettermost. You spread a handsomer tail than your fellows, you dress a finer top-knot . . . , she reviews you in competition, and selects you."[59] Clara is the principal "selector" of the novel; her choice is between Sir Willoughby Patterne, the pattern of the conventional English gentleman and a society founded according to the "Book of Egoism," and Vernon Whitford, "the new kind of thing,"[60] characterized, above all, by his capacity for sympathy and self-sacrifice. Clara's choice and the parabolic occasion for our faith in the future of the race is Vernon, and the choice is blessed not by the allusion to divine providence, characteristic of the earlier Victorian love parable of Dickens, Trollope, Thackeray,[61] and so on, but, as we have seen, by the Alpine metaphor of human nature liberated.

All this Stephen would have understood and approved. Where he would certainly have disagreed with Meredith's story is in its attitude towards science as the means of discovering the natural. *The Egoist* is clearly not looking to science to save civilization.[62] On the contrary, Meredith seems to see science as having inadvertently written the latest chapter in the "Book of Egoism." Willoughby, one recalls, is devoted to the modern desire for scientific knowledge as opposed to the classicist or philological training of his cousin Vernon. The reason is not far to seek. Science applied to our human nature, by Meredith's account, has only "introduced us to [an] o'er-hoary ancestry," taught us that self-preservation and the "mangling" of others is the animal root of our nature. "The Egoist is our fountain-head, primeval man; [in the Egoist] the primitive is born again, the elemental reconstituted. . . . Such we were, to such are we returning. . . . [Let man] haply relax the labour of his arms, however high up the stream, and back he goes . . . , to the early principle of our being, with seeds and plants, that are as carelessly weighed in the hand and as indiscriminately husbanded as our humanity."[63] What Meredith means by "science" here appears to be evolution as interpreted by the philosophy of Herbert Spencer, and one imagines he and Stephen must have had considerable discussion between them over what science actually does teach about our primitive nature (Stephen was, of course, developing the *Science of Ethics* in this period).

In *The Egoist* Meredith rejects what he takes to be the scientific reading of original human nature in favor of a more accurate "poetic" one: "Poets, on the other side, may be cited for an assurance that the primitive is not the degenerate: rather is he [the primitive] a sign of the indestructibility of the race, of the ancient energy in removing obstacles to individual growth; a sample of what we would be, had we his concentrated power. He is the original innocent, the pure simple. It is we who have fallen; we have melted into Society, diluted our essence, dissolved."[64] Again there is no disagreement with Stephen here over the essential goodness of the primitive, the indestructibility of our racial energy for survival through love. Where the two differ is over whether it is the scientist or the poet who is to be "cited" for this "assurance." Stephen would say the scientist, with the poet mimetically following his lead. For Meredith it is the poet, whose "pulse of imagination"[65] perceives truths about human nature overlooked by the scientist, and whose "condensing spirit"[66] provides us with an intelligible order by which to live. Presumably, Meredith would argue that it is the poet in Stephen and not the "matter-of-fact" scientific thinker who has reached the truth about human nature.

The differences between Meredith and Stephen, however, cannot be so easily reconciled. There remains a profound disagreement over the nature of the "ancient energy of the race," even though both writers understand it in some sense as a principle of love. This begins to emerge in *The Egoist*, when the standard positivist moral antithesis, egoist/altruist, is deconstructed by a third possibility. Clara's apparent choice is between Willoughby and Vernon, but Meredith also presents just the shadow of another possibility in Horace de Craye. What de Craye represents is a patently sexual and irresponsible, that is, antimarital love: "He was of the race of amorous heroes who glory in . . . subduing . . . : plucking her . . . in good old primitive fashion."[67] As of the writing of *The Egoist*, Meredith's comedic spirit cannot encompass a closure that even remotely approves such an alternative for Clara. Her "run" from convention goes no further than the breaking of an engagement in favor of a better marriage and to a conspicuously idealistic lover, such a lover as we shall see again when we come to a consideration of Hardy's version of the "new man's" way of loving in Angel Clare, arguably another fictional representative of Stephen. In Vernon's idealism, his preoccupation with the maintenance of Clara's purity, we find another crucial aspect of Stephen's character. To his second wife (the mother of Virginia) he once wrote, "You see, I have not got any saints and you must not be angry if I put you in the place where my saints ought to be."[68] This, as we remember from our discussion of the early George Eliot, is archetypally Comtean and closely related to Stephen's more formal moral theory, according to which the "sexual appetite" is recognized as being "at the root of all the social virtues" and at the same time feared as one of the most anarchic of human instincts. It must be transmuted by civilization into "unselfish affection" or "altruism."[69] The burden of transmutation is for Stephen, no less than for Lewes and George Eliot, placed on women. Accordingly, the explicit recognition of an active female sexuality that seeks expression outside marriage is taboo.

The Egoist is very much concerned to take us back to the sexual "roots" of altruism: The "love-season," writes Meredith, "brings the touchstone to our natures. I speak of love, not the mask . . . , but of the passion; a flame having, like our mortality, death in it as well as life. . . ." But more threateningly he wants to explore what for Stephen is absolutely forbidden ground, the "unsaintliness" of women, and specifically their desire to break out of the masculinist imprisonment of "purity": ". . . the devouring male Egoist prefers [women] as inanimate overwrought polished pure metal precious vessels, fresh from the hands of the artificer, for him to walk away with hugging, call all his own, . . . and forget that he stole them."[70] The portrayal of Clara is, for 1879, unusually frank in its suggestion that freedom for the woman means freedom to express herself sexually, freedom to find in a man like de Craye an attractive option for "selection."

Vernon, whose buried sexuality comes increasingly to the fore, eventually becomes for Clara a workable—and marriageable—alternative. In subsequent novels Meredith explores the theme with increasing candor, penetrating with his "pulse of imagination" an area of human naturalness that orthodox scientific discourse had, for the most part, avoided. *The Tragic Comedians* (1880) features a heroine, Clotilde, who must choose between an even more sexually energized man, even more of a social outcast, than de Craye and an asexual but conspicuously altruistic "prince" of the establishment. Her choice is unhesitantly the former to the horror, of course, of her bourgeois family. The preferred lover (Alvan) is killed in a duel by the second choice (Marko), whom she then marries with an implausibility that only highlights the pressure Meredith is under to remain within the bounds of convention. The true ending, the emotionally appropriate ending, however, is less a marriage than (metaphorically) an infidelity, possibly (and still metaphorically) a murder: "After a few months she buried [Marko]. From that day, or it may be, on her marriage day, her heart was Alvan's."[71]

In *Diana of the Crossways* (1885) the infidelity of the heroine is more than metaphorical. Not just engagement but marriage itself is portrayed as an imprisonment, the freedom, true self-realization, seems to lie only in adultery. "[Diana] called on her heart to glory in . . . the light of tried love, the love that defied the world. . . . She and [Percy] would at a single step give proof of their love: and this kingdom of love—how different from her recent craven languors!—this kingdom awaited her, was hers for one word. . . . She could hardly believe that it had come. . . . Resistance, nay, to hesitate at the joining of her life with his . . . accused her of worse than foolishness."[72] In the end, Diana does not actually commit adultery, but the unrepentant desire to do so would have been shocking enough, as, for that matter, would Meredith's entire project of making a heroine of a woman who spends most of her time defying the institution of marriage—without dying in the end.

Passing over the last two novels, *Lord Ormont and His Aminta* (1894) and *The Amazing Marriage* (1881; published 1895), both of which are firmly focused on "the great Marriage Question," we come to the most ambitious of the late novels and the least comedic of all Meredith's novels, *One of Our Conquerors* (1891). Its heroine lives with and has a child by a married man, and this, Meredith insists, is authorized by nature: "Nataly could argue her case in her conscience—deep down and out of hearing where women under scourge of the laws they have not helped decree may and do deliver their minds. She stood in the subterranean recess for Nature against the Institutions of Man. . . . [S]he had Nature's logic, Nature's voice for self-defence." Nataly does die, but her death is portrayed as a martyrdom that, in Meredith's most self-consciously epic novel, gives promise of a new social order to come which will accept the naturalness of sexual energy. "Even the rigorous in defence of righteous [social] laws are softened by a sinner's death to hear excuses, and may own a relationship, haply perceive the faint nimbus of the saint." Nature *"makes all sweet."*[73] In this revolutionary, distinctively un-Comtean redefinition of secular sainthood, Meredith's art, like George Eliot's before him, penetrates into regions that formal scientific discourse, by and large, avoided. But as we see in Nataly's martyrdom, so reminiscent of Maggie Tulliver's, the deeper and more plainspoken the penetration, the greater the risk to the comic spirit, the greater, that is, the danger of exposing an irreconcilable conflict between the desire to follow nature, on the one hand, and the constraint of the "social tissue," on the other.

The properly positivist way of resolving the conflict would be to allow science to pursue nature wherever it might lead and then to use the authority of science to validate the free expression of sexuality as indeed a natural, not just a "poetic," license. Impelled by so powerful an ideology as science had become in the second half of the century, social convention had to bend and harmony be reestablished between the natural self and society. Neither Stephen nor his positivist predecessors, including George Eliot, were quite prepared to pursue this strategy, but for a new generation of positivist thinkers, the late Victorian "sexologists," it became, as we shall see in chapter 10, a new route to the promised land.

But Meredith himself, finally, is too skeptical of the aims of science, too enamored of the self-generating, self-reflexive structures of art, and more particularly language, to accept such a prospective resolution. A side of him certainly wants to believe in the positivist faith that the scientific method will bring us at last to a conjunction of culture and nature, words and things, in short the elusive "language of nature" where we speak "so truthfully true."[74] But there is another, far more powerful, side of him that goes back to Carlyle's and the late George Eliot's faith in the power of the logic of symbols, in and of itself ungrounded and unverified. The "simple-seeming word is the triumph of the spiritual";[75] this gift does not simply "dazzle" and "tickle" us, but "strike[s] roots in the mind."[76] The poet's fascination with the figurative is so intense in Meredith's case that it must surely have suggested to him the possibility which for our own generation has become virtually another sort of faith, that one can never get beyond metaphor. As he wonderfully says at one point, "The banished of Eden had to put on metaphors, and the common use of them has helped largely to civilize us."[77] How else do his characters convey what convention outlaws or represses except through metaphor; how else does Meredith himself? Even the word "nature" itself can seem to Meredith a metaphor, the most powerful one, perhaps, at contemporary man's disposal. "We know not yet," Clara's father observes, "if nature be a fact or an effort to master one."[78]

Meredith is, indeed, more deeply ambivalent about the relation of language to reality than we have found any of our previous subjects to be. But the ambivalence is instructive. Insofar as he believes, as he clearly wants to believe, in the possibility of achieving a true or natural code of human behavior, he is very much in the positivist spirit of men like his admired Stephen. But insofar as he is unable, at last, to get beyond the "dazzle" of language, he is embarked on an altogether different course, parallel, if you like, to the one being far more purposefully traced by his German contemporary Nietzsche, for whom "to know is merely to work with one's favorite metaphors."[79] Meredith's irresolution before the prospect that Nietzsche gaily embraces we may fairly attribute to the timidity of a lesser mind. But that timidity is, at the same time, a nice measure of the terms in which the battle between positivism and spiritualism, science and poetry, will be waged at the close of the century. At issue, to use Meredith's own metaphor, will be whether the "root" of mind is nature or language.

Part Four

The Alienation of Mind

9

Reversing the Positivist Oracle: The Unvisionary Company of Darwin, Maudsley, and Hardy

What a book a devil's chaplain might write on the clumsy, wasteful, blundering, low, and horribly cruel works of nature!

—Darwin

LECTURING in 1879, Frederic Harrison, by then the preeminent voice of English Positivism (with a capital P), expressed a creed which may stand, *mutatis mutandis*, as the fundamental vision of all the writers whose work we have so far examined. The extension of science's domain from physical nature to the "crown and summary of all science," the study of man, he writes, has revealed to us a new "religious" order. Science has demonstrated the laws of "a Force towards which we can feel the highest sense of Sympathy, to whose service we can devote ourselves, whose mighty Power over us we cannot gainsay. . . . That Force is the vast and overwhelming consensus of all human lives, the complex movement of the ages through human civilization and thought." The "Realm of [natural] Law" and the "Realm of Love" can now be united under the dispensation of a "human Providence" as we pursue "the onward march of the human race, and its continual rising to a better mode of life."[1] It is this faith in the power of man's Promethean spirit, now scientifically rather than metaphysically validated, that underlies the logic of Mill, the psychology of Lewes, the fiction of George Eliot, and the ethics of Stephen. What we now turn to is the breakdown of that faith under the pressure of science itself and the advent of a new, philosophical pessimism in the century's last quarter, a pessimism of which Thomas Hardy becomes the preeminent English spokesman.

THE RISE OF SCIENTIFIC PESSIMISM

For a better indication of the direction in which contemporary thought was moving in the late 1870s we need to move from Harrison's paean to science and perpetual progress to a book published just two years earlier by James Sully (1842–1923). Sully, like Lewes, was a disciple of Mill and a student of the science of mind and was no less committed than Lewes (or Harrison) to the "religion" of science. The book he wrote is entitled *Pessimism: A History and a Criticism* (1877), and though his object is to demonstrate that there is no ground for adopting the pessimist's outlook, the fact that he found it necessary to argue at such length against that outlook is a fair indication of its growing currency. What concerns him is not simply a "temper of mind" that has found expression in various individuals throughout history but a rising philosophical movement: ". . . a considerable number of Englishmen are beginning to understand that pessimism also stands for a recent development of speculation which provides a complete theory of the universe, and which appears to be adopted, at least in the land of its birth [Germany], by a large and growing school." What this doctrine involves, Sully nicely summarizes. The pessimist condemns the world as "discordant or productive of misery"; he depreciates human nature and despairs of "man's capabilities of intellectual, moral, and social improvement." The blame for the new philosophy he places at the door of the usual suspect, German metaphysics, in particular the work of Arthur Schopenhauer (1788–1860) and his follower Eduard von Hartmann (1842–1906). What Sully is especially concerned to do is dispute the argument offered by von Hartmann that pessimism has a "scientific basis."

There is no need to detain ourselves with his lengthy refutation of this claim except to say Sully insists that modern science not only does not support Schopenhauer, von Hartmann, and others, but leads to entirely different conclusions such as we have just seen expressed by Harrison. Admittedly, Darwin presents a vision of human life as the product of random variation and painful struggle, but with the advent of human consciousness (a now familiar argument) things change: we gain conscious control of our environment and future development. Moving from biology to physics, and from the first to the second law of thermodynamics, he does admit a possible scientific basis for pessimism—modern physical science tells of "the dissipation of the whole of our solar system"—but immediately dismisses this as so remote an eventuality as to be "wholly inconceivable to our minds." In sum, despite efforts to "graft itself on modern science," pessimism is a product of a temporary "social sentiment," which science disposes of, as it does every other ungrounded product of man's residual penchant for metaphysical self-projection. That is, pessimism is cultural; optimism is natural.[2]

Sully's (and others') protestations notwithstanding, it is impossible not to draw a connection between late-century developments in science and a contemporaneous tendency to "theoretical" pessimism. Certainly, many Victorians did so. Responding to Sully's book in the new journal *Mind*, O. Plumacher finds the effort to dissociate modern pessimism from modern biology and physics naive. The emergence of mind, he argues, has not in the least reduced the cruelty of natural selection. "The extinction of one species by another more prolific does not seem to have been attended by more suffering than is involved in the rivalry of races. . . . Such things [science shows us] will continue as long as the evolution of nature and mind goes on." Even if, as Sully and the mainstream of contemporary science maintain, human evolution is tending towards some far-off triumph of pleasure over pain, altruism over egoism, such an eventuality is cold comfort "should it be the doom of organic creation to perish by a general refrigeration. . . ."[3] Similarly, for Francis Hueffer, writing on Schopenhauer in the year preceding Sully's book, the German philosopher's concept of will as "blindly [pursuing] its struggle for individualization" and in the process producing the "bewildering horror" of "species devouring species" is simply an inspired metaphysical anticipation of the world according to Darwin, the world we now understand ourselves to be living in.[4]

The point scarcely needs belaboring. By the late 1870s there began to emerge a distinctly negative reading of the meaning of science for the future of man. It was not by any means the majority view, certainly not among professional scientists. They had not fought the battle with the theologians and idealists to conclude that the scientific interpretation of life issued in Schopenhauer's invitation to universal suicide. Yet at the same time scientific knowledge was raising problems not easily ignored by the optimistically inclined. On the contrary, for those prepared to look, it seemed very much as if science, having confidently disposed of theism in favor of a proud vision of a "human providence," was now on its way to reducing the mind of man not simply to nature but to insignificance. What physical science reveals to us, writes Sidney Alexander in the *Contemporary Review* of 1893, is

the infinity of time and the immensity of space; and a dominant conception of our earth as a whirling atom . . . revolving at incredible speed in an unim-

portant system of heavenly bodies. This discovery of the real position of man
in the universe . . . has not failed, and cannot fail . . . to modify considerably
. . . our belief and practice. . . . [The] chief and greatest tendency of all this
set of facts and theories suggested by science . . . is towards the depreciation
of the value and importance of . . . the individual worker.[5]

It is Alexander's *angst* rather than Sully's faith that more nearly describes the direction in which scientific investigation was taking
philosophy by the century's close. Advances in biology, genetics, heat
theory, atomic theory, and astronomy, all worked relentlessly towards
the dehumanization of the world picture. As the modern historian of
science, Gerald Holton, puts it,

The reigning [cosmology] until about the mid-nineteenth century [pictured]
. . . a finite universe in time and space; a divine temple, God-given, God-
expressing, God-penetrated, knowable . . . [as completely] as the nature of
things admits in this mortal life.

   This representation was gradually supplanted by another, particularly in
the last half of the nineteenth century. The universe became unbounded,
"restless." . . . The clear lines of the earlier [cosmic structures] have been replaced by undelineated, fuzzy, smears. . . .

   And now a significant number of our most thoughtful scholars . . . seem to
fear that a third mandala is rising to take precedence over both of these—the
labyrinth with the empty center, where the investigator meets only his own
shadow. . . .

   It is therefore not surprising that [we] . . . find little comfort in the beauty
of scientific advances.[6]

What we need to identify more particularly before going forward are
the two principal sources of this third mandala in late-Victorian
science.

FROM DARWINISM TO NEO-DARWINISM:
THE IMPOSSIBILITY OF PROGRESS

Clearly the most devastating blow to scientific optimism was Darwin's
theory of evolution, if for no other reason than that it was the most
widely publicized of contemporary scientific concepts. As we have
seen, it was altogether possible for intelligent and sympathetic readers of Darwin to draw optimistic or melioristic conclusions from his
theory. Either one could find some sort of meaningful, quasi-divine
force driving the process of evolution: ". . . evolution of an orderly
Kosmos . . . by the continuous operation of mutual attractions according to . . . law . . . should furnish . . . the sublimest exemplification

of an Infinite Intelligence working out its vast designs. . . ."[7] Or one could believe, less mystically, that whatever chance and brutal struggle might have led to the emergence of the human mind, once it emerged things became meaningful and moral: ". . . from the time when . . . the intelligent and moral faculties became fairly developed in man he ceased to be influenced by 'natural selection. . . .' "[8] This second position is the one we have been most concerned to follow, forming as it did the foundation of the new scientific humanism. What we shall now need to consider is the persistence and eventual triumph of precisely that element in Darwin, which the British evolutionists, as Jacob Schurman observed, seem to have entered into something like a conspiracy to conceal (see above, p. 206).

George Bernard Shaw (1856–1950) early in this century described a sort of philosophical awakening characteristic of his generation. The Darwinian process, he says, seems relatively straightforward at first, but this is only because you do not "realize all that it involves." When its significance at last dawns on you, "your heart sinks into a heap of sand within you." What Shaw alludes to is not the fact of animal descent or the elimination of God or even the cruel struggle for existence. He is talking about the "chapter of accidents," as he says, that underlies the whole process of natural selection.[9] Nothing, finally, is more revolutionary in Darwinism and nothing less susceptible of melioristic revision than this concept of random variation. This, we now understand, is that most humiliating message of Darwinism, and we need not spend a great deal of time rehearsing again its philosophical consequences. Enough to bring these consequences more fully than we have so far done into the context of our distinctly modern *angst*, which we may do most economically by means of Hans Jonas' classic account in *The Phenomenon of Life*:

[Darwinism] completes the liquidation of immutable essences, and thus signifies the final victory of nominalism over realism. . . . This is a major philosophical event in that it powerfully confirms the anti-Platonism of the modern mind. If we add to this the absence of any teleological directedness, the evolutionary process presents itself as a sheer adventure with an entirely unforeseeable course. . . . The minimum left to the original essence of life is just self-preservation, which is analogous to the inertial laws ruling the conduct of a particle. . . . Mind was not foreseen in the amoeba, nor was the vertebrate structure, science no more than the opposable thumb: one and the other were elicited in due—but unforeseeable—course in the enormous span of the changing vital situation. . . . This reduction of the formal essence of life to the vanishing-point . . . , and correspondingly the throwing open of the indefinite horizon of situation for the evoking of possibilities which were not pre-existing potentialities, have a familiar ring to those conversant with contemporary philosophies of Man. Indeed nineteenth-century evolutionism, which completed the Copernican revolution in ontology, is an apocryphal ancestor . . . of present-day existentialism. The latter's encounter with "nothingness" springs from the denial of "essence" which blocked the recourse to an ideal "nature" of man.[10]

Jonas goes on to suggest the intimate connection between Darwinism and the nihilism of Nietzsche. Later I will develop what I take to be a still more relevant connection between Darwinism and Freud. In either case, these lines of intellectual filiation serve to highlight the thoroughly Quixotic nature of the mid-Victorians' efforts to enlist Darwin in the struggle for a new scientific religion. The "revolution in ontology" reduced mind to its vanishing point, and this was an even more devastating consequence of Darwinism than the prospect of a revolution in moral preconceptions, which we explored in the preceding chapter.

Yet another shadow needs to be added to the growing gloom of late-Victorian evolutionism. Insofar as it was possible to argue that the advent of mind introduced an entirely new, end-directed, and moral factor into the evolutionary process, at least for human beings, one could still, as we have seen Stephen do and as Darwin himself was inclined to do, make an argument for the transmission of acquired moral characteristics and hence the continued progress of the race. In this case it really need not matter that morality was fortuitous, only that, once with us in various superior individuals (superiority being determined largely by class and racial standing, as Darwin's cousin Francis Galton makes clear), it can by use and/or artificial selection be embedded in human nature.[11] But with the development of research into the genetic origin of organic mutations, it became increasingly apparent that it was biologically impossible to transmit any human adaptation, moral or otherwise, by inheritance. Here the figure to reckon with was August Weismann (1834–1914), who in 1885 proposed his theory of the "continuity of germ plasm," according to which the "germ track" ("genotype" as we would now say) is inherited quite independently of any influence from the individual body or "phenotype." Weismann's research, observes Ernst Mayr, excluded "all remnants of a belief in an inheritance of acquired characters or other kinds of soft inheritance."[12] Again, Jonas develops the philosophical repercussions of this biological discovery.

Weismann's theory of the continuity of the germ plasm is the clearest expression of . . . [a] new biological dualism. There is on the one hand the blind automatism of a germ [genetic] history enacted in the subterranean darkness which no light from the upper world penetrates; and on the other hand the upper world of the soma [individual organism] meeting the world in terms of life, pursuing its destiny, fighting its battles . . . —and all this being of no other consequence for the hidden charge than that of its being either continued or eliminated. The vicissitudes of the *germ's* history, as expressed in mutations, are entirely separate from the vicissitudes of the soma's history, uninfluenced by the whole drama of life enacted in the light. . . .[13]

Not only do we have with Weismann an apparent end to the hope that science will validate the possibility of moral progress, we also have a profound challenge to the idea, so sacrosanct among the Victorians (and still, of course, strong among ourselves), that the individual's experience of life can change his or her fundamental nature, can build "character."

DEGENERATION: THE IMPACT OF THE SECOND LAW OF THERMODYNAMICS

In applying evolution to man in 1871 Darwin could not, if he had wanted, have avoided addressing a question of increasing moment to the scientific community: Given that life has evolved and species have changed, must one assume that evolution, and particularly human evolution, is necessarily progressive? Darwin's response was guardedly optimistic:

To believe that man was aboriginally civilised and then suffered utter degradation [into the primitive tribes we find] in so many regions, is to take a pitiably low view of human nature. It is apparently a truer and more cheerful view that progress has been much more general than retrogression; that man has risen by slow and interrupted steps, from a lowly condition to the highest standard as yet attained by him in knowledge, morals and religion.[14]

Yet, at the same time, no one could read Darwin without being dismayed by the spectacle of extinguished species and, with the application of the theory to man, extinguished races. We must "keep steadily in mind that the increase of each species and each race is constantly checked in various ways; so that if any new check, even a slight one, be superadded, the race will surely decrease in number; and decreasing numbers will sooner or later lead to extinction. . . ."[15] This specter of extinction or, as it is more appropriately termed, *degeneration*, despite Darwin's and others' progressivist assurances, loomed ever larger in the imagination of the late nineteenth century, blending with and lending scientific support to a historicist trope of decline and fall that had haunted the Victorians at least since the publication of Carlyle's *French Revolution* (1837), intensifying, in millenarian fashion, as the century approached its close.

From the scientific perspective of Victorian England there were essentially two ways of understanding degeneration. One was as a medical and psychological problem and involved a growing awareness of the prevalence of physical and mental abnormality in advanced industrial society. The second was as a problem in physics and involved a growing awareness of the second law of thermodynamics and its implications. In the later nineteenth century these two understandings tended to converge, and it is not always easy to distinguish them.

We can trace serious scientific discussion of degeneration as a medical or psychological problem at least back to Bernard-Anz Morel's (1809–1873) influential *Traité des dégénérescences physiques, intellectuelles, et morales de l'espèce humaine* of 1857[16] (the same year as Baudelaire's *Fleurs du mal*) and see it, in general, as a topic of more interest on the Continent than in England. Among the English it is Henry Maudsley (1835–1918), more than anyone else, to whom we must look for an exemplary instance of degeneration theory. Maudsley, a late-Victorian follower of Comte, was one of the earliest of British psychologists to focus his attention on abnormal or pathological conditions of the mind. Although he began as a physiological psychologist (*Physiology and Pathology of the Mind*, 1867), he soon moved into wider philosophical explorations and, in the process, brought out the antithetical element of Comte's thought, the suppressed fear that the future of mankind may be not "order and progress" but dissolution and retrogression.

This transformation of Comte is particularly striking in Maudsley's major work, *Body and Will, Being an Essay Concerning Will in Its Metaphysical, Physiological, and Pathological Aspects* (1884). In the first two parts of the book he writes in an orthodox Comtean fashion (reminding one very much of Lewes) of the necessity of a positivist, as opposed to metaphysical, theory of mind, of the primacy of unconscious motivation, of the Lamarckian adaptation of the mind to the "social medium," and of the gradual ascendency of altruism over egoism. The principal distinction of his approach at this point, as against Comte's or Lewes', is his emphasis on *will*. He wants, not unlike George Eliot, to provide a positive interpretation of the will, probably with a view towards correcting the metaphysical accounts offered by the increasingly popular philosophies of Schopenhauer and von Hartmann.

Then, towards the close of the second part of the book, in the process of discussing the perennial egoism/altruism problem, Maudsley makes a radical departure from the positivist position as we have so far understood it. At present, he writes, "we fix attention too much perhaps on the process of evolution, to the overlooking of the correlative process of degeneration that is going on, not only in low but in high organisms, . . . not only in body but in mind; not only in individuals but in societies. . . ." The final third of the book is given over to a detailed account of contemporary mental degeneration, from which Maudsley draws the conclusion that English society and humanity in general are headed towards dissolution. "Without doubt there will be further great gains of evolution yet in the long run . . . all the signs point plainly to the conclusion that its range on earth is limited, its end . . . foredoomed in the future." And again, "What an awful contemplation, that of the human race bereft of its evolutional energy, disillusioned, without enthusiasm, without hope, without aspiration, without an ideal." We will all then realize the wisdom of Job and consider suicide a "sort of conclusive climax of pessimism."[17] Maudsley has replaced the metaphysical will of Schopenhauer with a positivist one, but he has come, nonetheless, to Schopenhauer's conclusion, not Comte's or Lewes' or George Eliot's.

What brings Maudsley to this position is, to begin with, his practical experience of the study and treatment of mental disease. His chapter on the "congenital deficience" of the will summarizes the wide variety of pathological conditions he had personally observed. Far from being evolved out of the race, they are, he is convinced, reproducing themselves at a formidable rate. This was not merely his own perception, but a widespread one among contemporary observers. J. Mortimer-Granville, writing in *The Nineteenth Century* in 1879, had no difficulty answering the provocative question posed in his title "Is Insanity Increasing?" It was, indeed, and, his statistics seemed to tell him, at almost twice the rate of the general population.[18] The principal force behind the infamous eugenics movement at the century's close was the sense of an impending crisis in the mental health of the nation owing to the excessive reproduction of the lower orders, where degeneracy was supposed to be concentrated.[19] Indeed, the inability to constrain one's sexual activity was in itself regarded as a sign of degeneracy. Where the eugenicists differed from Maudsley was in their confidence that something could be done to reverse the process. Having for the most part absorbed the neo-Darwinian lesson of Weismann and others, they thought in terms, not of improving degenerate germ plasm, but of preserving the purity of healthy germ plasm, health tending to be associated with the upper economic orders of the Caucasian race. The very desperation of this solution was a measure of the extent to which science seems to have darkened the future. On the one hand, psychology was discovering that a tendency towards degeneration might well be more operative in man than was evolution. On the other, modern genetic research was casting doubt on the possibility of doing anything to alter the process in the standard liberal way of inculcating cultural and moral ideas. What remained was a politically impractical and, for most, morally repugnant project for "breeding" degenerate tendencies out of the race.

The experience of working with "degenerates" and the conviction that degeneracy was rapidly increasing were instrumental in leading Maudsley (and others) to the conclusion that evolution had turned its corner, that devolution had become the new law of life. But there is another, more powerful source of Maudsley's gloom. The mental degeneracy that was the object of his professional attention as a psychologist, he comes to see eventually as part of a larger cosmic process of decline. What, he asks, is the "fundamental condition, of all progress from simple to complex combinations of matter" (i.e., of evolution)? He answers, ". . . we see plainly that the essential condition of all the successful becomings of things on earth . . . is the light and heat of the sun. . . . [And considering] that the sun is the immediate source of these energies, is it any wonder that Sun-worship was the religion of man at an early stage of his development? . . . [For] us practically and for our earth the sun is all in all, and . . . when its light and heat expire all those energies on earth which it animates will expire also." Is this expiration a real possibility? For Maudsley there is no doubt; the sun is in the process of dying and with it the "evolutional energy" that has produced the complex order of life that we now know: " . . . when [the sun] fails, as fail it one day must, there will be a . . . rapidly increasing degeneration of things, an undoing by regressive combinations. . . . This disintegrating process may be expected to take place first in the highest products of evolution. . . . The inevitable end of all that is done under the sun when the sun itself is exhausted is a world undone—a world, that is, become inorganic in the reverse way of that by which it became organic."[20] The explanation for mental pathology is finally not biological or psychological or even social, but cosmic.

What Maudsley's argument reflects is the growing currency of the second law of thermodynamics, or the law of entropy. Formulated by

Sadi Carnot (1796–1832) in 1824, elaborated upon by Helmholtz, R. Clausius (1822–1888), William Thomson, and Clerk Maxwell, the second law states that it is impossible for heat to pass from a colder to a warmer body unless some other change accompanies the process. In a closed system (one which exchanges no energy or matter with its surroundings) all forms of energy can be converted into one another but heat can never be converted entirely into any other form of energy. The result is a constant dissipation of energy into thermal energy at the expense of other forms. Ultimately this leads to what was called heat-death, a condition of maximum entropy in which all other expressions of energy as well as the structures which they created have "degenerated" into heat. What this meant to many physical scientists was that the solar system, inasmuch as it is a closed system, must inevitably run down with the consequence that the earth would become unfit for the habitation of man.[21] The theme is taken up by Spencer at the close of the *First Principles* (1862) and thus introduced into the mainstream of British philosophical discussion.

The tacit assumption that the sun can continue to give off an undiminished amount of light and heat through all future time is now abandoned. Involving as it does, under a disguise, the conception of power produced out of nothing, it is of the same order as the belief which misleads perpetual motion schemers. The spreading recognition of the truth that whatever force is manifested under one shape must previously have existed under another shape, implies recognition of the truth that the force known to us in solar radiation is the changed form of some other force, of which the Sun is the seat; and that, by the emission of these radiations, this other force is being slowly exhausted.

And from this point he proceeds to the unnerving question underlying his entire "synthetic philosophy." Does the doctrine of evolution imply, finally, a "Universal Death," which must inevitably come and "will continue indefinitely"?[22]

Spencer's way of formulating the question nicely brings out the price the positivist pays for reducing the energy we call consciousness to a physical basis, for seeing it, that is, as a transformation, through long aeons of evolution, of energy that has originated in the sun. In such a beginning of mind lies its end, an inevitable return to mere thermal energy and radical disorder. Those mid-Victorians who were aware of the logic imposed on the physicalist or evolutionist account of mind by the second law of thermodynamics tended either to ignore it (e.g., Lewes, Tyndall, and George Eliot); or to place it at so distant a point of futurity as to be, practically, ignorable (e.g., Sully, or

Spencer himself, who, in the end, answers his question by reference to a "period unimaginably remote" when there will be a mysterious "general renewal")[23]; or to exit the "closed system" of the "visible" universe altogether in search of the "unseen" universe, where God resides endlessly generating energy (e.g., Thomson, Tait, and Stewart; see above, p. 133).

What Maudsley's book represents is not simply an application of the second law to psychology, and, beyond this, to the situation of the human race in general, but also a relatively early example of complete acceptance of the philosophical implications of the second law without resort to the various defenses, scientific or metaphysical, customarily marshaled to contravene those implications. In effect, he brings the second law out from under the glare of the first and in the process reverses the optimistic bias that had characterized and continued to characterize physical and evolutionary theories in the second half of the century. In this he looks forward to Albert Einstein and the New Physics of the early twentieth century (as well as to such quasi-scientific efforts to connect the second law of thermodynamics with cultural decline as we find in the Adams brothers, Max Nordau, and Oswald Spengler).[24] As the Cambridge physicist A. S. Eddington put it in 1927, "We have to appeal to the outstanding law—the second law of thermodynamics—to put some sense into the world. . . . The law that entropy always increases . . . holds, I think, the supreme position among the laws of Nature. . . . [I]f your theory is found to be against the second law of thermodynamics, I can give you no hope. . . ."[25]

Whether the physicists' second law can "put some sense" into the world of biology is one of the most vexed questions of modern evolutionary theory. Obviously, the exhaustion of the sun's energy ultimately threatens the continuation of life on earth, but the direct connection made by Maudsley and others between the second law and what they took to be the rapid degeneration of life, particularly, human mental life, was a leap of imagination rather than a product of scientific logic. The biosphere is not a closed system, and there is ample energy available from outside to continue to propel the evolutionary process for aeons to come. In other words, it is hard to imagine how with the physicists' model of thermodynamics one could account for *fin-de-siècle* degeneration. From this standpoint, the Spencerian mode of postponing the effects of heat-death into the far distant future is much more plausible than Maudsley's rather melodramatic move from psychological effects to cosmic causes. Yet, Maudsley's position in the 1880s, unscientific though it may be, does look forward to the way the problem expresses itself in our own time, as a problem, that is, of finding in the biosphere itself an expression of the entropic principle, different in its mechanism from what one finds in cosmic entropy, but describing the same process of degeneration.

The key to the connection lies in the theory of information and the understanding of the gene as a storehouse of information which cannot be modified by the injection of energy from without, that is, arguably, a closed system and therefore subject to ever increasing entropy. For the late Jacques Monod, a prominent theorist of biological entropy, "there exists no conceivable mechanism whereby any instruction or piece of information [can] be transferred to DNA." Consequently, "the entire [biological] system is totally, intensely conservative, locked into itself, utterly impervious to any 'hints' from the outside world. . . . [This system] obviously defies any 'dialectical' description. It is not Hegelian at all, but thoroughly Cartesian: the cell is indeed a *machine*." Being a machine, it does not, then, contradict but conforms to the second law. "Evolution in the biosphere is . . . a necessarily irreversible process defining *a direction in time*; a direction which is the *same* as that enjoined by the law of increasing entropy. . . ."[26] If this is true, then we are not dealing with a comfortably indefinite period of waiting for the universe to use up the energy that fuels the biological system and the evolving world of human culture. We are talking, rather, of a particular closed system which appears not to be indefinitely evolving but to be running down quite independently of the solar system at large and with a far shorter "life-span."[27]

Monod has brought Maudsley and the entire strain of late nineteenth-century scientific pessimism up to date, and his conclusions may provide a fair summary of the movement of mind I have been outlining. The triumph of science

launched the evolution of culture on a one-way path; onto a track which nineteenth-century scientism saw leading infallibly upward to an empyrean noon hour for mankind, whereas what we see opening before us today is an abyss of darkness.

Modern societies . . . have not accepted—they have scarcely even heard—[science's] profounder message: the defining of a new and unique source of truth, and the demand for a thorough revision of ethical premises, for a total break with tradition. . . . Armed with all the powers, enjoying all the riches they owe to science, our societies are still trying to live by and to teach systems of values already blasted at the root by science itself.[28]

What I will be arguing for the remainder of this chapter is that in Thomas Hardy we find a Victorian who listened very closely indeed to the "profounder message" of science in its earliest whisperings. He made it, in an Arnoldian phrase (but in a far deeper sense than anything Arnold had in mind), his "criticism of life." The result was the most radical "revision of ethical premises" (to recur to Monod's language) to come out of the Victorian period. In chapter 10 we will turn to the distinctive philosophy of life and art to which these new scientific developments led him at the close of the century, a philosophy, I will argue, that effectively marks the end of the positivist enterprise, at least in its nineteenth-century form.

HARDY'S CRITICISM OF LIFE: THE NOVEL AND SCIENTIFIC PESSIMISM

The time is past, one hopes, when criticism can condescend to Hardy's thought in the manner T. S. Eliot did so much to encourage: "Hardy's art would have been better off with fewer ideas or none at all."[29] We understand, with Albert Guerard, that excessive concern for Hardy's philosophy of life obscures attention to his artistry;[30] or with Raymond Williams that such concern may cause us to overlook the rich social texture of his depictions of nineteenth-century country life.[31] Yet, at the same time, we are compelled, and perhaps by nothing so much as Hardy's own insistence, to recognize that he was always concerned "to spread over art the latest illumination of the time."[32] In this he simply followed a dominant precept of the Victorian aesthetic. As Stephen had said in words Hardy carefully recorded in his notebook, "A poet is great so far as he has set before us some impressive ideal of life. . . ."[33] Hardy, for all his notorious readiness to give way on almost any point to please the magazine readers, aspired to write on the level of the most philosophically conscious of novelists. He saw himself very much in the tradition of George Eliot and Meredith,[34] whereas of his contemporary Henry James he complained that James was too preoccupied with the "minutiae of manners" to be a great novelist.[35]

Let us, then, put aside for the moment the issue that is really at the heart of T. S. Eliot's and others' strictures on Hardy's ideas, the issue of whether they are an excrescence on his art, and take it as a given that Hardy did not think it worth writing without them. Let us consider these ideas, for the moment, as ideas only, with a focus on their relation to the specifically scientific concerns discussed in the previous sections. Having done this, we will be in a better position to judge, first, how "commonplace" they are (the epithet is Guerard's)[36] and, second, how they matter to his art.

It needs no ghost from the grave come back to tell us that Hardy's philosophy of life was the pessimistic one Sully had characterized in 1877 as a sign of the times. The fact of that philosophy, immediately apparent to the reader of the novels after 1878, was one of the two principal sources of the virulent criticism directed against him. The other was his closely related views on human love, to which we will give more attention in the next chapter.

Taking Hardy at a point late in his career when he had considerable opportunity to refine or outgrow his pessimism, we may consider the "Apology" to the 1922 volume of poems, *Late Lyrics and Earlier*. This is an essay he seems to have thought of as comparable to Wordsworth's *Preface* as a defense of unorthodox poetic practice.[37] It responds to a long line of attacks on his dark vision of life, but focuses on the recent criticism by his friend Frederic Harrison. Hardy finds a telling coincidence between the Positivist's unceremonious rejection of his pessimism and that of a Roman Catholic reviewer: ". . . when a Positivist and a Romanist agree there must be something wonderful in it, which should make a poet sit up."[38]

Hardy is considerably less absolute a pessimist in this essay than in earlier works, but his point is dismal enough. What the poet sits up to discover is that modern scientific optimism (à la Harrison) is at one with old unscientific religion in its faith in the value of human life. Hardy would like to believe in this alliance, to believe, as he puts it, in the "best consummation possible," which would be an "evolutionary meliorism." But this is a "forlorn hope," and the voices that most command his respect are those that disregard hope, the voices of "Schopenhauer, von Hartmann, and other philosophers down to Einstein."[39] Hardy cannot, after a lifetime of thinking about the problem of life, find among either optimists or meliorists an adequate rebuttal of pessimism. And although he is more conciliatory than usual towards his detractors in the "Apology," if we look back to an earlier, private response to essentially the same "forlorn hope," we will find him pretty definitive. After quoting from Sidney Alexander's 1893 rejection of philosophical pessimism—" 'In philosophy Schopenhauer has given place to Hegel—the hope of cosmic suicide to the thought of a spiritual society, the vision of that City of God to which the race of men is slowly climbing nearer. Pessimism has had its day' "—Hardy comments, "comforting but false."[40]

If one takes Hardy late in his career, as I have just done, it is easy to attribute his pessimistic outlook to Schopenhauer and von Hartmann, whom he began reading seriously in the early 1890s.[41] But neither Schopenhauer nor von Hartmann was a formative influence on Hardy, only further philosophical support for a position adopted quite independently of them. As he remarked to an early commentator, "My pages show harmony of view with Darwin, Huxley, Spencer, Comte, Hume, Mill, and others, all of whom I used to read more than Schopenhauer."[42] All these writers, of course, are preeminent figures in the development of the British scientific philosophy I have been tracing, and the point that Hardy wants to make is that he too is part of this tradition, that, for him, the road to pessimism was that paved by scientific thinkers. Granted that of the names listed only Darwin and Hume and the later Huxley contain the seeds of the pessimism he ultimately embraces, the point remains that what Hardy is describing is a way of thinking, an intellectual movement which, as we saw in the last section, and as he himself came to perceive, led, despite its initial promise, to despair over the human condition. "After infinite effort," he writes in his notebook in 1881, "trying to reconcile a scientific view of life with the emotional and spiritual . . . ," he had come to the conclusion that human emotions, morality, spirituality "have no place in a world of defect and it is a cruel injustice that they should have developed in it."[43] Darwin, first named on his list almost certainly because he was of first importance to Hardy, as we have seen, implicitly marked, if he did not explicitly approve, the reversal of the optimistic trend. It is "Darwinian theory" to which Hardy conspicuously alludes in the 1922 "Apology" as blocking modern literature's renewed romantic effort to evade the "truth" (the particular reference appears to be to Yeats's aesthetic mythologizing). Darwin's theory is the real, the properly scientific, basis of modern pessimism —and, as Hardy apparently believed, Einstein's theory of relativity, its latest confirmation.

Perhaps the best-known expression of what Hardy liked to call his "scientific realism" is his evocation of man's insignificance in the face of the cosmos. It is a theme we first see in distinctly scientific form in the passage in *A Pair of Blue Eyes* (1873) where Henry Knight hangs precariously on the face of a cliff overlooking the Channel. Knight, an exemplary modern thinker (he is modeled on Hardy's early mentor, Horace Moule, and has been further associated with Leslie Stephen),[44] finds himself in this predicament as the result of a "scientific experiment," and may be the first character in British fiction to mediate the thought of impending death with the contemplation, not of God or Country or his Beloved, but of the immensity of geological time. Beside the fossil record, which he sees a few inches before his face, his brief moment of consciousness is of little consequence: "He was to be with the small in his death."[45] From this perception follows a distinctly "unpoetic," or at least un-Wordsworthian, view of nature, which momentarily fills him with despair; nature is utterly oblivious of the welfare, not just of him as an individual, but of the entire race of man.

Knight survives, and Hardy makes little of this momentary (scientific) contemplation of the "Dark Valley and the unknown future beyond,"[46] but the experience will recur in one form and another throughout his fiction and poetry, becoming increasingly dominant and increasingly inescapable. Not just the characters but also the reader is made to feel it in the opening pages of *The Return of the Native* (1878), when Hardy directs our eye to the "Dark Valley" of Egdon Heath. In its primeval wildness with its ageless vegetation and geological structures, we are invited to see a "satire on human vanity." It is, in Hardy's metaphor, an "installment" of night come before "the final overthrow,"[47] a preview of the cosmic darkness that must finally engulf all human civilization. Or, again, in *Two on a Tower* (1882), where Hardy gives us his first scientist hero, the young astronomer St. Cleeve, we are invited to look at the "Dark Valley" of the heavens. There we find, says St. Cleeve, " 'Impersonal monsters, namely, Immensities' "; and he continues, " 'Until a person has sought out the stars and their interspaces, he has hardly learnt that there are things much more terrible than monsters of shape, namely, monsters of magnitude without known shape. Such monsters are the voids and waste places of the sky. . . .' " As Lady Constantine objects, the study of astronomy is not good for one: " 'It makes [one] feel human insignificance too plainly' "; it " 'annihilates' " one. The sense of human insignificance that accompanies the scientific recognition that "nothing is made for man" ultimately saps the will to live.[48] It is the most important emotion Hardy has to convey, and in virtually every novel it has its representative, the antithesis, as it were, to George Eliot's prophetic aspirer to a new totality: Manston in *Desperate Remedies* (1871), Knight in *A Pair of Blue Eyes*, Boldwood in *Far from the Madding Crowd* (1874), and so on, to Jude Fawley. Modern science, as Hardy sees it, returns human consciousness to a primitive anxiety over the unintelligibility of the universe, and with a vengeance. In experiencing this anxiety his isolated country characters are at one with his most sophisticated representatives of the modern spirit.

As we have seen, Darwinism, and in particular the doctrine of natural selection, meant the end of any teleological, let alone providential, interpretation of life. This was not something Darwin was comfortable expressing in his published work, but in private correspondence he risked more. "I cannot persuade myself," he wrote to Asa Gray in 1860, "that a beneficent and omnipotent God would have designedly created Ichneumonidae with the express intention of their feeding within the living bodies of caterpillars, or that a cat would play with mice."[49] Hardy had no difficulty absorbing this subtext of the *Origin*. Nowhere in his work is the notion that the world is under the dispensation of divine intention presented other than ironically. As soon as one of his characters praises the action of providence, we can be sure that he or she is about to suffer inexplicably. As Thomas Vargish has lately pointed out, the "providential aesthetic" that everywhere characterizes the structure of Victorian fiction, even the fiction of such a nonbeliever as George Eliot, ends with Hardy.[50]

But Hardy goes further. The overthrow of the providential view of life was not, as we have seen, the most devastating blow struck by Darwinism. The full implication of Darwin's theory is the problemization of all order. Again, Hans Jonas: "The evolutionary process presents itself as a sheer adventure with an unforeseeable course." Darwin himself could not accept this—even in private.[51] Hardy, however, is not afraid to take "a full look at Worst,"[52] which in this case means insisting on what Darwin suppresses. It is always chance or brute force that shapes human destiny in his imaginative world, never the human will and, certainly, never divinity.

> —Crass Casualty obstructs the sun and rain,
> And dicing Time for gladness casts a moan. . . .
> These purblind Doomsters had as readily strown
> Blisses about my pilgrimage as pain.
>
> ("Hap," lines 11–14)

There is no need to dwell upon this point. No feature of Hardy's world view has been more fully discussed in the criticism. Dramatically, it involves him in the repeated presentation of the irony of human expectations. With few exceptions, and these only in the very early works, nothing that anyone plans, or "schemes" (one of Hardy's favorite words for human intentionality), ever works out.

Of course, our sense of order finds itself continually mocked by the radical "schemelessness" of nature, for the very concept of order is a fortuitous product of our evolution, rooted not in any structure in things but in the gratuitous, purely random development of consciousness. "A woeful fact," Hardy writes in 1889,"—that the human race is too extremely developed for its corporeal condition. . . . It may be questioned if Nature, or what we call Nature, so far back as when she crossed the line from invertebrates to vertebrates, did not exceed her mission."[53] And the corollary of this is that the age-old injunction to conform to nature, the foundation of the scientific humanism we have earlier explored, is utterly wrongheaded.[54] Mill, and following him Huxley, had by the 1870s recognized the futility of finding in nature a sanction for man's moral views.[55] But Hardy had no such residual faith as Huxley's, for example, that "intelligence and will, guided by sound principles of investigation, and organised in a common effort, may modify the conditions of existence . . . [and even] the nature of man himself. . . ."[56] As we will see in detail later, for Hardy whatever shapes human consciousness projects are doomed to a constant debilitating conflict with the "corporeal" both in the world and, still more, in the self.

Hardy's refusal to allow human consciousness to transcend the scandal of its accidental origins was no doubt confirmed (and given sharper intellectual definition) by his exposure to August Weismann's work in genetics. He had read about Weismann as early as 1882[57] and was actually reading his *Essays on Heredity* by 1890.[58] His novelistic interest in the subject begins with *The Mayor of Casterbridge* (1886), subtitled "A Story of a Man of Character," which we may read as being about the *immutability* of character. It continues more prominently in *Tess of the d'Urbervilles* (1891), and is virtually an obsession in *Jude the Obscure* (1896) and *The Well-Beloved* (1897). Tess, Jude, Sue, and Jocelyn are all conspicuously fixed by heredity. As J. Hillis Miller has noted in the case of the last novel, the "ultimate grimness" of that novel owes much to Weismann's theory of the "immortality of the germ plasm."[59] We may note now for further development later that in both *Jude the Obscure* and *The Well-Beloved* Hardy's treatment of the fatality of heredity is inseparable from the question of incestuous love as he attempts to underline the radically unprogressive, self-repetitive nature of reproduction. In this he seems almost deliberately to controvert Huxley's persistent statement of the positivist faith that "much might be done to change the nature of man himself." Consider, for a prime example, says Huxley, "the suppression of the sexual instinct between near relations,"[60] which, indeed, Hardy does and finds this ground-rock evidence that culture can modify nature disconcertingly shaky.

Although degeneration is not a necessary consequence of Weismann's "hard inheritance," Hardy by the 1880s clearly conflates the two. Recognition of contemporary thought on heat-death is certainly implicit in his 1878 presentation of Egdon Heath with its allusion to that "final overthrow" when the entire earth will be as black, as sunless, as the heath. The heath simply absorbs the Promethean energy of all the novel's protagonists, above all, Eustacia, though it is the eponymous native Clym Yeobright who presents us, finally, with the characteristic fate of its inhabitants, the gradual "attenuation" of spiritual light.[61] The theme of energy loss, both solar and spiritual, is united with what we may more properly speak of as biological degeneration in *The Woodlanders*, where the persistent images of cold or dying light are interwoven with the degeneration of nature and this in turn with the deformation of modern society: "On older trees still than these huge lobes of fungi grew like lungs. Here as everywhere, the Unfulfilled Intention, which makes life what it is, was as obvious as it could be among the depraved crowds of a city slum. The leaf was deformed, the curve was crippled, the taper was interrupted; the lichen ate the vigour of the stalk, and the ivy slowly strangled to death the promising sapling."[62] Giles Winterbourne, the "pastoral king" of this consciously deformed pastoral novel, has descended directly from Gabriel Oaks and Diggory Venn, but unlike these earlier figures he does not marry the heroine at last, thus depriving us altogether of a comedic alternative to nature's slow decline. On the contrary, his intimacy with nature implicates him more completely than any of the novel's more sophisticated characters in the inevitability of degeneration.

The imaginative linking of cosmic, biological, and mental decay, which is so pronounced in *The Woodlanders* (1887), continues in *Tess of the d'Urbervilles* and *Jude the Obscure*. Hardy refers to Tess repeatedly as the descendant of an "exhausted line"[63] and ultimately sacrifices her on the altar of an exhausted solar worship. Tess, the antiquity of her genotype notwithstanding, remains to the end "pure," in Hardy's special sense of the term. The same cannot be said for Jude Fawley and Sue Bridehead, cousins whose genetic "flaw" (Jude's family name contains the word) makes them and their offspring as openly "degenerate" as any characters Hardy or, for that matter, the *enfant terrible* of French naturalism, Emile Zola,[64] ever created—which contemporary reviewers were quick to observe. This is the psychic counterpart of an atmospheric "obscurity" or sunlessness that dominates their world more completely than that of any other novel, including *The Return of the Native*.[65] In these last novels it is difficult not to see evidence of

Hardy's reading in and about Henry Maudsley's work, which had caught his imagination at least as early as the mid-1880s.[66]

Guerard, in his effort to distract our attention from Hardy's ideas, suggests that as a thinker he was rather less interesting than Comte or Bergson,[67] the point being, presumably, that Hardy's philosophy is not even up to the standards of second- or third-rate professionals. We have not yet come to what is most original about Hardy's interpretation of life—as against what he was borrowing more or less wholesale from contemporary science. But even from what we have seen, it is aparent that Guerard's choice of philosophers with which to associate Hardy is singularly inappropriate. Comte, as the founding father of the philosophical faith in the power of science to deliver us from intellectual and social anarchy, and Bergson, as a descendant (with William James) of later nineteenth-century science's preoccupation with the physical power of psychic energy, both believed in the capacity of science to define a new, forward-looking humanism. Hardy, we see, read the meaning of contemporary science quite differently. Much later in his career Comte and Bergson became for him, respectively, the high priest and belated epigone of a discredited faith.[68] So Guerard has chosen to illustrate Hardy's philosophical weakness with representatives of an intellectual tradition which, it may be fairly argued, it is precisely Hardy's philosophical strength to have challenged. No more than Comte does Hardy deny the power of scientific knowledge as the key to man's situation in the world. But he understands, as Comte (and Bergson) did not, that the knowledge science leads us to must fundamentally revise our understanding of what it means to be human—and this in the last quarter of the nineteenth century is, to recur to and revise Guerard's estimate, very interesting.

But Guerard's complaint, in the end, is less about the quality of Hardy's ideas than their tendency to get in the way of a proper appreciation of his artistic achievement. I will discuss the relation between Hardy's scientific pessimism and his artistry in detail in the next chapter. For the moment we may simply note that the science Hardy brought to art marked the definitive end of an aesthetic movement, the movement which, in seeking to reformulate the Promethean or humanistic aspirations of the romantic revolution in positive rather than metaphysical terms, issued in the triumph of "classical realism" (Lukács' term[69]) in the mid- and later nineteenth-century novel. To put the point paradigmatically, Hardy effectively reversed the effort to affirm a purely human providence which reaches its artistic apogee in England in the fiction of George Eliot. Hers is the thesis to which he is self-consciously writing the antithesis. By the time he came to *The Return of the Native*, he had lost whatever positivist faith he might once have held and begun to experiment with an alternative vision, or better, given Clym Yeobright's fate, with what one does and how one writes in the absence of vision. For George Eliot that visionless possibility could still be blocked by the "force of the imagination that pierces and exalts solid fact"[70] or, to recur to the splendid formulation of *Middlemarch*, the "inward light which is the last refinement of Energy capable of bathing even the ethereal atoms in ideally illuminated space."[71] Hardy's fiction is, finally, about that illuminated space as illusion and along with it the totalizing project of a "perfect interchange between science and art; offering the most direct alliance between intellectual conquest and the social good"[72] that underlies all George Eliot's work. For a genuine "scientific realism" there can be no attainment of oneness, only a confrontation with primal darkness and disorder. In Hardy's failed Promethean myths the "mythopoetic force of the Faustian soul," in Spengler's phrase, is at last "returning to its origins,"[73] and this could not help but have aesthetic consequences.

10

"The Best Consummation Possible": Psychical Entropy in Hardy and Freud

And now I think the meaning of the evolution of civilization is no longer obscure to us. It must present the struggle between Eros and Death . . . as it works itself out in the human species. This struggle is what all life essentially consists of. . . . And it is this battle of the giants that our nursemaids try to appease with their lullaby about Heaven.

—Freud

In the preface to *Two on a Tower* (1882), Hardy brings out a contrast that is characteristic of his work. Behind this "slightly built romance," he says, is a "wish to set the emotional history of two infinitesimal lives against the stupendous background of the stellar universe." The conclusion we are meant to draw is that, of "these contrasting magnitudes," the smaller, the love relationship between the protagonists, "might be the greater to [us] as men."[1]

Love, for Hardy, lies at the absolute center of human interest. Our infinitesimal lives may count for little beside the immensity of the universe, but insofar as they matter at all to us, it is by virtue of our preoccupation with love. This may at first glance seem unexceptional enough in a novelist. The novel, as Trollope says, is virtually synonymous with the love interest.[2] But what is distinctive about Hardy as novelist is not so much the inevitability of the love theme as its all-absorbing intensity. Not religion or morality or social order or art or anything else, but love is what keeps us going in the face of the obliterating background of the cosmos. This peculiarity of Hardy's fiction did not go unnoticed by his contemporaries. Reviewing Hardy's career up to and including *Two on a Tower*, the "sexologist" Havelock

Ellis (1859–1939) had this to say about his achievement: "Looking at [Hardy's works] as a whole, what one observes about them first is that they are all love-stories. There is something very fresh and delightful, turning from the writers with whom love is only interesting from the moral problems it involves . . . to find a writer . . . who has little to say about . . . morals . . . , and yet thinks love is the chief business of life, and can devote himself so frankly to the rendering of its devious ways."[3] We could do worse than keep Ellis' insight squarely before us in our modern approaches to Hardy, to recognize that in no other major Victorian novelist, with the possible exception of Emily Brontë, is the relation between the sexes so consuming. Hardy, as D. H. Lawrence well knew, was his proper artistic progenitor.

What we now consider is the issue of how Hardy's determination, not to evade the most disconcerting implications of contemporary scientific realism, bears upon this preoccupation with the "devious ways" of love. It is a theme we have touched upon as early as our discussion of Comte's notion of sexual instinct as the basis of social cohesion and Mill's quite different misgiving that (scientific) analysis of human motivation might reduce our behavior to merely sensual causes. And we have come back to it in one way and another with all our principal figures. Now with Hardy it must become the center of our concern. As with earlier Victorian positivists we have found, either by influence or coincidence of thought, reflections of more famous (but not necessarily more accomplished) Continental thinkers—Goethe, Comte, Helmholtz, Wundt, Taine, Durkheim—so with Hardy we will find a formidable German analogue. In his prolonged, artist's effort to unravel the true meaning of science for human love, he resembles no one so much as Sigmund Freud, who, like Hardy's own Jude, we may perhaps regard as the prophet of a lost cause, the discoverer of an insurmountable "division" at the heart of the scientific philosophy and its program for regenerating society.

EROS AND PHILOSOPHY

Ellis' distinction between Hardy's interest in love itself as opposed to "moral problems" may strike us as odd, since it is apparent that Hardy does not consider love relationships independently of the moral problems they raise. But Ellis' point is more intelligible if we consider the context of nineteenth-century fiction. The intrinsic attractions of love stories aside, love issuing in marriage performed a crucial thematic function. It signified the essential health of society. To the novelist, like Scott or Dickens or Trollope, who still believed in the Christian God, love was indeed a divine law, and the final marriage of the ideal couple, a symbol of God's providence, the pervasive reality of human misery and wickedness notwithstanding. For those novelists, such as George Eliot or Meredith, who were prepared to do without God, love was not the dispensation of any otherworldly overseer but a psychological reality, an ineffaceable ingredient of our "common nature," from which, as we have seen, the scientific philosopher could work up, in the manner of Comte, Lewes, Stephen, and others, to the ideal of social unity and social good. In this context, we understand better that what Ellis admires in Hardy and identifies as a revolutionary gesture is Hardy's willingness to portray human love without making any clear connection between his characters' love for one another and the moral health of society.

Hardy only gradually articulated the full extent of the problem of love as he saw it, partly, of course, because of social prohibitions, but also because he himself needed to break free of the very powerful assumptions about love and social morality I have alluded to. Like George Eliot he never believed that the "divine tenderness" he speaks of in the preface to *Two on a Tower* was divine in any but a figurative sense; but unlike George Eliot, he obviously had doubts as well about its tenderness, or, at least, was more prepared to explore these doubts openly. He closes *Far from the Madding Crowd* by placing his lovers as George Eliot had placed Adam and Dinah, on a hill overlooking the recovered Eden, and trying very hard, though with considerably less conviction that his predecessor, to affirm the transcendent value of "substantial affection," as opposed to merely temporary "passion." This is such a love, he wants to say, as comes only after painful experience and, interestingly enough, a frank and equal sharing of *labor* between the sexes. This is such a love as "many waters cannot quench, nor the floods drown, beside which the passion usually called by the name is evanescent as steam."[4] It is such a love, in short, that defies death and consequently, to return to George Eliot's great point, is "hardly distinguishable from religious feeling." In later novels, indeed, in *Far from the Madding Crowd* itself, "passion" is never for Hardy as "evanescent as steam." Far more than George Eliot, even in her most forthright recognitions of the "mixed" nature of love, he needs to express the demonic, the profoundly disruptive, force of human sexuality. Arthur's offstage seduction of Hetty or Maggie's barely suppressed desire for the engaged Stephen, are, after all, pretty tame beside Boldwood's suicide upon being deprived of Bathsheba or Eustacia Vye's insistent call to Wildeve. What happens in Hardy is that the "evanescent" passion that courts rather than transcends death becomes less and less qualified or controlled by the dream of "substantial affection."[5] *Caritas*, altruism, all but evaporates in the face of a too substantial eros.

Two on a Tower, the first Hardy novel to excite widespread moral indignation, is something of a halfway house. Hardy can still technically, if disingenuously, affirm of it that "there is hardly a single caress in the book outside legal matrimony, or what was intended to be."[6] But by the time he comes to *The Woodlanders* (1887) he is openly condemning marriage as an institution and, still more subversively, treating the whole notion of altruistic love with its "indifference to the attribute of sex" as the illusion of "an abstract humanism."[7] Hardy's fully developed treatment of love in the last three novels will be the subject of further discussion below. Enough has been said at this point to indicate, if such indication is necessary at this advanced date in Hardy studies, that his novelistic treatment of love has one persistent tendency and that is towards the conclusion that love, sublimate it as we may, comes down, at last, to sexual desire.

Those familiar with Hardy's life can easily enough locate the sources of this understanding of love in his own experience of loving as he saw it among country people and encountered it in his own complicated relations with women. The confidence to write about it, the conviction that it had become an intellectual necessity to write about it, these almost certainly came to him from his reading. Schopenhauer is an obvious influence, for by at least the early 1880s and certainly by the time of *Tess of the d'Urbervilles* (1891), Hardy would have understood that one of Schopenhauer's distinctions as a thinker was the treatment of human sexuality as a philosophically serious subject.[8] "[N]o one," writes the German, "can doubt either the reality or the importance of [human sexuality]; . . . one ought . . . to be surprised that a thing which plays . . . so important a part in human life has hitherto practically been disregarded by philosophers altogether. . . ." And what a philosophy of love must begin with is one simple proposition: ". . . all love, however ethereally it may bear itself, is rooted in the sexual impulse alone, nay, it absolutely is only a more definitely determined, specialized and indeed in the strictest sense individualised sexual impulse."[9] But Hardy hardly needed to go to Schopenhauer for this insight. There was another source nearer to hand with which he was intimately familiar, the source that heads up his famous list of British influences who mattered more to him than any Germans.

In *The Descent of Man,* parts 2 and 3 of which are on "sexual selection," Hardy might well have had his earliest exposure to Schopenhauer's point. As Darwin subsequently observes, his own extensive discussion of the sexual instinct in the *Descent* is closely related to the philosopher's assertion that sexuality "is really of more importance than all other ends of human life."[10] What Hardy would have taken away from Darwin's book—published in the same year he published his first novel—is not simply an extensive demonstration that human love rests, finally, on the same instinctual drives as the coupling of all other species, but perhaps even the persistent pattern of his fiction from *Desperate Remedies* on, two or more men competing for the sexual attentions of one woman. Sexual selection by Darwin's account, we have seen in the discussion of Meredith, requires "a struggle between the males for the possession of the female,"[11] and on this struggle, more than on the natural selection of the *Origin,* will depend the future of the human species.

Freud, of course, would also draw heavily on Darwin (as well as Schopenhauer) to develop his own theory of love. Using the same critical sources, Hardy in the last novels anticipates Freud in administering what the latter has called the third great scientific blow to human pride. First came the Copernican revolution that marked the advent of man's alienation from the center of the cosmos, then the Darwinian revolution that reduced man's mind to a biological accident, and, finally, the one that bears Freud's own name, which undermined the rational basis of all man's cultural structures, that great "fabric of good," as George Eliot had called it.[12]

TESS OF THE D'URBERVILLES: A POSITIVIST ALLEGORY MANQUÉ

As we consider, says Freud, how unsuccessful all our advances in civilization have been in preventing suffering, a suspicion gradually dawns upon us that "what we call our civilization is largely responsible for our misery, and that we should be much happier if we gave it up and returned to primitive conditions."[13] Precisely this suspicion had evidently dawned on Hardy early on in his career, for reviewing his work from *Desperate Remedies* onward, we find no more persistent theme than man's discontent with civilization, a discontent, he tells us plainly enough, that requires "desperate remedies," although, as we will see, it finally becomes a question with him of whether any remedy is possible.

Tess of the d'Urbervilles is the climactic retelling of a story Hardy had told many times before, the perennial Victorian tragedy of the "fallen woman," or in the country phrase he probably preferred, the "ruined maid." What the story usually involves, in Hardy's telling, is a woman whose sexual desires have led her to pre- or extramarital sexual or quasi-sexual experience, which she must keep secret on pain of rejection by her present lover/husband and the society in which she lives. Exposure of the secret, which, metaphorically, is simply the secret of suppressed sexuality, results either in immediate catastrophe, as in the case of Eustacia Vye or Lucetta Templeman, or in a lingering decline towards alienation and death, as we see most notably with Tess. These women are usually unable or unwilling to articulate their inner agony. Either they lack sufficient self-knowledge or they (not to mention their creator) fear the social repercussions of a frank expression of their feelings. An exception is Felice Charmond, the fallen woman of the novel immediately preceding *Tess of the d'Urbervilles*, who has the education as well as the independence of mind to say what she means. More to the point, Hardy, now (1887) secure as a major novelist, is himself feeling independent enough to move into more explicit statements of what he thinks lies at the heart of human tragedy. "Women," says Felice when she confronts the shallowness of Fitzpiers' masculine "passions," "are always carried about like corks upon the water of masculine desires. . . . I hope I have not alarmed you; but Hintock has the curious effect of bottling up the emotions till one can no longer hold them; I am often obliged to fly away and discharge my sentiments somewhere, or I should die outright"; again and still more desperately, "O! why were we given hungry hearts and wild desires if we have to live in a world like this? Why should Death alone lend what Life is compelled to borrow—rest? . . . The terrible insistencies of society—how severe they are, and cold, and inexorable. . . . O, I am afraid of them. . . ."[14] Of course, masculine desires are also deep-seated and socially repressed—one thinks immediately of Boldwood or Henchard or Jude—but women are, for Hardy, the real test case. As we have seen, contemporary society seemed to many Victorians to stand or fall on maternal tenderness abstracted from sexual desire, on belief in a special female purity, and we recall that even so independent a woman as George Eliot was unable to disentangle herself from this powerful ideology.

In *Tess of the d'Urbervilles* Hardy returns to the predicament of Felice Charmond and makes it the focus of his story. For the first time in his fiction there are no male competitors to distract our attention from the female's suffering. The issue he places defiantly before the reader on the very title page (and elaborates in the preface) is whether a woman can fall and still in some higher sense remain "pure," which, more broadly, is really the issue of whether desire can ever free itself from the "terrible insistencies of society" to regain a paradise of life rather than death. The biblical metaphor, of course, is very much to the point. *Tess of the d'Urbervilles* shares with *The Return of the Native* and *The Mayor of Casterbridge* an ambition to rewrite in novelistic form one of the great myths of Western civilization. The foundations of the two earlier stories are classical, from Aeschylus' *Prometheus Bound* and Sophocles' *Oedipus Rex*, and the Greeks have left their mark on Tess's story as well. Torn between public opinion and private feeling she is Hardy's Antigone. But here, as with George Eliot's *The Mill on the Floss*, the myth Hardy seeks most to recast is that of the Fall. Like George Eliot or, for that matter, his beloved Shelley, Hardy wants to tell again why Eve fell and, as with these predecessors, the telling of why leads to the vexed question of whether what has been lost can be regained.

There are "two forces . . . at work here as everywhere," Hardy says of Tess's effort to survive after Angel's desertion of her, "the inherent will to enjoy, and the circumstantial will against enjoyment."[15] This is the essential antithesis on which this novel, like all Hardy's fiction, is structured. What distinguishes *Tess of the d'Urbervilles* is that the precise nature of the opposing forces is so much more definitively drawn and their opposition so much more carefully balanced than in his earlier fiction. The inherent will to enjoy is quite simply the desire for pleasure that culminates in the sexual act. The circumstantial will against enjoyment is the code of morality of any given society. These appear to be Hardy's equivalent of God and Satan in this retelling of Eve's story, although, as we will see, the opposition is not as conceptually neat as such a Blakean formula suggests.

Taking the second term first, we find that Hardy's treatment of the social forms or codes that entrap man is both more inclusive and psychologically more sophisticated in *Tess of the d'Urbervilles* than in the earlier fiction. An intricate matrix of cultural structures and differences conditions the behavior of the characters. There is no single community like Casterbridge or Hintock that supplies the norm, but a multiplicity of communities, each, as Hardy suggests, with its separate "code" of conduct[16] in and out of which the heroine moves, receiving from each its special restraining or distorting "trace":[17] the peasant "fetishes" imbibed at her mother's knee; the "standard knowledge" and second language learned at the national school;[18] religious beliefs learned from her parish priest; class and sexual roles learned from both Alec and Angel; the discipline of the new technological age learned from the relentless rhythm of the threshing machine; and, ultimately, "justice" learned from the state and its executioner. As Raymond Williams has observed, Hardy takes second place to no Victorian novelist in his grasp of the complexity of contemporary society, and in no Hardy novel is that complexity more impressively orchestrated than in *Tess of the d'Urbervilles*.[19] By the 1890s Hardy has not only intellectually absorbed but also imaginatively captured his friend and mentor Leslie Stephen's point about the all-pervasive influence of the "social tissue." What, of course, he lacks is Stephen's faith in the healthiness of that tissue.

No less interesting is Hardy's new preoccupation with *how* the social matrix becomes part of the individual's psychological structure. He can speak in terms that may well remind us of the cultural Lamarckianism we have seen in Lewes and in Stephen, of the social code as if it becomes somehow physically inscribed upon the mind. The famous passage following the seduction (or rape) of Tess provides a striking example. The sexual penetration of Tess is of little consequence beside the social "traces" the act inscribes on the "tissue" of her mind. The pattern of that mind, once fine as gossamer, now becomes "coarse." She must henceforth think of herself and view all her relations with the world as if she were impure and thus forever alienated from the possibility of experiencing true love: "An immeasurable social chasm was to divide our heroine's personality thereafter from that previous self of hers. . . ."[20] J. Hillis Miller has splendidly explicated this passage with the deconstructivist end in view of showing that whatever social pattern is inscribed on Tess here or anywhere in the narrative is without origin—a point to which we will need to return.[21]

At the moment what we need to note is that Hardy presents the effects of social structure on the individual as alterations in the individual's *perception* of the world rather than in some underlying or substantial self or character. So at the beginning of the next "phase" of the story, Tess returning home as fallen woman perceives her native vale differently from the way she perceived it as a "maiden" (the title of the story's first phase). The "familiar green world," once beautiful to her, is now "terribly beautiful . . . , for since her eyes last fell upon it she had learnt that the serpent hisses where the sweet birds sing, and her views of life had been totally changed for her by the lesson."[22] A few pages later and still more explicitly:

> . . . her whimsical fancy would intensify natural processes around her till they seemed a part of her own story. Rather they became part of it; for the world is only a psychological phenomenon, and what they seemed they were. . . .
> But this encompassment of her own characterization, based on shreds of convention, peopled by phantoms and voices antipathetic to her, was a sorry and mistaken creation of Tess's fancy—a cloud of moral hobgoblins. . . . It was they that were out of harmony with the actual world, not she.[23]

Or we may go further forward in the story to what amounts to Tess's second fall from grace when Angel discovers on their wedding night that she is not a virgin. Here the perceptual shift is in him and is no less a product of the "moral hobgoblins" society has imprinted on his consciousness: ". . . the complexion even of external things seemed to suffer transmutation as her announcement progressed. . . . And yet nothing had changed since the moments when he had been kissing her; or rather nothing in the substance of things."[24] What has happened is that Angel's Shelleyan image of Tess as the ideal counterpart[25] has simply dissolved and with it an entire moral order, essentially, if godlessly, Christian, in which eros must always be subordinated to agape: ". . . reillumination as to the terrible and total change that her confession had wrought in his life, in his universe, returned to him. . . . This was what their *Agape* had come to."[26]

Both characters, in short, suffer rather literally from what we may call moral vision. Socially generated patterns of belief or ideologies unconsciously condition the way one *perceives* the world, so that the world is always in some degree a structure not simply of one's senses but also of society's beliefs. So often does Hardy make this point in *Tess of the d'Urbervilles* that it is evident he means us to notice it. "Daze my eyes," exclaims John Durbeyfield in response to the revelation that he is a fallen aristocrat,[27] and, of course, this is precisely what the information, the new, unexpected social "trace" on his consciousness does, and thus begins the tragedy. Everyone's eyes in this story are in some way socially dazed so that nothing is seen as it is but always through an "ideal photosphere."[28] What has led Hardy to this preoccupation with perception "is partly his delighted discovery in 1886 that Impressionism is even more suggestive in the direction of literature than in that of art . . . ," from which standpoint the novel's pervasive "photospheric" effects are perhaps an effort to extend a painterly technique to literature[29] (Roman Polanski's film of the novel attempts to transmute these effects back to visual imagery). But more important, I suspect, was Hardy's reading in contemporary epistemology and psychology as he prepared for the writing of *Tess of the d'Urbervilles*, notably, in T. H. Green's *Introductions to Hume's "Treatise on Human Nature"* (1874), Mill's *An Examination of Sir William Hamilton's Philosophy* (1865), Spencer's *Principles of Psychology* (1855), W. K. Clifford's "On the Nature of Things in Themselves" (1878), and George Romanes' "The World as Eject" (1886).[30] Whether Hardy was turning to these works for the first time or, as is more likely, returning to them to refresh his memory on particular points, he seems to have wanted theoretical background on the issue with which they are all most concerned, the "relativity of knowledge," the issue, as we have seen, of the extent to which our subjective consciousness determines the form of external things. More particularly, he would have found in Clifford's essay (and Romanes' critique of it) what we have already noticed in George Eliot, that we interpret the world through images relative to, that is, conditioned by, our social context.[31]

But where Hardy derived his notion of the social perception of reality is of less moment than the point that his philosophical reading of the period immediately preceding the writing of *Tess of the d'Urbervilles* shows him focusing on that most fundamental issue of the difference between what the mind perceives and what is actually there. This in turn may help us understand that what Hardy is doing in the novel is recasting this important midcentury debate in his own distinctive terms. The scientific solution to the problem, as we have seen, is to work out a methodology by which one can ensure that one's mental forms will eventually coincide with the forms of nature. This desired solution Hardy, in fact, copies from the *Encyclopaedia Britannica*: ". . . science reaches its true form only when the order of thought is made one with the order of nature."[32] What must strike us, finally, about *Tess of the d'Urbervilles* is that Hardy has clearly come to believe there is no relationship between the "order of thought" and the "order of nature." The former is a self-generating social phenomenon, which, far from corresponding at any point to nature, distorts it to fit its own (to return to Darwinism) merely random structures.

Turning now to that other term of Hardy's central thematic opposition, the "will to enjoy," we note another philosopher Hardy was beginning to take seriously before and during the writing of *Tess of the d'Urbervilles*. Although Hardy appears not to have read seriously in Schopenhauer until 1891, he was reading about him in Sully and elsewhere at the same time he was studying the epistemological issues we have just been considering.[33] He would have known from these readings what little use Schopenhauer had for the Kantian exaltation of the forms of thought and what he proposed to substitute for them as his own ultimate reality. How this might have contributed to *Tess of the d'Urbervilles* is clear enough from the passage he cites from an 1886 exposition of Schopenhauer in a French periodical: "Si nous regardons du dehors, ce ne sont pas nos *perceptions* changeant[e]s, nos *pensées* contradictoires, nos *conceptions* abstraites ou vides; ce sont nos *affections*, ce sont nos désirs, ce sont nos *passions* qui seules constituent notre moi. . . ."[34] While this passage would have told Hardy nothing he did not already believe about human nature, the authority of the great philosopher that lies behind it might well have encouraged him to present sexual passion in *Tess of the d'Urbervilles* as the force which alone gives us joy or hope of paradise on earth.

Every earlier novel has its moments when the "appetite for joy which pervades all creation"[35] seems at last on the verge of freeing itself from conventional restraints and taking over the lives of the characters. These are among the most powerful scenes in Hardy's fiction. They accompany the touch or the kiss out of wedlock in the drama of individual love and, in the community, the ritual or seasonal dance. In the latter, the individual loses himself or herself in a Dionysian ecstasy and is delivered to the freedom of the body.

The enchantment of the dance surprised [Eustacia]. A clear line of difference divided like a tangible fence her experience within this maze of motion from her experience without it. . . . Whether [Wildeve's] personality supplied the greater part of this sweetly compounded feeling, or whether the dance and the scene weighed the more therein, was a nice point upon which Eustacia herself was entirely in a cloud. . . . The dance had come like an irresistible attack upon whatever sense of social order there was in their minds, to drive them back into the old paths. . . .[36]

Because it transcends the individual conscience and because of its embodiment of the universal desire for sexual freedom, the dance, for Hardy, as for Nietzsche,[37] symbolizes what one may call a *religious* possibility, where religion means the experience of a universal human bond. In Hardy the country dance becomes a metaphor for the only totality we can hope for. It is his version of George Eliot's Hebrew hymn of the divine unity (see above, p. 155). But at the same time, Hardy's prophecy reverses George Eliot's (of *Daniel Deronda*). Not man's refined energy of imaginative, that is, aesthetic, ordering, but the unrefined energy that underlies and drives it is what Hardy celebrates in *Tess of the d'Urbervilles*. The symbol-making power that George Eliot comes at last to see as man's highest accomplishment, his road to the New Jerusalem, Hardy treats as a socially generated form of repression.

In *Tess of the d'Urbervilles*, Hardy approaches nearer than anywhere else the promised end of sexual transcendence, which is probably why it tends for modern readers to be the most admired of his novels. In Tess's "pilgrimage," Irving Howe has acutely observed, "is Hardy's greatest tribute to the possibilities of human existence." But then Howe mars the point by adding, ". . . for Tess is one of the greatest triumphs of civilization."[38] It is precisely because the novel displays so richly before us the "invincible instinct"[39] for life *in spite of* civilization that it seems the one point in all Hardy's fiction where he is on the very verge of finding an alternative to human defeat. Nature, which in the immediately preceding novel (*The Woodlanders*) is, like the novel's gardener, Giles Winterbourne, sickening (degenerating) unto death, now bursts forth with a beauty and a profusion beyond anything found in Hardy since *Far from the Madding Crowd* and with a new insistence, absent in that earlier novel, on the utterly promiscuous procreative energy that drives it: "Amid the oozing fatness and warm ferments of the Froom Vale, at a season when the rush of juices could almost be heard below the hiss of fertilization, it was impossible that the most fanciful love should not grow passionate. The ready bosoms existing there were impregnated by their surroundings."[40] This is the Hardy that Gillian Beer has associated with the " 'affirmation of the free play of the word,' " the "writerly" Hardy, whom she seeks to rescue from the "crushing" drive of his plots.[41]

The plot does ultimately strangle this force of life, requiring, as it does, the death of the life force's principal human embodiment, Tess, but not before we have seen a full realization of what life might be like without the constraints of the social rubric. We see enough, in short, to suggest that "metaphysical comfort" Nietzsche finds at the heart of tragedy, the recognition "that life is at the bottom of things, despite all the changes of appearance, indestructibly powerful and pleasurable."[42] Tess, having missed her dance with Angel at the outset of the novel, recovers him in Edenic Talbothays, where she experiences what Hardy deliberately sets up as a revelation, a vision into the sexual sublime. In the company of the "suitable partner," taken up by the "rhythmic pulsation" of life and surrounded by the "hiss" of its fertility, she moves spontaneously into the dance, forgetting the "lack of everything to justify its existence in the eye of civilization." Angel advances to embrace her and she yields "to his embrace with unreflecting inevitableness" and sinks "upon him in her momentary joy, with something very like an ecstatic cry." For the Victorian reader no less than for Hardy's lovers, "a veil [has] been whisked aside."[43]

But, of course, this is not the end. Angel will desert Tess upon learning of her "impurity," susceptible as he is to the "appalling" power of sublimation.[44] He returns too late to save her from going back to Alec but effectively precipitates the crime that leads to her execution. She becomes a sacrificial victim, as Hardy symbolically suggests in the Stonehenge scene, to social structures that go back to the very origins of man's religious impulse, his desire for a cultural totality that will insulate him from the chaos of physical nature not only without but also within him. Why must the story end this way? Why could not Angel return in time? Why could not Tess have left Alec? Or failing all else, why after her sacrifice could not Hardy have left us with some sense of tragic renewal, some sense of the inevitable resurgence of that "recuperative power"[45] of nature of which he had made so much throughout the novel? Why, instead, are we left with a parodic echo of Milton, an image of Angel going hand-in-hand from the lost paradise, with a pale shadow of Tess, the conventionally pure Liza Lu, as if nothing had been gained, after all, from such suffering?

These are questions that go directly to the heart of the problem we have with all of Hardy and perhaps especially with this novel. Lawrence, who saw more of himself in Hardy than in any other predecessor, defines the problem thus: "Nothing in his work is so pitiable as his clumsy efforts to push events into line with his theory of being, and to make calamity fall on those who represent the principle of Love. He does it exceedingly badly, and owing to his effort his form is execrable in the extreme."[46] Lawrence is saying that Hardy's answer to our question of why is simply a doctrinaire pessimism: in our "blighted world"[47] these things are bound to happen; or in Hardy's own well-known words, "In the ill-judged execution of the well-judged plan of things the call seldom produces the comer, the man to love rarely coincides with the hour for loving. . . . [S]uch completeness is not to be prophesied, or even conceived as possible."[48] Lawrence is right. This is "clumsy." Yet ruminations on inevitable doom repeatedly interrupt the story, culminating in that most notorious clumsiness, the arrival of the "President of the Immortals, in Aeschylean phrase"[49] to finish Tess off.

The reason for the gloom, as Lawrence suggests, is intellectual. Specifically, it is the expression of that reading and thinking on the consequences of modern science that I have outlined in the last chapter. But the question is not now about the philosophical provenance of Hardy's gloom but about the relation of intellectual or philosophical conceptions to his art. There appears to Lawrence, to Guerard (see above, p. 232), and to Beer a fundamental incongruity between Hardy's engagement with contemporary ideas and his engagement with life itself, especially life as found in the "fetishistic" (Comte's term[50]) or primitive form he sought to capture. That incongruity strikes us perhaps more in *Tess of the d'Urbervilles* than anywhere else, and we need to explore its causes.

"The best tragedy," writes Hardy upon completing *Tess of the d'Urbervilles*, "is that of the WORTHY encompassed by the INEVITABLE." This is unexceptional enough. It becomes problematic only when we ask what constitutes the inevitable, as we can see more clearly in a later attempt at definition. "Tragedy may be created by an opposing environment either of things inherent in the universe, or of human institutions. If the former be the means exhibited and deplored, the writer is regarded as impious; if the latter, as subversive and dangerous. . . ."[51] The ambivalence we see here is crucial, and we have, of course, seen it before in a slightly different form in George Eliot. In tragedy the worthy is defeated by the inevitable, but is that inevitable cosmic, that is, is it built into the nature of things, or is it social, the product of conventions that alienate us from our natural or healthy selves?

What *Tess of the d'Urbervilles* portrays as worthy is the life/love energy, the "inherent will to enjoy." What is "inevitable" is the "circumstantial will against enjoyment," which I earlier defined, following Hardy's own lead, as constraining social structures. Now, insofar as these structures are manmade, one assumes they can be man unmade, initially by such critical realism as Hardy is directing against them, ultimately by political action. Definitions of purity can be changed, marriage laws can be repealed, and so on. In this understanding, man's tragic condition is remediable. Beyond the particular, painful historico-political situation is a future in which there need no longer be victims. That Hardy wants to write this kind of tragedy—"social tragedy," Raymond Williams has called it[52]—is nowhere more evident than in his preoccupation with the specifically epistemological dimension of social structure. Neither biological nor transcendent, but ideological, the structures through which we read life are eminently susceptible of reform. Angel's is a case in point. He is a conspicuously modern thinker, a man notable for his open-mindedness, his willingness to learn new ideas and discard old ones. Although it takes him too long, he does learn the new idea it is most important for him to learn: female purity is not a matter simply of physical intactness. With him there is, surely, a revolutionary change of moral perspective, and he is, at the novel's close, as liberated as his creator. Angel, then, is the hero of liberalism, the character who, by example and precept, offers the possibility of progress. He is the prophetic hero for whom ideas/symbols are the key to changing the world and transcending the tragic, a proper descendant of Daniel Deronda.

Whether, then, we approach the novel from the direction of Tess, which is to say from Hardy's fullest embodiment of natural energy, or, of Angel, Hardy's fullest embodiment of cultural progressivism, the result is the same: the story shows us Hardy working harder than in any novel since the pastoral *Far from the Madding Crowd* to create an image of hope, of paradise regainable, to give us, as he says at the climactic moment of Tess and Angel's sexual revelation, a "new horizon."[53] Because that new horizon seems so possible, because at every step of the way Hardy seems to say to us as never before, "I am writing to free you," we feel, as never before, the jolt of that other, more characteristic, voice of his interrupting to say with Schopenhauer that true tragedy offers no new horizon, only "the scornful mastery of chance, the irretrievable fall of the just and the innocent."[54]

Aesthetically, the superimposition of this darker plot on a novel that wants so much to give us a remediable or visionary (social) tragedy may well be a mistake. As Lawrence says, it has an "execrable" effect on form, forcing into unresolved contiguity two incongruous structures of life. Intellectually, however, it was a necessity for Hardy. He does not simply say, as he does in the earlier cosmic tragedies (*The Return of the Native* and *The Mayor of Casterbridge*), "there is no altering—so it must be,"[55] but asks, no less insistently than his betrayed readers— *why* must it be? Why can we not unmake the "social rubric"[56] and return if even momentarily to the real, the genuinely "pure" life of nature? Why is "such completeness . . . not to be prophesied"? The answer at this point in Hardy's career goes beyond the new scientific realism set up, as it were, on Aeschylean buskins, as Crass Casualty. Hardy is seeking a more intimate answer, one that sees man's irremediably tragic destiny as emanating, not from the cosmos without, but from the radically conflicted workings of the mind itself.

Frederic Harrison called *Tess of the d'Urbervilles* a "positivist allegory,"[57] a strangely inappropriate judgment. Yet there is perhaps a way in which we can render it meaningful, a way which Harrison, to give him his due, may well have had somewhere in mind. With his irrepressible optimism, he may have considered that Tess's tragedy was regenerative and that Angel and Liza Lu were actually going somewhere at the close. If so, that somewhere would be in the direction of the affirmation of the natural self untrammeled by society's laws. And, still more, he probably understood perfectly well the revolutionary interpretation Hardy is offering of the natural self as essentially sexual. Such a vision could, indeed, be incorporated into the positivist program, for the late-century sexologists, Carl Ulrichs, Richard von Krafft-Ebing, Albert Moll, Havelock Ellis, Edward Carpenter, and others, were all descendants of the scientific or physiological movement in psychology we initially examined in Lewes.[58] Here for example is Edward Carpenter writing almost contemporaneously with *Tess of the d'Urbervilles*:

With the regeneration of our social ideas, the whole conception of sex as a thing covert and to be ashamed of . . . will have to be regenerated. . . . [A] healthy delight in, and cultivation of, the body and all its natural functions, and a determination to keep them pure and beautiful . . . , will have to become a recognized part of national life. The Lord has indeed driven us out of Paradise. . . . Will the man or woman, or race . . . , never come, to whom love in its various manifestations shall be from the beginning a perfect whole, pure and natural, free and standing sanely on its feet?[58]

Carpenter's answer, obviously, is yes; science is on its way to bringing us back to the garden in this franker version of Comte's return to the fetishistic mode of social relations.

Tess of the d'Urbervilles might, then, be read as a positivist allegory in the sense just described—if, that is, we ignore the superimposition of the pessimistic plot, which Lawrence, who is, after all, closer to the nineteenth-century sexologists in spirit than is Hardy, calls the suppression of love. But the "clumsy" overlaying of the spontaneous, natural will to enjoy with the pessimistic plot is Hardy's way of definitively separating himself from even this most liberated of positivist visions. Lawrence was to mock the scientific prophylaxis with which Freud sanitized his penetration of the dark passages of human sexuality.[59] Hardy (as well as Freud) might well turn that criticism back on Lawrence. Lawrence, the least scientific of thinkers, had nonetheless a properly positivist faith in the natural. It was not for nothing that Bertrand Russell found him so fascinating. Hardy, far from suppressing the principle of love, looks all too closely at it, finding with his imaginative insight or, rather, his insight into the ways of the imagination, antinomies the sexologists could not or would not see.

JUDE THE OBSCURE: TRAVERSING THE SPACE
FROM DARWIN TO FREUD

The last two novels are as close as Hardy ever came to autobiography. The one, *Jude the Obscure* (1896), shows us the hero as would-be Victorian prophet searching for a creed. The other, *The Well-Beloved* (1897), gives us the portrait not just of the young but also of the middle-aged and old man as artist. As representations of the self, or two aspects of the self, thinker and artist, these stories are remarkable inversions of what we expect of the great Victorian genre of *Bildungsroman*, for the point of the one is antiprophetic and that of the other is antiartistic. There is, at last, no approach either to a new, totalizing creed or to a new aesthetic shape in which to embody it. Hardy is no Carlyle, no Tennyson, no Arnold, above all, no George Eliot. For him they are, like the ghosts Jude finds amid the stones of Christminster, elusive shadows of an achievement that is unattainable, not simply for him personally, but, as Hardy now unambiguously says, for mankind. We will look first at *Jude the Obscure* and the failed prophetic search, and then turn to Hardy's view of art in the last novel (I am considering *The Well-Beloved* the last novel because, though begun before *Jude the Obscure*, it was not completed until after Jude was published), where we will find the position that must close this study, that of a radical incompatibility between science, on the one hand, art and the aesthetic totalization of society, on the other.

Jude is a character we have seen in various guises throughout Hardy, broadly speaking, the intellectual, the "new man," familiar with the best that is thought and known in his generation and seeking with it to come to some understanding of the world (other examples are Henry Knight, Clym Yeobright, George Somerset, Edred Fitzpiers, and, above all, Angel Clare). But at the same time, several things distinguish Jude from his predecessors, not least of all his eponymous status. In no other Hardy novel is the intellectual/prophetic hero so central. As we have seen, Hardy's imaginative interest in the hero's female counterpart always tends to eclipse him. Here, as in no previous work, we witness the step-by-step struggle for an intellectual vantage point from which the world will at last make sense, such a struggle as governs the plot of *Wilhelm Meister, Sartor Resartus, Daniel*

Deronda, Marius the Epicurean, and so on. Only the subplot of Angel's education, all but the last phase of which happens offstage, comes close to what Hardy is now doing, and Jude, in this sense, is Angel redux, without the burden of Angel's excessively Christian and conventional upbringing.

But if Hardy has made the archetypal Victorian search for a world view central to this novel, it is with the end in view of making explicit the point never fully conceded in earlier novels: that the pursuit is foredoomed to failure. From Jude, Hardy methodically removes any possibility of achieving the longed-for understanding, leaving him at last in a situation of absolute confusion or, again, nonvision. As the protagonist says on his final ironic return to the New Jerusalem of Christminster, the "intellectual granary of the nation,"[60]

I am in a chaos of principles—groping in the dark—acting by instinct. . . . Eight or nine years ago when I came here first, I had a neat stock of fixed opinions, but they dropped away one by one; and the further I get the less sure I am. I doubt if I have anything more for my present rule of life than following inclinations which do me and nobody else any harm. . . . I perceive there is something wrong somewhere in our social formulas: what it is can only be discovered by men or women with greater insight than mine,—if, indeed, they ever discover it—at least in our time.[61]

Sue, the most intellectual (and prophetlike) of all Hardy's women, reiterates the point with her own version of nonvision, which, we may recognize, undoes the great Arnoldian prophecy with which Hardy had long grappled: "There is something external to us which says, 'You shan't!'" Or we may turn to Phillotson, who started Jude on his intellectual pilgrimage, but must finally concede that "cruelty is the law pervading all nature and society; and we can't get out of it if we would."[62]

Both Phillotson's conclusion and Sue's, in their different ways, refer the cause of human entrapment to something "external" to ourselves that makes for misery, the old "defect of nature." Such externalization, as I have argued, is the characteristic sign of Hardy's relation to the new scientific pessimism. For Hardy's own distinctive development of this pessimism, a development that brings together his own experience of life and art with the gloomy message of contemporary science, we need to look to Jude, who achieves the greatest "insight" of anyone in Hardy's fiction. Whatever external causes block our access to happiness, the ultimate block is within. "There's more for us to think about in [the] . . . hungry heart," Sue says at one point, "than in all the stars of the sky."[63] This psychological or internal nemesis

Hardy had begun fully to grasp and imaginatively to embody in the absolutely circular, nonprogressive career of Michael Henchard, who, one recalls, ends almost exactly where he begins. The point was deepened in *Tess of the d'Urbervilles*, in which the circularity of human suffering is not limited to the individual self but has ancient family roots, as Tess herself at last understands all too well: " . . . your nature and your past doings have been just like thousands' and thousands', and . . . your coming life and doings'll be like thousands', and thousands'."[64] The inescapable family curse, the curse, in effect, of the human race, is back with a vengeance in *Jude the Obscure*, only now Hardy has set it as his task to try to define it psychologically. What precisely is it in us, rather than external to us, that says, "You shan't"?

The novel takes up again the question of natural joy uninhibited by social convention, the potential vision underlying Tess's story. In Hardy's recurrent use of the Shelleyan motif of male and female "counterparts"[65] in search of one another, Jude and Sue are counterparted as no other characters in his fiction and, more wonderful still, granted the opportunity to conduct their love relationship outside marriage. Here at last are characters who live in a social world, which, for all its conventionality, does at least permit divorce. They can extricate themselves from bad marriages and live together, the Laon and Cythna of an ideal love.[66] The consequences are, of course, the most disasterous of any relationship in all of Hardy, and Sue's reaction to the disaster may be read as a direct response to the previous novel's glimpse of hope: "'We went about loving each other too much. . . . We said—do you remember?—that we would make a virtue of joy. I said it was Nature's intentions, Nature's law and *raison d'être* that we should be joyful in what instincts she offered us—instincts which civilization had taken upon itself to thwart. . . . And now Fate has given us the stab in the back for being such fools as to take Nature at her word!'"[67] The impossibility of joy, which neither Sue nor anyone in the novel can do anything but feel, Hardy tries intellectually to account for, and the effort takes him on a remarkably precocious journey beyond joy.

Hardy's lovers characteristically have a Shelleyan penchant for idealizing the object of their sexual desire. What Hardy seems to want to say about idealization by the time he comes to *Tess of the d'Urbervilles* is that it is the product of civilization engrained in us by numerous texts. In *Jude the Obscure*, he again examines this process of idealization; indeed, it absorbs his interest more completely than in any earlier novel. But now his approach is different in two ways. First, he seeks to explore in depth what he has only touched upon in earlier works, the continuity between the idealization of the woman (or man) and the idealization that produces religious and moral beliefs. Second, he has shifted his focus from the way in which ideals are socially generated and imbedded in the individual's consciousness (the theme of Lewes' scientific psychology and Stephen's scientific ethics) to an entirely different psychological process, namely, the way in which they arise in the first place. It is an essential part of his conception of Jude as prophet that we should have an opportunity to see in him how vision develops from within and takes over an individual's life.

The sources of Jude's great ideal, the ideal of pursuing knowledge, are not, at first, clearly revealed. All we see is how it possesses his childish imagination in the symbolic form of the distant city of Christminster, full at once of light and music, calling to him as the New Jerusalem: "We are happy here."[68] If we are to say anything of how this ideal comes to exercise such "a hold on his life,"[69] it must be that childhood misery and deprivation demand some compensation. Hardy himself offers only one "nucleus of fact"[70] to explain Jude's obsession, which is that the far-off city contains the one man who was ever kind to him and whose knowledge and purpose he revered. This is Phillotson, the village teacher, who seems to have served the orphan boy as a surrogate parent, and it is, in fact, with the deprivation of this "father figure" at age 11 that the story begins.

The vision of the "tree of knowledge"[71] once established in Jude's mind keeps its hold until it is eclipsed by awakening sexual desire, which Hardy portrays in the first part as a purely physical force, an animal "magnetism"[72] that opposes and destroys Jude's scholarly aspirations. Arabella "was a complete and substantial female animal— no more, no less; and Jude was almost certain that to her [among the other girls] was attributable the enterprise of attracting his attention from dreams of the humaner letters to what was simmering in the minds around him."[73] Later, after marrying and falling out of love with Arabella, he contemplates the pathos of the human situation in which man's efforts to make himself "superior to the lower animals" and a contributor "to the general progress of his generation" can simply be canceled by a "transitory instinct which had nothing in it of the nature of vice, and could only at the most be called weakness."[74] We note how thoroughly Hardy has reversed the rhetoric of *Tess of the d'Urbervilles*. There the antithesis is between a healthy, joy-giving "force" of desire and the ideal constraints of convention, the "social rubric," with the latter triumphant. Here sexuality is presented as unclean, like the offal Arabella flings at Jude, and aggressive, even mutilating; the ideal world is the object of an antithetic drive towards a realm of wholeness, sanity, and light. Although Jude's visionary aspirations are always defeated by his sexual impulse, like the "pulse of [organic] life" in *Tess of the d'Urbervilles*, those aspirations keep reviving. Jude's spontaneous resumption of his quest after the exit of Arabella to Australia, then, parallels but inverts Tess's purely physical and emotional "rally" after the stigma of her illegitimate child is removed by death.

In the second part of *Jude the Obscure*, Hardy approaches the relation between the sexual and the ideal from a very different perspective. In the now mature Jude, the antithesis initially established between sexuality and idealization ceases to be so clearcut. The pursuit of the ideal, originally fixed on the image of Christminster, once he is in that town, begins to focus on a woman, much as Angel's vague desire for "intellectual liberty"[75] transfers itself to Tess at Talbothays: "The consciousness of [Sue's] living presence stimulated him. . . . [H]e began to weave . . . fantastic daydreams [about her]."[76] But now in Hardy's treatment of this Shelleyan (or Platonic) condensation of the ideal, there is perhaps less a new understanding of what is going on than a new willingness to speak explicitly about it. The idealizing gesture, he makes clear, is deeply ambivalent, generated as a defense against, displacement of, sexual desire, the exigencies of which Jude knows all too well:

. . . the emotion which had been accumulating in his breast as the bottled-up effect of solitude . . . insensibly began to precipitate itself on this half-visionary form. . . .

. . . She would be to him a kindly star, an elevating power, a companion in Anglican worship. . . .

. . . To an impressionable and lonely young man the consciousness of having at last found anchorage for his thoughts, which promised to supply both social and spiritual possibilities, was like the dew of Hermon, and he remained throughout the service in a sustaining atmosphere of ecstasy.

Though he was loth to suspect it, some people might have said to him that the atmosphere blew as distinctly from Cyprus as from Galilee.

And rather more directly: ". . . he could not altogether be blind to the real nature of the magnetism."[77] The scene of their initial encounter is, of course, the cathedral at Christminster, so that her image can never really be disengaged in Jude's mind from the God she serves.

This merging of sexual desire with religion through the medium of the idealized woman is as striking a symbolic presentation as anything we have in Victorian fiction of what Freud was shortly to term "sublimation" and describe perhaps nowhere more appositely for our purposes than in the essay on Leonardo with its discussion of what motivates the scholar, the obsessive seeker after knowledge: "The sexual instinct . . . is endowed with a capacity for sublimation: that is, it has the power to replace its immediate aim by other aims which may be valued more highly and which are not sexual."[78] And although Freud's etiology of religion as sublimation is considerably more complex than the simple displacement of one form of "ecstasy" by another that Hardy suggests here, it remains true that religion for him is rooted in human sexuality, which it masks or disguises.[79] In his famous phrase, it is "the universal obsessional neurosis."[80] That Hardy imaginatively anticipates Freudian sublimation is less surprising than his willingness to expatiate upon it. What is most shocking about the passage just quoted, finally, is less the dramatic presentation of Jude's ambivalent feeling than the narrator's explanation of it. Victorian readers might happily luxuriate in the transmutation of sexual desire into religious ecstasy—they had long been doing so—but to be told frankly what was going on, and what they as readers were collaborating in, was something else entirely.

By the time we get through the second part, then, we have a significant revision of the relationship between desire and idealization from what we saw "At Marygreen." Idealization, whether of the woman or of the world (in the case of Jude's prophetic vocation), has its origin in desire, which it sanitizes, makes socially acceptable. But what had earlier been portrayed as a simple antithesis—desire disrupts idealization—is now more complexly understood as a symbolic transmutation of one term into another—desire sublimates itself into the ideal, it generates, that is, the symbolic negation of itself. The consequences of this new relationship are formidable from any standpoint, but perhaps particularly from that of the positivist. The ideal ceases altogether to be something we can reconcile with any real; rather, it becomes in its very essence, an evasion of the real. We cannot even say of it, as George Eliot does in her late pragmatistic compromise with positivism, that it is a "noble" fiction that gives practical shape to our inarticulate yearning for the good; rather, it now becomes a defense, a deception, by which we attempt to disguise what we can never reconcile with the noble. "[U]nlike hunger or even the defense of ego, sexuality," writes Paul Ricoeur, "gives rise to imagination . . . but in an unrealistic mode, . . . the semantics of desire is a semantics of delusion."[81] Jude has just begun to understand this when, at the close of the second part, he abandons his Christminster ambitions, recognizing them as an "imaginative world he had lately inhabited, in which an abstract figure, more or less himself, was steeping his mind in a sublimation of the arts and sciences, and making his calling and election sure to a seat in the paradise of the learned." Beneath the illusion Jude now sees the "real Christminster life," which, in Hardy's account of it at this point, is the life of common working men and "frolicsome girls who made advances—wistful to gain a little joy."[82]

Had Hardy a still more precocious psychoanalytical awareness, he might have given us in the first part a history of Jude's childhood that would have shown the origins of the boy's visionary character in his familial relations, as Freud was to do, for example, with his reconstruction of Leonardo's childhood. But in Hardy's treatment of Jude's relationship with his cousin we find some very suggestive explorations. The ideal female counterpart in Shelley's myth of love is often presented as a sister. In the original version of *The Revolt of Islam*, for example, Laon and Cythna were brother and sister, and in *Epipsychidion* the poet addresses Emily as both "sister" and "spouse." As Earl Wasserman has observed, the double relationship of sister and lover had special significance for Shelley, representing for him the most perfect possible union of "coequal souls derived from a common source."[83] Nor was Shelley (any more than Byron) speaking merely metaphorically of the lover as sister.

Hardy clearly responded to this particular subtext of the Shelleyan myth. Incest is a hidden preoccupation in the novels from as early as *Desperate Remedies*, where Miss Aldcliffe strives to arrange a marriage between her son Manston and her own namesake, Cytherea (cf. Shelley's "Cythna"), whom she has adopted as a surrogate daughter. In *The Return of the Native* Clym and Thomasin, cousins raised as siblings, are considered likely mates. Grace Melbury and Giles in *The Woodlanders*, again quasi-siblings, are engaged to marry. Alec and Tess share the same family name, and so on. The approaches to the subject, as we see, are discreet. But in *Jude the Obscure* Hardy at last gives us lovers who are, in fact, members of the same family, and the blood connection is very much to the point. There were "crushing reasons," the narrator tells us, why Jude should not fall in love with his cousin. One, obviously, is that he is already married, but the other is new, at least as a theme Hardy is prepared to write about: ". . . in a family like his own where marriage usually meant a tragic sadness, marriage with a blood-relation would duplicate the adverse conditions, and a tragic sadness might be intensified to a tragic horror"[84]—which, of course, is what happens.

In the next novel, *The Well-Beloved*, the tragedy is muted, but the incest motif is, if anything, intensified. Jocelyn, in falling in love with Avice Caro, her daughter, and then her granddaughter, falls in love with an island family like his own and hence one to which he must be related. Indeed, it is the blood or "racial" connection that is all Hardy can offer to explain this otherwise irrational pursuit of the Well-Beloved: ". . . in her nature, as in his, was some mysterious ingredient sucked from the isle; otherwise a racial instinct necessary to the absolute unison of a pair. Thus, . . . he could not love long . . . a woman other than of [his own] . . . race, for her lack of this groundwork of character."[85] The attraction is, as its object's name perhaps suggests, a "dear vice," and one Hardy appears to have had not a little experience of. His willingness to write openly about it in these last two novels is not the least of their claims to being autobiographical, indeed, confessional texts.[86]

Not the autobiographical provenance of the theme, however, but Hardy's effort to come to some kind of philosophical understanding of it concerns us. On one level, the love for the cousin/sister is a desire to return to "one in whom seemed to linger as an aroma all the charm of his youth and early home."[87] In the psychoanalytic terms that Hardy's treatment of love in these last two novels seems to demand, the protagonist Jude or Jocelyn, disconcerted (as both are) by adult, genital sexuality, seeks a return to an earlier, less threatening stage of the libido, where the love object is a sibling or, more fundamentally still, a parent, a phenomenon Freud calls regression.

At every stage in the course of development through which all human beings . . . pass, a certain number are held back; so there are some who have never got over their parents' authority and have withdrawn their affection from them either very incompletely or not at all. . . .

The closer one comes to the deeper disturbances of psychosexual development, the more unmistakably the importance of incestuous object-choices emerges. . . . Girls with an . . . exaggerated horror of the real demands made by sexual life have an irresistible temptation . . . to conceal their libido behind an affection which they can express without self-reproaches, by holding fast . . . to infantile fondness . . . for their parents or brothers and sisters.[88]

Freud's example here is feminine, but the regressive syndrome is transsexual, as we see in the study of Leonardo, where regression is intimately linked with the adolescent male's sublimation of desire into artistic and intellectual pursuits.

Yet the fact is that Freud does consider the female especially liable to this "psychoneurotic" disturbance.[89] In *Jude the Obscure*, both cousins are sexually regressive, but it is Sue in whom regression has rendered adult, or genital, sexuality absolutely repulsive. Hardy's treatment of her abnormality, which begins in earnest in the third part of the novel (with its Sapphic epigraph), is easily the most daring treatment of human sexuality in his novels and among the most daring in Victorian literature. In Sue, Hardy describes a relation between civilization and sexuality quite different from what we have seen in *Tess of the d'Urbervilles*. There female sexuality is what civilization represses. In the later novel civilization is seen as having created a form of sexuality (genital) which is repugnant to the female and from which she seeks to escape. Thus Jude analyzes her problem in terms that would have fit nicely with the treatment of sexuality in *Tess of the D'Urbervilles* (and, as we have seen, among the contemporary sexologists): "'You only think you like [sexual love]; you don't: you are quite a product of civilization.'" Civilization, that is, teaches us to dislike and fear sex. But Sue responds with a far more subtle perception. "'Indeed I am not. . . . I crave to get back to the life of my infancy and its freedom.'" And somewhat later: "'You called me a creature of civilization . . . ,' she said. . . . 'It was very odd you should have done that.' 'Why?' 'Well, because it is provokingly wrong. I am a sort of negation of it.'"[90] She then goes on to confess an early Platonic relationship with a young man, the essence of her confession being that such relationships—and she is attempting to form a similar one with Jude—are for her a way of avoiding the adult sexual activity that society demands of a wife. Society's views "'of the relations of man and woman are limited. . . . [Its] philosophy only recognizes relations based on animal desire. The wide field of strong attachment where desire plays, at least, only a secondary part, is ignored by them—the part of—who is it?—Venus Urania.'"[91] Sue's regressiveness, again, is but an extreme form of Jude's, for whom, as we have seen, preference for her over Arabella signifies on some level a preference for sister/mother love over adult sexuality, his sexual pressure on Sue notwithstanding.

My object in all this is not to set Hardy up as a pioneer of the heartland of psychoneurosis but to make a metapsychological point that takes us back to the question of science and culture. At the root of both Jude's and Sue's regressiveness, Hardy seems to suggest, is a common psychic phenomenon. When Sue comes to Jude's rooms at night wet from swimming the river to escape her school, he "palpitates" with a sense of "what counterparts they were." Because she is soaked through, he has her change into his clothes with the effect that the female counterpart suddenly becomes the image of the self: "Sitting in his only arm-chair he saw a slim and fragile being masquerading as himself. . . ."[92] In *The Well-Beloved*, that epitome of the Shelleyan search for a counterpart, the identification of the female antitype with the self is even more explicit. Jocelyn's repeated discovery of the well-beloved in Avice and her descendants is understood, to paraphrase Hardy, as the soul's confrontation with itself. For this reduction of the ideal other to a projection of self, Hardy would have found ample authority in Shelley himself. "We are born into the world," writes the poet, "and there is something within us which from the instant that we live and move thirsts after its likeness. . . . We dimly see within our intellectual nature a miniature as it were of our entire self. . . ."[93] But as well as looking back to Shelley, Hardy is looking forward (as does Shelley himself) to the Freudian concept of narcissism.

This relatively late development in psychoanalytic theory postulates a love object prior even to the love of the mother and makes its first significant appearance in *Totem and Taboo* (1913):

> If we trace back the development of libidinal trends as we find them in the individual from their adult forms to the first beginnings in childhood, an important distinction emerges. . . . Manifestations of the sexual instincts can be observed from the very first, but to begin with they are not yet directed towards any external object. The separate instinctual components of sexuality work independently of one another to obtain pleasure and find satisfaction in the subject's own body. This stage is known as auto-eroticism. . . . [The sexual] object is not an external one, extraneous to the subject, but is [one's] own ego, which has been constituted at about this same time. . . . [T]his new stage . . . we have given . . . the name of "narcissism."[94]

The reason Freud found it "expedient and indeed indispensable" to introduce this new stage into his libidinal theory was to explain how sexual instincts are cathected into mental structures, or in terms of the perennial nineteenth-century problem which we have encountered throughout this study, how body becomes mind. The ego, the image of the self, is the first structural whole the developing mind realizes and as such forms the foundation of all future mental organization. *Totem and Taboo* is, after all, about the origin of religion, and specifically (as with Comte's earlier discussion of the same subject) the origin of religion in "animism." The theory of narcissism is meant to describe the original strategy by which we come, in Freud's terms, to "*over*-value" our own mental acts or conceptualizations and project them onto the external world: "Primitive men and neurotics . . . attach a high valuation—in our eyes an *over*-valuation—to psychical acts. . . . This is the origin of their belief in the omnipotence of thought, their unshakable confidence in the possibility of controlling the world. . . ." [95]

In future refinements the theory becomes the keystone of Freud's theory of culture, the means by which he reduces all our mental organization of experience to a desire to regress to the source of order in the original conception of the wholeness or oneness of the self: "[Man] is not willing to forego the narcissistic perfection of his childhood; and when . . . he can no longer retain that perfection, he seeks to recover it in the new form of an ego ideal. What he projects before him as his ideal is the substitute for the lost narcissism of his own childhood. . . ."[96] What for Shelley, and before him Plato, had been a metaphorical return to an original "prototypical" self, in which that self is made to stand for a metaphysical or transcendent principle of perfection—"a soul within our soul that describes a circle around its proper paradise, which pain, sorrow, and evil dare not overleap"[97]— becomes in Freud a literal return to a stage of individual development at which an inchoate instinct, the sexual drive, first fixes itself (cathects) upon an ideal object, the ego. The sense of perfection experienced in this original cathexis of instinct is psychological rather than metaphysical and, finally, illusory, in Freud's special sense of that word: "What is characteristic of illusions is that they are derived from human wishes. . . . Thus we call a belief an illusion when a wish-fulfillment is a prominent factor in its motivation, and in doing so we disregard its relations to reality. . . ."[98] These illusions, these moral and religious beliefs we have about the world and which we call culture, ultimately defy the positivists' criterion of verification because they are not, after all, statements about the world. They are strategies by which man seeks at once relief from his instinctual burden and recompense for the necessity of sacrificing instinctual satisfaction.

Freud may, as we see, abandon the crucial positivist criterion of verification in his analysis of cultural beliefs, but, of course, he himself is altogether a product of the positivist tradition, a rigorous devotee of science who, in Habermas' wonderful phrase, ended by presenting the positivist logic with a scrap it could not digest.[99] Freud is the natural continuator of Darwin's Copernican revolution. Where Darwin in

1871 definitively reunites man with nature by finding at the core of his being the same instinctual drives that motivate the unreflecting organisms "below" him, Freud describes the process, the "economy," by which those drives are transmuted into cultural ideals. In this sense, we may regard his theory of mind as the culmination (if an ironical one) of the positivist assault on metaphysics announced by Comte more than half a century earlier. As Stephen Draenos has lately put it,

> The key to Freud's vision and to the place of his thought within Western speculation about man can be stated simply: psychoanalysis realizes the end of metaphysics by elaborating the meaning of Darwinism for human self-understanding. . . .
>   . . . The ultimate aim of the psychology of the unconscious is to fulfill the scientifically ordained destiny of metaphysics by transforming it into metapsychology. . . . For what ultimately sustains metaphysical illusions are the urgent needs welling up from within, which the wishful impulses populating the unconscious represent. . . . By treating the metaphysical answers to the ultimate questions of existence as unconscious manifestations of human psychology, Freud could hope to translate transcendental illusions into scientific truths, to capture the human essence within the cognitions of science.[100]

The object of the Freudian enterprise is to explain how what Darwinism had identified as a chance event, the human mind, comes to imperialize a world with which it is radically out of sorts, to find human meaning where none, in fact, exists. Again, Draenos: "The necessary correlate to science's disclosure that nature is itself devoid of meaning is that all meaning is psychogenic—that it must arise from the depths of human subjectivity." Meaning "is necessarily construed as a projective illusion of psychical factors and relations that have their true reality in the wordless depths of the unconscious."[101]

Draenos' excellent account helps us to an understanding of the critical point of intersection between Freud and Hardy, the point at which the latter, indeed, anticipates the former in the development of the nineteenth-century science of mind. It is not simply that Hardy has, in the manner we are familiar with in novelists, portrayed certain psychological realities that psychologists proper were later to incorporate into their systems. Hardy precedes Freud in the much more significant metapsychological project of pursuing the implications of Darwinism for human self-understanding. No less than Freud he appears in the last novels to have understood that all cultural idealization, all meaning, is psychogenetic, an elaborate strategy of desire. The structures of human belief are ultimately unverifiable, not, as the earlier positivists would have it, because mind cannot *know* the thing-in-itself, but because they are, in their very nature, falsifications, psychogenetic flights from a thing-in-itself that we fear to know.

But there is a still more decisive parting of the ways between Freud and the positivist tradition that engendered his thought. The fundamental psychic duality that he eventually postulates at the center of the human condition is unresolvable. There can be, that is, no progress from division to wholeness of self, only an unending, repetitive conflict of opposing impulses. In the late Freud the essential positivist faith that we are moving, through science, ever closer to perfection becomes just another metaphysical illusion:

It may be difficult . . . , for many of us, to abandon the belief that there is an instinct towards perfection at work in human beings, which has brought them to their present high level of intellectual achievement and ethical sublimation and which may be expected to watch over their development into supermen. I have no faith, however, in the existence of any such internal instinct. . . . What appears in . . . human individuals as an untiring impulsion towards further perfection can easily be understood as a result of the instinctual repression upon which is based all that is most precious in civilization. The repressed instinct never ceases to strive for complete satisfaction; which would consist in repetition of the primary experience of satisfaction. [Since such a return to primary satisfaction is impossible,] there is no alternative but to advance in the direction which is still free—though with no prospect of bringing the process to a conclusion or of being able to reach the goal.[102]

Norman Brown makes a pivotal distinction in his account of Freud between antithetical and dialectical opposition. The concept of *dialectical* opposition, which we associate with the Hegelian-Marxist tradition, but which has its positivist form as well, as we saw in our discussion of Comte, is of an opposition that progressively leads towards utopic synthesis, a reconciliation of subject and object, self and other, the return, in short, at the end of history to primal wholeness or totality. *Antithetical* opposition, however, is endlessly recurrent, and it is this kind of opposition that Freud's theory at last leaves us with. The later "Freud's therapeutic pessimism," writes Brown, "is grounded in his hypothesis of the eternal and irreconcilable struggle of life and death in every organism, producing in every human being the 'spontaneous tendency to conflict' and manifesting itself in neurotic patients as an unconscious resistance to cure, a kind of 'psychical entropy.'"[103]

It is precisely this condition of antithetical opposition within the self, or psychical entropy, that Hardy in the last two novels seems definitively to substitute for an external or cosmic nemesis as the source of human tragedy. Waiting at Melchester for Sue, Jude is, as always, disappointed and in his disappointment spontaneously "projects" his mind into a future where he imagines Sue in an ideal love relationship surrounded by happy children "more or less in her own likeness." But immediately he catches himself up and recognizes that his imagined "new beginning" is an illusion, for "every desired renewal of an existence is debased by being half alloy."[104] The metallurgical metaphor is absolutely right, for it makes the point that the problem is not external but incorporated into the self and its expectations.

The alloy, or duality, the late Freud finds at the center of human nature is, as we know, between eros, the sexual instinct, and thanatos, the death instinct. Observing patients' compulsion to repeat unpleasurable experience, Freud postulates in *Beyond the Pleasure Principle* (1920) a more primitive instinct underlying the drive for pleasure or sexual instinct: "There really does exist in the mind a compulsion to repeat which overrides the pleasure principle."[105] This instinct is the expression of the "*conservative* nature of living substance" in its tendency towards "the restoration of an earlier state of things." The "final goal of all organic striving" is not "a state of things which has never yet been attained," but "an *old* state of things, an initial state from which the living entity has at one time or other departed and to which its development leads. If we are to take it as a truth that knows no exception that everything living dies for *internal* reasons—becomes inorganic once again—then we shall be compelled to say that '*the aim of all life is death*.'"[106] The "first instinct" is the desire to return to an inanimate, original state. Against this desire, the search for pleasure or eros becomes our primary defense, and the two great impulses battle it out not only in the life of the individual but, as Freud came increasingly to believe, also in the history of civilization. Man's "aggressive instinct is the derivative and the main representative of the death instinct which we have found alongside of Eros and which shares world-dominion with it. And now, I think the meaning of the evolution of civilization is no longer obscure to us. It must present the struggle between Eros and Death, between the instinct of life and the instinct of destruction, as it works itself out in the human species."[107]

We are reminded of Comte's ambivalence about whether the germ of human nature is fundamentally altruistic and unifying or egoistic and disintegrating. It is an ambivalence, we have seen, that continued to dog positivist psychology, morality, and social theory throughout the century. Its resolution up to this point had been a matter of either taking it on faith that altruism (a sanitized or sublimated eros) is primary and egoism (a sanitized or sublimated thanatos) is secondary, or, more characteristically, constructing a theory of culture governed by an aesthetic or self-formative principle that conduces to the triumph of native altruism over native egoism. In Freud's revolutionary reworking of this perennial positivist dilemma, not only is the instinctual duality stripped of its civilized disguise—altruism becomes eros; egoism becomes aggression and desire for death—but also civilization itself becomes, in his wonderful metaphor, a mere "lullaby" about heaven sung to us all (as to Mirah Lapidoth) in our cradles, an elaborate placebo devised by humankind to hide from itself the irremediable discontent built into, alloyed with, its very nature.

Surely, Jude illustrates this flaw in the nature of our psychic economy. But still more does Sue. In her we see more clearly than in any other Hardy character the "colossal inconsistency" that at once longs for sexual gratification and is repulsed by it, encourages love but then punishes the lover for offering it: ". . . she would go on inflicting such pains again and again, and grieving for the sufferer again and again. . . ."[108] Or we may look ahead to *The Well-Beloved*, where the "compulsion to repeat" becomes so prominent a motif[109] that, while it effectively destroys our interest in the story, it nonetheless brings out the antithetical opposition within the self in virtually allegorical relief. Jocelyn futilely pursues his Shelleyan counterpart (his "lullaby") through three generations only to marry at last the only woman he had a chance of obtaining, the one, after all, who represents what he truly wants. Marcia, "the old tabernacle in a new aspect,"[110] suddenly reveals herself to Jocelyn at the close, "an old woman, pale and shrivelled, her forehead ploughed, her cheek hollow, her hair white as snow," in short, a virtual deathshead.[111] In their marriage Hardy gives us a deliberate parody of the all-powerful Victorian symbol of moral and social health, hope in the future, and so on, and effectively closes an epoch. Marriage, the consummate union with the well-beloved for reconciliation of desire and duty, can no longer be translated into the prophetic promise of "new beginnings." In Hardy there are no new beginnings, only the reiteration of Jude's radically antiprophetic burden: the "universal wish not to be." "Weddings," as Widow Edlin says at the end of *Jude*, "be funerals."[112]

Returning to the question of tragedy with which I closed the last section, we see that the hesitation observed in *Tess of the d'Urbervilles* between two opposing concepts of the tragic, the social and the cosmic, resolves itself in *Jude the Obscure*. The opposition to human happiness is not in human institutions but in human nature; as Hardy says

in the later novel, things are not merely obstructive, they are antagonistic. In such a world we may well ask with Jude (and Job), "Where-
fore is the light given to him that is in misery?"[113] The "dialectical
drive toward knowledge and scientific optimism has succeeded in
turning tragedy from its course," Nietzsche had regretfully written
some 20 years before. In Hardy's last novels we would no doubt have
found an excellent confirmation of the corollary of that observation.
Real tragedy can be reborn "only when science [has] at last been
pushed to its limits. . . ."[114] In Hardy, as in the late Freud, the logic
of a scientific theory of mind is pursued to the point of rendering the
century's proud positivist vision of a "religion of humanity" yet
another metaphysical illusion. Romantic Prometheanism revised by
scientific method proves no more liberating than romanticism itself,
and we return, at last, to just such a tragic conception of the human
situation as Nietzsche tells us characterized the pagan world. "Begotten by accident and toil," man has only one good: "not to have been
born, not to *be*, to be *nothing*."[115]

ART AND SCIENCE: AN ANTITHETICAL OPPOSITION

One may well ask why Hardy, having arrived at such wisdom, continued to write, as of course he did, for another 30 years. The compulsion to find one's way out of this dismal circle, is one likely answer.
But closer to the mark in Hardy's case is a no less compulsive effort to
satisfy a demanding aesthetic conscience, to find the appropriate artistic form for this postpositivist and posthumanist vision of man's situation.

Hardy shares with Matthew Arnold, whose critical intelligence he
greatly admired, the conviction that there exists a causal relationship
between the dominant intellectual outlook of a period and its literary
forms. Of course, Arnold regretted the relationship in his own era,
considering his age lacked "intellectual deliverance," that it was, as
we might now say, ideologically underdetermined. For him, the only
strategy left to the artist in such a situation was to imitate the forms
of a previous "deliverance" (notably, the Periclean one of fifth-century
Greece) while patiently awaiting or, better yet, promoting through
criticism a new structure of belief suitable to the modern age, which
he had no doubt criticism eventually would produce. This new intellectual deliverance, and the social totality ("culture") he assumed
would go with it, must be the historically enabling condition of great
literature. Such literature, by Arnold's still classicist definition, would

be consummately "architectonic"—expressive of the grand style, as he had come to understand it through his reading of the Bible, Homer, and above all, Sophocles.[116]

For Hardy there is no faith that history will lead to any new intellectual deliverance. Yet he retains Arnold's aesthetic model to the extent that he commits himself to finding an artistic form that will reflect the situation to which the best that is thought and known, namely, contemporary science, has brought his generation, and this is the recognition of the distinct possibility that society is not only intellectually undelivered but undeliverable. "[I have] tried to spread over art the latest illumination of the time," he writes in another journal entry; and right on its heels, the attempt "has darkened counsel in respect of me."[117] In the paradoxical relationship so central to Hardy's work, the light of knowledge inevitably brings darkness, obscurity.

But more to the present point, self-consciousness about the artistic form into which he must cast the "latest illumination of the time" is everywhere present in his work, from the very first, unpublished novel, which he announced was without a plot,[118] to those late prefaces to the poetry, which insist in one way and another that his poems are really a series of fugitive pieces with "little cohesion of thought."[119] The essential direction and outcome of this aesthetic self-consciousness I can briefly indicate in the space that remains. What we will see, not surprisingly, is a "progress" that effectively reverses the revaluation of symbolic expression that Lewes and George Eliot had achieved, reducing the aesthetic act to an utterly ironic, albeit inescapable, that is, obsessive, gesture.

In *The Return of the Native*, Michael Millgate tells us, Hardy strives "more deliberately than ever before to make . . . an unmistakable work of art. . . ."[120] The previous novel, *The Hand of Ethelberta* (1876), one of several he wrote about being an artist, gives us a metropolitan heroine who abandons writing unconventional love poetry in favor of telling popular stories to upper-class audiences, her object being, as she says, strictly "utilitarian"—to achieve financial security and social status. Having thus dramatized a concern intimately related to the development of his own literary career, Hardy returns with a vengeance not only to his native Wessex (county) matter, but also, in a sense, to his native or original intention to write not fiction but poetry. *The Return of the Native*, like Aeschylus' *Prometheus Bound* or Shakespeare's *Lear*, on both of which it clearly draws, aims to render the unaccommodated human condition and to render it in something that has at least seemed to most readers like tragic form.[121]

That the *form* is very much the issue, Hardy makes clear from the outset. There is a question, he says on the novel's third page, of whether the "reign of . . . orthodox beauty is not approaching its last quarter." A new kind of beauty or form is required by art, a "chastened sublimity . . . in keeping with the more thinking among mankind."[122] And again, much later in the narrative, describing his exemplar of the modern spirit, Clym Yeobright, he speaks of the need for a "new artistic departure." "The truth seems to be that a long line of disillusive centuries has permanently displaced the Hellenic idea of life. . . . That old fashioned revelling [in the ideal] grows less and less possible as we uncover the defects of natural laws, and see the quandary that man is in by their operation."[123] So much—as I read this—for Matthew Arnold's Hellenism with its hankering after a bygone aesthetic ideal, its ultimate evasion of the modern spirit. To write in the modern spirit, Hardy is saying here, requires the "disillusioned" recognition of the fundamental defect in our human situation. But how does one express a defect, an absence, formally, aesthetically?

Immediately after describing *The Return of the Native* as the most self-conscious of Hardy's tragedies, a recent critic goes on to say it is also the least successful. This is true if classical tragic form is, in the end, what Hardy was actually after, but I doubt that it was. A tragic shape does exist in the narrative, and a tragic hero or, rather, heroine. Eustacia Vye is Hardy's new Prometheus, the thwarted bearer of light who tries valiantly to extricate herself from the darkness of Egdon Heath. Her story occupies the first five books—acts, if you like—of the drama, and in death she seems, indeed, to assume something like the tragic mask: "The expression of her finely carved mouth was pleasant, as if a sense of dignity had just compelled her to leave off speaking. . . . The stateliness of look . . . had at last found an artistically happy background."[124] But the hero of the book, the eponymous native who returns, is Clym, and his story continues beyond this "artistically happy," this conspicuously architectonic, Hellenic closure in a sixth book, an "Aftercourse," which clearly aims at undermining the neatness of the foregoing tragic structure by emphasizing its unreality. Eustacia Vye and Wildeve's story was "enlarged, distorted, touched up, and modified" until the "original reality" bore but a "slight resemblance" to the "counterfeit presentation. . . . Misfortune had struck them gracefully, cutting off their erratic histories with a catastrophic dash, instead of, as with many, attenuating each life to an uninteresting meagreness. . . ."[125] The attenuation of life to an uninteresting meagreness, its inevitable return, in the story of Clym, to the chaos and obscurity of the heath, is the self-consciously untragic, the farcical or absurd, shape that Hardy wants somehow to capture in this fiction. *The Return of the Native* is not an unsuccessful tragedy so much as a criticism of tragic form and, at the same time, a tentative movement towards a "new artistic departure," one, as it seems, that strives for the attenuation or release of formal tension: an expected form materializes only to be dissolved or disrupted as unrealistic.

The tragic form appears to most readers to be what Hardy is again after in the later, far more accomplished, narrative of *Tess of the d'Urbervilles*. As with *The Return of the Native*, there is, as we have seen, a struggle to define a tragic structure *within* the narrative, but, again, one must doubt whether that structure encloses the narrative or was ever meant to.[126] Again, as we have seen, neither Aeschylus nor the Prometheus myth inspires the tragic gesture in this novel so much as the Bible, Milton, and the myth of the Fall.[127] Angel and Tess are types of Adam and Eve,[128] and if we regard the seven structural "phases" of the narrative in the context of the biblical-cum-Miltonic story, we find that Tess first falls from innocence, or "purity" (first and second phases), and then receives a second chance at paradise in her relationship with Angel (third and fourth phases). We have up to this point (roughly halfway through the narrative) not only a reenactment of the fall but also an apparent redemption as promised by both Genesis and *Paradise Lost*. The potential redemption in Hardy's story is an entirely secular or natural one involving a descent down Egdon's uncongenial slopes into the idyllic setting of the Froom Vale and a no less idyllic love relationship with Angel. In this, Hardy departs from his orthodox sources to join Wordsworth in suggesting that the scene of redemption can be this natural world rather than the next. But he goes beyond Wordsworth (and anticipates Lawrence) by making his natural paradise at once radically material and explicitly sexual.

But that is not really a possibility beyond the pseudo-Eden of Froom Vale. From the moment of Tess's confession of sexual experience, which brings to a close the paradisiac interlude, the path of the narrative reproduces (in the fifth through seventh phases) much the same process of "attenuation" we observed in the final book of *The Return of the Native*, only at much greater length. Though Tess may die suddenly, catastrophically, at the hands of the executioner, that death is but the anticlimax of the wearing down of her will to live. Not only she, but her race, is, in Hardy's metaphor, a "spent force"; she "drifts . . . like a corpse upon the current, in a direction dissociated from the living will."[129] This drift towards annihilation, like Clym's, is symbolically associated with the return of all nature to primal darkness, as we see in the scene at Stonehenge amongst the conspicuously antiarchitectonic fragments (ruins) of sun worship. The possibility of any sort of redemption, and with it a congenial, intelligible shape to life/art, is not simply excluded, it is mocked. To call Tess an epic heroine, as Peter Morton has lately done (on the ground that she bears the genotype of her race),[130] and thereby to suggest that Hardy as novelist, like George Eliot, is consciously trying to create a new epic form for the scientific age, surely is to misread him. No less aware than George Eliot of the novel's epic and tragic potential, its potential to revive the ancient forms of human transcendence, he understands that what he wants to say in the novel, his particular reality, is, after all, antiepical, antitragic, perhaps even antinovelistic.

In the last novel Hardy develops to a fault a narrative form of unprogressive repetition with which he had been experimenting since at least as early as the consummately circular *Mayor of Casterbridge*, a form (if that is the word) that seeks to reflect the attenuation of all structural energy, to reflect, that is, psychical entropy. *The Well-Beloved* (1897) is Hardy's fullest portrait of the artist, but with a signal difference from similar portraits by his nineteenth-century predecessors. Rather than taking us up to the young man's arrival at his artistic vocation, he takes us, as it were, down from that moment to the old man's disillusionment with art, or at least the kind of art that has made him successful. The novel is a *Künstlerroman* in reverse. Like virtually all Hardy's artist-figures, Jocelyn Pierston is a worker in stone, a sculptor whom contemporaries consider the Praxiteles of his age, its most accomplished shaper of ideal beauty. The cause of his success is portrayed as psychopathetic (as the subtitle indicates, this is the "sketch of a temperament"): "Jocelyn threw into plastic creations that ever-bubbling spring of emotion which, without some conduit into space, will surge upwards and ruin all but the greatest men. It was probably owing to this . . . that he was successful in his art. . . ."[131] This facility at transforming "ruinous" emotional (libidinal) energy into a civilized "conduit" is also, however, a "curse"[132]—a word choice that suggests the obsessiveness of the idealizing or aesthetic impulse.

Only when the energy of desire wanes with old age is the curse removed, a change symbolically marked by a life-threatening fever: "Pierston was conscious of a singular change in himself. . . . The malignant fever . . . had taken something away from him, and put something else in its place. . . . [This was the] strange death of the sensuous side of [his] nature."[133] The "something else" that has taken the place of desire is something very close to a longing for death, embodied, as we have seen, in the decaying features of his first love, Marcia Benscombe, "the image and superscription of Age."[134] With this parabolic victory of thanatos over eros, already seen in the contemporaneous *Jude the Obscure* but now more deliberately than ever before applied to the meaning of art, art in its customary, idealizing sense ceases to matter. "Pierston never again saw his studio or its contents. He had been down there but a brief while when, finding his sense of beauty in art and nature absolutely extinct, he directed his agent in town to dispense the whole collection. . . . "[135]

Pierston is not Hardy. The aesthetic idealizations of life he produces, Hardy, we have seen, consciously resisted at least as early as *The Return of the Native*. Yet the conclusion of the novel, namely, that the revelation of the truly well-beloved as death means an end of the artist's desire to form ideal wholes from the "stupendous inanimate,"[136] is very close, indeed, to Hardy's own situation, an expression not only of his own, but also of his generation's attempts to relate the emerging meanings of science to aesthetic production. Particularly pertinent is Pierston's final recognition that he has, for some 40 years, pursued the wrong line in art, the wrong genre, for, of course, with *The Well-Beloved* Hardy has come to the end of his career as a novelist. What he understands, one suspects, is that to write in the novel form, however subversively, is still to accept the progressivist, totalizing ideology implicit in that form in what Lukács has called its classical state, its aspiration to be the epic of the modern world. George Eliot clearly believed in this ideology as she sought in her last two novels to produce that "perfect interchange between science and art. . . ." Her oracle of epic wholeness is still essentially positivist; Lukács' (at least in *The Theory of the Novel*) is residually metaphysical. Hardy, at last, rejects both positivist and metaphysical totalities in the interests of a radically dehumanized science and directly confronts the emptiness, the compulsiveness, of our need to "give a geometrical shape" to our stories of life.[137]

The year after publishing *The Well-Beloved* Hardy came out with his first volume of poetry and continued to write in this form until the end of his life. He liked to talk about the change in generic venue as if poetry somehow gave him more license for expressing his unpopular views.[138] But the object in going over to verse seems to me to have had less to do, after all, with a desire to reduce the pain inflicted by critics than with Hardy's persistent Arnoldean pursuit of an aesthetic form appropriate to "scientific realism." The philosopher in him may have arrived at the "coming universal wish not to be," but the inveterate and, as he now seems to have recognized, obsessive artist persisted in wanting to find out how that wish might best be "structured."

The process of collecting individual poems into single volumes always gave Hardy an opportunity he seemed eager to embrace to act as if the production of these poems were somehow out of his control, "automatic." In one preface after another, we find him insisting that his poems are "dramatic" in the special sense that they are "impersonations" of the views of others, not himself, and that, in those cases in which they are clearly lyrical, they represent not any firmly held, systematic belief but contrasting moods and fancies. Moreover, the collections as wholes are, he insists, not wholes at all. They have no "cohesion" or "concord" but are simply "unadjusted impressions" and "diverse readings" of phenomena. These are not expressions of modesty, still less of failure. In their conspicuous evasion of authorial and authorizing intentionality, they mean to announce something like an aesthetic principle, one aimed at conveying nothing so much as the "sense of disconnection."[139]

Paul Bourget (1852–1935), a French novelist and theorist of decadence who, like Hardy, sought to describe the relation between art and what he took to be the profoundly pessimistic message of modern science, concluded that the new aesthetic must be one of "analysis" (rather than synthesis), in which "form" would reflect the impossibility of wholeness.[140] The parts "which comprise the total organism cease . . . to subordinate their energy to the energy of the whole, and the anarchy which results constitutes the decadence of the whole. . . . A decadent style [accordingly] is one in which the unity of the book breaks down in order to give place to the independence of the page, or the page breaks down to give place to the independence of the sentence, and the sentence, to give place to the independence of the word."[141] Some such self-consciously entropic effect is almost certainly what Hardy is increasingly after in the late volumes of poetry.

But we may, at least, consider Hardy's situation as artist in the scientific age from a more general and more radical perspective. Bourget observes at the close of an essay, from which Hardy, in fact, quotes, that there is an "irreducible antithesis" between "art and science." In interpreting reality, he says, art "deforms" it whereas science expresses it "naked," without anthropomorphic or sentimental distortions. Science is the "absence of style," for "style" implies "inexactitude."[142] As the more intelligent artists come to understand this distinctly modern situation, Bourget writes in another essay (in this case on Flaubert), they realize they can no longer hope to find an absolute order either in man or in the external world, and consequently, like Flaubert, they place "this absolute both outside [man] and outside things, in the work of art, [in] the Written Sentence [la Phrase Ecrite]." In this way the artist endeavors to establish an "existence" that will transcend the universal ruin ("l'universelle caducité").[143]

From this strategy one might trace a now perhaps excessively familiar descent from Flaubert to Nietzsche to Derrida, the last of whom has provided Miller with some of the finest insights we have lately had into Hardy's art. But Hardy—and here I find myself at odds with the deconstructivist reading of this author—could not ignore or bracket, any more than Bourget, the reality of universal *caducité* in favor of an aesthetic or writerly absolute. Rather, he tried somehow to embody what was more and more appearing to be an irreducible antithesis between the interests of art and the interests of science. Miller has plausibly identified Hardy's artistic procedure as one version or another of an "interminable" repetition of structures expressive of an "impasse [which] is not the confrontation of a definite obstacle to further thought but a searching for a definitive end which can never be found."[144] But in my own reading, Hardy does indeed believe that he has found the definitive end, the "metalinguistic reality" or thing-in-itself, which he is striving to imitate. The repetition of aesthetic (symbolic) structuring exists for him, not as an absolute (as for Neitzsche or Derrida or Miller), but as an accident of evolution. From this standpoint, he is not compulsively resisting confrontation with the absence of a "definitive end." On the contrary, he is expressing the consequences of an end that seems to him all too definitively, that is, scientifically, present.

11

Conclusion:
Towards the New Century

... we may conclude that just as science ... leads to the imaginary, so life leads us to the impossible. ...

—Hans Vaihinger

"SCIENCE . . . leads to the imaginary"[1]: Vaihinger's point (from *The Philosophy of "As If,"* 1911) nicely summarizes some 75 years of intense speculation on the method and meaning of science. The point, as Vaihinger argues it, is safely epistemological. Nineteenth-century scientific philosophers, although they might have begun by setting themselves the task of overthrowing the unreal, the imaginary constructions of metaphysics, repeatedly came back, in one way and another, to the realization that the initial move in the development of any scientific knowledge, whether of the natural or the human world, must be some sort of imaginary projection. As Vaihinger's mentor, F. A. Lange (1828–1875), had earlier put it in his famous *Geschichte des Materialismus* (1866), scientific thought always begins outside the material or natural, in "aesthetic principles," for we "cannot do away with the fact that our mind is so constituted as ever anew to produce within itself a harmonious picture of the world. . . ."[2] Whether in its general assumption of a harmoniously ordered world, or in its particular hypothetical projections about some aspect of that world, nineteenth-century scientific philosophy, positivism, kept coming back to the "imaginary," the "aesthetic." Or one may put the point another way: it kept coming back, consciously or unconsciously, to Kant.[3] This we have seen and seen often enough, one hopes, to preserve us from belief in that truly imaginary being, a serious positivist thinker who was unaware of the necessary intervention of the mind's

280

intentional structures between himself or herself and the world as in itself it really is.

What came to demarcate the scientific epistemology from the metaphysical, on the one side, the purely aesthetical (emerging in the work of Pater, Wilde, Nietzsche, and others, and about which more in a moment), on the other, was insistence on the criterion of verification. Imaginative projections were a necessary preliminary to scientific explanation, but no scientific explanation could be truly scientific until verified by one logical strategy or another. The constructions of the mind must ultimately be proved to coincide in their essential outlines with the structures of the world. Even for Vaihinger's exceptionally liberal methodology (it has been called idealistic positivism, or fictionalism), this is a sine qua non: Hypothesis always "claims or hopes to coincide with some perception in the future. It . . . demands *verification.*"[4]

Where positivism departs from the criterion of verification, it begins to become something else. We have seen this, notably in the instance of the late George Eliot, who moves in a direction I have considered anticipatory of pragmatism. We have also seen it in the late Hardy, who moves towards insights we attribute to a different intellectual tradition altogether (psychoanalysis), but one no less derivative from the root of nineteenth-century positivism. More important, we have seen what sort of "divisions" or discontinuities within the positivist episteme have compelled these very different divagations.

What the two artists have in common is, paradoxically, a sort of "imaginative realism" that scientists proper tend to avoid, a willingness to consider the "inharmonious" possibility either that the human mind is inherently incapable of ever, by any logical strategy, comprehending the true structure either of the world or of the self (the pragmatist position), or—and here the skepticism moves from the epistemological towards an ontological plane—that there is nothing in reality that can correspond to the structures of the mind, mind and nature being two completely antithetical entities. In this latter case we may say that science has led to the imaginary in a rather different, considerably more threatening, sense than what Vaihinger has in mind. It has led to the proposition that there is no thinking at all, no human interpretation, and consequently no human value which is not essentially and irremediably imaginary, that is, ironic.

The difference between George Eliot's position and Hardy's comes down not to faith or lack of faith in verification; they are beyond that.

Rather, it comes down to how much stock one is prepared to place in the constructions of the human mind in and of themselves. George Eliot, aware as she is of the discrepancy between those mental images and the way the world and our inner selves actually may be, nonetheless falls back on an arbitrary valuation of our mental images (altruism is good, egoism is evil) and on the confidence that they can eventually remake the real, that they have the *energy* to change whatever nature has given us, externally or in the self. This is, as I have argued, a belated, if demystified, romanticism. Thomas Hardy, on the contrary, treats the mind's constructions as imaginary evasions of a natural reality we fear to confront and cannot possibly alter. "*Timor fecet deos,*" Kant had said, in criticism of the primitive mentality, and then added in the keynote of the Enlightenment spirit, "*Ratio facit Deus.*"[5] With Hardy (as with Freud) the Enlightenment is thoroughly dead. The god Reason—"the speculative interest of reason," which, according to Kant, makes "it necessary to regard all order as if it had originated in the purpose of a supreme wisdom"[6]—has simply become one of the host of discredited idols, created by the alienated mind. Add to the radical disjunction Hardy finds between mind and world, the further demoralization of a belief, derived in part from the deterministic or "structuralist" moral theory of his friend Stephen among others, in part from developments in contemporary evolutionary and energy theory, that the spiritual force of neither one prophetic individual (George Eliot's "massive being") nor the entire race is sufficient to change what nature has given, and one has the full measure of the pessimism to which the Victorian positivist tradition, in spite of itself, led. Where does one go from there?

A recent historian of ideas has written an excellent account of the distinctive philosophical character of our own era. Tracing a line of development through what he calls the "prophets of extremity"—Nietzsche, Heidegger, Foucault, and Derrida—Allan Megill argues that the dominant philosophy of the later twentieth century has become "aestheticism," by which he means the "tendency to see 'art' or 'language' or 'discourse' or 'text' as constituting the primary realm of human experience. . . . The irony that pervaded modernism tried to uncover a Man or Culture or Nature or History underlying the flux of surface experience. In postmodernism, this has given way to a new irony, one that holds these erstwhile realities to be textual fictions. We are seen as cut off from 'things' and confined to a confrontation with 'words' alone."[7] It would perhaps not be too great a presumption to suggest that Megill has, in effect, written a sequel to the story I have just completed: twentieth-century "aestheticism," broadly speaking, is not simply a reaction to but, more precisely, an inevitable outgrowth of late nineteenth-century positivism, just as the latter was itself both a reaction against and an inevitable outcome of that earlier, distinctly metaphysical, aestheticism that we call the romantic movement (Megill is well aware of the romantic roots of his twentieth-century prophets).

But, as the passage from Megill just quoted indicates, the twentieth-century aesthetic movement in philosophy has actually had, not one, but two emanations, a modernist (early twentieth-century) and postmodernist (later twentieth-century) one. His distinction between the two is that the postmodernists, whom he, in fact, is writing about, have arrived at a "new," all-consuming irony. For them aesthetic structures, quite appropriately reduced by Megill to symbols or words, have been absolutely dissociated ("cut-off") from "things." What began by asserting itself as the "primary realm of human experience" has ended—and here Megill could perhaps have been more precise—by being the *only* available realm of human experience.

This distinction between what amounts to degrees of aestheticism, roughly speaking, parallels the two departures from nineteenth-century positivism I have just described. Early twentieth-century modernism, admittedly more neo-Kantian than pragmatist, is not that far removed from George Eliot's celebration of the ultimate efficacy of symbolic form. One could quite conceivably draw a line of philosophical filiation from *Daniel Deronda*, or for that matter from Lewes' late work (which, as we have seen, has a distinctly neo-Kantian provenance), to the Marburg school, culminating perhaps in Ernst Cassirer, whose philosophy in so many ways seems to capture the essence of modernism: "In language, in religion, in art, in science, man can do no more than to build up his own universe—a symbolic universe that enables him to understand and interpret, to articulate and organize, to synthesize and universalize his human experience."[8] For Cassirer, as for George Eliot, this symbolic (aesthetic) synthesis (totalization) of experience, for all its apparent autonomy, remains anchored in some "thing," let us say, recurring to Megill's list, Culture or History, though certainly not Nature. Later twentieth-century, that is, postmodernist, aestheticism is not that far removed from the conclusion Hardy is approaching at the close of his career. Our human symbolic structures are absolutely aesthetic or imaginary in the sense of being random, accidental, ultimately irrelevant or alienated orderings of a world we cannot know. There is no "thing" behind them, certainly not Nature, but also not even Man or Culture or History, inasmuch as all these signs, implicitly deified by their capitals, have traditionally signified entities with an origin in—to recall Kant's phrase—"supreme wisdom," a wisdom which implicitly celebrates our human right to reign in this world and define its order. Hardy's late work, that is, really does seem to take us a long way towards Foucault's reading of man as a post-Kantian "invention of recent date. And one perhaps nearing its end."[9]

What do I mean to suggest by these rather far-flung connections? First, simply a historicist point about the dialectical continuity of philosophical development, the naivete of believing in radical disjunctions and innovations. But also I am urging a related rhetorical point about another sort of naivete that would oversimplify not only history but also one's present philosophical antagonists in the interests of establishing an easy superiority over beliefs or positions that may never have had any serious exponents.

But these points about continuity and fair play aside, I do not want to close by obscuring fundamental differences. The end of the nineteenth-century positivist tradition, as I have traced it in the later Darwin, in Hardy, and in Freud, is obviously a good way from the beginning of the modernist/postmodernist movement Megill describes. It became rather, the *occasion* for the rise to prominence of a thoroughgoing philosophical aestheticism. To vary Vaihinger's formula with which we began, the growing scientific recognition of "the impossibility of life" as we would like to believe in it compelled philosophy towards a new and increasingly unqualified privileging of the imaginary. Humanity followed, as Arnold would have put it, its inerradicable "instinct of self-preservation."[10]

The key transitional figure is certainly Hardy's contemporary Friedrich Nietzsche (1844–1900). For modernists and especially postmodernists alike he has become the true precursor in the last century. "Nietzsche," says Megill, "stands as the founder of what became the aesthetic metacritique of 'truth.' . . ."[11] But there are several Nietzsches. The one Megill has in mind is the one alluded to at the end of my discussion of Meredith, the one who gaily embraces the prospect of the aesthetic or figurative as ultimate reality, for whom, that is, "it is only as an aesthetic phenomenon that existence and the world are eternally justified."[12] To this "extreme" of aestheticism none of my Victorian prophets of science, understandably, ever came. But with another, more anxious, Nietzsche, they might well have identified. "One question there is that seems to lie like lead upon our tongues," laments a somewhat shakier sage, "the question whether we can consciously remain in falsehood and, if we must, whether death would not be preferable."[13] Jürgen Habermas perspicaciously— and, it would appear in defiance of the modernists/postmodernists— finds in this other Nietzsche the "last chapter" of nineteenth-century positivism.[14] Only the positivist's final frustration at the impossibility of anchoring mind in an innocent nature can have issued in such a bitter question. This is also the Nietzsche to whom Freud could most closely relate, the realist Freud that Jacques Derrida cannot accept, for whom the pain within a still substantial self is of more moment, finally, than the imaginary text we weave to avoid it,[15] the Freud for whom, at last, "science is no illusion."[16]

On this point we may perhaps make our final demarcation of the tradition we have been following. However conscious they may have come to be of the illusions science could perpetrate about itself and its capacity to deliver the human world from indeterminacy, these Victorian positivists still believed that science itself was no illusion, dangerous as that belief increasingly became to their human self-esteem. One wonders whether the newest moderns are as unflinching, after all, as the latest Victorians; whether it takes more intellectual courage to postulate absence than to confront a presence that seems utterly impervious to our imaginings. Are Megill's prophets actually on the extremity or simply trying to get back from it?

Notes

Index

Notes

Chapter 1. Modes of Totality

1 Charles Dickens, *Great Expectations* (Harmondsworth: Penguin Books, 1965), p. 246.
2 Ibid., p. 35.
3 G. W. F. Hegel, *The Phenomenology of Mind*, trans. J. B. Baillie (New York: Harper and Row, 1967), p. 465.
4 Georg Lukács, *The Theory of the Novel: a Historico-Philosophical Essay on the Forms of Great Epic Literature*, trans. Anna Bostock (Cambridge, Mass.: MIT Press, 1971), pp. 32, 56. For the best exposition of Lukács' connection between totality and literary form, see J. M. Bernstein, *The Philosophy of the Novel: Lukács, Marxism, and the Dialectics of Form* (Minneapolis: University of Minnesota Press, 1984), esp. ch. 2.
5 Dickens, *Great Expectations*, p. 472.
6 Ibid., p. 493.
7 Katherine Everett Gilbert and Helmut Kuhn, *A History of Aesthetics*, 2nd ed. (New York: Dover, 1972), p. 428.
8 Martin Jay, *Marxism and Totality: the Adventures of a Concept from Lukács to Habermas* (Berkeley: University of California Press, 1982), p. 51.
9 Georg Lukács, *History and Class Consciousness: Studies in Marxist Dialects*, trans. Rodney Livingstone (Cambridge, Mass.: MIT Press, 1971), pp. 10, 12–13.
10 For a comprehensive survey of modern Marxist concepts of totality, see Jay, *Marxism and Totality*.
11 F. M. Turner, *Between Science and Religion: the Reaction to Scientific Naturalism in Late Victorian England* (New Haven: Yale University Press, 1974), p. 9. See also Walter F. Cannon, "The Normative Role of Science in Early Victorian Thought," *Journal of the History of Ideas* 25 (1964): 487–502; and Susan Faye Cannon, *Science in Culture: the Early Victorian Period* (New York: Dawson, 1978), esp. ch. 1. The present study, however, takes issue with S. F. Cannon's thesis that science somehow diminished in intellectual authority after Darwin's *Origin*.
12 Louis Althusser, *For Marx*, trans. Ben Brewster (London: Verso Editions, 1979), p. 25.
13 I am indebted to Diana Postlethwaite's fine book, *Making It Whole: a Victorian Circle and the Shape of Their World* (Columbus, Ohio: Ohio State University Press, 1984), which exhibits a comparable concern with the positivist pursuit of totality, though her approach as well as most of her characters is quite dif-

ferent from mine. Her story, moreover, is about the *making* of the whole; mine has more to do, at last, with its *unmaking*.

14 Allen Tate, *On the Limits of Poetry: Selected Essays: 1928–1948* (New York: Swallow Press and William Morrow, 1948), pp. 9, 5, 11.

15 See Jonathan Culler, *On Deconstruction: Theory and Criticism after Structuralism* (Ithaca: Cornell University Press, 1982), pp. 23, 178.

16 R. G. Collingwood as quoted by Hans-Georg Gadamer in *Truth and Method* (New York: Crossroad, 1975), p. 467.

17 Theodor W. Adorno, "Introduction," in *The Positivist Dispute in German Sociology*, Theodor Adorno et al., trans. Glyn Adey and David Frisby (London: Heinemann, 1976), p. 14.

18 H. Stuart Hughes, *Consciousness and Society: the Reorientation of European Social Thought, 1890–1930* (New York: Vintage, 1958).

19 Richard J. Bernstein, *Beyond Objectivism and Relativism: Science, Hermeneutics and Praxis* (Oxford: Blackwell, 1983), p. 4.

20 Emile Littré, cited by D. B. Charlton in *Positivist Thought in France during the Second Empire, 1852–1870* (Oxford: Clarendon, 1959), p. 53.

21 Thomas Carlyle, *Sartor Resartus: the Life and Opinions of Herr Teufelsdröckh* in *Works*, Centenary ed. (London: Chapman and Hall, 1896), 1: 131.

22 Walter Simon, *European Positivism in the Nineteenth Century: an Essay in Intellectual History* (Ithaca: Cornell University Press, 1963), pp. 3–4.

23 The point is developed at length by both Charlton and Simon.

24 See Karl R. Popper, "Reason or Revolution," in *The Positivist Dispute*, Adorno et al., p. 299; see also Popper's distinction between his position and positivism in *The Logic of Scientific Discovery* (New York: Harper and Row, 1965), pp. 34ff.

25 I have already noted Charlton's and Simon's histories. For Positivism in Great Britain see J. E. McGee's standard survey, *A Crusade for Humanity: the History of Organized Positivism in England* (London: Watts, 1931); for more up-to-date and stimulating accounts see Christopher Kent's *Brains and Numbers: Elitism, Comtism, and Democracy in Mid-Victorian England* (Toronto: University of Toronto Press, 1978); and Martha S. Vogeler's magisterial *Frederic Harrison: the Vocations of a Positivist* (Oxford: Clarendon, 1984).

26 Leszek Kolakowski, *The Alienation of Reason: a History of Positivist Thought*, trans. Norbert Guterman (New York: Doubleday, 1968), p. 3.

27 Auguste Comte, *The Positive Philosophy*, trans. Harriet Martineau (New York: Calvin Blanchard, 1855), pp. 25–26. I will continue to use shortened forms of Comte's French titles (in this case, *Cours*) in the text and notes.

28 Leslie Stephen, *History of English Thought in the Eighteenth Century* (New York: Harcourt, Brace and World, 1962), 1: 1.

29 David Hume, *A Treatise of Human Nature*, ed. Ernest C. Mossner (Harmondsworth: Penguin Books, 1969), pp. 233–34.

30 Cannon, "The Normative Role of Science," p. 487.

31 Maurice Mandelbaum, *History, Man, and Reason: a Study in Nineteenth-Century Thought* (Baltimore: Johns Hopkins University Press, 1971), p. 11.

32 Comte, *The Positive Philosophy*, p. 30.

33 John Stuart Mill, *A System of Logic Ratiocinative and Inductive: Being a Connected View of the Principles of Evidence and the Methods of Scientific Investigation*, ed.

J. M. Robson, in *Collected Works*, ed. F. E. L. Priestly and J. M. Robson (Toronto: University of Toronto Press, 1963–), 8: 833.

34 See F. A. Hayek, *The Counter-Revolution of Science: Studies in the Abuse of Reason* (London: Collier-Macmillan, 1955), pp. 13–14.

35 Comte, *The Positive Philosophy*, pp. 457, 463, 464.

36 Alan Swingewood, "Comte, Marx, and Political Economy," *Sociological Review*, n.s., 18 (1970): 345–46.

37 See Karl R. Popper, *The Poverty of Historicism* (London: Routledge and Kegan Paul, 1961), ch. 2.

38 Herbert Marcuse, *Reason and Revolution: Hegel and the Rise of Social Theory* (Atlantic Highlands, N.J.: Humanities Press, 1983), pp. 344–45.

39 Jürgen Habermas, "The Analytical Theory of Science and Dialectics," in *The Positivist Dispute*, Adorno et al., pp. 142–43.

40 Comte, *The Positive Philosophy*, p. 516.

41 Ibid., pp. 831–32.

42 Ibid., p. 391.

43 For Comte's relation to modern socialism see Willard Wolfe, *From Radicalism to Socialism: Men and Ideas in the Formation of Fabian Socialist Doctrines, 1881–1889* (New Haven: Yale University Press, 1975), ch. 1.

44 *Auguste Comte and Positivism, the Essential Writings*, ed. Gertrude Lenzer (New York: Harper and Row, 1975), p. 42. The passage is from "Plan of the Scientific Operations Necessary for Reorganizing Society" (1822).

45 Auguste Comte, *System of Positive Polity*, trans. J. H. Bridges et al. (London: Longmans, Green, 1875–1877), 1: 261. Simon discusses the Comtist concept of "spiritual power" in *European Positivism*, pp. 34ff.

46 Simon correctly observes that psychology, having been dismissed in the *Cours*, comes back as "ethics" in the *Système* (*European Positivism*, p. 28).

47 Comte, *System*, 1: 552–59, 189.

48 Richard Rorty, *Consequences of Pragmatism (Essays: 1972–1980)* (Minneapolis: University of Minnesota Press, 1982), p. xvi.

49 Moritz Schlick, "The Turning Point in Philosophy" in *Logical Positivism*, ed. A. J. Ayer (New York: Macmillan, 1959), p. 56.

50 Ibid., pp. 214, 226.

51 The movement from old to new positivism is described in detail by David F. Lindenfeld in *The Transformation of Positivism: Alexius Meinong and European Thought, 1880–1920* (Berkeley: University of California Press, 1980).

52 Mill, *System of Logic*, in *Collected Works*, 8: 3–4.

53 Comte, *System*, 2: 185, 186, 202, 214, 219–20.

54 Kolakowski, *The Alienation of Reason*, p. 214.

55 Comte, *The Positive Philosophy*, pp. 381–82.

56 "At last in Ernst Brücke's Physiology Laboratory I found rest and satisfaction—and men too, whom I could respect and take as my models. . . ." Quoted from Freud by Ernest Jones in *The Life and Work of Sigmund Freud*, ed. Steven Marcus and Lionel Trilling (Harmondsworth: Penguin Books, 1961), p. 61.

57 Comte, *The Positive Philosophy*, pp. 384, 386.

58 Jacques Monod, *Chance and Necessity: an Essay on the Natural Philosophy of Modern Biology*, trans. Austryn Wainhouse (New York: Random House, 1972), pp. 172–73.

59 Jürgen Habermas, *Knowledge and Human Interests*, trans. Jeremy J. Shapiro (Boston: Beacon Press, 1971), pp. 68–69.

60 Charles Dickens, *Hard Times* (Harmondsworth: Penguin Books, 1969), p. 52.

61 Adorno, "Introduction," in *The Positivist Dispute*, Adorno et al., p. 51. For a characteristic modern positivist trivialization of "fancy," see Hans Reichenbach, *The Rise of Scientific Philosophy* (Berkeley: University of California Press, 1951), p. 312.

62 J. S. Mill, *Essays on Politics and Society*, ed. J. M. Robson, in *Collected Works*, 18: 137.

63 Immanuel Kant, *Critique of Judgment*, trans. J. H. Bernard (New York: Hafner Publishing Co., 1968), pp. 157–58.

64 Gadamer, *Truth and Method*, pp. 73ff.

65 Ibid., p. 76.

66 Ibid., p. 79.

67 Ibid., p. 5.

68 In particular I note Postlethwaite's discussion of him in *Making It Whole*.

69 Herbert Spencer, *The Principles of Psychology* (New York: Appleton, 1910), 2: 627, 648.

70 Peter Morton, *The Vital Science: Biology and the Literary Imagination, 1860–1900* (London: George Allen and Unwin, 1984), pp. 6, 17. Morton is much indebted to Lovejoy, an affiliation, as he says, "obvious on every page" (p. 15).

Chapter 2. An Initial Parting of the Ways

1 Auguste Comte, quoted by Christian Cherfils, *L'Esthétique positiviste, exposé d'ensemble d'après les textes* (Paris: Libraire Leon Vauier, 1909), p. 117; my translation.

2 Auguste Comte, *The Positive Philosophy*, trans. Harriet Martineau (New York: Calvin Blanchard, 1855), p. 569.

3 Ibid., p. 837.

4 Emile Littré, *Auguste Comte et la philosophie positive*, 2nd ed. (Paris: Hachette, 1864), part 3, ch. 2; J. S. Mill, *Auguste Comte and Positivism*, ed. J. M. Robson in *Collected Works*, ed. F. E. L. Priestly and J. M. Robson (Toronto: University of Toronto Press, 1963), 10: 292ff.

5 J. S. Mill, *The Earlier Letters, 1812–1848*, ed. Francis E. Mineka, in *Collected Works*, 12: 487.

6 Comte, *The Positive Philosophy*, p. 452.

7 Comte, *System of Positive Polity*, trans. J. H. Bridges et al. (London: Longmans, Green, 1875–1877), 1: xi–xii.

8 Ibid., p. xi. As Mill carefully explains in *Auguste Comte*, "religion" here is to be understood in its "ordinary sense" as "a creed, or conviction, claiming authority over the whole of human life . . ." (*Collected Works*, 10: 332). In such a sense the concept in no way implies belief in God. George Eliot will pick up this "ordinary sense" of the word as a totalizing social belief in her later fiction, a belief that literally "binds together" (Latin *re* + *ligare*).

9 See J. S. Mill, *A System of Logic Ratiocinative and Inductive, Being a Connected View of the Principles of Evidence and the Methods of Scientific Investigation*, ed. J. M. Robson, in *Collected Works*, 8: ch. 12, "Of the Logic of Practice, or Art: Including Morality and Polity."

10 Comte, *System*, 1: 225.

11 Ibid., p. 227.

12 Ibid., p. 228.

13 Ibid., p. 253.

14 Ibid., 2: 207.

15 Ibid., pp. 211–12.

16 Ibid., 1: 249. The best discussion of Comte's aesthetic theory is in Arline Rei-lein Standley's *Auguste Comte* (Boston: Twayne, 1981), ch. 5. But Standley does not adequately develop the relation among aesthetic projection, scientific method, and language in the later Comte.

17 J. S. Mill, *Autobiography*, ed. J. M. Robson, in *Collected Works*, 1: 141, 143.

18 Ibid., p. 151.

19 J. S. Mill, "Remarks on Bentham's Philosophy," ed. J. M. Robson, in *Collected Works*, 10: 12–13.

20 Ibid., p. 93.

21 Ibid., p. 92.

22 Mill, *Autobiography*, in *Collected Works*, 1: 139.

23 Ibid., p. 153.

24 Mill, *Earlier Letters*, in *Collected Works*, 12: 101.

25 Mill, "Bentham," in *Collected Works*, 10: 95.

26 J. B. Schneewind, "Introduction," in *Mill's Ethical Writings*, ed. J. B. Schnee-wind (New York: Collier-Macmillan, 1965), p. 23. See also Joseph Margolis, "Mill's *Utilitarianism* Again," in J. S. Mill's *Utilitarianism with Critical Essays*, ed. Samuel Gorovitz (Indianapolis: Bobbs-Merrill, 1971), pp. 378–79.

27 Mill, *Autobiography*, in *Collected Works*, 1: 143, 153.

28 J. M. Robson, "J. S. Mill's Theory of Poetry," in *Mill: a Collection of Essays*, ed. J. B. Schneewind (Garden City, N.Y.: Doubleday, 1968), pp. 256–77. Robson's single essay comes closer to the spirit of Mill's theory of poetry and that theory's relation to the main body of his philosophy than these two book-length studies: Thomas Wood's *Poetry and Philosophy: a Study in the Thought of John Stuart Mill* (London: Hutchinson, 1961); and F. Parvin Sharpless' *Literary Criticism of J. S. Mill* (The Hague: Mouton, 1967).

29 Mill, *Utilitarianism*, ed. J. M. Robson, in *Collected Works*, 10: 217.

30 See R. F. Harrod, "Utilitarianism Revised" in *Utilitarianism with Critical Essays*, ed. Gorovitz, pp. 86–87.

31 Mill, *Autobiography*, in *Collected Works*, 1: 142–43.

32 Margolis, "Mills *Utilitarianism* Again," p. 379.

33 Mill, *Autobiography*, in *Collected Works*, 1: 221.

34 J. S. Mill, *Utilitarianism, Liberty, Representative Government* (London: Dent, 1910), p. 115. R. P. Anschutz in his classic study of Mill elaborates on the conflict between Mill's ethic of individualism and traditional utilitarianism: "He failed to develop [his notion of individualism] into a coherent system of ethics; and his attempt to graft it on to the system of utility ended . . . in utter confusion. . . . The principle of individuality provides Mill with a strong argument . . . for the widest possible extension of representative government, since he holds that participation in democratic institutions alone can provide the education necessary for the full development of individuality. But the same principle also leads him to be extremely apprehensive of the actions that democratic states may take in the interests of the majority" (*The Philosophy of J. S. Mill* [Oxford: Clarendon, 1953], pp. 27–28).

35 Mill, *Earlier Letters*, in *Collected Works*, 13: 487.

36 Mill, *System of Logic*, in *Collected Works*, 7: 221.

37 Mill, *Autobiography*, in *Collected Works*, 1: 221.

38 Comte, *System*, 1: 419.

39 Mill, *Autobiography*, in *Collected Works*, 1: 217.

40 Mill, *Auguste Comte*, in *Collected Works*, 10: 292.

41 Ibid., p. 291.

42 Mill, *System of Logic*, in *Collected Works*, 7: 284.

43 See Oskar Alfred Kubitz, *Development of John Stuart Mill's "System of Logic"* (Urbana, Ill.: University of Illinois Press, 1932), ch. 4.

44 Mill, *System of Logic*, in *Collected Works*, 7: 432. There is an extensive literature on Mill's dispute with Whewell, but note especially, Anschutz, *The Philosophy of J. S. Mill*, ch. 9; Alvar Ellegård, "The Darwinian Theory and Nineteenth-Century Philosophies of Science," *Journal of the History of Ideas* 18 (1957): 362–93; E. W. Strong, "William Whewell and John Stuart Mill: Their Controversy about Scientific Knowledge," *Journal of the History of Ideas* 16 (1955): 209–31; H. T. Walsh, "Whewell and Mill on Induction," *Philosophy of Science* 29 (1962): 279–84.

45 See Larry Laudan, *Science and Hypothesis: Historical Essays on Scientific Methodology* (Dordrecht, Holland: D. Reidel, 1981), pp. 10–15.

46 Mill, *System of Logic*, in *Collected Works*, 7: 490–99.

47 Cited by Laudan in *Science and Hypothesis*, p. 151.

48 Mill, *Autobiography*, in *Collected Works*, 1: 255.

49 Laudan, *Science and Hypothesis*, p. 158.

50 Jeremy Bentham, *The Theory of Fictions*, ed. C. K. Ogden (Paterson, N.J.: Littlefield, Adams, 1959), p. 18.

51 Comte, *System*, 1: 358–68.

52 S. F. Barker, *Induction and Hypothesis: a Study of the Logic of Confirmation* (Ithaca: Cornell University Press, 1957), p. 134.

53 Comte, *System*, 1: 405.

54 Ibid., p. 421.

55 Ibid., p. 449.

56 Auguste Comte, *Synthèse subjective ou système universal des conceptions propres a l'état normal de l'humanité* (Paris: Victor Dalmont, 1856), pp. 35–43; my translation.

57 Ibid., p. 29; my translation.

58 Mill, *System of Logic*, in *Collected Works*, 8: 888.

59 Ibid., p. 895.

60 Mill, "Coleridge," ed. J. M. Robson, in *Collected Works*, 10: 119.

61 Karl Pearson, *The Grammar of Science* (London: Macmillan, 1892), p. 30.

62 Karl R. Popper, *The Logic of Scientific Discovery* (New York: Harper and Row, 1965), p. 32.

63 Paul Feyerabend, *Against Method: Outline of an Anarchistic Theory of Knowledge* (London: Humanities Press, 1975), pp. 23, 26.

64 Mary Hesse, *The Structure of Scientific Inference* (Berkeley: University of California Press, 1974), p. 3.

65 Michael Ermarth, *Wilhelm Dilthey: the Critique of Historical Reason* (Chicago: University of Chicago Press, 1978) pp. 17–18.

66 Ibid., pp. 18–19; the quoted phrase at the close is from Wilhelm Dilthey's

Gesammelte Schriften (Stuttgart: B. G. Teubner; and Göttingen: Vandenhoeck and Ruprech, 1914–1977), 5: 145.

67 For more on the concept of intentionality, see two classic studies: G. E. M. Anscombe, *Intention* (Ithaca: Cornell University Press, 1957); Georg Henrik von Wright, *Explanation and Understanding* (Ithaca: Cornell University Press, 1971).

Chapter 3. The Biological Structure of Thought

1 T. H. Green, "Mr. Herbert Spencer and Mr. G. H. Lewes: Their Application of the Doctrine of Evolution to Thought," part 2, *Contemporary Review* 31 (1878): 769. Frederic Harrison found that Lewes' *History of Philosophy* influenced the late Victorians more "than any single book except Mr. Mill's *Logic*." Cited by Anna Kitchell in *G. H. Lewes and George Eliot* (New York: John Day, 1933), p. 46.

2 Kitchell, *G. H. Lewes and George Eliot*, p. 40.

3 John Halperin, ed., *The Theory of the Novel: New Essays* (New York: Oxford University Press, 1974), p. 8. Halperin places Lewes as the best English-speaking critic of the novel up to James.

4 G. H. Lewes Journals, 3 April 1860, Beinecke Library, Yale University. This is, in fact, just two weeks before his 43rd birthday.

5 G. H. Lewes, "Percy Bysshe Shelley," *Westminster Review* 35: 319.

6 See, e.g., Benedetto Croce, *Aesthetic as Science of Expression and General Linguistic*, trans. Douglas Ainslie (New York: Noonday Press, 1968). Hegel "refused to evade the logical exigencies of his system and proclaimed the mortality, nay, the very death of art" (p. 302).

7 See J. S. Mill, *The Earlier Letters, 1812–1848*, ed. Francis Mineka, in *Collected Works*, ed. F. E. L. Priestly and J. M. Robson (Toronto: University of Toronto Press, 1963–), 13: 466, 470–71, 484.

8 G. H. Lewes, "The Modern Metaphysics and Moral Philosophy of France," *British Foreign Quarterly* 15 (1843): 400 ff. For Mill's influence on Lewes' move toward Comte, see *Earlier Letters*, in *Collected Works*, 13: 527, 667.

9 G. H. Lewes, *A Biographical History of Philosophy* (London: George Routledge and Sons, 1845–1846), p. 614.

10 Ibid., pp. xviii–xix.

11 G. H. Lewes, *Problems of Life and Mind* (London: Trübner, 1874–1879), 1 (*The Foundations of a Creed*, i): 2–3. There are five volumes to this series, the last two published posthumously. Reference will be made to the volume and page, not to the several "series."

12 Lewes, *Biographical History*, p. 637.

13 Northrop Frye, *Anatomy of Criticism: Four Essays* (New York: Atheneum, 1966), p. 5.

14 G. H. Lewes, "The Errors and Abuses of Criticism," *Westminster Review* 38 (1842): 481.

15 The evidence for this reading is found in Lewes' very substantial essay on Hegel's *Vorlesungen über die Ästhetik* ("Hegel's Aesthetics," *British and Foreign Review* 13 [1842]: 1–40); but see also by Lewes: "The Errors and Abuses of Criticism"; "Character and Works of Goethe" (*British and Foreign Quarterly* 14

[1843]: 78–135); "Augustus Wilhelm Schlegel" (*Foreign Quarterly Review* 32 [1843]: 160–81); "State of Criticism in France" (*British and Foreign Quarterly* 16 [1844]: 327–62); "Lessing" (*Edinburgh Review* 82 [1845]: 451–70).

16   Lewes, "Hegel's Aesthetics," p. 44.

17   Lewes, "Augustus Wilhelm Schlegel," pp. 162, 181.

18   See G. H. Lewes' 1861 Notebook, p. 4, Beinecke Library, Yale University.

19   The comparison is stimulated by Harry Levin's situating of Taine as the principal critical theorist of the French realists: "Their critic is, inevitably, Taine" (*The Gates of Horn: Study of Five French Realists* [New York: Oxford University Press, 1963], p. 7). Lewes stands in a comparable position to the mid- and later Victorian realists. He was a wider-ranging critic than Taine and certainly better informed on contemporary science.

20   I am indebted to the following for their efforts to synthesize Lewes' critical theory: R. L. Brett, "George Henry Lewes, Dramatist, Novelist, Critic" (*Essays and Studies* 2 [1958]: 101–20); Morris Greenhut, "George Henry Lewes and the Classical Tradition in English Criticism" (*Review of English Studies* 24 [1948]: 126–37), and "George Lewes as a Critic of the Novel" (*Studies in Philology* 45 [1948]: 491–511); Edgar W. Hirshberg, *George Henry Lewes* (New York: Twayne, 1970), ch. 3; Alice Kaminsky, ed., *George Lewes as Literary Critic* (Syracuse, N.Y.: Syracuse University Press, 1968); Hock Guam Tjoa, *George Henry Lewes: a Victorian Mind* (Cambridge, Mass.: Harvard University Press, 1977), ch. 2. Few, however, seem inclined to allow Lewes as much stature as I do in the history of criticism. R. L. Brett places him as the most important critic between Coleridge and Arnold ("George Henry Lewes," p. 120). My own comparison of him with Coleridge aims to bring out what Arnold, for example, lacks—his extraordinarily broad philosophical background.

21   Richard von Mises, *Positivism: a Study in Human Understanding* (Cambridge, Mass.: Harvard University Press, 1958), p. 262.

22   Ernst Cassirer, *An Essay on Man: Introduction to a Philosophy of Human Culture* (New York: Bantam, 1970), p. 152.

23   Alexander Bain, *The Emotions and the Will*, 3rd ed. (London: Longmans, Green, 1875), pp. 227–28. Still the best survey of this earlier scientific or empiricist aesthetic is Gordon MacKenzie's *Critical Responsiveness: a Study of the Psychological Current in Later Eighteenth-Century Criticism* (Berkeley: University of California Press, 1949).

24   Paul de Man, "Sign and Symbol in Hegel's Aesthetics," *Critical Inquiry* 8 (1982): 763–64.

25   Cited by Linda Nochlin in *Realism* (Harmondsworth: Penguin Books, 1971), p. 14.

26   G. H. Lewes, *The Life of Goethe*, 3rd ed. (London: Smith Elder, 1875), pp. 409, 447.

27   George Eliot, *Adam Bede* (Harmondsworth: Penguin Books, 1980), p. 221.

28   Cited by Lewes in *Problems*, 1 (*Foundations of a Creed*, i): 195, from Auguste Comte, *Système de politique positive, ou traité de sociologie instituant la religion de humanité* (Paris: Mathias, 1851–54) 2: 382; my translation.

29   Frye, *Anatomy*, p. 74.

30   Jacques Derrida, *Margins of Philosophy*, trans. Alan Bass (Chicago: University of Chicago Press, 1982), pp. 20, 11.

31   See, for example, Lewes, *Life of Goethe*, pp. 51–55.

32 G. H. Lewes, "Balzac and George Sand," *Foreign Quarterly Review* 33 (1844): 291.

33 See, e.g., Edmund Husserl, *Logical Investigations*, trans. J. N. Findlay (New York: Humanities Press, 1970), pp. 90–97.

34 Lewes, *Problems*, 1 (*Foundations of a Creed*, i): vi.

35 Robert Thomson, *The Pelican History of Psychology* (Harmondsworth: Penguin Books, 1968), p. 27. Edwin Boring appears close to sharing this view and scarcely mentions Lewes: ". . . we can afford to pass him by" (*A History of Experimental Psychology*, 2nd ed. [New York: Appleton-Century-Crofts, 1957], p. 244).

36 See Edmund Husserl on the subject in *The Crisis of European Sciences and Transcendental Phenomenology: an Introduction to Phenomenological Philosophy*, trans. David Carr (Evanston, Ill.: Northwestern University Press, 1970), esp. pp. 191–215.

37 S. T. Coleridge, *Biographia Literaria or Biographical Sketches of My Literary Life and Opinions*, ed. James Engell and W. Jackson Bate (Princeton: Princeton University Press, 1983), p. 304.

38 S. T. Coleridge, "The Aeolian Harp," line 26.

39 George Eliot, *Middlemarch* (Harmondsworth: Penguin Books, 1965), pp. 855–56.

40 Cited by Ronald Bush in *T. S. Eliot: a Study in Character and Style* (Oxford: Oxford University Press, 1983), p. 5.

41 J. S. Mill, *Auguste Comte and Positivism*, ed. J. M. Robson, in *Collected Works*, 10: 269.

42 G. H. Lewes, *Comte's Philosophy of the Sciences, Being an Exposition of the Principles of the "Cours de philosophie positive" of Auguste Comte* (London: George Bell and Sons, 1878), pp. 213ff.

43 See Alexander Bain, *Autobiography* (London: Longmans, Green, 1904), pp. 216ff.

44 Robert M. Young, *Mind, Brain, and Adaptation in the Nineteenth Century: Cerebral Localization and Its Biological Context from Gall to Ferrier* (Oxford: Clarendon, 1970), pp. 101–14. See also Boring, *History of Exprimental Psychology*, p. 240.

45 Young concedes that for Bain introspection remained, after all, the " 'alpha and omega of psychological inquiry' " (*Mind, Brain, and Adaptation*, p. 108). Young is quoting from Bain's *Autobiography*, p. 242.

46 Lewes, *Comte's Philosophy*, p. 174.

47 For Lewes' reading in Müller and the others named see, e.g., *The Physiology of Common Life* (Edinburgh: Blackwood, 1859–1860), 2: 50 (Müller); 1: 211 (Brücke); 2: 23 (Dubois-Reymond); 1: 108 (Moleschott). Vogt he would have read by at least 1862 in preparing his book on Aristotle (see *Aristotle* [London: Smith, Elder, 1864], pp. 197, 218).

48 For a comprehensive history of the movement (which begins in earnest in the 1850s), see Frederick Gregory, *Scientific Materialism in Nineteenth-Century Germany* (Dordrecht, Holland: D. Reidel, 1977), esp. part 2.

49 Cited by Yehuda Elkana, *The Discovery of the Conservation of Energy* (London: Hutchinson, 1974), p. 104.

50 G. H. Lewes, "Balzac and George Sand," pp. 283–85.

51 G. H. Lewes, "*Ruth* and *Villette*," *Westminster Review* 59 (1852): 490. We are so preoccupied with Lewes' relationship as a critic to George Eliot that we tend

to overlook his fascination with this earlier female novelist, whose reputation he did much to promote. See Gary Franklin, "Charlotte Brontë and George Henry Lewes," *PMLA* 51 (1936): 518–42.

52   G. H. Lewes, "Julia von Krudener as Coquette and Mystic," *Westminster Review* 57 (1852): 162.

53   Lewes, "Balzac and George Sand," pp. 281ff.

54   Lewes, *The Physiology of Common Life*, 2: 12.

55   Ibid., p. 15.

56   Lewes, *Problems*, 1 (*Foundations of a Creed*, i): 138.

57   Ibid., 3 (*The Physical Basis of Mind*): 42.

58   Auguste Comte, *System of Positive Polity*, trans. J. H. Bridges et al. (London: Longmans, Green, 1875–1877), 1: 11–12.

59   Nelson Goodman, *Languages of Art: an Approach to a Theory of Symbols* (Indianapolis: Bobbs-Merrill, 1968), p. 38. George Levine has provided us with an excellent application of this principle to actual works of Victorian fiction in *The Realistic Imagination: English Fiction from Frankenstein to Lady Chatterley* (Chicago: University of Chicago Press, 1981).

60   G. H. Lewes, "The Lady Novelists," *Westminster Review* 58 (1852): 131.

61   G. H. Lewes, "Historical Romance," *Westminster Review* 43 (1846): 47.

62   Lewes, "Balzac and George Sand," pp. 266, 268–70.

63   Lewes, "*Ruth* and *Villette*," pp. 483, 485, 490–91.

64   Lewes, "Balzac and George Sand," p. 273. Balzac, Lewes also observes in this essay, portrays adultery as the "norm" of society, and this makes his work unrealistic.

65   G. H. Lewes, "The Three Fausts," *British and Foreign Quarterly* 18 (1844): 87–89. Lewes here consciously challenges the romantic notion that art is the highest expression of truth. This leads him to a revision of the romantic reading of Goethe's *Faust* as promulgated most notably by Carlyle in the 1830s. But note that Lewes' later *Life of Goethe* is dedicated to Carlyle.

66   G. H. Lewes, "*Shirley*," *Edinburgh Review* 91 (1850): 160.

67   J. S. Mill, *A System of Logic Ratiocinative and Inductive, Being a Connected View of the Principles of Evidence and the Methods of Scientific Investigation*, ed. J. M. Robson, in *Collected Works*, 8: 848.

68   Lewes, "The Lady Novelists," p. 130.

69   G. H. Lewes, "Goethe as a Man of Science," *Westminster Review* 58 (1852): 479.

70   Lewes, *Life of Goethe*, p. 356. For a modern view of Goethe's contribution in his field see Timothy Lenoir, "The Eternal Laws of Form: Morphotypes and the Conditions of Existence in Goethe's Biological Thought," in *Goethe and the Sciences: a Reappraisal*, ed. Frederick Amrine, Francis J. Zucker, and Harvey Wheeler, Boston University Studies in the Philosophy of Science, no. 97, 1987, pp. 21–24.

71   See: *The Leader* 4: 617–18 (25 June 1853), 1073–75 (5 November 1853); G. H. Lewes, "Life and Doctrine of Geoffroy St. Hilaire," *Westminster Review* 61 (1854): 165–90.

72   Lewes, *Life of Goethe*, pp. 350–51.

73   Lewes, "Life and Doctrine of Geoffroy St. Hilaire," p. 176. For a detailed listing of this phase of biological thought see E. S. Russell, *Form and Function: a*

Contribution to the History of Animal Morphology (Chicago: University of Chicago Press, 1982), chs. 4 and 5.

74   George Eliot, *Middlemarch*, p. 178.

75   Lewes, *Physiology of Common Life*, 2: 70. The experience of actually identifying the biological forms of thought, which Lewes clearly sought, has approached being possible only in our own time. Here, for example, is Melvin Konner describing his excitement and empirical confidence at viewing the pyramidal cells of the brain: ". . . somehow it is structure—that most ancient of biological subjects—seen and drawn or photographed through the microscope . . . that persuades at last" (*The Tangled Wing: Biological Constraints on the Human Spirit* [New York: Harper and Row, 1983], p. 61).

76   G. H. Lewes, "Realism in Art: Recent German Fiction," *Westminster Review* 70 (1858): 489.

77   Ibid., pp. 493–95.

78   G. H. Lewes, *The Principles of Success in Literature* (Westmead, Eng.: Gregg International Publishers, 1969), pp. 40–41. These essays were originally published in the *Fortnightly Review,* May to November 1865.

79   James Sully, *Sensation and Intuition* (London: Henry S. King, 1874), pp. 269–70. Sully's principal example of this aesthetic presentation of unity or type of character is, interestingly, George Eliot (p. 267).

80   Morris Greenhut has written well on the neoclassical bias of Lewes' criticism, finding in it an important precursor of Matthew Arnold's aesthetic. What Greenhut does not note is the radical difference between Lewes' scientific and Arnold's humanistic reasons for adopting the neoclassical posture (see "G. H. Lewes and the Classical Tradition in English Criticism," *Review of English Studies* 24 [1948]: 127–31).

81   Auguste Comte, *The Positive Philosophy*, trans. Harriet Martineau (New York: Calvin Blanchard, 1855), p. 498.

82   Lewes, *Comte's Philosophy*, p. 263.

83   Comte, *The Positive Philosophy*, p. 506.

84   Comte, *System*, 1: 75–76.

85   Lewes, *Comte's Philosophy*, p. 262.

86   Comte, *System*, 1: 285.

87   Ludwig Feuerbach, *The Essence of Christianity*, trans. George Eliot (New York: Harper and Row, 1957), pp. 71–72.

88   George Eliot, *Daniel Deronda* (Harmondsworth: Penguin Books, 1967), p. 50.

89   George Eliot, *Middlemarch*, p. 194.

90   George Eliot, *The Mill on the Floss* (Harmondsworth: Penguin Books, 1979), p. 263.

Chapter 4. A World Wrapped In Words

1   Quoted by John Morley in "The Life of George Eliot," *Macmillan's Magazine* 51 (1885): 254.

2   Suzanne Graver, *George Eliot and Community: a Study in Social Theory and Fictional Form* (Berkeley: University of California Press, 1984), p. 3.

3   Lucien Goldmann, *Towards a Sociology of the Novel*, trans. Alan Sheridan

(London: Tavistock, 1975), pp. 1–8. Goldmann is, of course, drawing heavily on Lukács.

4   George Eliot, *The Mill on the Floss* (Harmondsworth: Penguin Books, 1979), p. 320.

5   Ibid., p. 363.

6   Sally Shuttleworth, *George Eliot and Nineteenth-Century Science: the Make-Be-lieve of a Beginning* (Cambridge: Cambridge University Press, 1984), p. 204. Shuttleworth, like Graver, is concerned with George Eliot's theory of an organic society. But far more than Graver she develops the specifically scientific basis of that theory. The result is the most comprehensive study we now have of George Eliot's use of contemporary scientific thought. Although I emphasize different aspects of George Eliot's relation to science and disagree with some of Shuttleworth's conclusions about the aesthetic and political consequences of the relationship, I am, nonetheless, deeply indebted to Shuttleworth's wide-ranging scholarship and penetrating analyses. For a thorough account of George Eliot's relation to Positivism, see Martha Vogeler, "George Eliot and the Positivists," *Nineteenth-Century Fiction* 35 (1980): 406–31.

7   G. H. Lewes, *Problems of Life and Mind* (London: Trübner, 1874–1879), 1 (*The Foundations of a Creed*, i): 3.

8   Ibid., 2: 147.

9   George Eliot, *Mill on the Floss*, p. 100.

10 Ibid., p. 164. The reference is to Aristotle's concept of heroic action as requiring a certain magnitude.

11 *George Eliot's Life as Related in Her Letters and Journals*, ed. J. W. Cross (New York: AMS Press, 1970; reprinted from 1885 ed.), pp. 425–26.

12 Ibid.

13 George Eliot, *Mill on the Floss*, pp. 91, 69, 320, 362.

14 *George Eliot's Life*, ed. Cross, p. 427.

15 An important point of difference between Shuttleworth's and my interpretations of George Eliot's relation to scientific thought lies in my belief that physics, notably energy theory, was probably more important to George Eliot than biology and organicism, though, as we will see, the two fields bear heavily on one another in the later nineteenth century.

16 George Eliot, *Adam Bede* (Harmondsworth: Penguin Books, 1980), p. 326.

17 George Eliot, *Daniel Deronda* (Harmondsworth: Penguin Books, 1967), p. 476.

18 George Eliot, *Adam Bede*, p. 477. The passage, however, is problematically placed in the chapter entitled "The Verdict," in which Hetty is condemned for child murder.

19 Ibid., pp. 229, 222.

20 Gillian Beer has written well on Hetty's antithetical role in the novel: "The broken, interrupted and agonised narrative of Hetty's experience proves to be the major story that the book must tell, and only Dinah among the characters is permitted to hear it fully" (*George Eliot* [Bloomington: Indiana University Press, 1986], p. 69).

21 The phrase is derived from George Eliot's "Nature . . . has a language of her own, which she uses with strict veracity . . ." (*Adam Bede*, p. 197).

22 A literary "genus" identified by George Eliot in an early article in the *West-*

minster Review (October 1856). See *Essays of George Eliot*, ed. Thomas Pinney (New York: Columbia University Press, 1963), pp. 335ff.

23 George Eliot, *Adam Bede*, p. 52.

24 Ibid., pp. 75–76.

25 See, e.g., Ellen Moers, *Literary Women* (London: The Women's Press, 1978), p. 194.

26 George Eliot, *Adam Bede*, p. 576.

27 But she does not go further than Ludwig Feuerbach; see, *The Essence of Christianity*, trans. George Eliot (New York: Harper and Row, 1957), p. 27.

28 Ibid., p. 48.

29 George Eliot, *Adam Bede*, p. 410.

30 Ibid., p. 500.

31 Ibid., pp. 584, 500. Like Shuttleworth, I am struck with the relative "stasis" of *Adam Bede's* world, but I find more "shadows" in it than she does; cf. her pp. 49–50.

32 George Eliot, *Mill on the Floss*, p. 69.

33 Ibid., p. 464.

34 G. H. Lewes, *Aristotle* (London: Smith, Elder, 1864), pp. 71–72.

35 George Eliot, *Mill on the Floss*, p. 209.

36 See F. Max Müller, *Lectures on the Science of Language* (London: Longmans, Green, 1885), 2: 385–86, 391–93. The lectures were originally delivered in 1861–1864. For George Eliot's familiarity with these lectures see *The George Eliot Letters*, ed. Gordon Haight (New Haven: Yale University Press, 1954–1978), 4: 8, 160. That "great and delightful book," she called the "first series" of Müller's lectures.

37 George Eliot, *Mill on the Floss*, p. 362; from the chapter entitled "A Variation of Protestantism Unknown to Bossuet."

38 Ibid., p. 183.

39 Ibid., pp. 624–25.

40 Ibid., pp. 507–8.

41 As early as 1848, George Eliot was writing of her deep "yearning . . . [for] the time when the miserable reign of Mammon shall end . . ." (*George Eliot Letters*, ed. Haight, 1: 267).

42 George Eliot, *Mill on the Floss*, p. 91.

43 Ibid., p. 20.

44 Thomas à Kempis is also a favorite of Comte's: "In reading [the *Imitation*], we may, by merely substituting humanity for God, continually recognize the spontaneous presentiment of the normal harmony of our existence . . ." (*System of Positive Polity*, trans. J. H. Bridges et al. [London: Longmans, Green, 1875–1877], 3: 460).

45 Lewes, *Problems*, 1 (*Foundations of a Creed*, i): 4.

46 George Eliot, *Mill on the Floss*, p. 125.

47 Ibid., pp. 588–89.

48 Ibid., p. 320.

49 Ibid., p. 366.

50 George Eliot, *Daniel Deronda*, p. 596. For Mordecai the "seed of fire" is the leaven that will promote the growth of a new "enlarging belief."

51 George Eliot, *Mill on the Floss*, p. 208.

52 Felicia Bonaparte, *The Triptych and the Cross: the Central Myths of George Eliot's Imagination* (New York: New York University Press, 1979), p. 10.

53 George Eliot, *Romola* (Harmondsworth: Penguin Books, 1980), p. 391.

54 Bonaparte, *The Triptych*, p. 7.

55 See my "George Eliot's 'Brother Jacob': Fable and the Physiology of Common Life" (*Philological Quarterly* 64 [1985]: 17–35) for a discussion of this story as an experiment in relating literary symbolization to Lewes' contemporary work in physiological psychology.

56 George Eliot, *Romola*, p. 649.

57 Ibid., p. 76.

58 George Eliot, *Mill on the Floss*, p. 222.

Chapter 5. A New Theory of the Symbol

1 Ernst Cassirer, *The Problem of Knowledge: Philosophy, Science and History since Hegel*, trans. William H. Woglom and Charles W. Hendel (New Haven: Yale University Press, 1950), pp. 3–5, 41–42; Maurice Mandelbaum, *History, Man, and Reason: a Study in Nineteenth-Century Thought* (Baltimore: Johns Hopkins University Press, 1971), pp. 292–98.

2 John T. Merz, *A History of European Thought* (Edinburgh: Blackwood and Sons, 1928), 2: 491.

3 For Helmholtz's relation to and departure from the German materialist tradition discussed in ch. 3, see: Yehuda Elkana, *The Discovery of the Conservation of Energy* (London: Hutchinson, 1974), ch. 5; Frederick Gregory, *Scientific Materialism in Nineteenth-Century Germany*, Boston University Studies in the History of Science, no. 1, 1977, ch. 7; Thomas E. Willey, *Back to Kant: the Revival of Kantianism in German Social and Historical Thought, 1860–1914* (Detroit: Wayne State University Press, 1978), pp. 25–26.

4 Cassirer, *Problem of Knowledge*, p. 3.

5 Hermann von Helmholtz, *Treatise on Physiological Optics*, trans. from 3rd ed. by T. P. C. Southhall (New York: Dover Publications, 1962), 3: 1, 170. The passages quoted are unchanged from the original 1867 edition of vol. 3 of *Treatise*, which Lewes would have read.

6 Mandelbaum, *History, Man, and Reason*, p. 16.

7 Ernst Cassirer, "Structuralism in Modern Linguistics," *Word* 1 (1945): 120. See also David Katz, *Gestalt Psychology, Its Nature and Significance* (trans. Robert Tyson [London: Methuen, 1951]) on the roots of the Gestaltist understanding of perception.

8 Lewes admired Helmholtz's work enough to make a special effort to visit him on his German trip of 1868 (G. H. Lewes Journals, January 1868, Beinecke Library, Yale University), and was reading him regularly in 1869 while working on what was to become *Problems* (G. H. Lewes Diaries, January–February 1869, Beinecke Library, Yale University). Lewes' first published mention of Helmholtz is in connection with Goethe's methodology in G. H. Lewes, *The Life and Works of Goethe with Sketches of His Age and Contemporaries from Published and Unpublished Sources* (London: D. Nutt, 1855), p. 141.

9 G. H. Lewes, *Problems of Life and Mind* (London: Trübner, 1874–1879), 1 (*The Foundations of a Creed,* i): 175.

10 Ibid., pp. v–vi.

11 G. H. Lewes, Prolegomena to *The History of Philosophy*, 3rd ed. (London: Longmans, Green, 1867), pp. xciv–xcvi. This may be the work he refers to as an introduction to a proposed magnum opus on the mind in his journals (G. H. Lewes Journals, 8 November 1862 and 1 January 1863, Beinecke Library, Yale University).

12 Lewes, *History of Philosophy*, p. xcix.

13 Lewes, *Problems* 1 (*Foundations of a Creed*, i): 165, 185, 188–89. One repeatedly notices in Lewes, as in George Eliot, a fascination with the metaphor of the web for both social and cosmic totality.

14 Ibid., pp. 192–93. This discussion of Lewes' mature philosophical concept of realism develops further the general account offered by Jack Kaminsky in "The Empirical Metaphysics of G. H. Lewes" (*Journal of the History of Ideas* 13 [1952]: 314–32), a pioneering study of Lewes and the first in this century to take him seriously as a philosopher. Kaminsky is not, however, concerned to bring out the crucial impact of Helmholtz on Lewes' thought after 1860.

15 Lewes, *History of Philosophy*, p. xxxi.

16 G. H. Lewes, *Aristotle* (London: Smith, Elder, 1864), p. 100.

17 Lewes, *History of Philosophy*, p. xxxiii.

18 Ibid., pp. xxxvii, lxv.

19 Ibid., p. lxxxv.

20 Lewes, *Problems*, 1 (*Foundations of a Creed*, i): 3–7.

21 Ibid., pp. 16, 17, 48.

22 Ibid., pp. 135–37, 315–17.

23 See Larry Laudan, *Science and Hypothesis: Historical Essays on Scientific Method*, University of Ontario Series in Philosophy of Science, no. 19, 1981, chs. 7, 9, and 11.

24 Lewes, *Problems*, 1 (*Foundations of a Creed*, i): 32, 37, 289.

25 Ibid., p. 326

26 Ibid., p. 296.

27 See, e.g., Frank Kermode, *The Sense of an Ending: Studies in the Theory of Fiction* (London: Oxford University Press, 1966), ch. 2; and Edward W. Said, *Beginning: Intentions and Methods* (Baltimore: Johns Hopkins University Press, 1975), pp. 49, 78.

28 Hans Vaihinger, *The Philosophy of "As If": a System of the Theoretical, Practical, and Religious Fictions of Mankind*, trans. C. K. Ogden (London: Routledge and Kegan Paul, 1924), p. 271.

29 This is evident from his complete revision of the section on Kant for the 1867 edition of the *History of Philosophy*, as well as the extensive reference to Kant throughout the Prolegomena to that volume.

30 Lewes, *Problems*, 1 (*Foundations of a Creed*, i): 299–301.

31 Vaihinger will make the same point some 40 years later (see, e.g., *The Philosophy of "As If,"* p. 49).

32 Lewes, *Problems*, 1 (*Foundations of a Creed*, i): 304–5.

33 Ibid.

34 G. H. Lewes, *The Principles of Success in Literature* (Westmead, Eng.: Gregg International, 1969), p. 18. Published originally from May to November 1865 in the *Fortnightly Review*, this is surely the long-meditated "Ariadne" book on scientific aesthetics.

35 Ibid., p. 42.

36 Ibid., p. 45.
37 Ibid., p. 55.
38 Ibid., p. 56.
39 Lewes, *Problems*, 1 (*Foundations of a Creed*, i): 456–57.
40 Ibid., p. 471.
41 K. K. Collins has given us an excellent acount of George Eliot's role in editing Lewes' posthumous work ("G. H. Lewes Revised: George Eliot and the Moral Sense," *Victorian Studies* 32 [1977–1978]: 465–92). But I think Collins may exaggerate the degree to which George Eliot pushed the late Lewes in a Kantian direction (p. 476). As I have shown, Lewes, probably inspired by Helmholtz, was already sympathetically reconsidering Kant on the mental constitution of reality as early as the mid-1860's. On the other hand, Collins is right to emphasize the presence of a distinct split between George Eliot and Lewes in moral and social theory, a split I will address at length in the next chapter. George Eliot was definitely not in a "parasitical" intellectual relationship to Lewes, "like mistletoe" (shades of Trollope's Eleanor Bold), as David Williams has lately concluded in his account of Lewes' life (*Mr. George Eliot: a Biography of George Henry Lewes* [London: Hodder and Stroughton, 1983], p. 277).
42 Lewes, *Problems*, 5: 457–62, 484–85, 494–95.
43 Ibid., pp. 470–71.
44 Ibid., pp. 485, 494, 495. 496.
45 Ludwig Wittgenstein, *Philosophical Investigations*, trans. G. E. M. Anscombe, 3rd ed. (New York: Macmillan, 1958), pp. 6, 137. See also K. T. Fann, *Wittgenstein's Conception of Philosophy* (Berkeley: University of California Press, 1971), pp. 63ff.
46 Peter Winch, *The Idea of a Social Science and Its Relation to Philosophy* (London: Routledge and Kegan Paul, 1958), pp. 23, 72.
47 Ernst Mayr, *The Growth of Biological Thought: Diversity, Evolution, Inheritance* (Cambridge, Mass.: Harvard University Press, 1982), p. 686.
48 Lewes, *Problems*, 3 (*The Physical Basis of Mind*): 110, 134. Srilekha Bell provides a comprehensive account of Lewes' relation to Darwinism in "George Henry Lewes: a Man of His Time," *Journal of the History of Biology* 14 (1981): 277–98. I find a sharper difference between Darwin and Lewes on evolution, however, than does Bell.
49 Lewes, *Problems*, 3 (*Physical Basis of Mind*): 102–6.
50 Thomas Huxley, "On the Hypothesis That Animals Are Automata, and Its History," in *Collected Essays* (New York: Appleton, 1894), 1: 239–40.
51 Lewes, *Problems*, 3 (*Physical Basis of Mind*): 408.
52 Ibid., pp. 326, 329.
53 Ibid., 4 (*The Study of Psychology*): 131, 139.
54 Ibid., 3 (*Physical Basis of Mind*): 337–42.
55 Edwin G. Boring, *A History of Experiemental Psychology* (New York: Appleton-Century-Crofts, 1957), p. 316.
56 See, e.g., G. H. Lewes Journals, 15 July 1866, 29 June and 28 August 1867, 10 January 1868, Beinecke Library, Yale University. Wundt was another German psychologist (besides Helmholtz) Lewes took pains to meet on his 1868 German trip.
57 Wilhelm Wundt, *Lectures on Human and Animal Psychology*, trans. from 2nd

German ed. by T. E. Creighton and E. B. Tichner (London: Swan Sonnenschein, 1894), pp. 442, 450.

58 Ibid., p. 427.

59 Wundt's controversy with Mach and Avenarius and the impact it had on Dilthey are discussed by Kurt Danziger in "The Positivist Repudiation of Wundt" (*Journal of the History of the Behavioral Sciences* 15 [1979]: 205–30; see esp. pp. 211–14).

60 Lewes, *Problems*, 4 (*Study of Psychology*): 144–45, 136–38.

61 Ibid., p. 79.

62 See, e.g., Samuel Butler, *Life and Habit* (London: A.C. Fifield, 1916), passim, but esp. ch. 13, "Lamarck and Mr. Darwin": "Mr. Darwin has made us all feel that in some way or other variations *are accumulated,* and that evolution is the true solution. . . . Nevertheless, I cannot think that 'natural selection,' working upon small, fortuitous, undefinite, unintelligent variations, would produce the results we see around us" (p. 261); "[I cannot] believe in an origin of species which does not resolve itself mainly into sense of need, faith, intelligence, and memory" (p. 272).

63 Lewes, *Problems*, 1 (*Foundations of a Creed*, i): 141, 162–65.

64 Ibid., 4 (*Study of Psychology*): 71.

65 Ibid., pp. 151–52.

66 Francis Galton, Darwin's cousin, published "A Theory of Heredity" in 1876 (*Journal of the Anthropological Institute of Great Britain and Ireland* 5: 329–48), which anticipated some of Weismann's arguments against soft inheritance. W. His's *Unsere Körperform und das physiologische Problem ihrer Entstehung* came out in 1874 (see Ernst Mayr, *Growth of Biological Thought*, pp. 695–98). Lewes was personally acquainted with Galton, and His was one of the men he visited on his 1868 German trip (*The George Eliot Letters*, ed. Gordon S. Haight [New Haven: Yale University Press, 1954–1978], 6: 6, 4: 459).

67 Lewes, *Problems*, 4 (*Study of Psychology*): 153, 165.

68 Ibid., 1 (*Foundations of a Creed*, i): 139.

69 Ibid., 5: 457.

70 Ibid., 4 (*Study of Psychology*): 102–3, 109–11, 165.

71 Wundt, *Lectures*, p. 428.

72 Lewes, *Problems*, 5: 459, 457.

73 Ibid., 4 (*Study of Psychology*): 80.

74 Ibid, 5: 496.

75 Definitively described by Daniel J. Kevles in *In the Name of Eugenics: Genetics and the Use of Human Heredity* (New York: Alfred A. Knopf, 1985), ch. 2.

Chapter 6. From New Physics to New Jerusalem

1 Stuart Peterfreund, "The Re-Emergence of Energy in the Discourse of Literature and Science," *Annals of Scholarship: Metastudies of the Humanities and Social Sciences* 4 (1986–1987): 27, 36, and passim.

2 *The George Eliot Letters*, ed. Gordon S. Haight (New Haven: Yale University Press, 1954–1978), 4: 210.

3 John Tyndall, *Fragments of Science: a Series of Detached Essays, Addresses, and Reviews* (New York: Appleton, 1897), 1: 17.

4 Ibid., 2: 180.

5   It has been related in a number of books, but perhaps most definitively in Yehuda Elkana's *The Discovery of the Conservation of Energy* (London: Hutchinson Educational, 1974); see esp. ch. 5, on Helmholtz's contribution.

6   P. M. Harman, *Energy, Force, and Matter: the Conceptual Development of Nineteenth-Century Physics* (Cambridge: Cambridge University Press, 1982), p. 3. See also Harold I. Sharlin, *The Convergent Theory: the Unification of Science in the Nineteenth Century* (London: Abelard-Schuman, 1966), p. 118.

7   Tyndall, *Fragments*, 1: 6. Paul L. Sawyer has written of Tyndall's love of the dramatic in "Ruskin and Tyndall: the Poetry of Matter and the Poetry of Spirit," in *Victorian Science and Victorian Values: Literary Perspectives*, ed. James Paradis and Thomas Postlewait (New Brunswick, N.J.: Rutgers University Press, 1985), pp. 228–33.

8   Auguste Comte, *The Positive Philosophy*, trans. Harriet Martineau (New York: Calvin Blanchard, 1855), p. 28.

9   Cited by Alvar Ellegård, in "The Darwinian Theory and Nineteenth-Century Philosophies of Science," *Journal of the History of Ideas* 18 (1957): 372.

10 Ibid.

11 Ibid., p. 367.

12 Ibid., p. 371.

13 James Thomson and Peter Guthrie Tait, *Treatise on Natural Philosophy* (Oxford: Oxford University Press, 1867). Cited by Cosbie Smith in "A New Chart for British Natural Philosophy: The Development of Energy Physics in the Nineteenth Century," *History of Science* 16 (1978): 259. Smith writes at length on the force/energy distinction. See also D. F. Moyer, "Energy, Dynamics, Hidden Machinery: Rankine, Thomson, and Tait, Maxwell," *Studies in History and Philosophy of Science* 8 (1977): 251–69.

14 Balfour Stewart and Peter Guthrie Tait, *The Unseen Universe of Physical Speculations on a Future State* (London: Macmillan, 1886), p. 271. See also P. M. Heimann, "*The Unseen Universe*: Physics and the Philosophy of Nature in Victorian Britain," *British Journal for the History of Science* 6 (1972–73); Heimann discusses the "theistic interpretation" of the conservation of energy.

15 For Tyndall's relation to Huxley, see Sawyer, "Ruskin and Tyndall," pp. 227–28.

16 G. H. Lewes, *Aristotle* (London: Smith, Elder, 1864), pp. 123, 95.

17 *George Eliot Letters*, ed. Haight, 5: 400, 416.

18 Ibid., 6: 79.

19 G. H. Lewes, *Problems of Life and Mind* (London: Trübner, 1874–1879), 2 (*Foundations of a Creed*, ii): 349.

20 Ibid., pp. 346, 363, 380, 383.

21 Ibid., p. 401.

22 See K. K. Collins, "G. H. Lewes Revised: George Eliot and the Moral Sense," *Victorian Studies* (1978): 463–92: ". . . portions of the third series of *Problems of Life and Mind* are distinctly stamped with George Eliot's own temperament" (p. 465); see also above, p. 304, n. 41.

23 George Eliot, *Middlemarch* (Harmondsworth: Penguin Books, 1965), p. 427.

24 Ibid., pp. 68, 846, 51, 109, 112, 50, 25.

25 Ibid., pp. 665, 88.

26 See, e.g., David P. Deneau, "Eliot's Casaubon and Mythology," *American Notes and Queries* 6 (1968): 125–27.

27 George Eliot, *Middlemarch*, p. 46.

28 Ibid., p. 520. Note the use of the crucial "seed" metaphor that we found in *The Mill on the Floss*.

29 Ibid., p. 519.

30 The relation between Lydgate and Lewes and, beyond that, between *Middlemarch* and *Problems of Life and Mind*, vols. 1 and 2, has been splendidly explored by George Levine in "George Eliot's Hypothesis of Reality" (*Nineteenth-Century Fiction* 35 [1980]: 1–28). I owe much to this article, but hope I have extended its perceptions in new directions. See also Michael York Mason, "*Middlemarch* and Science: Problems of Life and Mind," *Review of English Studies* 22 (1971): 151–69.

31 George Eliot, *Middlemarch*, p. 120.

32 Ibid., p. 324.

33 Ibid., pp. 173, 175.

34 Auguste Comte, *A System of Positive Polity*, trans. J. H. Bridges et al. (London: Longmans, Green, 1975–1977), 1: x.

35 George Eliot, *Middlemarch*, pp. 177–78.

36 Lewes defended Schwann against Huxley's early criticism of his and Schleiden's claim to be the formulators of the cell theory. Huxley's article was in *The British and Foreign Medical Review* of October 1853; Lewes responded in the *Leader* of 5 November 1853 (pp. 1073–75). Among other things, Lewes rejected the concept of a "cell-force," which Huxley appeared to endorse (p. 1074). This may well have been the opening engagement in an ongoing intellectual battle between these two great Victorian scientists.

37 George Eliot, *Middlemarch*, p. 194.

38 G. H. Lewes, *History of Philosophy*, 4th ed. (London: Longmans, Green, 1871), 2: 388.

39 George Eliot, *Middlemarch*, p. 178–79; her actual phrase is "whose distinguished mind is a little spotted with commonness; who is a little pinched . . . with native prejudices; or whose better energies are apt to lapse down the wrong channel. . . ."

40 For an account of the linking together of the two stories see Gordon S. Haight, *George Eliot: a Biography* (New York: Oxford University Press, 1968), pp. 431–32.

41 George Eliot, *Middlemarch*, p. 194.

42 Levine has made this point in "George Eliot's Hypothesis of Reality," pp. 12–13.

43 George Eliot, *Middlemarch*, p. 380.

44 Ibid., p. 374.

45 Shuttleworth has noted the importance of the concept of energy in *Middlemarch*, but relates George Eliot's use of it too closely to Lewes'. My own reading sees her as consciously diverging from Lewes on this critical issue.

46 John Tyndall, "Scientific Limits of the Imagination" (an address to the British Association, 19 August 1868), in *Essays on the Use and Limit of the Imagination in Science* (London: Longmans, Green, 1870); pp. 55–58, 61.

47 John Tyndall, "Scientific Use of the Imagination" (a paper delivered to the British Association, 16 September 1870), *Fragments*, 2: 131, 107.

48 Ibid., pp. 108–9.

49 George Eliot, *Middlemarch*, p. 210.

50 Ibid., pp. 816, 210, 841.

51 Ibid., pp. 174, 183.

52 His "hair seemed to shake out light" (quoted, ibid., p. 241); see Brian Swann, "*Middlemarch* and Myth," *Nineteenth-Century Fiction* 28 (1973–1974): 210–14.

53 George Eliot, *Middlemarch*, pp. 502–3.

54 Ibid., p. 506.

55 I disagree, then, with Graham Martin's argument in his excellent, but I think insufficiently sympathetic, Marxist critique of George Eliot's politics. The mental energies she admires are idealizing energies, as Martin indicates, but idealizing energies specifically directed to coping with the "embroiled medium" of social reality, the "massive sense of wrong in a class." Where she perhaps goes wrong, at least from a traditional Marxist perspective such as Martin's, is in her skepticism over the ability of this practical, political energy to make a difference after all, a point we shall be addressing in the next section. See Graham Martin, "George Eliot and Political Change," in *Critical Essays on George Eliot*, ed. Barbara Hardy (New York: Barnes and Noble, 1970), pp. 133–50. William Myers' "George Eliot: Politics and Personality" (in *Literature and Politics*, ed. John Lucas [London: Methuen, 1971]) is closer to the mark; see esp. pp. 111–12.

56 George Eliot, *Middlemarch*, pp. 890, 896.

57 Ibid., pp. 31, 112, 235.

58 Ibid., pp. 462, 532, 580, 86, 789.

59 Ibid., p. 819.

60 The "central theme" of all George Eliot's fiction, maintains Felicia Bonaparte, is "the progress of Western civilization" ("*Middlemarch*: the Genesis of Myth in the English Novel: the Relationship between Literary Form and the Modern Predicament," *Notre Dame English Journal* 8 [1981]: 110); see also Michael York Mason, "*Middlemarch* and History," Nineteenth-Century Fiction 25 (1971): 417–31.

61 George Eliot, *Middlemarch*, p. 224.

62 Ibid., p. 392. See also Frank Kermode, *Continuities* (London: Routledge and Kegan Paul, 1968), pp. 143ff.

63 George Eliot, *Middlemarch*, pp. 224, 245–46.

64 Herodotus was the first of the ancient historians to see the process of history as a progress towards human perfection. See Herbert J. Muller, *The Uses of the Past* (New York: Mentor, 1954), pp. 108–10.

65 George Eliot, *Middlemarch*, p. 123.

66 See Simon Pembroke, "Woman in Charge: the Function of Alternatives in Early Greek Tradition and the Ancient Idea of Matriarchy," *Journal of the Warburg and Courtland Institute* 30 (1967): 1–35. The passage quoted from Herodotus is on p. 2 of Simon's article.

67 George Eliot, *Middlemarch*, pp. 896, 894.

68 Ibid., p. 896.

69 Herodotus, *The Histories*, trans. Aubrey de Selincourt (Harmondsworth: Penguin Books, 1954), p. 117. Cyrus blocks the current of the Gyndes, "making it so weak that even a woman" could cross it. George Eliot may also have had in mind the immediately preceding account of the Babylonian queen Nitocris, who "changed the course" of the Euphrates in defense of her realm.

70 George Eliot, *Middlemarch*, p. 170. I read *Middlemarch* as more self-con-

sciously subversive of male authority than do Sandra Gilbert and Susan Gubar. George Eliot is, indeed, as they argue, afraid of the demonic potential for disruption in women (as in men), a point we will take up below. But I do not see Dorothea's "submission" to the patriarchy as an expression of George Eliot's fear of that demonic energy. Rather, it is deliberately presented as a political tragedy, the result of social structures that George Eliot wants changed. See Gilbert and Gubar, *The Madwoman in the Attic: the Woman Writer and the Nineteenth-Century Literary Imagination* (New Haven: Yale University Press, 1979), pp. 510ff.

71 John Morley, "The Life of George Eliot," *Macmillan's Magazine* 51 (1885): 254.

72 George Eliot, *Middlemarch*, p. 894.

73 Ibid., p. 633.

74 J. H. Miller, "Narrative and History," *English Literary History* 41 (1974): 469. Both Levine in "George Eliot's Hypothesis of Reality" (p. 6) and Postlethwaite in *Making It Whole* (p. 253) take issue with Miller from a "realist" position. Neither, however, seems to me to have located the exact focus or center of the real in *Middlemarch*, the center, that is, of energy.

75 George Eliot, *Middlemarch*, p. 427; note also the passage from the *Spanish Gypsy* Levine quotes in his article "George Eliot's Hypothesis of Reality": "Speech is but the broken light upon the depth / Of the unspoken . . ." (*The Spanish Gypsy*, Cabinet ed. [London: Blackwood and Sons, n.d.], 28: 104).

76 J. Hillis Miller, "Optic and Semiotic in *Middlemarch*" in *The Worlds of Victorian Fiction*, ed. Jerome H. Buckley, Harvard English Studies, no. 6 (Cambridge, Mass.: Harvard University Press, 1975), p. 144.

77 George Eliot, *Middlemarch*, pp. 243, 510. See also Barbara Hardy, "*Middlemarch* and the Passions," in *This Particular Web: Essays in "Middlemarch*," ed. Ian Adams (Toronto: University of Toronto Press, 1975), pp. 3–21.

78 Miller, "Optic and Semiotic," p. 144.

79 George Eliot, *Daniel Deronda*, p. 95.

80 Ibid., p. 202; see also, the epigraph to ch. 38 for a conspicuous reference to Prometheus as a tragic model. The motif is carefully woven throughout the narrative.

81 This Alan Minitz makes clear in *George Eliot and the Novel of Vocation* (Cambridge, Mass.: Harvard University Press, 1978), pp. 163ff.

82 Levine, "George Eliot's Hypothesis of Reality," p. 22.

83 Henry James, "*Daniel Deronda*: a Conversation" (1876), in *George Eliot: the Critical Heritage*, ed. David Carroll (New York: Barnes and Noble, 1971), p. 420.

84 George Eliot, *Daniel Deronda*, p. 160; Gwendolen figures prominently in Nina Auerbach's list of Victorian "serpent-women" in *Woman and the Demon: the Life of a Victorian Myth* (Cambridge, Mass.: Harvard University Press, 1982), p. 8.

85 George Eliot, *Daniel Deronda*, pp. 210, 219, 367, 723, 413, 229.

86 Ibid., pp. 380, 485.

87 Lewes, *Problems*, 4 (*Study of Psychology*): 102.

88 George Eliot was almost certainly encouraged in this concept of personality by a growing, quasi-scientific interest in psychic force in the early 1870s that led to the founding of the Society for Psychic Research, two of whose earliest supporters, F. W. M. Myers and Edward Gurney, she had become close to between the writing of *Middlemarch* and *Daniel Deronda*, and one of whom,

Gurney, may have provided her with a model for Deronda. Always on the edge of spiritualism, these researchers attempted nonetheless to ground their thought in a scientific theory of energy conversion. Their main concern was with the power of individual personality to move others by an exertion of psychic energy. Gurney was said (by Lady Battersea) to have particularly admired *Deronda* because "it contains one grand idea: How one fine nature can become the salvation of a narrow egotistical one, how it can open the gates of heaven to a poor earth-bound soul" (quoted by Alan Gauld, *The Founders of Psychical Research* [New York: Schocken Books, 1968], pp. 175–76). See also Haight, *George Eliot*, pp. 463–65, 488.

89 George Eliot, *Daniel Deronda*, p. 532.
90 Ibid., pp. 412–13.
91 Ibid., p. 814.
92 Ibid., p. 625.
93 Sally Shuttleworth has written on energy transference and partiality in *George Eliot and Nineteenth-Century Science: the Make-Believe of a Beginning* (Cambridge: Cambridge University Press, 1984). But for her, *Deronda* ultimately "undermines . . . conceptions of the self as a unified directory force, and of society as the free interaction of autonomous entities" (p. 195). My own view, as will become clear, is that the novel, in fact, strongly supports such conceptions of the self or the subjective (just as does Comte's late work) and marks the reversal of the "organicist" conception of self and society, as Shuttleworth defines it, in George Eliot's earlier novels.
94 George Eliot, *Daniel Deronda*, p. 35.
95 Ibid., pp. 224, 522, 208, 225.
96 Ibid., p. 523.
97 Ibid., p. 527; see also p. 530: "Mordecai's mind wrought . . . constantly in images. . . ."
98 Ibid., p. 206.
99 Ibid., pp. 571–72; this passage needs to be read in conjunction with Lewes' effort to get from scientific to moral hypotheses in *Problems*, 1 (see above, p. 113).
100 Ibid., pp. 819–20.
101 Ibid., p. 802; see also p. 590: "Israel is the heart of mankind. . . . "
102 Here, indeed, there may be a genuine anticipation of deconstructionism; cf. Jacques Derrida, "Freud and the Scene of Writing," in *Writing and Difference*, trans. Alan Bass (Chicago: University of Chicago Press, 1978), p. 201: ". . . psychic life is neither the transparency of meaning nor the opacity of force but the difference within the exertion of forces."
103 George Eliot, *Daniel Deronda*, p. 686.
104 Comte, *System*, 1: xxi.
105 Ibid., p. 253.
106 Ibid., p. 18.
107 See my "*Sartor Resartus* and the Inverse Sublime: the Art of Humorous Deconstruction," in *Allegory, Myth, and Symbol*, ed. Morton Bloomfield (Cambridge, Mass.: Harvard University Press, 1981), pp. 293–312.
108 Philip P. Wiener, *Evolution and the Founders of Pragmatism* (Cambridge, Mass.: Harvard University Press, 1949), p. 101.

109 William James, *The Meaning of Truth*, in *Works*, ed. Frederick H. Burkhardt (Cambridge, Mass.: Harvard University Press, 1975), 1: 50–51.

110 Lewes also was well versed in Lotze's work on psychology; see, e.g., G. H. Lewes Diaries, August-September 1869, Beinecke Library, Yale University.

111 James, *Meaning of Truth*, in *Works*, 1: 40–41.

112 William James, *The Will to Believe*, in *Works*, 4: 9.

113 Richard Rorty, *Consequences of Pragmatism (Essays: 1972–1980)* (Minneapolis: University of Minnesota Press, 1982), pp. xvi–xvii.

114 Leszek Kolakowski, *The Alienation of Reason: a History of Positivist Thought*, trans. Norbert Guterman (New York: Doubleday, 1968), pp. 154–60.

115 As I have earlier done in my "Symbolic Representation and the Means of Revolution in *Daniel Deronda*" (*Victorian Newsletter* 59 [1981]: 30).

116 George Eliot, *Daniel Deronda*, p. 50.

117 The title of book 1 is, of course, "The Spoiled Child."

118 George Eliot, *Daniel Deronda*, p. 71.

119 Ibid., p. 94. Gwendolen had a "liability . . . to fits of spiritual dread . . . [,] an undefined feeling of unmeasurable existence aloof from her in the midst of which she was helplessly incapable of asserting herself."

120 Ibid., p. 523.

121. Ibid., pp. 685–86.

122 Ibid., p. 685. Note the persistent use of the energy metaphor "current" in the key passages of these last two works (cf. the blocked "current" at the close of *Middlemarch*).

123 Ibid., p. 695.

124 Ibid., p. 803.

125 Ibid., p. 842.

Chapter 7. Beyond Humanism

1 Leslie Stephen, *Hours in a Library* (New York: G. P. Putnam, 1907), 4: 154–55; he found "something jarring and depressing in the later work" (p. 180); this is a characteristic aversion to the "depressing," which we will explore in the next chapter. One notes that at the close of his career Stephen directly attacks the pragmatist position, with which I have associated George Eliot, in "The Will to Believe" (*Agnostic Annual* [1898]: 14–22; see esp. p. 22).

2 F. W. Maitland, *The Life and Letters of Leslie Stephen* (London: Duckworth, 1906), p. 229: "I write such a quantity of rubbish . . . that I lose all appetite for writing of a more satisfactory sort" (letter to J. R. Lowell, 29 January 1872).

3 Ibid., p. 232.

4 Leslie Stephen, *Essays on Freethinking and Plainspeaking* (London: Longmans, Green, 1873), pp. 68, 113, 111.

5 Ibid., pp. 327–28.

6 "I [did not discover] that my creed was false, but that I had never really believed in it" (Maitland, *Life and Letters*, p. 145).

7 The title of an 1872 essay in *Fraser's Magazine*, which became ch. 2 of *Freethinking*.

8 Maitland, *Life and Letters*, p. 245.

9   Noel Annan, *Leslie Stephen: the Godless Victorian* (London: Weidenfeld and Nicolson, 1984), pp. 39–42.

10   Matthew Arnold, *St. Paul and Protestantism*, in *Complete Prose Works*, ed. R. H. Super (Ann Arbor: University of Michigan Press, 1961–1977), 6: 126.

11   Leslie Stephen, "Mr. Matthew Arnold and the Church of England," *Fraser's Magazine* 82 (1870): esp. pp. 427–429.

12   Arnold, *St. Paul and Protestantism*, in *Complete Prose Works*, 6: 29–30.

13   Ibid., p. 71.

14   Ibid., p. 127.

15   Ibid., pp. 152–53.

16   Ibid., pp. 170–71.

17   The phrase recurs in various forms throughout *Literature and Dogma*; see, e.g., Arnold, *Complete Prose Works*, 6: 196.

18   Ibid., p. 174.

19   Arnold, "The Study of Poetry," in *Complete Prose Works*, 9: 161–62.

20   Arnold, *Literature and Dogma*, in *Complete Prose Works*, 6: 199.

21   Although not published in book form until 1873, *Literature and Dogma* began coming out in *Cornhill Magazine* in July 1871. Stephen's article was published in February 1872.

22   Stephen, *Freethinking*, pp. 45–46, 49, 50, 52, 58–59.

23   Ibid., p. 150.

24   Ibid., pp. 144–46.

25   Ibid., pp. 357, 362.

26   I, therefore, disagree with S. O. A. Ullman, who maintains that it is "as a critic that Stephen will be remembered longest" (*Men, Books, and Mountains: Essays by Leslie Stephen*, ed. S. O. A. Ullman [Minneapolis: University of Minnesota Press, 1956], p. 11). Stephen himself did not see criticism as his major work; it was something, rather, that he "stumbled into" (Maitland, *Life and Letters*, p. 170).

27   J. S. Mill, "Remarks on Bentham's Philosophy," ed. J. M. Robson, in *Collected Works*, ed. F. E. L. Priestly and J. M. Robson (Toronto: University of Toronto Press, 1963–), 10: 910.

28   Ibid., p. 8.

29   G. E. Moore, *Principia Ethica* (Cambridge: Cambridge University Press, 1968), p. 40.

30   Mill, "Whewell on Moral Philosophy," ed. J. M. Robson, in *Collected Works*, 10: 171.

31   John Plamenatz, *The English Utilitarians* (Oxford: Blackwell, 1966), p. 145.

32   J. B. Schneewind has made a commanding case for Sidgwick's significance as well as produced a definitive study of mid-Victorian ethical debate in *Sidgwick's Ethics and Victorian Moral Philosophy* (Oxford: Clarendon, 1977).

33   Ibid., pp. 62, 212, 232.

34   See Paul Levy, *Moore: G. E. Moore and the Cambridge Apostles* (Oxford: Oxford University Press, 1981), pp. 59, 152–53.

35   Henry Sidgwick, *The Methods of Ethics*, 3rd ed. (London: Macmillan, 1884), p. 2.

36   Ibid., p. 71.

37   Ibid., p. 504; see also Schneewind, *Sidgwick's Ethics*, p. 212.

38   Leslie Stephen, "Sidgwick's *Methods of Ethics*," *Fraser's Magazine* 91 (1875): 307.

39 Ibid., p. 307; see also p. 323.

40 Leslie Stephen, *The Science of Ethics*, 2nd ed. (London: Smith, Elder, 1907), pp. 55–70.

41 Leslie Stephen, "An Attempted Philosophy of History," *Fortnightly Review* 33 (1880): 680.

42 Maitland, *Life and Letters*, p. 172.

43 Ibid., p. 73.

44 Leslie Stephen, "The Comtist Utopia," *Fraser's Magazine* 80 (1869): 2, 14. Stephen is, of course, referring to the social disorder related to the passage of the Second Reform Bill (1867), the subject also of Arnold's contemporaneous *Culture and Anarchy*, which offers quite another solution to the problem.

45 Auguste Comte, *System of Positive Polity*, trans. J. H. Bridges et al. (London: Longmans, Green, 1875–1877), 1: 12.

46 See Willard Wolfe, *From Radicalism to Socialism: Men and Ideas in the Formation of Fabian Doctrines, 1881–1889* (New Haven: Yale University Press, 1975), ch. 1, for an account of the roots of Fabianism in the scientific sociology of Comte.

47 Stephen, *Freethinking*, pp. 246, 271, 153, 261.

48 Sidgwick, *Methods of Ethics*, pp. 115–17.

49 See Plamenatz, *The English Utilitarians*, p. 30.

50 David Hume, *An Enquiry into the Principles of Morals* (Chicago: Open Court, 1930), p. 109.

51 Maitland, *Life and Letters*, p. 489.

52 Stephen, "An Attempted Philosophy of History," p. 695.

53 J. H. Bridges, "Evolution and Positivism," *Fortnightly Review* 28 (1877): 106.

54 For Positivist antipathy to Darwinism see H. Eisen, "Herbert Spencer and the Spectre of Comte," *Journal of British Studies* 7 (1967–1968): 65–66.

55 T. H. Huxley, "Evolution and Ethics," in *Collected Essays* (New York: Appleton, 1894), 9: 82.

56 Quoted by R. C. Lewontin, Steven Rose, and Leon J. Kamin, *Not in Our Genes: Biology, Ideology, and Human Nature* (New York: Pantheon Books, 1984), p. 26. See Richard Hofstadter's definitive study, *Social Darwinism in American Thought* (Philadelphia: University of Pennsylvania Press, 1944); see also Barry Barnes and Steven Shapin's revision of the "question of 'links' between Darwin and social Darwinism" in "Darwin and Social Darwinism: Purity and History," in *Natural Order: Historical Studies of Scientific Culture*, ed. Barry Barnes and Steven Shapin (Beverly Hills: Sage Publications, 1979), pp. 125–42.

57 Jacob G. Schurman, *The Ethical Import of Darwinism* (New York: Charles Scribner's Sons, 1887), p. 126; compare, e.g., Robert Young, "Darwinism and the Division of Labour," *Listener* 88 (1972): 202–3.

58 The tradition is described by Ashley Montague, *Darwin: Competition and Cooperation* (New York: H. Schuman, 1952).

59 Stephen Jay Gould, *Ever Since Darwin: Reflections in Natural History* (New York: W. W. Norton, 1977), p. 24: Darwin "espoused but feared to expose something he perceived as far more heretical than evolution itself: philosophical materialism . . ."; hence "Darwin's delay" in publishing the *Origin*.

60 Charles Darwin, *The Descent of Man and Selection in Relation to Sex*, 2nd ed. (London: John Murray, 1885), pp. 98, 99, 119, 125.

61   W. K. Clifford, *Lectures and Essays*, ed. Leslie Stephen and Frederick Pollock, 2nd ed. (London: Macmillan, 1886), p. 291.

62   The debate is reviewed and exemplified in *Morality as a Biological Phenomenon: the Presuppositions of Sociobiological Research*, ed. Gunther S. Stent (Berkeley: University of California Press, 1980); see esp. Stent's introduction.

63   Stephen, *The Science of Ethics*, p. 88.

64   Ibid., p. 339.

65   Ibid., e.g., p. 87.

66   Leslie Stephen, "Social Macadamisation," *Fraser's Magazine* 86 (1872): 150, 159–60.

67   Leslie Stephen, *The English Utilitarians* (New York: P. Smith, 1950), pp. 293–96, 342–43.

68   Maitland, *Life and Letters*, p. 351.

69   Indeed, we should now be better able to appreciate the new method of ethical analysis Stephen is proposing (against Mill, Spencer, and others), familiar as we are with the modern debate between "holism" and "individualism" as means of explaining historico-sociological phenomena. See the classic exchange between Ernest Gellner ("Holism versus Individualism in History and Sociology") and T. W. N. Watkins ("Historical Explanation in the Social Sciences"), reprinted in *Theories of History* (ed. Patrick Gardiner [New York: Collier-Macmillan, 1959]). "Holism" or "organicism," says Watkins, maintains that "social systems constitute 'wholes' at least in the sense that some of their large-scale behavior is governed by macro-laws which are essentially *sociological*. . . ." In contrast, "the central" assumption of the individualistic position . . . is that no social tendency exists which could not be altered *if* the individuals concerned both wanted to alter it and possessed the appropriate information" (pp. 505, 506).

70   Henry Sidgwick, "The Science of Ethics by Leslie Stephen," *Mind* 7 (1882): 573–74.

71   Stephen, *Science of Ethics*, p. 17.

72   Ibid., p. 29.

73   Ibid., pp. 114ff.

74   Ibid., p. 30.

75   Gordon S. Haight, *George Eliot: a Biography* (New York: Oxford University Press, 1968), p. 464.

76   Auguste Comte, *The Positive Philosophy*, trans. Harriet Martineau (New York: Calvin Blanchard, 1855), p. 831.

77   Stephen, *Science of Ethics*, p. 36.

78   Ibid., p. 100.

79   Ibid. For a discussion of later nineteenth-century views of the autonomy of language, see Linda Dowling's pathbreaking *Language and Decadence in the Victorian Fin de Siècle* (Princeton: Princeton University Press, 1986), pp. 61ff.

80   George Eliot, *Middlemarch* (Harmondsworth: Penquin Books, 1965), p. 448.

81   Claude Lévi-Strauss, *The Savage Mind* (Chicago: University of Chicago Press, 1962), p. 252.

82   For both Durkheim's and Lévi-Strauss's relation to Comte see C. R. Badcock, *Lévi-Strauss: Structuralism and Sociological Theory* (London: Hutchinson, 1975), e.g., pp. 28, 45.

83   Emile Durkheim, *The Division of Labor in Society*, trans. George Simpson

(Glencoe, Ill.: Free Press, 1933), p. 228.

84 Talcott Parsons, *The Structure of Social Action: a Study in Social Theory with Special Reference to a Group of European Writers* (Glencoe, Ill.: Free Press, 1949), ch. 9.

85 Stephen, *Science of Ethics*, pp. 106, 115, 116, 135, 208. Here Stephen may be showing the influence of Spencer and his anthropologist disciple Edward B. Tylor. Of all nineteenth-century evolutionists, writes Marvin Harris, Spencer "approached most closely to the understanding of sociocultural phenomena in terms of evolving systems" (*The Rise of Anthropological Theory: a History of Theories of Culture* [New York: Crowell, 1968], p. 208). See Spencer's *Principles of Sociology* (New York: Appleton, 1910), and Tylor's *Primitive Culture: Researches into the Development of Mythology, Philosophy, Religion, Language, Art and Custom* (New York: Henry Holt, 1874), esp. ch. 1. The difference between Stephen and Spencer is that, for all his interest in the "system" of culture, Spencer does not see it as ultimately constraining or determining individual action.

86 Stephen, *Science of Ethics*, pp. 136–37.

87 Ibid., pp. 143, 160.

88 Durkheim, *On Suicide: A Study in Sociology,* trans. John A. Spaulding and George Simpson (New York: The Free Press, 1951), pp. 208–16.

89 See Stephen, *Science of Ethics*, ch. 9, sec. 2.

90 Ibid., p. 362.

91 Maitland, *Life and Letters*, p. 274. Maitland is quoting Hardy, who was quite close to Stephen; see, e.g., pp. 263–64.

Chapter 8. Science and the Comedic Vision

1 Q. D. Leavis, "Leslie Stephen: Cambridge Critic," in *A Selection from Scrutiny,* comp. F. R. Leavis (Cambridge: Cambridge University Press, 1968), 1: 23–24.

2 Desmond MacCarthy, "Leslie Stephen: the Leslie Stephen Lecture Delivered before the University of Cambridge on 27 May 1937" (Cambridge: Cambridge University Press, 1937), p. 11.

3 Matthew Arnold, "Wordsworth," in *Complete Prose Works*, ed. R. H. Super (Ann Arbor: University of Michigan Press, 1961–77), 9: 48.

4 MacCarthy, "Leslie Stephen," p. 23.

5 Leavis, "Leslie Stephen," p. 25.

6 Ibid.

7 Arnold, "Wordsworth," in *Complete Prose Works*, 9: 46.

8 Noel Annan, *Leslie Stephen: His Thought and Character in Relation to His Time* (Cambridge, Mass.: Harvard University Press, 1952), p. 255. In the revised and expanded version of his book Annan significantly qualifies this statement (having read René Wellek on Stephen), but seems, nonetheless, to come round to the view that the two are in the same camp as literary *moralists*, a point I will be taking issue with (see Annan, *Leslie Stephen: the Godless Victorian* [London: Weidenfield and Nicolson, 1984], p. 320).

9 Arnold, "Heinrich Heine," in *Complete Prose Works*, 3: 121–22.

10 Arnold, *God and the Bible*, in *Complete Prose Works*, 7: 377–78.

11 Stephen, *Hours in a Library* (London: G. P. Putnam's Sons, 1907), 3: 140–42.

12 Arnold, "Wordsworth," in *Complete Prose Works*, 9: 44, 48.

13 Ibid., pp. 49–51.

14 Ibid., pp. 161–62.

15 Stephen, *Hours*, 3: 128

16 Leslie Stephen, *English Literature and Society in the Eighteenth Century* (London: Duckworth, 1903), p. 5.

17 René Wellek recognizes Stephen's commitment to the sociological method of criticism, but considers it subordinate, after all, to his moralism: "The moralistic point of view overrides . . . the social point of view in Stephen" (*A History of Modern Criticism: 1750–1950* [New Haven: Yale University Press, 1965], 4: 188). From my discussion in the previous chapter it should be apparent that for Stephen there is little distinction between the moral and the sociological. Surveying the history of the sociological approach in her excellent *Aesthetics and the Sociology of Art* ([London: George Allen and Unwin, 1983], pp. 22ff.), Janet Wolff appears to have little interest in the extent to which that approach derives from other than Marxist sources. A Comtist or positivist sociology of art was well developed in Great Britain (I say nothing of the Continent) long before the appearance of Christopher Caudwell; we find it, notably, in the works of Stephen, his close friend John Morley, and J. A. Symonds.

18 Wellek, *Modern Criticism*, 4: 27. Yet, as I will argue, Stephen is the more genuinely sociological critic, the closer follower of Comte. The best account of Taine's criticism—and its interests outside sociology—is Sholom T. Kahn's *Science and Aesthetic Judgment: a Study in Taine's Critical Method* (London: Routledge and Kegan Paul, 1953), see esp. ch. 9, "The Psychological Core . . . ."

19 Stephen, "Taine's History of English Literature," *Fortnightly Review* 20 (1873): 693–94.

20 Stephen, *Hours*, 1: 174.

21 Ibid., 2: 210, 217.

22 Ibid., p. 186.

23 Wellek, *Modern Criticism*, 4: 28–29.

24 Hippolyte Taine, *History of English Literature*, trans. H. Van Laun (London: Chatto and Windus, 1907), 1: 10–11, 17–25, 8, 33.

25 Ibid., pp. 34–35.

26 E.g., Colin Evans, *Taine: Essai de biographie interieure* (Paris: Librairie Nizet, 1975): "The Conclusion that forces itself upon us is that Taine . . . did not renounce [Hegel's] metaphysic and [instead] made it his business to prove its rationality, a posteriori. . . . [He] wished to take this 'magnificent hypothesis' of Hegel and try to give it a foundation" (pp. 222–23; my translation).

27 Stephen, "Art and Morality," *Cornhill Magazine* 32 (1875): 92, 96.

28 Ibid., p. 100.

29 Stephen, "Genius and Vanity," *Cornhill Magazine* 35 (1877): 671; Stephen is not directly applying these concepts of martyrdom and an inescapable labyrinth to *Middlemarch*, but his use of them to make his point about the romantic illusion of genius, surely, is drawing on that novel, which he cites in the same paragraph.

30 Ibid., pp. 680–82. The probable allusion to Shelley ("not the work of a solitary legislator") recalls George Eliot's scientific revision of Shelley's Promethean myth in *Daniel Deronda*.

31   Stephen, *History of English Thought in the Eighteenth Century* (London: Smith, Elder, 1903), 2: 330.

32   Ibid., pp. 332, 337, 369, 371, 379.

33   Ibid., pp. 456, 381, 382, 451.

34   Stephen, *English Literature and Society*, p. 125.

35   The rise of the "new [scientific] philology" is described by Linda Dowling in *Language and Decadence in the Victorian Fin de Siècle* (Princeton: Princeton University Press, 1986), esp. ch. 2, "The Decay of Literature."

36   Edward B. Tylor, *Primitive Culture: Researches into the Development of Mythology, Philosophy, Religion, Language, Art and Custom* (New York: Henry Holt, 1874), 1: 299, 315.

37   Stephen, *English Thought*, 2: 335.

38   Stephen, *Hours*, 4: 86, 37.

39   Stephen, *Studies of a Biographer* (New York: G. P. Putnam's Sons, 1907), 2: 82, 106, 109, 110.

40   Arnold, "Science and Literature," in *Complete Prose Works*, 10: 6.

41   Leslie Stephen, "The Moral Element in Literature," *Cornhill Magazine* 43 (1881): 48.

42   Henry Sidgwick, "The Science of Ethics by Leslie Stephen," *Mind* (1876) 1: 582; see also Sidgwick, "Spencer's *Data of Ethics*," *Mind* 5 (1880): 218–220.

43   The strain continues in our own era. See, e.g., Charles T. Lumsden and Edward O. Wilson, *Promethean Fire: Reflections on the Origin of Mind* (Cambridge, Mass.: Harvard University Press, 1983), p. 184. Significantly, Wilson and Lumsden look back to the "inspired visionaries" Comte and Spencer, whose scientific optimism they now see renewed by modern sociobiology (p. 171).

44   Henry Sidgwick, "Theory of Evolution in Its Application to Practice," *Mind* 1 (1876): 65–66. Huxley makes the same point more famously 17 years later; see "Evolutionary Ethics" in *Collected Essays* (New York: Appleton, 1894), 9: passim.

45   Charles Darwin, *The Descent of Man and Selection in Relation to Sex*, 2nd ed. (London: John Murray, 1885), pp. 124–25.

46   Jacob G. Schurman, *The Ethical Impact of Darwinism* (New York: Charles Scribner's Sons, 1887), pp. 140–41. Cf. John Dewey's better-known conclusions along the same lines in *The Influence of Darwin on Philosophy and Other Essays in Contemporary Thought* (Bloomington, Ind.: Indiana University Press, 1965), pp. 10–11.

47   Dewey, *Influence of Darwin*, p. 15.

48   See Theodosius Dobzhansky, *Mankind Evolving: the Evolution of the Human Species* (New Haven: Yale University Press, 1962), esp. ch. 12, for a modern version of this late-Victorian faith.

49   The *Life and Letters of Charles Darwin*, ed. Francis Darwin (New York: Appleton, 1893), 1: 282.

50   Leslie Stephen, "The Decay of Literature," *Cornhill Magazine* 46 (1882): 612.

51   See Lionel Stevenson, *The Ordeal of George Meredith: a Biography* (New York: Charles Scribner's Sons, 1953), pp. 156, 186–87, 235; see also *The Letters of George Meredith*, ed. C. L. Cline (Oxford: Clarendon, 1970), 2: 658, 674–75, 731.

52 Stevenson, *Ordeal of George Meredith*, p. 231.

53 Ibid., p. 308. Contrasting himself with George Eliot, Meredith asserts that he always "draws from the life."

54 Donald D. Stone has nicely placed Meredith as the last major Victorian novelist to resist the movement towards decadence and naturalism (*Novelists in a Changing World: Meredith, James, and the Transformation of English Fiction in the 1880's* [Cambridge, Mass.: Harvard University Press, 1972], pp. 88–89). See also Stevenson, *Ordeal of George Meredith*, p. 231.

55 Stephen, "The Alps in Winter," *Cornhill Magazine* 35 (1877): 353. For Meredith's reading of the essay, see *Letters*, ed. Cline, 2: 566.

56 George Meredith, *The Egoist*, in *Works* (New York: Charles Scribner's Sons, 1910), 14: 332.

57 Ibid., 13: 1. For Carlyle's use of the comic spirit see my "*Sartor Resartus* and the Inverse Sublime: the Art of Humorous Deconstruction," in *Allegory, Myth and Symbol*, ed. Morton W. Bloomfield (Cambridge, Mass.: Harvard University Press, 1981), pp. 293–312. The concept of metaphor I develop in this essay may be, finally, the most important link between Carlyle's and Meredith's comic spirit.

58 I am indebted to Carolyn William's "Natural Selection and Narrative Form in *The Egoist*" (*Victorian Studies* 27 [1983]: 53–79).

59 Meredith, *The Egoist*, in *Works*, 13: 43; cf. Darwin, *Descent of Man*, pp. 210–12.

60 Meredith, *The Egoist*, in *Works*, 13: 28.

61 Thomas Vargish has described the central position of this "Providential aesthetic" in earlier Victorian fiction in *The Providential Aesthetic in Victorian Fiction* (Charlottesville: University of Virginia Press, 1985). The novels examined in the present book are nothing if not expressions of the collapse of that aesthetic under the pressure of advancing scientific knowledge.

62 Meredith's quarrel with the contemporary gospel of science comes out as early as *The Ordeal of Richard Feverel*; see Irving Buchen, "*The Ordeal of Richard Feverel*: Science versus Nature," *English Literary History* 19 (1962): 47–66.

63 Meredith, *The Egoist*, in *Works*, 14: 182.

64 Ibid.

65 Ibid., p. 183.

66 Ibid., 13: 2.

67 Ibid., p. 260.

68 Annan, *Leslie Stephen* (1952), p. 75.

69 Stephen, *Science of Ethics*, pp. 212–13.

70 Meredith, *The Egoist*, in *Works*, 13: 130–32.

71 Meredith, *Tragic Comedians*, in *Works*, 15: 200.

72 Meredith, *Diana of the Crossways*, in *Works*, 16: 280–82.

73 Meredith, *One of Our Conquerors*, in *Works*, 17: 285, 120, 506.

74 Meredith, *The Egoist*, in *Works*, 13: 188.

75 Ibid., p. 12.

76 Meredith, *Diana*, in *Works*, 16: 2.

77 Ibid., p. 275. Meredith's preoccupation with figurative language has long been the subject of commentary, but Michael Sprinker has put Meredith's situation in the later novels particularly well: "The origin of language, the zero level of metaphorical discourse, the language of transparency, must perpetually elude the writer, as Meredith shows. His later novels recognize the

impossibility of such a language, while longing for a time and space in which this language could exist" (" 'The Intricate Evasions of As': Meredith's Theory of Figure," *Victorian Newsletter* 53 [1978]: 13). I find Meredith less comfortable than Sprinker does in this Derridean world, but applaud Sprinker's demonstration of Meredith's linguistic sophistication. See also Deborah S. Austin's pioneering "Meredith on the Nature of Metaphor," *University of Toronto Quarterly* 27 (1957): 96–101; Stone, *Novelists in a Changing World*, pp. 154–172; Gillian Beer, "*One of Our Conquerors*: Language and Music" in *Meredith Now: Some Critical Essays*, ed. Ian Fletcher (London: Routledge and Kegan Paul, 1971), pp. 265–80.

78 Meredith, *The Egoist*, in *Works*, 14: 262.
79 Cited by Hans Vaihinger, *The Philosophy of "As If": a System of the Theoretical, Practical, and Religious Fictions of Mankind*, trans. C. K. Ogden (London: Routledge and Kegan Paul, 1924), p. 344.

Chapter 9. Reversing the Positivist Oracle

1 Frederic Harrison, *The Philosophy of Common Sense* (New York: Macmillan, 1907), pp. 414–15.
2 James Sully, *Pessimism: a History and a Criticism* (London: Henry S. King, 1877), pp. 2–3, 5, 384–87, 396, 448.
3 O. Plumacher, "Pessimism," *Mind* 4 (1879): 85–86, 87.
4 Francis Hueffer, "Arthur Schopenhauer," *Fortnightly Review* 26 (1876): 789–90. The late 1870s abound in articles that find pessimism an all-too-plausible outcome of modern science. See, e.g., Henry Maudsley, "Materialism and Its Lessons," *Fortnightly Review* 32 (1879): 244–60; Edwin Wallace, "The Philosophy of Pessimism," *Westminster Review* 105 (1876): 124–65. As the latter concludes, "Cassandra's voice is heard throughout our magazines and novels" (p. 165).
5 Sidney Alexander, "Pessimism and Progress," *Contemporary Review* 63 (1893): 78.
6 Gerald Holton, *Thematic Origins of Scientific Thought: Kepler to Einstein* (Cambridge, Mass.: Harvard University Press, 1973), pp. 35–36.
7 William Carpenter, "The Doctrine of Evolution in Its Relation to Theism," in *Nature and Man: Essays Scientific and Philosophical* (London: Kegan Paul, Trench, 1888), p. 396.
8 Alfred R. Wallace, *Contributions to the Theory of Natural Selection* (London: Macmillan, 1870), p. 316.
9 Cited by Basil Willey, *Darwin and Butler: Two Versions of Evolution* (London: Chatto and Windus, 1960), p. 60.
10 Hans Jonas, *The Phenomenon of Life: Toward a Philosophical Biology* (New York: Harper and Row, 1966), pp. 45–47.
11 See Francis Galton, *Hereditary Genius: an Inquiry into Its Laws and Consequences* (London: Watts, 1869), esp. pp. 338–61. But see as well Daniel J. Kevles' study of the late-Victorian, early-modern eugenics movement, of which Galton is the founding father (*In the Name of Eugenics: Genetics and the Uses of Human Heredity* [New York: Alfred A. Knopf, 1985]).
12 Ernst Mayr, *The Growth of Biological Thought: Diversity, Evolution and Inheritance* (Cambridge, Mass.: Harvard University Press, 1982), p. 698.
13 Jonas, *Phenomenon of Life*, pp. 52–53.

14 Charles Darwin, *The Descent of Man and Selection in Relation to Sex*, 2nd ed. (London: John Murray, 1885), p. 145.

15 Ibid., pp. 191–92.

16 Max Nordau in his classic study of degeneration identifies Morel as the first to grasp clearly the concept of degeneracy in the sense of "morbid deviation from an original type" (*Degeneration*, trans. from 2nd German ed. [New York: Appleton, 1895], pp. 15–17). Caesare Lombroso and Henry Maudsley (about whom more below) are also listed as important scientific pioneers of the subject. An English student of the subject not mentioned by Nordau is Ray E. Lankester, whose *Degeneration: a Chapter in Darwinism* came out in 1880. Lankester was a personal friend of Hardy, and the latter would almost certainly have known his book (see Florence E. Hardy, *The Later Years of Thomas Hardy: 1892–1928* [New York: Macmillan, 1930], pp. 18, 34).

17 Henry Maudsley, *Body and Will, Being an Essay Concerning Will in Its Metaphysical, Physiological, and Pathological Aspects* (New York: Appleton, 1884), pp. 183–84, 316, 323, 330.

18 J. Mortimer-Granville, "Is Insanity Increasing?" *Nineteenth Century* 5 (1879): 524.

19 See Kevles, *In the Name of Eugenics*, ch. 5.

20 Maudsley, *Body and Will*, pp. 318–20.

21 The history of the development of the second law of thermodynamics is told by Stephen G. Brush in *The Temperature of History: Phases of Science and Culture in the Nineteenth Century* (New York: Burt Franklin, 1978), ch. 3. Brush's generalization on the cultural implications of the two laws is very much to the point of the present study: "The first law of thermodynamics (conservation of energy) . . . provided an organizing principle for the science of the realist period. Likewise the second . . . (dissipation of energy) . . . provided a disorganizing principle which turned out to be highly appropriate for [the late nineteenth century] . . ." (p. 29). See also P. M. Harman, *Energy, Force, and Matter: the Conceptual Development of Nineteenth-Century Physics* (Cambridge: Cambridge University Press, 1982), ch. 3; and Harold I. Sharlin, *The Convergent Century: the Unification of Science in the Nineteenth Century* (London: Abelard-Schuman, 1966), ch. 2. For Thomson's and Maxwell's particular contributions to the debate over the second law see E. E. Daub's excellent "Maxwell's Demon," reprinted in *Darwin to Einstein: Historical Studies on Science and Belief,* ed. Colin Chant and John Fauvel (London: Longmans, Green, 1980), pp. 222–35.

22 Herbert Spencer, *First Principles* (New York: Appleton, 1910), p. 454.

23 Ibid., pp. 484–85.

24 See Brush, *Temperature of History*, chs. 7 and 8.

25 A. S. Eddington, *The Nature of the Physical World* (Cambridge: Cambridge University Press, 1927), p. 67. See also Jonathan Powers, *Philosophy and the New Physics* (London: Methuen, 1982), ch. 3.

26 Jacques Monod, *Chance and Necessity: an Essay on the Natural Philosophy of Modern Biology*, trans. Austryn Wainhouse (New York: Random House, 1972), pp. 110–11, 123.

27 The point is argued at length and in far greater technical detail by Daniel R. Brooks and E. O. Wiley in their recent *Evolution as Entropy: Toward a Unified Theory of Biology* (Chicago: University of Chicago Press, 1986); see esp. pp.

34–44. Brooks and Wiley, like Monod, are centrally concerned with the relation between entropy and genetic information (see, e.g., pp. 41–49, 134–39, 292–98).

28 Monod, *Chance and Necessity*, pp. 170–71.

29 Quoted by Samuel L. Hynes in *The Pattern of Thomas Hardy's Poetry* (Chapel Hill: University of North Carolina Press, 1956), p. 34.

30 Albert J. Guerard, *Thomas Hardy: the Novels and Stories* (Cambridge, Mass.: Harvard University Press, 1949), pp. 7–9.

31 Raymond Williams, *The English Novel from Dickens to Lawrence* (London: Hogarth Press, 1984), pp. 116–18.

32 Florence Hardy, *The Later Years of Thomas Hardy*, p. 104.

33 Thomas Hardy, *Literary Notebooks*, ed. Lennart A. Björk (London: Macmillan, 1985), 1: 137; the passage is from Stephen's "The Moral Element in Literature."

34 See ibid., 2: 121, 208, 406. When he speaks of George Eliot's art being "impaired" by the "deepening sense of pain in the world" brought on by her studies of science (p. 208), he is speaking as well, surely, of his own situation.

35 Florence Hardy, *Early Life*, p. 277.

36 Guerard, *Hardy*, p. 7.

37 Thomas Hardy, *Personal Writings: Prefaces, Literary Opinions, Reminiscences*, ed. Harold Orel (Lawrence, Kans.: University of Kansas Press, 1966), p. 51.

38 Ibid., p. 53. Harrison's words in the *Fortnightly Review* of 1920, as recorded by Orel, were, "This monotony of gloom . . . is not human, not social, not true" (p. 266).

39 Ibid., pp. 57–58, 52.

40 Hardy, *Literary Notebooks*, 2: 55. See also above, p. 221.

41 See Mary Kelly, "Hardy's Reading in Schopenhauer: *Tess of the d'Urbervilles*," *Colby Library Quarterly* 18–19 (1982): 183–98.

42 Cited by Carl J. Weber, *Hardy of Wessex: His Life and Literary Career* (New York: Columbia University Press, 1965), pp. 246–47.

43 Florence Hardy, *Early Life*, p. 192.

44 See Tess Cosslett, *The "Scientific Movement" and Victorian Literature* (Brighton, Eng.: Harvester Press, 1982), pp. 135–37.

45 Thomas Hardy, *A Pair of Blue Eyes*, in *Novels* (London: Macmillan, 1952–1964), 10: 241.

46 Ibid., p. 245. See Gillian Beer's important comment on this passage as a measure of the "scale of the human" in *Darwin's Plots: Evolutionary Narrative in Darwin, George Eliot, and Nineteenth-Century Fiction* (London: Routledge and Kegan Paul, 1983), p. 248.

47 Hardy, *The Return of the Native*, in *Novels*, 11: 6, 3, 4.

48 Hardy, *Two on a Tower*, in *Novels*, 14: 33, 32.

49 *The Life and Letters of Charles Darwin*, ed. Francis Darwin (New York: Appleton, 1893), 1: 554–55.

50 Thomas Vargish, *The Providential Aesthetic in Victorian Fiction* (Charlottesville: University of Virginia Press, 1985), pp. 53–55.

51 See *Life and Letters*, ed. F. Darwin, 2: 105.

52 The phrase is from Hardy's poem "In Tenebris II" and is quoted prominently

by him in the 1922 "Apology." For the best account of Hardy's uncompromisingly pessimistic reading of Darwin, see Roger Robinson's excellent "Hardy and Darwin," in *Thomas Hardy: the Writer and His Background*, ed. Norman Page (London: Bell and Hyman, 1980), pp. 128–50.

53 Florence Hardy, *Early Life*, pp. 285–86.

54 From this standpoint I find it difficult to understand what Donald Davie means when he insists on Hardy's "scientific humanism" (*Thomas Hardy and British Poetry* [Oxford: Oxford University Press, 1972], pp. 5–7).

55 See Oma Stanley, "T. H. Huxley's Treatment of 'Nature' " (*Journal of the History of Ideas* 18 [1957]: 120–27) for an account of this crucial shift in Mill's and Huxley's attitudes.

56 Thomas Huxley, "Evolution and Ethics," in *Collected Essays* (New York: Appleton, 1894), 9: 85. As James G. Paradis acutely observes, much of Huxley's social theory comes, in the end, from Thomas Carlyle (*T. H. Huxley: Man's Place in Nature* [Lincoln: University of Nebraska Press, 1978], p. 49).

57 Hardy, *Literary Notebooks*, 1: 148.

58 Florence Hardy, *Early Life*, p. 301. Weismann's work did not become widely known in Great Britain until the controversy with Spencer conducted in the pages of the *Contemporary Review* from 1893 to 1895. Peter Morton discusses Hardy's use of Weismann in *Tess*, as well as *Jude* and the *Well-Beloved*, in *"Tess of the d'Urbervilles*: a Neo-Darwinian Reading," *Southern Review* 7 (1974). My addition of *Casterbridge* to the list of late works influenced by Weismann is owing primarily to the great pains Hardy takes in that novel to demonstrate the radically unprogressive career of his hero, who ends literally where he began.

59 J. Hillis Miller, *Fiction and Repetition: Seven English Novels* (Cambridge, Mass.: Harvard University Press, 1982), p. 169.

60 Thomas Huxley, "Evolution and Ethics," in *Collected Essays*, 9: 116.

61 Hardy, *The Return of the Native*, in *Novels*, 11: 453.

62 Hardy, *The Woodlanders*, in *Novels*, 18: 59.

63 E.g., Hardy, *Tess of the d'Urbervilles*, in *Novels*, 12: 45, 139, 241, 436. "I . . . am . . . but a d'Urberville . . . and—we are all gone to nothing" (p. 241). For Hardy's sense of his own family line as exhausted, see Michael Millgate, *Thomas Hardy: a Biography* (Oxford: Oxford University Press, 1982), pp. 293–94; he considered calling the novel "Tess of the Hardys."

64 Hardy began reading Zola while working on *Tess*; see Robert Gittings, *Thomas Hardy's Later Years* (Boston: Little, Brown, 1878), p. 68. Reviewers were quick to associate *Jude* with Zola's work (ibid., p. 81).

65 We seem seldom to emerge from the fog and gloom with which the novel begins until the close when the sun shines brightly (and ironically) enough on Jude's death and funeral.

66 Hardy, *Literary Notebooks*, 2: 102, 112.

67 Guerard, *Hardy*, p. 7.

68 Hardy, *Literary Notebooks*, 2: 80. Florence Hardy, *Later Years*, p. 271: "I fear that [Bergson's] philosophy is . . . only our old friend dualism in a new suit of clothes. . . ."

69 See Georg Lukács, *Studies in European Realism* (New York: Universal Library, 1964), esp. the preface; see also Everett Knight, *A Theory of the Classical Novel*

(London: Routledge and Kegan Paul, 1969), ch. 3, "The Classical Novel as an Art Form."

70 George Eliot, *Daniel Deronda* (Harmondsworth: Penguin Books, 1967), p. 431.

71 George Eliot, *Middlemarch* (Harmondsworth: Penguin Books, 1965), p. 194.

72 Ibid., p. 174.

73 Oswald Spengler, *The Decline of the West*, trans. C. F. Atkinson (New York: Knopf, 1962, abridged ed.), pp. 219–20.

Chapter 10. "The Best Consummation Possible"

1 Thomas Hardy, *Two on a Tower*, in *Novels* (London: Macmillan, 1952–1964), 14: v.

2 "[I]t is from novels that the crowd of expectant readers and ready pupils obtain that constant flow of easy teaching which fills the mind of all readers with continual thoughts of love." Anthony Trollope, "Novel-Reading" (1879) in *Nineteenth-Century British Novelists on the Novel*, ed. George L. Barnett (New York: Appleton-Century-Crofts, 1971), p. 204.

3 Havelock Ellis, "Thomas Hardy's Novels," *Westminster Review* 119 (1883), p. 356.

4 Hardy, *Far from the Madding Crowd*, in *Novels*, 3: 456–57.

5 Ibid., p. 457.

6 Hardy, *Two on a Tower*, in *Novels*, 14: v.

7 Hardy, *The Woodlanders*, in *Novels*, 18: 108.

8 James Sully had made this point in *Pessimism: a History and a Criticism* (London: Henry and King, 1877), pp. 89–90. Hardy's first (surviving) notebook entry on Schopenhauer is from late 1881 (*Literary Notebooks*, ed. Lennart A. Björk [London: Macmillan, 1985], 1: 141). Mary Kelly ("Hardy's Reading in Schopenhauer . . . ," *Colby Library Quarterly* 18–19 [1982]: 183) places Hardy's first reading of (as opposed to about) Schopenhauer in 1883. Edmund Gosse's contention that Hardy was not influenced by Schopenhauer may be true enough with regard to Hardy's philosophical pessimism, which I have argued can be better explained by his reading in science, but Schopenhauer's views on love may well be another matter.

9 Arthur Schopenhauer, *Selections*, ed. DeWitt H. Parker (New York: Charles Scribner's Sons, 1928), p. 335.

10 Darwin is here quoting Schopenhauer in the second edition of *The Descent of Man and Selection in Relation to Sex* ([London: John Murray, 1885], p. 586) and referring to the article "Schopenhauer and Darwinism" in the *Journal of Anthropology* for 1871.

11 Darwin, *Descent of Man*, p. 212.

12 "[T]he theories of Darwin . . . strongly attracted me," writes Freud, "for they held out hopes of an extraordinary advance in our understanding of the world"; quoted by Ernest Jones in *The Life and Work of Sigmund Freud*, abridged version, ed. Lionel Trilling and Steven Marcus (Harmondsworth: Pelican Books, 1964), p. 54. The three scientific blows to human pride are described by Freud in "A Difficulty in the Path of Psychoanalysis" (1917), in *The Standard Edition of the Complete Psychological Works of Sigmund Freud*, ed. James

Strachey (London: Hogarth, 1953–1974), 17: 139–43. For a detailed account of the impact of Darwin on Freud, see Frank J. Sulloway, *Freud, Biologist of the Mind: Beyond the Psychoanalytic Legend* (New York: Basic Books, 1979), pp. 238–76.

13 Freud, *The Future of an Illusion*, in Standard Edition, 21: 86.

14 Hardy, *The Woodlanders*, in *Novels*, 18: 228, 237.

15 Hardy, *Tess of the d'Urbervilles*, in *Novels*, 12: 365.

16 "Every village has its idiosyncrasy, its constitution, often its own code of morality" (ibid., p. 75).

17 Ibid., p. 91.

18 "Between the mother, with her fast perishing lumber of superstitions, folk-lore, dialect, and orally transmitted ballads, and the daughter, with her trained National teachings and Standard knowledge under an infinitely Revised Code, there was a gap of two hundred years . . ." (ibid., pp. 23–24).

19 Raymond Williams, *The English Novel from Dickens to Lawrence* (London: Hogarth Press, 1984), pp. 106–17.

20 Hardy, *Tess*, in *Novels*, 12: 91.

21 J. Hillis Miller, *Fiction and Repetition: Seven English Novels* (Cambridge, Mass.: Harvard University Press, 1982), pp. 117–20.

22 Hardy, *Tess*, in *Novels*, 12: 96.

23 Ibid., p. 108.

24 Ibid., p. 291.

25 One early title for *Tess* was "Too Late, Beloved!" (Michael Millgate, *Thomas Hardy: a Biography* [Oxford: Oxford University Press, 1982], p. 299), which is very close to "The Well-Beloved," the title of the next novel. The phrase itself is from Shelley's *Epipsychidion* (lines 131–32). Hardy, as Avron Fleischman notes, quoted and alluded to Shelley's work perhaps more than to any other excepting the Bible and Shakespeare (*Fiction and the Ways of Knowing: Essays on British Novels* [Austin: University of Texas Press, 1978], p. 119).

26 Hardy, *Tess*, in *Novels*, 12: 295.

27 Ibid., p. 5.

28 Ibid., p. 134.

29 Florence Emily Hardy, *The Early Life of Thomas Hardy: 1840–1891* (London: Macmillan, 1928), p. 241. J. M. Bullen's study of Hardy's use of painterly techniques admirably demonstrates that "perhaps more than any other Victorian novelist Hardy employed the visual image to communicate meaning and feeling." For Bullen's discussion of Hardy's use of the impressionists, see *The Expressive Eye: Fiction and Perception in the Work of Thomas Hardy* (Oxford: Clarendon, 1986), pp. 181–82, 185.

30 Thomas Hardy, *Literary Notebooks*, ed. Lennart A. Björk (London: Macmillan, 1985), 1: 171–74.

31 We "ascribe to Society ejective existence: we habitually think of the whole of human thought and feeling as a psychological complex, which is other than . . . a mere shorthand enumeration of all the thoughts and feelings of all individual human beings. . . . [I]t is with this . . . imago condition of the world-eject [as determined by social preconceptions] that we have to do. . . . [This is] the world-eject in its highest conceivable stage of evolution" (George J. Romanes, "The World as Eject," *Contemporary Review* 50 [1886]: 52–53).

32 Hardy, *Literary Notebooks*, 1: 171.

33 Ibid., p. 170.

34 Ibid., p. 183. "If we consider further, it isn't our changing perceptions, contradictory thoughts, our abstract or empty conceptions, but our affections, our desires, our passions that constitute our self" (my translation). The reaction against rationalism may remind us of what Comte was doing almost contemporaneously in the *Cours*, with the crucial difference that Comte was not prepared to identify "affection" with sexual desire.

35 Hardy, *Tess*, in *Novels*, 12: 244.

36 Hardy, *The Return of the Native*, in *Novels*, 11: 310–11. The second chapter of *Tess*, of course, centers on a country dance, with Tess wanting a male partner. See also the more explicitly Dionysian dance of chapter 10.

37 Nietzsche also relies heavily on Schopenhauer; see, e.g., Friedrich Nietzsche, *The Birth of Tragedy*, trans. Walter Kaufman (New York: Vintage, 1967), pp. 51–52.

38 Irving Howe, *Thomas Hardy* (London: Weidenfeld and Nicolson, 1968), pp. 130–31.

39 Hardy, *Tess*, in *Novels*, 12: 127.

40 Ibid., p. 190.

41 Gillian Beer, *Darwin's Plots: Evolutionary Narrative in Darwin, George Eliot, and Nineteenth-Century Fiction* (London: Routledge and Kegan Paul, 1983), p. 248. Beer is quoting from Derrida.

42 Nietzsche, *Birth of Tragedy*, pp. 7, 8; cited by Alexander Nehamas, *Nietzsche: Life as Literature* (Cambridge, Mass.: Harvard University Press, 1985), p. 43.

43 Hardy, *Tess*, in *Novels*, 12: 190, 192, 187, 193, 194.

44 Tess "was appalled by . . . [Angel's] will to subdue the grosser to the subtler emotion, . . . the flesh to the spirit" (ibid., p. 313).

45 Ibid., p. 126.

46 D. H. Lawrence, *Selected Literary Criticism*, ed. Anthony Beal (New York: Vintage, 1966), p. 189. This, of course, is another version of Beer's criticism.

47 Hardy, *Tess*, in *Novels*, 12: 34.

48 Ibid., pp. 48–49. The passage draws heavily on Shelley's Platonic myth of the search for the ideal "anti-type," which Hardy in this and the next two novels is consciously reversing. See Shelley's short essay "On Love" for the most economical expression of the myth.

49 Hardy, *Tess*, in *Novels*, 12: 508.

50 See Comte's *System of Positive Polity*, trans. J. H. Bridges et al. (London: Longmans, Green, 1875–1877), 3: 101. Science, says Comte, eventually takes us back to the healthy moral state of "fetishism," from which we have departed.

51 Florence Emily Hardy, *The Later Years of Thomas Hardy, 1892–1928* (London: Macmillan, 1930), pp. 14, 44.

52 See Raymond Williams, *Modern Tragedy* (Palo Alto, Calif.: Stanford University Press, 1966), part 2, ch. 3, "Social and Personal Tragedy. . . ."

53 Hardy, *Tess*, in *Novels*, 12: 194.

54 Cited by Williams, *Modern Tragedy*, p. 37. This is a type of tragedy, in Williams' account, which is diametrically opposed to social tragedy.

55 Hardy, *The Mayor of Casterbridge*, in *Novels*, 9: 384.

56 Hardy, *Tess*, in *Novels*, 12: 244.

57 See Hardy, *Literary Notebooks*, 1: 324.

58 Edward Carpenter, *Love's Coming-of-Age* (Chicago: Charles Kerr, 1902), pp. 23–24, 27–28. Peter Gay has lately devoted a good deal of attention to the late-century sexologists in *The Bourgeois Experience: Victoria to Freud*, vol. 2, *The Tender Passion* (New York: Oxford University Press, 1986), ch. 4; see also Sulloway, *Freud, Biologist of the Mind*, ch. 8.

59 D. H. Lawrence, *Fantasia of the Unconscious* (Harmondsworth: Penguin Books, 1971), p. 19 (this volume also contains *Psychoanalysis and the Unconscious*).

60 Hardy, *Jude*, in *Novels*, 6: 178. Christminster as the goal of Jude's intellectual pilgrimage is several times compared with the New Jerusalem, see pp. 124ff., 396.

61 Ibid., p. 394.

62 Ibid., pp. 407, 384.

63 Ibid., p. 335. Cf. Tess's attribution of human fatality to the stars at the outset of her story (*Tess*, in *Novels*, 12: 34).

64 Hardy, *Tess*, in *Novels*, 12: 162. J. Hillis Miller has explored at length the preoccupation with circularity or repetition in *Tess* in *Fiction and Repetition: Seven English Novels* (Cambridge, Mass.: Harvard University Press, 1982), pp. 116–46.

65 Hardy, *Jude*, in *Novels*, 6: 172.

66 Laon and Cythna are the lovers in Shelley's *Revolt of Islam*.

67 Hardy, *Jude*, in *Novels*, 6: 408–9.

68 Ibid., p. 22.

69 Ibid., p. 20.

70 Ibid.

71 Ibid., p. 24.

72 Ibid., p. 44.

73 Ibid., p. 42.

74 Ibid., pp. 70–71.

75 Hardy, *Tess*, in *Novels*, 12: 151.

76 Hardy, *Jude*, in *Novels*, 6: 104.

77 Ibid., pp. 105, 107, 108.

78 Freud, "Leonardo da Vinci and a Memory of His Childhood," in *Standard Edition*, 11: 78. Leon Waldoff has spoken very generally of the relation between Hardy's concept of psychological determinism and Freudianism in "Psychological Determinism in *Tess*" in *Critical Approaches to the Fiction of Thomas Hardy*, ed. Dale Kramer (New York: Barnes and Noble, 1979), pp. 135–54.

79 Freud, "Leonardo," in *Standard Edition*, 11: 123.

80 Freud, *The Future of an Illusion*, in *Standard Edition*, 21: 43.

81 Paul Ricoeur, *Freud and Philosophy: an Essay on Interpretation*, trans. Denis Savage (New Haven: Yale University Press, 1970), p. 271.

82 Hardy, *Jude*, in *Novels*, 6: 133, 140.

83 Earl Wasserman, *Shelley: a Critical Reading* (Baltimore: Johns Hopkins University Press, 1971), p. 420.

84 Hardy, *Jude*, in *Novels*, 6: 105.

85 Hardy, *The Well-Beloved*, in *Novels*, 16: 76; see also p. 106.

86 Millgate has noted the close connection between Sue Bridehead and Hardy's sister Mary in *Thomas Hardy: a Biography*, pp. 351–53.

87 Hardy, *The Well-Beloved*, in *Novels*, 16: 107.

88 Freud, *Standard Edition*, 7: 227–28.

89 Ibid.

90 Hardy, *Jude*, in *Novels*, 6: 165, 176.

91 Ibid., p. 201.

92 Ibid., p. 173. A canceled version of the passage is more direct: Jude saw "himself done into another sex . . ." (Millgate, *Thomas Hardy: a Biography*, p. 352).

93 P. B. Shelley, *Complete Works*, ed. Roger Ingpen and Walter E. Peck (New York: Gordian Press, 1965), 6: 201.

94 Freud, *Totem and Taboo*, in *Standard Edition*, 13: 88–89.

95 Ibid., p. 89.

96 Ibid., 14: 94.

97 Shelley, *Complete Works*, 6: 202.

98 Freud, *Future of an Illusion*, in *Standard Edition*, 21: 31.

99 Jürgen Habermas, *Knowledge and Human Interests*, trans. Jeremy J. Shapiro (Boston: Beacon Press, 1971), p. 189.

100 Stephen Draenos, *Freud's Odyssey: Psychoanalysis and the End of Metaphysics* (New Haven: Yale University Press, 1982), pp. 69, 79.

101 Ibid., pp. 143, 148.

102 Freud, *Beyond the Pleasure Principle*, in *Standard Edition*, 18: 42.

103 Norman O. Brown, *Life against Death: the Psychoanalytic Meaning of History* (Middletown, Conn.: Wesleyan University Press, 1959), p. 81. A connection between Freud's concept of the "death instinct" and the second law of thermodynamics was made early on by Siegfried Bernfield and Sergei Feitelberg in "Principles of Entropy and the Death Instinct" (*International Journal of Psychology* 12 [1931]: 61–81).

104 Hardy, *Jude*, in *Novels*, 6: 212.

105 Freud, *Beyond the Pleasure Principle*, in *Standard Edition*, 18: 22.

106 Ibid., pp. 36–38. J. Hillis Miller has drawn attention to the intriguing connection between Hardy's *The Well-Beloved* and Freud's *Beyond the Pleasure Principle* in *Fiction and Repetition*, p. 169.

107 Freud, *Future of an Illusion*, in *Standard Edition*, 21: 69. Freud also uses the metallurgical metaphor to describe the inescapable antinomy of these new forces: they "are alloyed with each other" in our human nature (p. 66).

108 Hardy, *Jude*, in *Novels*, 6: 210.

109 Cf. J. Hillis Miller in *Fiction and Repetition*, pp. 147–75.

110 Hardy, *The Well-Beloved*, in *Novels*, 16; the title of chapter 7, third part.

111 Ibid., p. 212.

112 Hardy, *Jude*, in *Novels*, 6: 406, 493. See Alan Friedman, *The Turn of the Novel* (New York: Oxford University Press, 1967), pp. 73–74, for a related argument on this passage as marking an important "turn" in the novel.

113 Hardy, *Jude*, in *Novels*, 6: 488.

114 Quoted by Williams, *Modern Tragedy*, p. 41.

115 Nietzsche, *Birth of Tragedy*, p. 42.

116 For Arnold's concept of the relation between intellectual deliverance and architectonic, classical forms, see my *The Victorian Critic and the Idea of History: Carlyle, Arnold, and Pater* (Cambridge, Mass.: Harvard University Press, 1977), pp. 140–52.

117 Florence Hardy, *The Later Years*, p. 104.

118 Millgate, *Thomas Hardy: a Biography*, p. 108.

119 *Thomas Hardy's Personal Writings*, ed. Harold Orel (Lawrence, Kans.: University of Kansas Press, 1966), pp. 38–39.

120 Millgate, *Thomas Hardy: a Biography*, p. 198.

121 Dale Kramer, *Thomas Hardy: the Form of Tragedy* (Detroit: Wayne State University Press, 1975), p. 48.

122 Hardy, *Return*, in *Novels*, 11: 5.

123 Ibid., p. 197.

124 Ibid., p. 448.

125 Ibid., p. 453.

126 But cf. Kramer, *Thomas Hardy*, pp. 134–35.

127 See, e.g., Robert Gittings, *Thomas Hardy's Later Years* (Boston: Little, Brown, 1978), p. 68: *Tess* has "the emotional force of a universal poem, as moving as the expulsion from Paradise" in Milton's epic.

128 Hardy, *The Well-Beloved*, in *Novels*, 12: 167.

129 Ibid., p. 484.

130. Peter Morton, *The Vital Science: Biology and Literary Imagination, 1860–1900* (London: George Allen and Unwin, 1984), p. 176.

131 Hardy, *The Well-Beloved*, in *Novels*, 16: 49.

132 Ibid., p. 32.

133 Ibid., p. 109.

134 Ibid., p. 212.

135 Ibid., pp. 213–14.

136 Ibid., p. 104.

137 Ibid., p. 216.

138 Florence Hardy, *The Later Years*, pp. 57–58.

139 *Personal Writings*, ed. Orel, pp. 38–39, 43, 48, 61.

140 See, e.g., Paul Bourget, *Essais de psychologie contemporaine* (Paris: Librairie Plon, 1924), 2: 156: "The novel of . . . minute analysis . . . is . . . what best conforms to our age of universal calculation" (my translation). Hardy may have been thinking of Bourget's concept of analytic art, as expressed here and elsewhere in *Essais*, when he wrote in his journal for 4 March 1886 that "novel writing as an art" had reached the "analytic stage" (Florence Hardy, *Early Life*, p. 232). The passage from Bourget above was published in 1885; Hardy was reading in the *Essais* by at least 1887 (see Hardy, *Literary Notebooks*, 1: 207).

141 Bourget, *Essais*, 1: 20 (my translation here and in the following quotations from *Essais*): Bourget is writing in the context of an essay on Baudelaire's poetry.

142 Ibid., 2: 183.

143 Ibid., 1: 170.

144 Miller, *Fiction and Repetition*, p. 174.

Chapter 11. Conclusion

1 Hans Vaihinger, *The Philosophy of "As If": a System of the Theoretical, Practical and Religious Fictions of Mankind*, trans. C. K. Ogden (London: Routledge and Kegan Paul, 1924), p. 44.

2 Frederich Albert Lange, *The History of Materialism*, trans. Ernest C. Thomas, 3rd ed. (London: Kegan Paul, Trench, Trübner, 1925), p. 341.

3 For an account of the later nineteenth-century return to Kant, see Thomas E.

Willey, *Back to Kant: the Revival of Kantianism in German Social and Historical Thought, 1860–1914* (Detroit: Wayne State University Press, 1978).

4 Vaihinger, *Philosophy of "As If,"* p. 85.

5 Immanuel Kant, *Critique of Judgment,* trans. J. H. Bernard (New York: Hafner, 1968), p. 297.

6 Immanuel Kant, *The Critique of Pure Reason,* trans. F. Max Müller (New York: Macmillan, 1911), p. 551.

7 Allan Megill, *Prophets of Extremity: Nietzsche, Heidegger, Foucault, Derrida* (Berkeley: University of California Press, 1987), p. 2.

8 Ernst Cassirer, *An Essay on Man: an Introduction to a Philosophy of Human Culture* (New York: Bantam Books, 1970), p. 244.

9 Michel Foucault, *The Order of Things: an Archeology of the Human Sciences* (New York: Vintage Books, 1970), p. 387.

10 Matthew Arnold, *Complete Prose Works,* ed. R. H. Super (Ann Arbor: University of Michigan Press, 1960–1977), 10: 63.

11 Megill, *Prophets of Extremity,* p. 33.

12 Friedrich Nietzsche, *The Birth of Tragedy,* cited by Megill in *Prophets of Extremity,* p. 2.

13 Friedrich Nietzsche, cited by Vaihinger in *The Philosophy of "As If,"* p. 345.

14 Jürgen Habermas, *Knowledge and Human Interests,* trans. Jeremy J. Shapiro (Boston: Beacon Press, 1968), p. 299.

15 The best discussion I know of Derrida's ambiguous relation to Freud is Stephen W. Melville's in *Philosophy Beside Itself: On Deconstruction and Modernism* (Minneapolis: University of Minnesota Press, 1986), pp. 84–97.

16 Sigmund Freud, *The Future of an Illusion,* in *The Standard Edition of the Complete Works,* ed. and trans. James Strachey (London: Hogarth, 1953–1974), 21: 56.

Index

Adams, B., 230
Adams, H. B., 230
Adorno, T. W., 27
Aeschylus: Hardy's use of in *Return*, 247, 273; Hardy's use of in *Tess*, 253, 255, 275. *See also* Prometheus myth
Aesthetic idealization: Kant on, 27–30, 111; Comte on in relation to historical change, 34, 38; and scientific method, 53–55, 111, 280–81; Helmholtz on, 103–5; Vaihinger on, 111, 280–81; and morality, 114–18; Stephen versus Arnold on, 194–204
Aesthetic totalization: as a romantic philosophy, 5–7; and M. Arnold, 167–74, 200, 204; Hardy's opposition to, 257, 276–77
Aestheticism: as a Victorian philosophy, 64, 167–74, 192–93, 207; as a modernist and postmodernist philosophy, 65–67, 282–84
Aesthetics: romantic, 5, 63; Comte on, 33–39; Mill on, 39–44; Lewes on scientific, 62–67, 76–84, 113–14; empiricist, 65, 296n23; Stephen on scientific, 194–204; Hardy on scientific, 234, 272–79
Affectivism: as principle of aesthetic value, 37
Agape: and eros in Hardy, 249
Albert, H., 15
Alexander, S., 221–22, 233
Alison, A.: and empiricist aesthetics, 65
Allen, G., 31, 81
Althusser, L., 7
Altruism: Comte on, 17–18, 20, 36, 76, 82–83, 157, 270; versus egoism, 40, 97, 123–28, 186–87, 205–6, 227; J. S. Mill on, 40–42; Bentham on, 43–44; Lewes on, 76, 82–83, 123–28; and sexual desire, 83, 90–93, 145, 209–13, 270–71; G. Eliot on, 90–101, 145–48, 161–63;

Stephen on evolutionary, 178–83, 205–6; Meredith on, 209–13; Maudsley on, 227; Freud on, 270–71
Anglo-American critical tradition, 8–9
Antigone, 148, 247
Aristotle: on mimesis, 65, 67; Lewes on, 65, 67, 107; G. Eliot on, 87; on tragedy, 87, 99; on metaphor, 99; on scientific method, 107; on causality, 131
Arnold, M.: contrasted with Lewes as critic, 60, 296n20, 299n80; as biblical critic, 169–71, 171–72, 195–96; Stephen on, 169–74, 184, 191, 194–200, 204; on science, 170–71, 204, 284; on Wordsworth, 172, 194–96; on poetry, 172–73, 196; on humanism, 184, 192–96, 284; as cultural conservative, 191; as literary critic, 192–96, 296n20, 299n80; on philosophy in literature, 195–96; 232, 272; Hardy's use of, 232, 257, 258, 272–74, 278; on Hellenic form, 273–74
Art. *See* Aesthetics
Associationism: Lewes' reaction against, 68, 70–71, 74; Bain as pre-eminent Victorian representative, 70–71; J. S. Mill on, 76, 175, 184; and Helmholtz, 104; and Sidgwick's ethics, 176–77
Atomic theory, 50, 141, 143
Avenarius, R., 122, 305n59

Bacon, F.: and inductivism, 47, 129; Lewes on, 105; and hermeneutics, 129; and correspondence theory, 129, 159; Bentham on, 175
Baer, K. E. von, 77
Bain, A., 64–65, 68, 70–71. *See also* Associationism
Balzac, H. de, 72, 75, 86, 97
Barker, S. F., 49
Baudelaire, C. P., 226
Beesly, E. S., 30
Beneke, F. E., 68